Chitose Is in the Ramune Bottle

Bonus Short Story

A Bun on the Rooftop at Lunch Break

It was lunchtime, the day that Kenta was harassed by Atomu and his gang. I had some stuff on my mind, so I made up an excuse for Yuuko and the other people I usually ate lunch with, then headed to the rooftop alone with a filled hot dog bun I'd bought.

For whatever reason, I didn't feel like eating right away, so instead, I went to lie down and gazed at the sky. The sky, as blue as a swimming pool in summer, sparkled so brightly I had to close my eyes.

For a while, I let my mind wander among various pointless things.

There was a screech as the door opened, then quietly closed. *Clunk, clunk, clunk.* The sound of polite footsteps approached.

Regular students generally weren't allowed on the roof, so it must have been one of my friends who knew I had a key.

"I thought I'd find you here."

The voice that floated down to my supine form was the exact one I'd been expecting.

"Saku, want to eat lunch together?"

I responded without opening my eyes. "Yua, if you stand over me like that, I'll be able to see your underwear."

Whap. A light tap on my forehead.

"I knew you'd say that, so don't worry. I've taken the proper precautions."

Relieved to hear that, I opened my eyes to see Yua crouched down, holding a wrapped bento box. She had her skirt tucked neatly between her knees.

I hoisted myself up. "How'd you know I was up here?"

"You had this look on your face. I could tell you were going to go curl up in a ball by yourself."

"I was lying flat on my back, actually. But semantics aside, what are you doing here?"

Yua looked away awkwardly, then mumbled, "I guess I just didn't want you to have to ruminate alone."

I let forth a brief laugh and opened the paper bag by my side. I pulled out my split bun filled with egg salad and took a bite before speaking again. "You really helped today."

Yua spread out her bento lunch, which she'd made for herself as usual. "That's not true. I couldn't really do anything," she said apologetically.

"You're not very good at dealing with people like Atomu's group, huh?"

"Not necessarily. I'm plenty used to being around people who put on an arrogant, tough-guy front, after all."

"Ouch, Yua."

We both giggled over her smooth insult.

Once we regained our composure, I spoke again. "Man, it really was a good thing you were there, Yua. Kenta would have been in real trouble if he'd been alone."

"Like I said, I really didn't do anything except stand there, you know? You're the one who saved the day, Saku," Yua said as she delicately grasped a piece of yellow omelet with her chopsticks.

"Isn't it nice having someone stand by you, though?"

"…Hmm, well, I guess I can understand that."

She sounded a little down, and when I looked over at her…

"Here, you need veggies."

She stuck out her hand, clutching a bright-red round cherry tomato. She must have been concerned that I was only eating a filled hot dog bun for lunch.

"Mm, thanks."

Taking care not to brush against her fingertips, I plucked it out of her hand with my lips. A sharp sweetness and sourness burst inside my mouth, flowing over my tongue.

"I think you're fine the way you are, Saku," said Yua.

"Huh…?"

"You take things on by yourself, get all confused, lose your way, but still put on a cool front and forge forward anyway… I think Yamazaki appreciates that, too."

"Yua…"

It was as if she'd read my innermost thoughts. I didn't

know what to say.

It's all right. It's all right. Those words kept coming.

"And if the time ever comes when you lose sight of yourself..." Her voice was gentle, like a warm embrace.

"I'll chew you out like you wouldn't believe, you hear?"

Yua gave me a wide grin.

I was so pleased—and so embarrassed. "I'll be sure to be careful. You're pretty scary when you're mad, Yua," I responded breezily.

"I was about to give you a piece of fried chicken, but I guess I won't."

"No, no, I didn't mean it! You're a graceful domestic goddess with a smile that could brighten anyone's day!"

"Tch, Saku..."

We both laughed together, shoulders shaking.

My egg-salad-filled hot dog bun, with Yua's piece of fried chicken sandwiched inside it, tasted sweet and a little salty. *Just like the two of us today*, I thought to myself.

Chitose Is in the Ramune Bottle

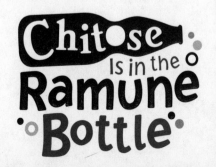

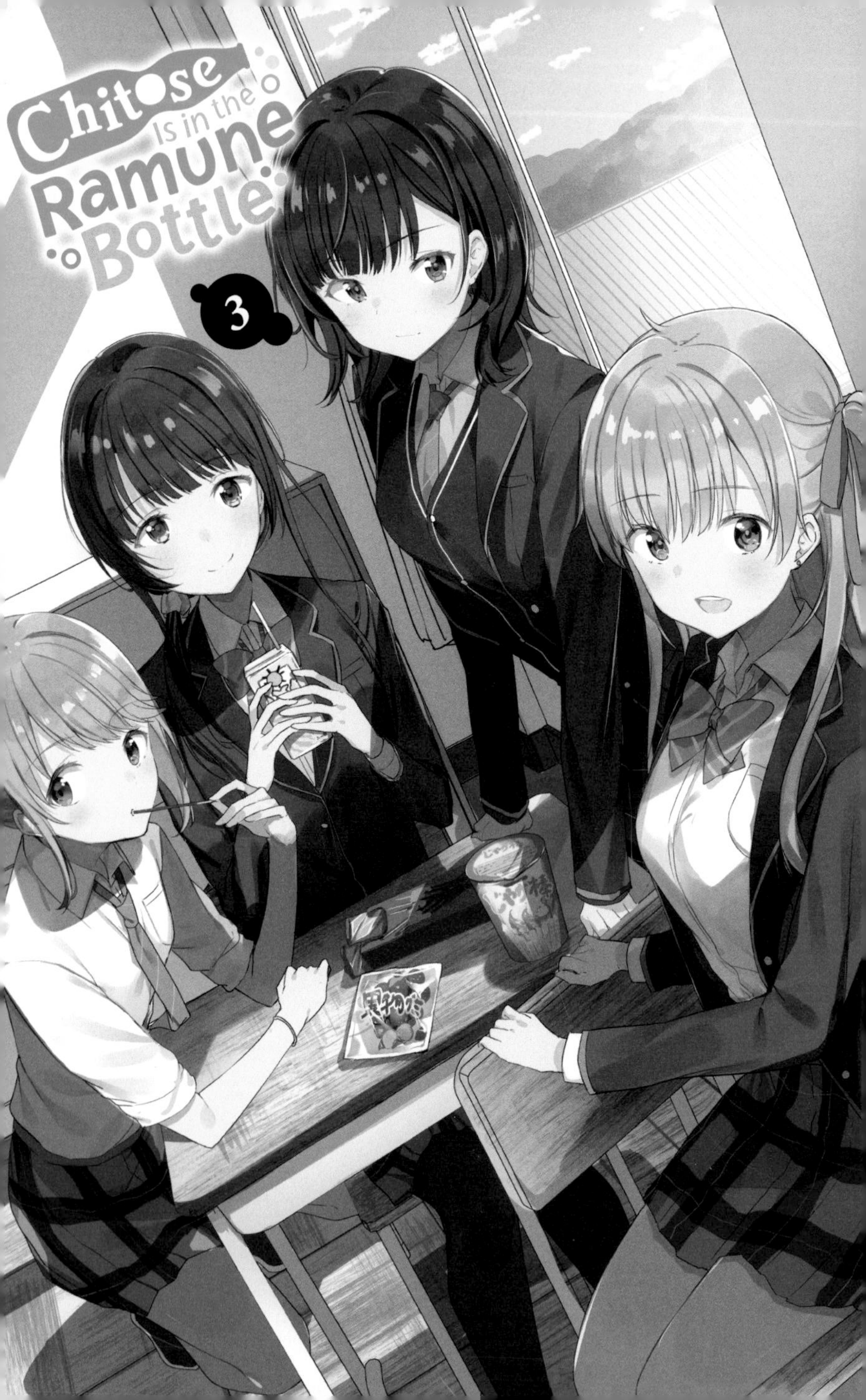
Chitose Is in the Ramune Bottle
3

CONTENTS

Chitose Is in the Ramune Bottle

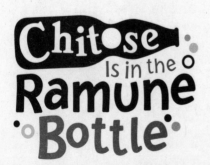

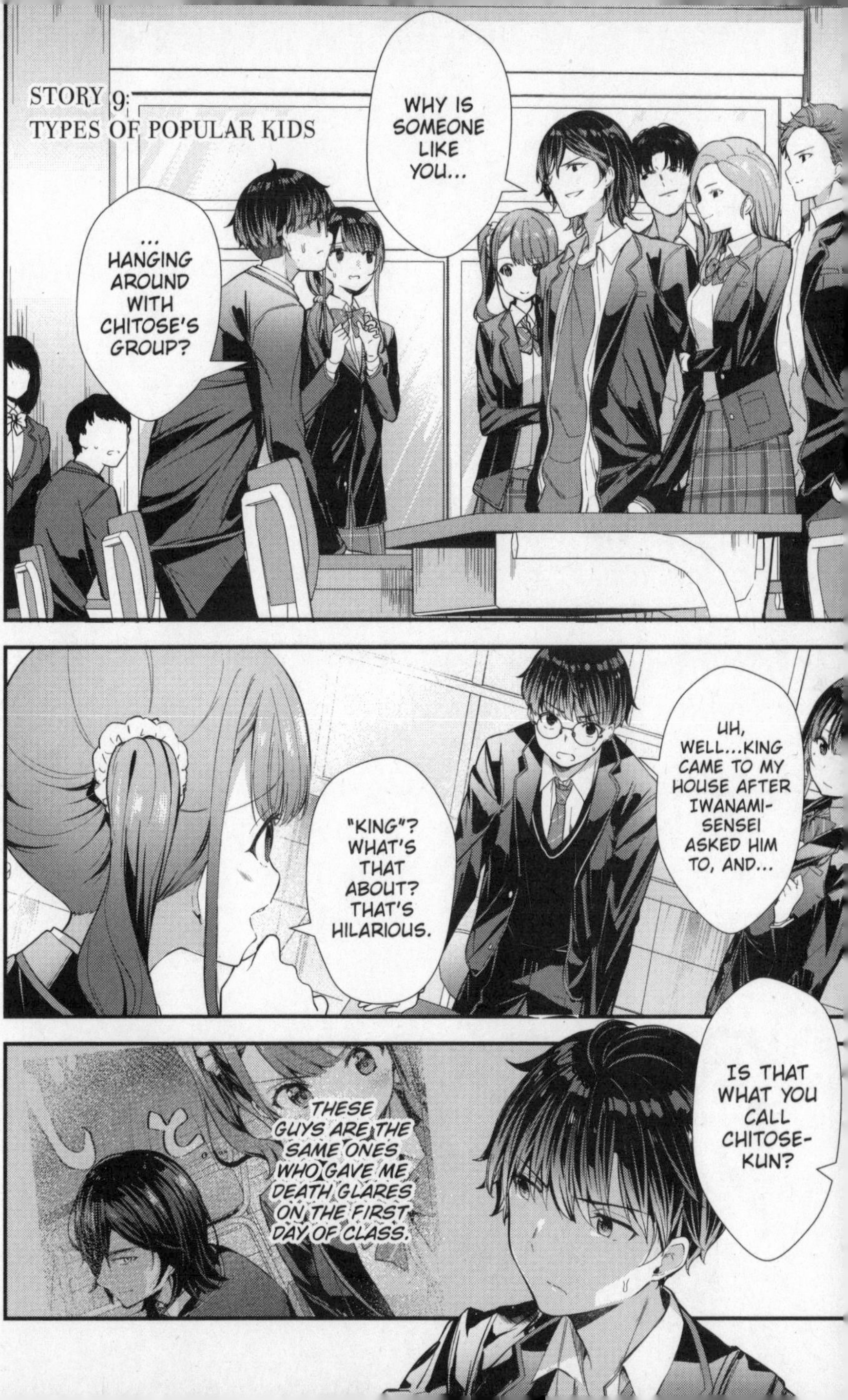
STORY 9: TYPES OF POPULAR KIDS
WHY IS SOMEONE LIKE YOU...
...HANGING AROUND WITH CHITOSE'S GROUP?
UH, WELL...KING CAME TO MY HOUSE AFTER IWANAMI-SENSEI ASKED HIM TO, AND...
"KING"? WHAT'S THAT ABOUT? THAT'S HILARIOUS.
IS THAT WHAT YOU CALL CHITOSE-KUN?
THESE GUYS ARE THE SAME ONES WHO GAVE ME DEATH GLARES ON THE FIRST DAY OF CLASS.

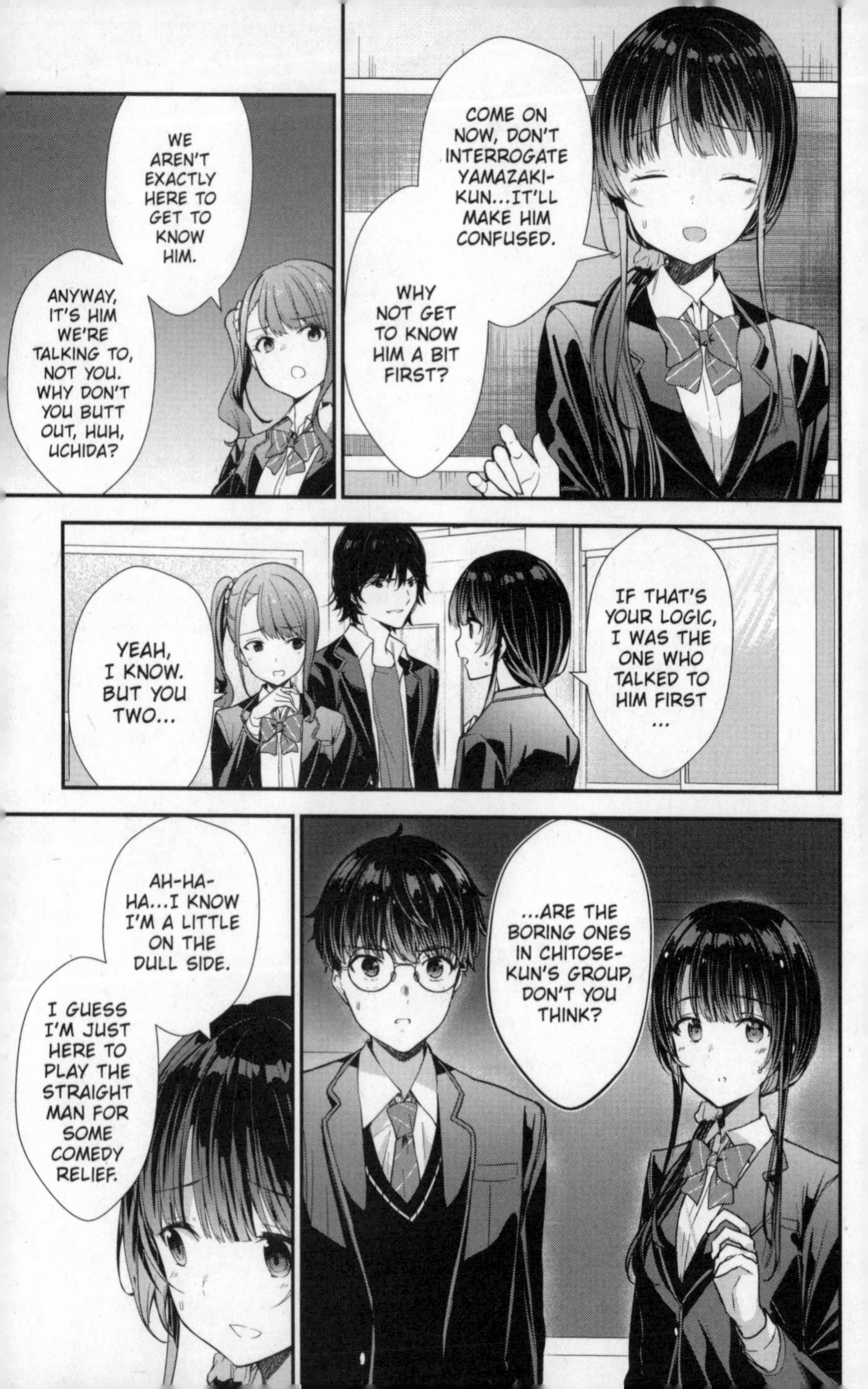
COME ON NOW, DON'T INTERROGATE YAMAZAKI-KUN...IT'LL MAKE HIM CONFUSED.
WHY NOT GET TO KNOW HIM A BIT FIRST?
WE AREN'T EXACTLY HERE TO GET TO KNOW HIM.
ANYWAY, IT'S HIM WE'RE TALKING TO, NOT YOU. WHY DON'T YOU BUTT OUT, HUH, UCHIDA?
IF THAT'S YOUR LOGIC, I WAS THE ONE WHO TALKED TO HIM FIRST...
YEAH, I KNOW. BUT YOU TWO...
...ARE THE BORING ONES IN CHITOSE-KUN'S GROUP, DON'T YOU THINK?
AH-HA-HA...I KNOW I'M A LITTLE ON THE DULL SIDE.
I GUESS I'M JUST HERE TO PLAY THE STRAIGHT MAN FOR SOME COMEDY RELIEF.

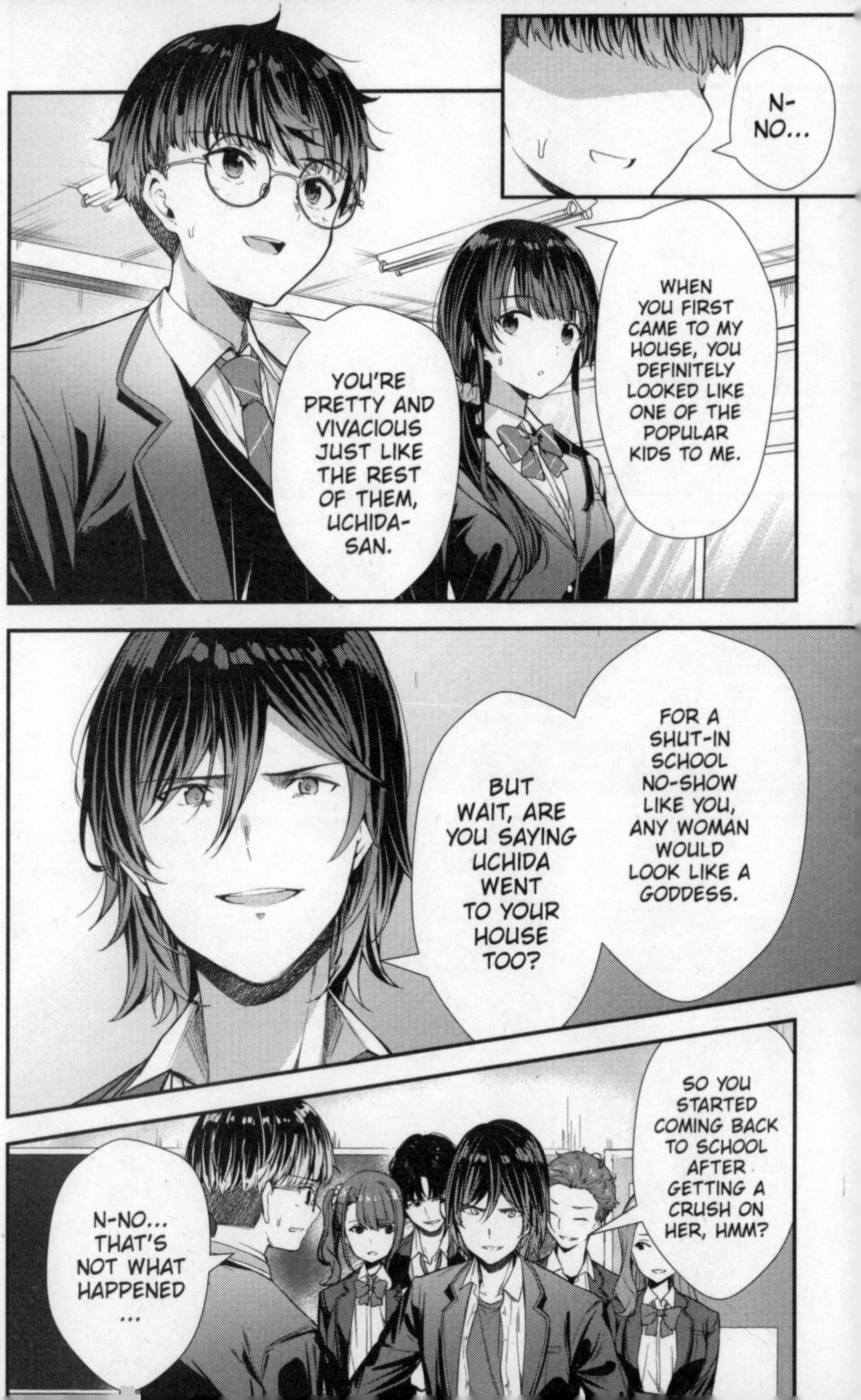
N- NO...
WHEN YOU FIRST CAME TO MY HOUSE, YOU DEFINITELY LOOKED LIKE ONE OF THE POPULAR KIDS TO ME.
YOU'RE PRETTY AND VIVACIOUS JUST LIKE THE REST OF THEM, UCHIDA-SAN.
FOR A SHUT-IN SCHOOL NO-SHOW LIKE YOU, ANY WOMAN WOULD LOOK LIKE A GODDESS.
BUT WAIT, ARE YOU SAYING UCHIDA WENT TO YOUR HOUSE TOO?
SO YOU STARTED COMING BACK TO SCHOOL AFTER GETTING A CRUSH ON HER, HMM?
N-NO... THAT'S NOT WHAT HAPPENED...

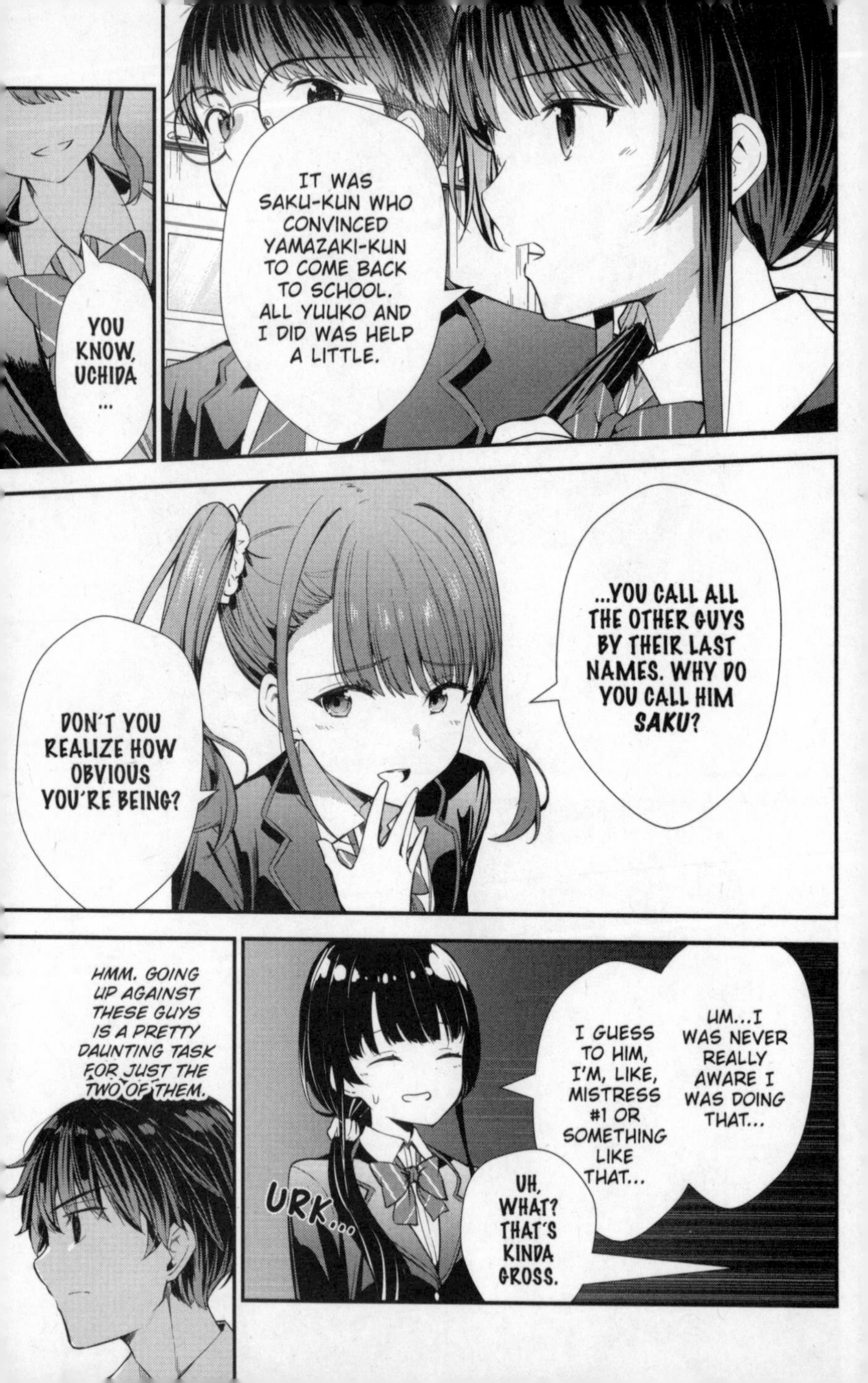
IT WAS SAKU-KUN WHO CONVINCED YAMAZAKI-KUN TO COME BACK TO SCHOOL. ALL YUUKO AND I DID WAS HELP A LITTLE.
YOU KNOW, UCHIDA...
...YOU CALL ALL THE OTHER GUYS BY THEIR LAST NAMES. WHY DO YOU CALL HIM SAKU?
DON'T YOU REALIZE HOW OBVIOUS YOU'RE BEING?
UM...I WAS NEVER REALLY AWARE I WAS DOING THAT...
I GUESS TO HIM, I'M, LIKE, MISTRESS #1 OR SOMETHING LIKE THAT...
UH, WHAT? THAT'S KINDA GROSS.
URK...
HMM. GOING UP AGAINST THESE GUYS IS A PRETTY DAUNTING TASK FOR JUST THE TWO OF THEM.

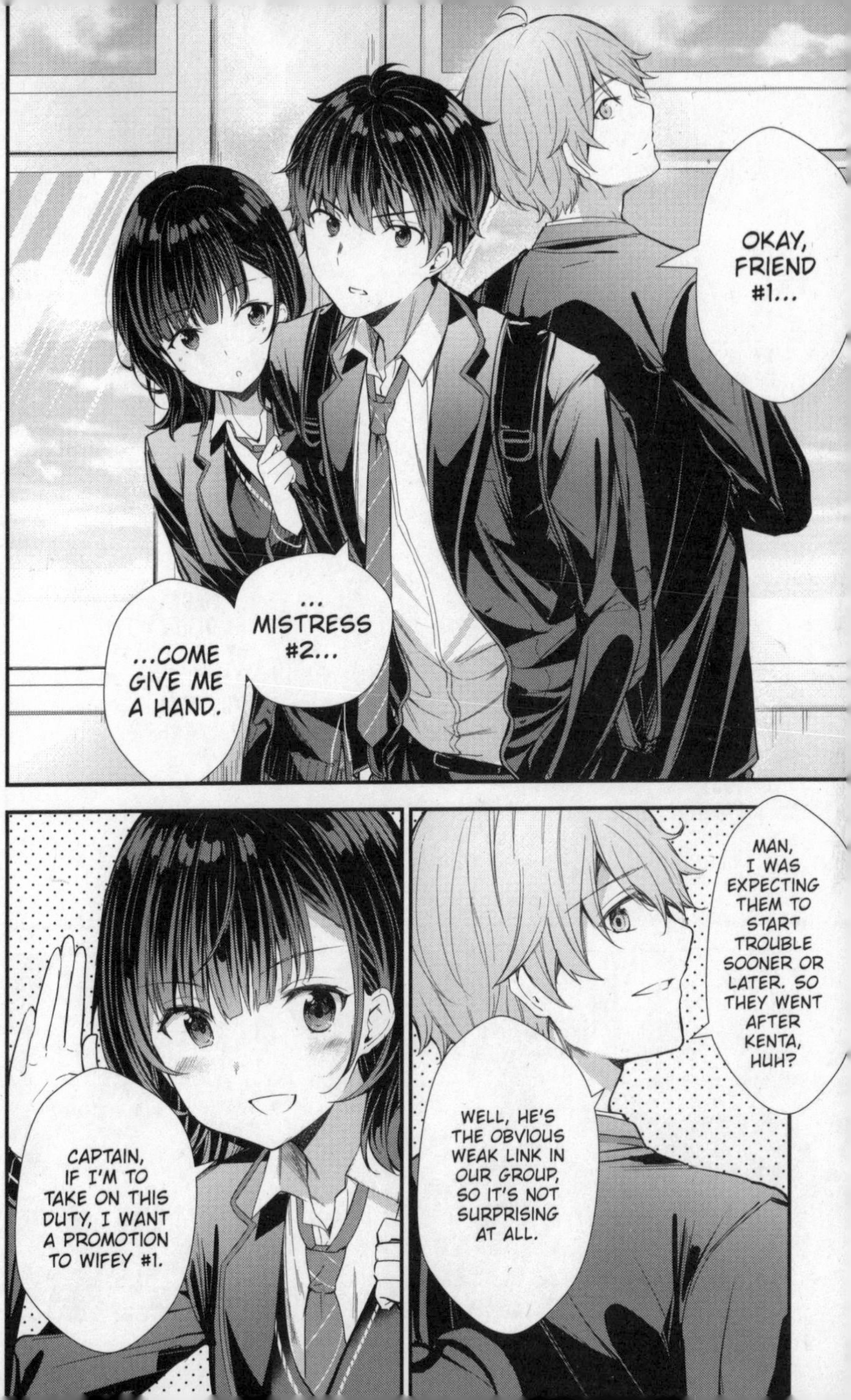
OKAY, FRIEND #1...
... MISTRESS #2...
...COME GIVE ME A HAND.
MAN, I WAS EXPECTING THEM TO START TROUBLE SOONER OR LATER. SO THEY WENT AFTER KENTA, HUH?
WELL, HE'S THE OBVIOUS WEAK LINK IN OUR GROUP, SO IT'S NOT SURPRISING AT ALL.
CAPTAIN, IF I'M TO TAKE ON THIS DUTY, I WANT A PROMOTION TO WIFEY #1.

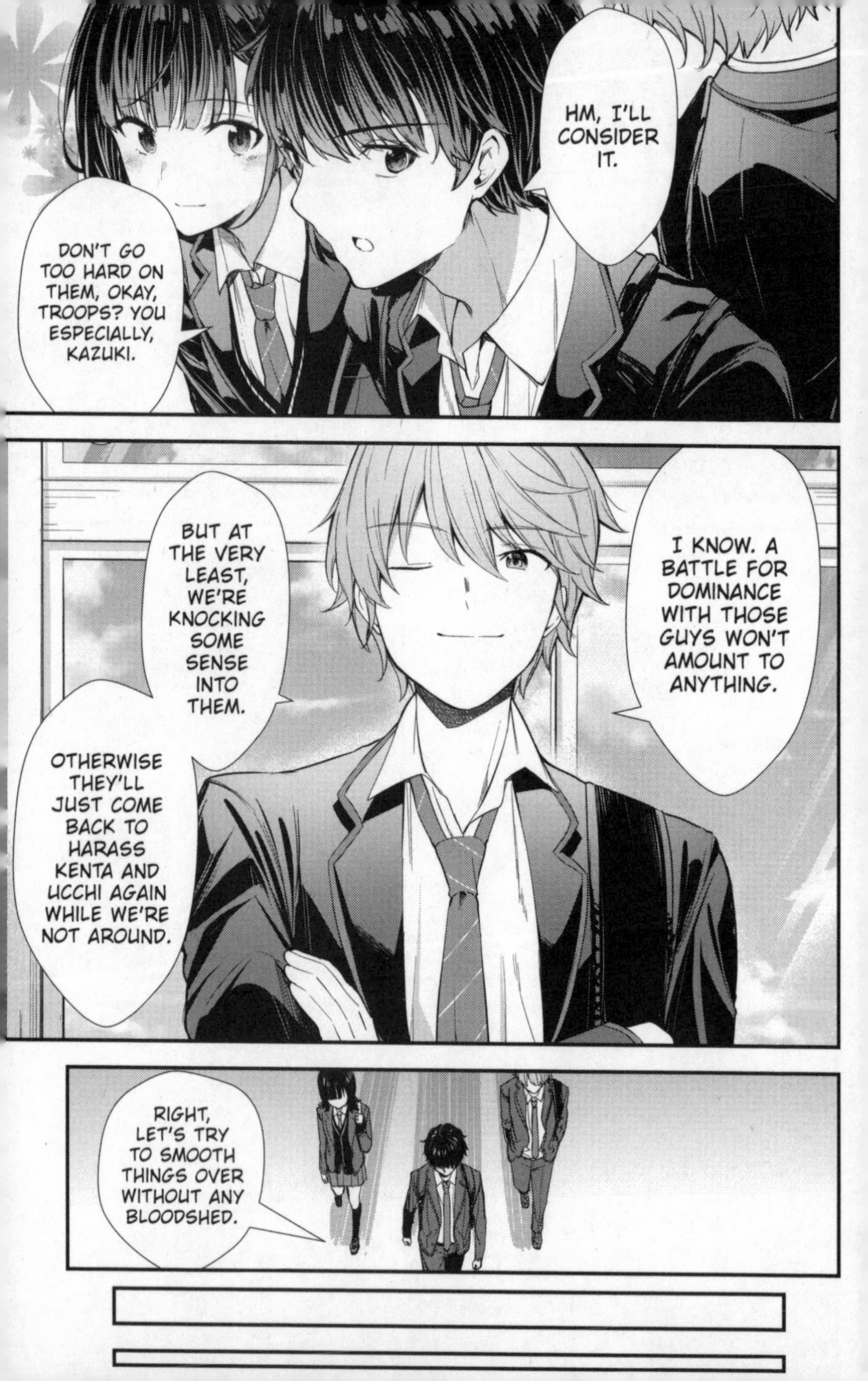
HM, I'LL CONSIDER IT.
DON'T GO TOO HARD ON THEM, OKAY, TROOPS? YOU ESPECIALLY, KAZUKI.
I KNOW. A BATTLE FOR DOMINANCE WITH THOSE GUYS WON'T AMOUNT TO ANYTHING.
BUT AT THE VERY LEAST, WE'RE KNOCKING SOME SENSE INTO THEM.
OTHERWISE THEY'LL JUST COME BACK TO HARASS KENTA AND UCCHI AGAIN WHILE WE'RE NOT AROUND.
RIGHT, LET'S TRY TO SMOOTH THINGS OVER WITHOUT ANY BLOODSHED.

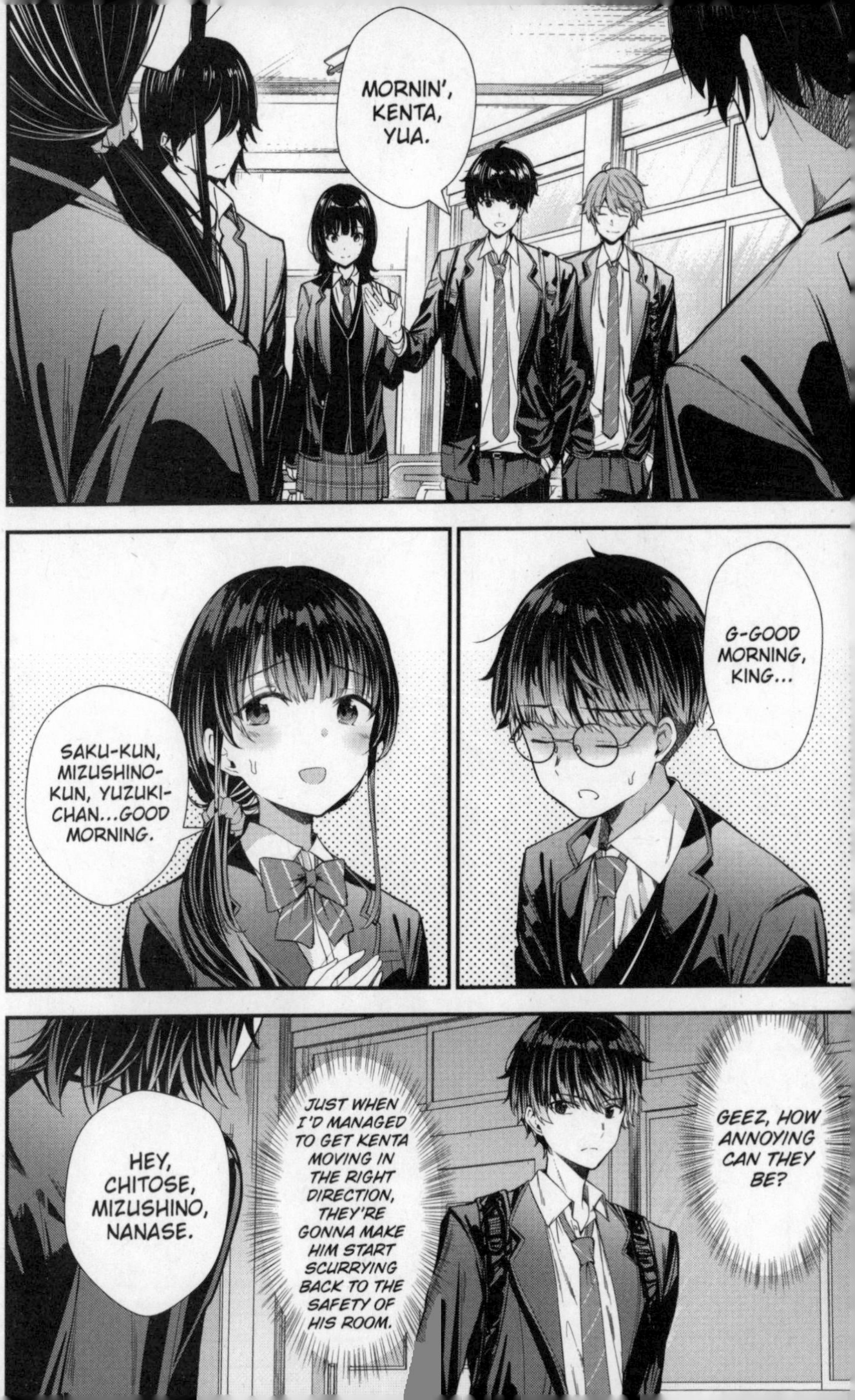
MORNIN', KENTA, YUA.
G-GOOD MORNING, KING...
SAKU-KUN, MIZUSHINO-KUN, YUZUKI-CHAN...GOOD MORNING.
GEEZ, HOW ANNOYING CAN THEY BE?
JUST WHEN I'D MANAGED TO GET KENTA MOVING IN THE RIGHT DIRECTION, THEY'RE GONNA MAKE HIM START SCURRYING BACK TO THE SAFETY OF HIS ROOM.
HEY, CHITOSE, MIZUSHINO, NANASE.

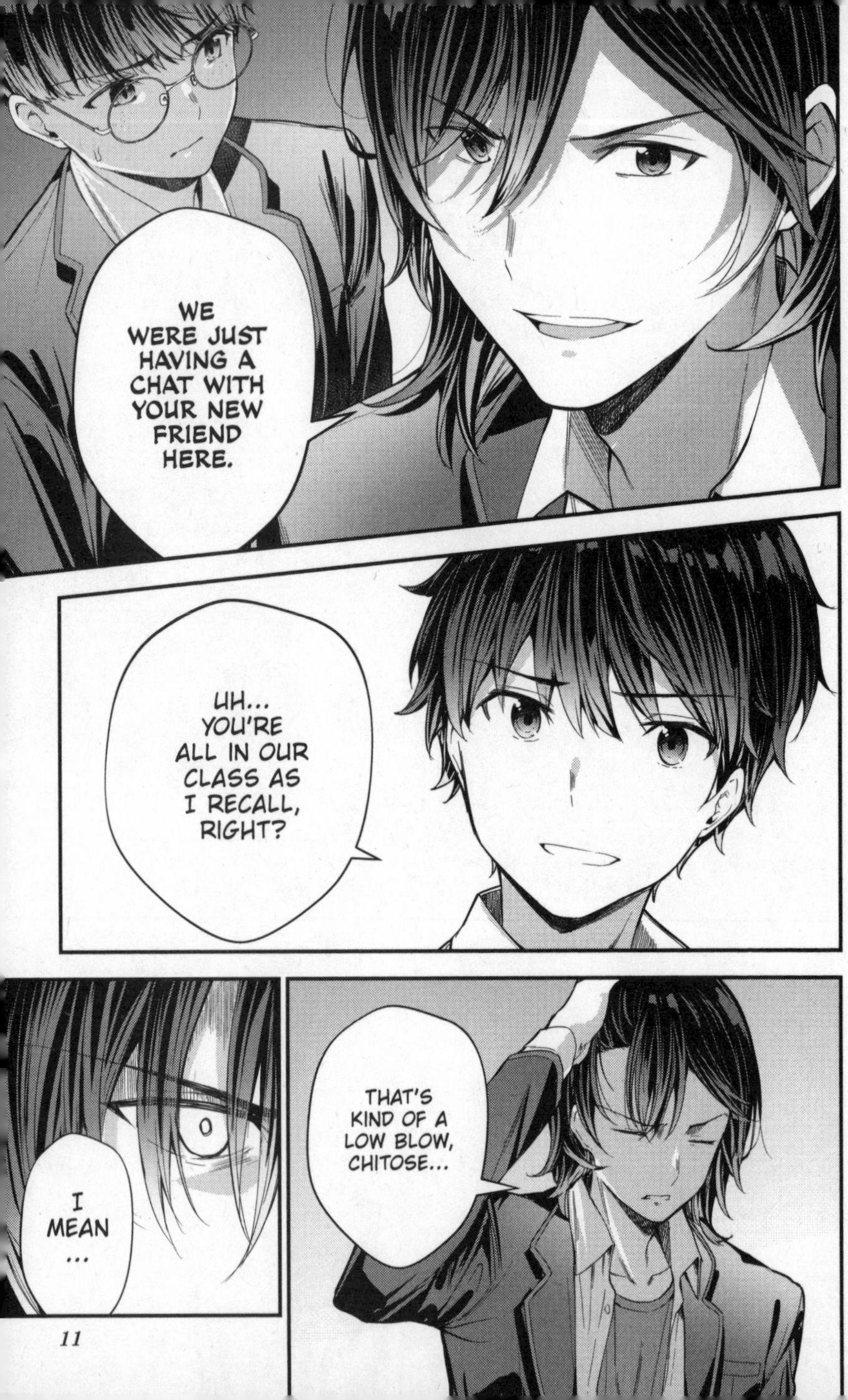
WE WERE JUST HAVING A CHAT WITH YOUR NEW FRIEND HERE.
UH... YOU'RE ALL IN OUR CLASS AS I RECALL, RIGHT?
THAT'S KIND OF A LOW BLOW, CHITOSE...
I MEAN ...

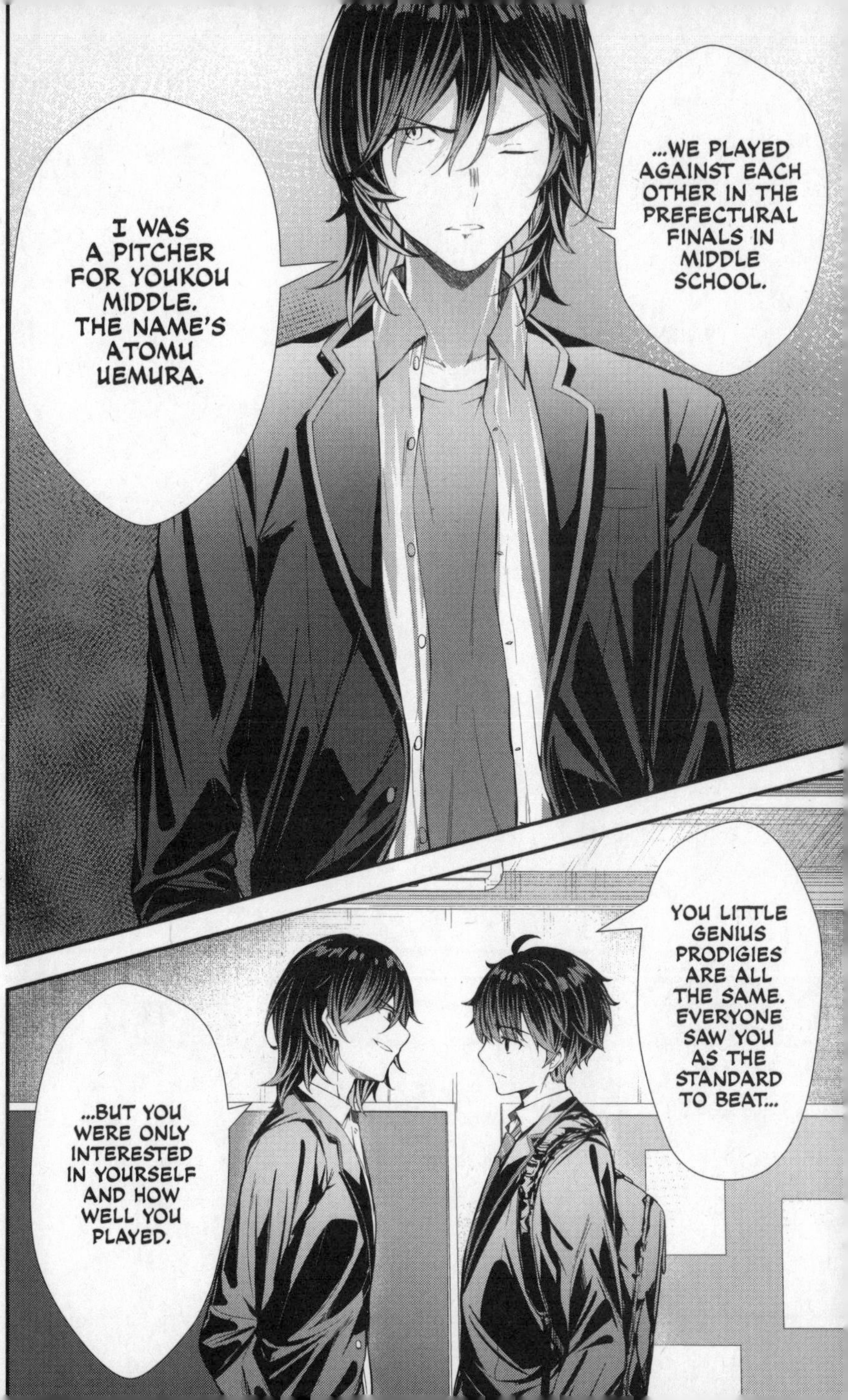
...WE PLAYED AGAINST EACH OTHER IN THE PREFECTURAL FINALS IN MIDDLE SCHOOL.
I WAS A PITCHER FOR YOUKOU MIDDLE. THE NAME'S ATOMU UEMURA.
YOU LITTLE GENIUS PRODIGIES ARE ALL THE SAME. EVERYONE SAW YOU AS THE STANDARD TO BEAT...
...BUT YOU WERE ONLY INTERESTED IN YOURSELF AND HOW WELL YOU PLAYED.

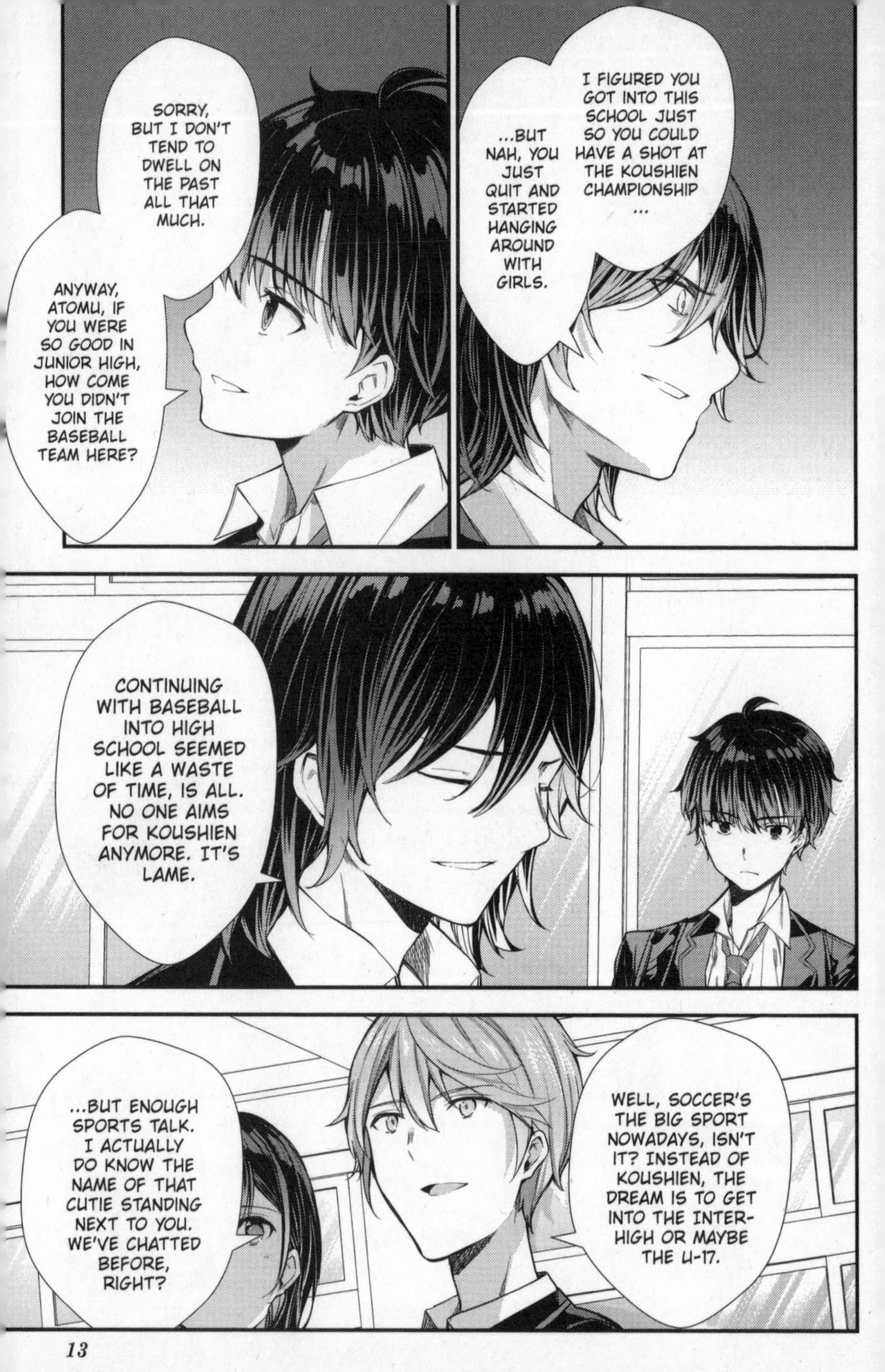
I FIGURED YOU GOT INTO THIS SCHOOL JUST SO YOU COULD HAVE A SHOT AT THE KOUSHIEN CHAMPIONSHIP ...
...BUT NAH, YOU JUST QUIT AND STARTED HANGING AROUND WITH GIRLS.
SORRY, BUT I DON'T TEND TO DWELL ON THE PAST ALL THAT MUCH.
ANYWAY, ATOMU, IF YOU WERE SO GOOD IN JUNIOR HIGH, HOW COME YOU DIDN'T JOIN THE BASEBALL TEAM HERE?
CONTINUING WITH BASEBALL INTO HIGH SCHOOL SEEMED LIKE A WASTE OF TIME, IS ALL. NO ONE AIMS FOR KOUSHIEN ANYMORE. IT'S LAME.
WELL, SOCCER'S THE BIG SPORT NOWADAYS, ISN'T IT? INSTEAD OF KOUSHIEN, THE DREAM IS TO GET INTO THE INTER-HIGH OR MAYBE THE U-17.
...BUT ENOUGH SPORTS TALK. I ACTUALLY DO KNOW THE NAME OF THAT CUTIE STANDING NEXT TO YOU. WE'VE CHATTED BEFORE, RIGHT?

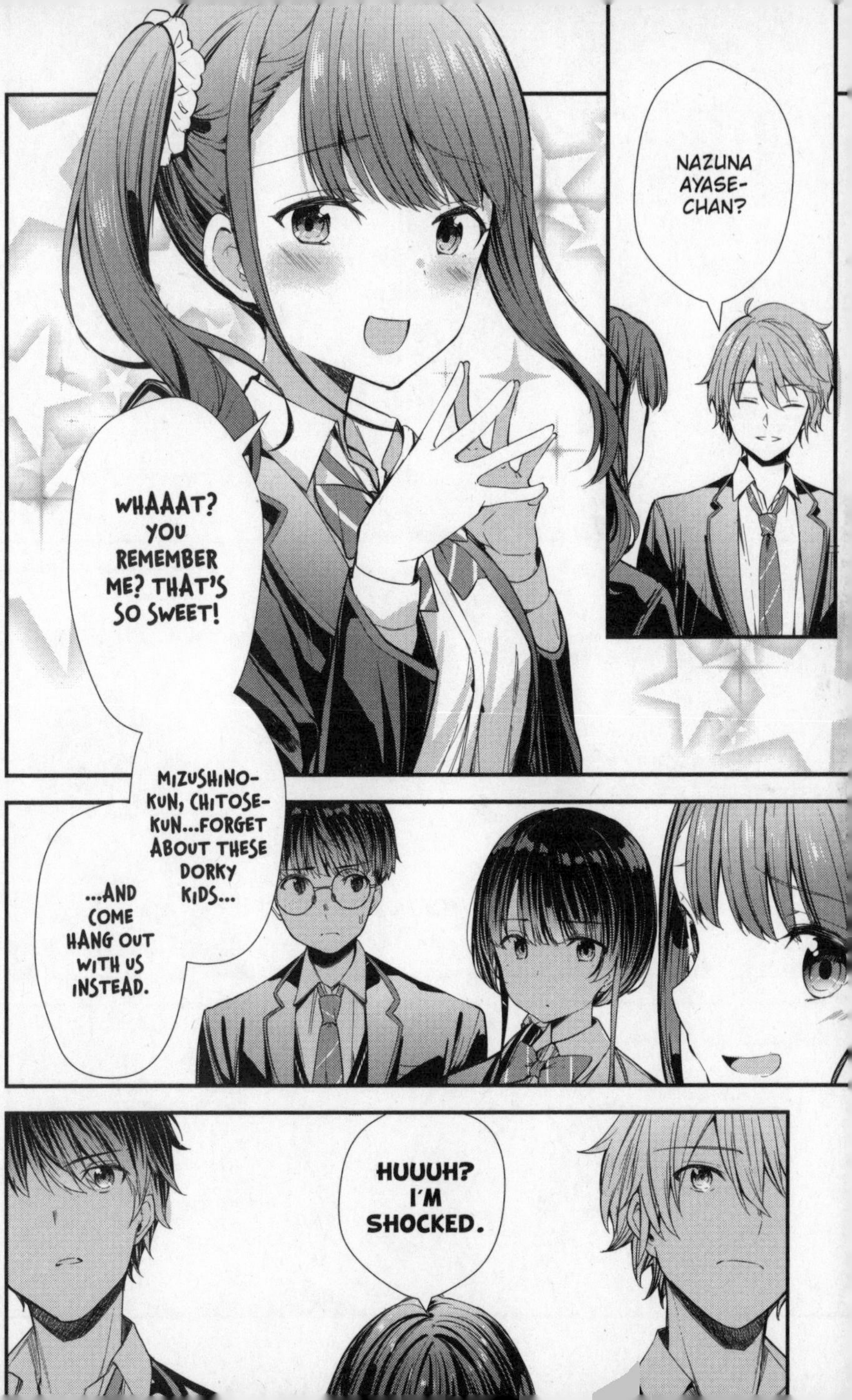
NAZUNA AYASE-CHAN?
WHAAAT? YOU REMEMBER ME? THAT'S SO SWEET!
MIZUSHINO-KUN, CHITOSE-KUN...FORGET ABOUT THESE DORKY KIDS...
...AND COME HANG OUT WITH US INSTEAD.
HUUUH? I'M SHOCKED.

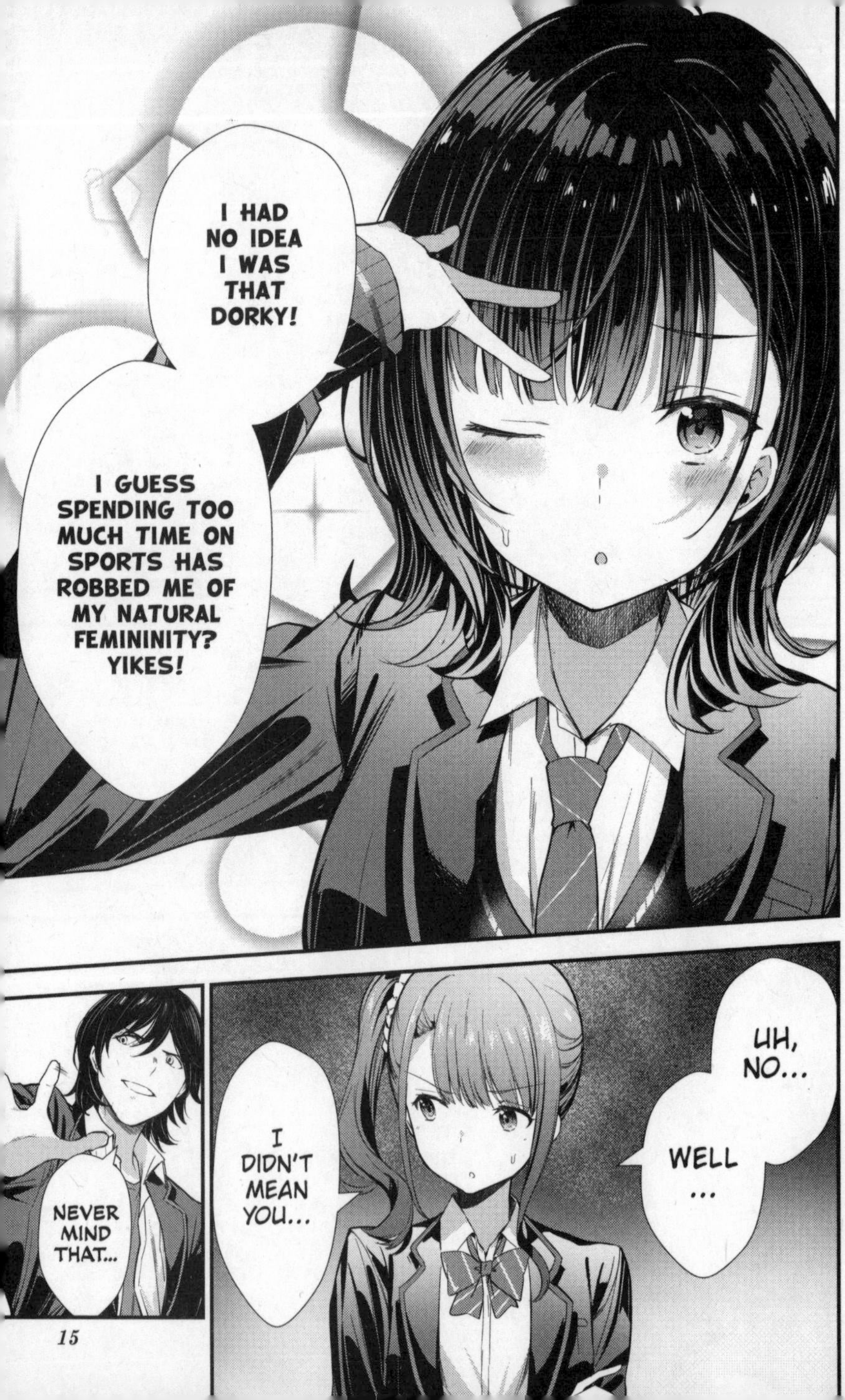
I HAD NO IDEA I WAS THAT DORKY!
I GUESS SPENDING TOO MUCH TIME ON SPORTS HAS ROBBED ME OF MY NATURAL FEMININITY? YIKES!
UH, NO...
WELL ...
I DIDN'T MEAN YOU...
NEVER MIND THAT...

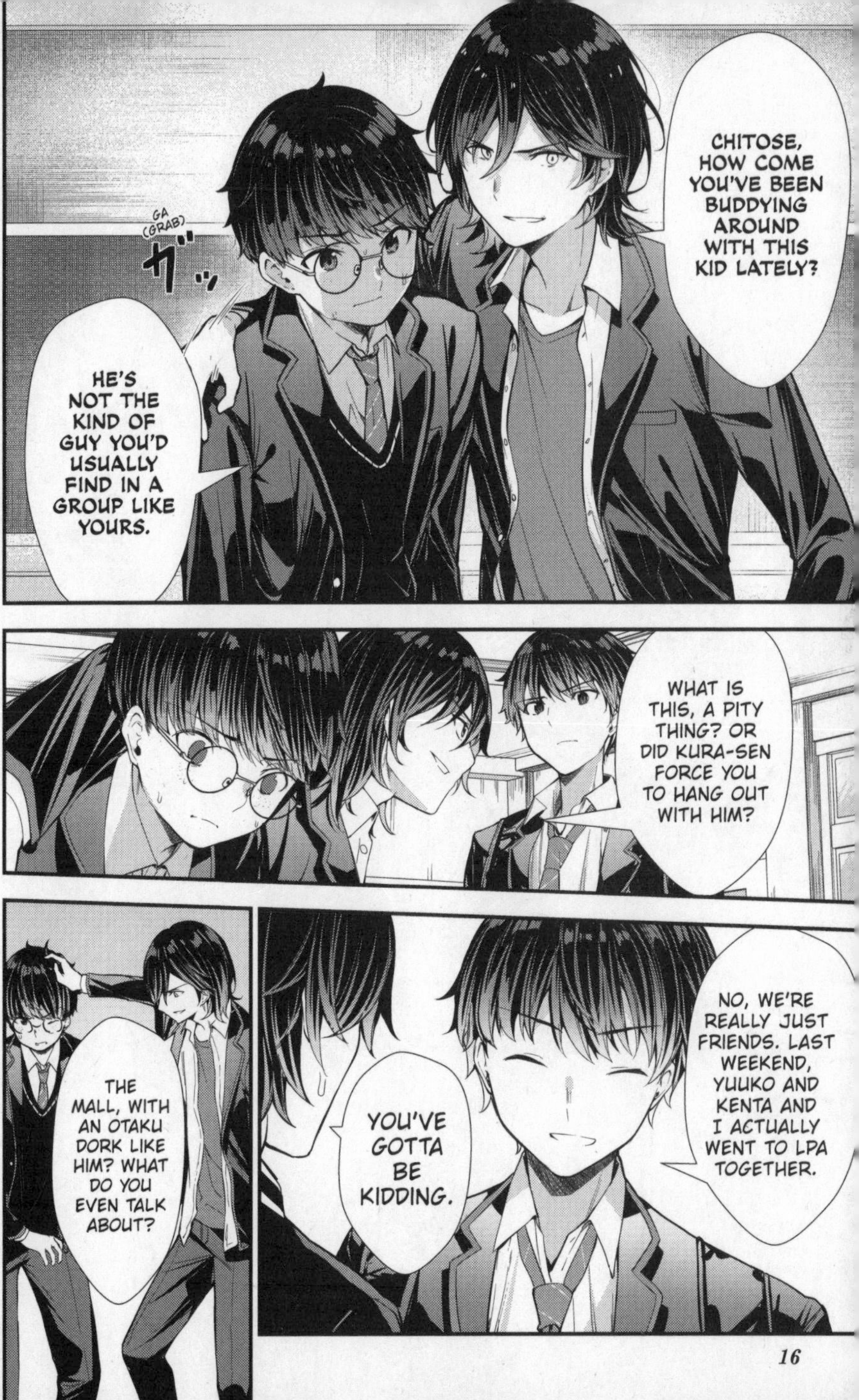
CHITOSE, HOW COME YOU'VE BEEN BUDDYING AROUND WITH THIS KID LATELY?
GA (GRAB)
ガッ
HE'S NOT THE KIND OF GUY YOU'D USUALLY FIND IN A GROUP LIKE YOURS.
WHAT IS THIS, A PITY THING? OR DID KURA-SEN FORCE YOU TO HANG OUT WITH HIM?
NO, WE'RE REALLY JUST FRIENDS. LAST WEEKEND, YUUKO AND KENTA AND I ACTUALLY WENT TO LPA TOGETHER.
YOU'VE GOTTA BE KIDDING.
THE MALL, WITH AN OTAKU DORK LIKE HIM? WHAT DO YOU EVEN TALK ABOUT?

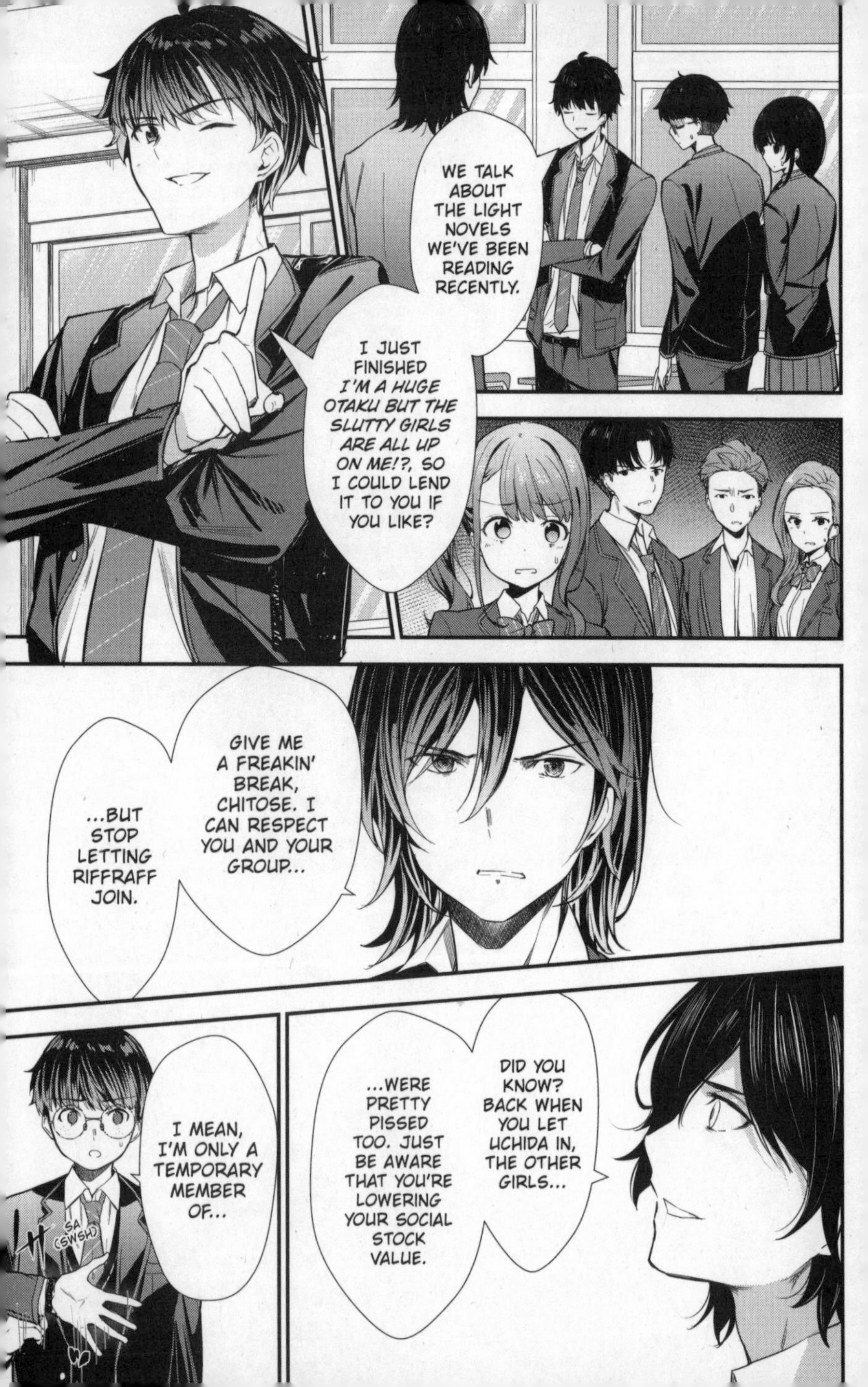
WE TALK ABOUT THE LIGHT NOVELS WE'VE BEEN READING RECENTLY.
I JUST FINISHED *I'M A HUGE OTAKU BUT THE SLUTTY GIRLS ARE ALL UP ON ME!?*, SO I COULD LEND IT TO YOU IF YOU LIKE?
GIVE ME A FREAKIN' BREAK, CHITOSE. I CAN RESPECT YOU AND YOUR GROUP...
...BUT STOP LETTING RIFFRAFF JOIN.
DID YOU KNOW? BACK WHEN YOU LET UCHIDA IN, THE OTHER GIRLS...
...WERE PRETTY PISSED TOO. JUST BE AWARE THAT YOU'RE LOWERING YOUR SOCIAL STOCK VALUE.
I MEAN, I'M ONLY A TEMPORARY MEMBER OF...
SA (SWSH)

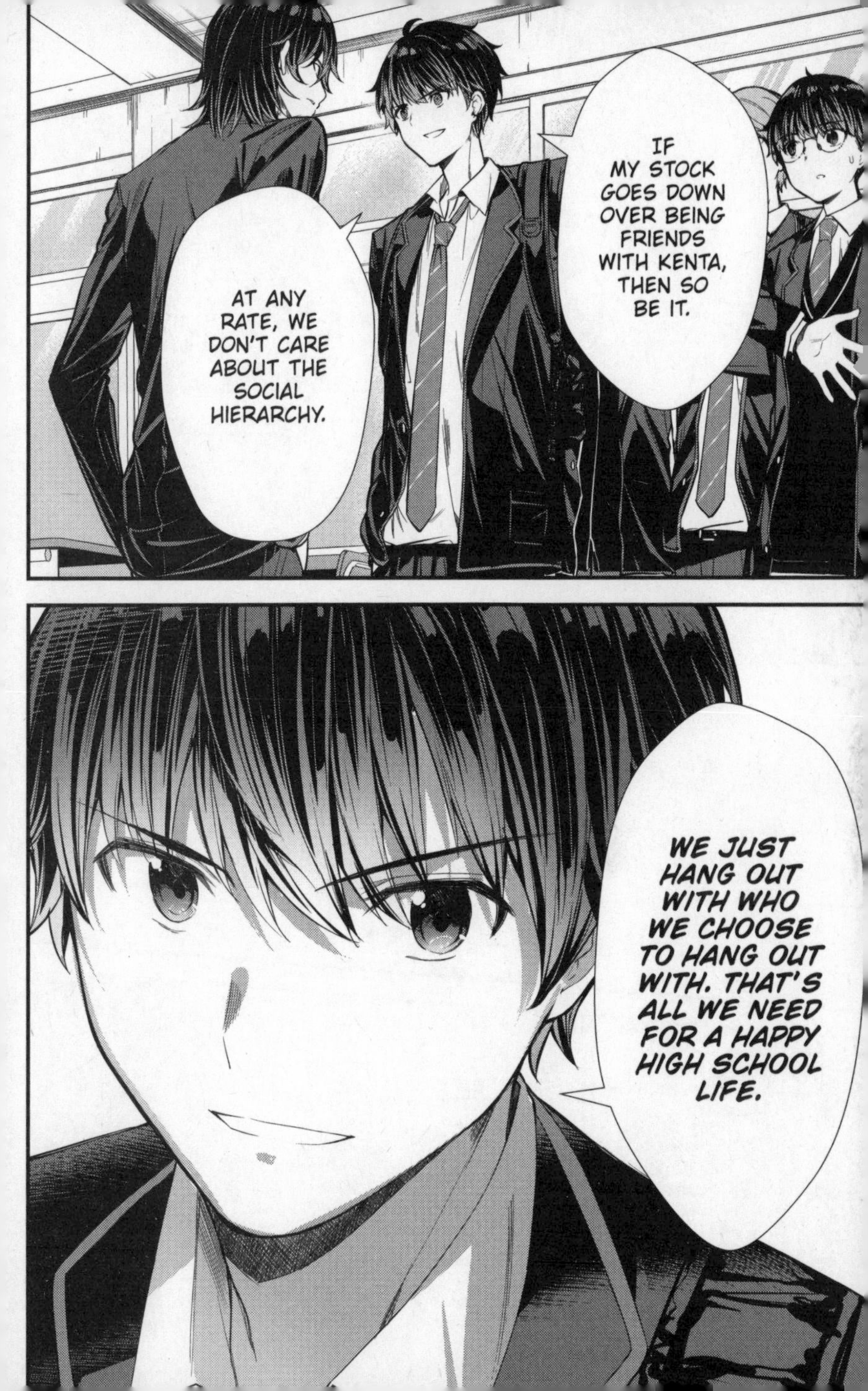
IF MY STOCK GOES DOWN OVER BEING FRIENDS WITH KENTA, THEN SO BE IT.
AT ANY RATE, WE DON'T CARE ABOUT THE SOCIAL HIERARCHY.
WE JUST HANG OUT WITH WHO WE CHOOSE TO HANG OUT WITH. THAT'S ALL WE NEED FOR A HAPPY HIGH SCHOOL LIFE.

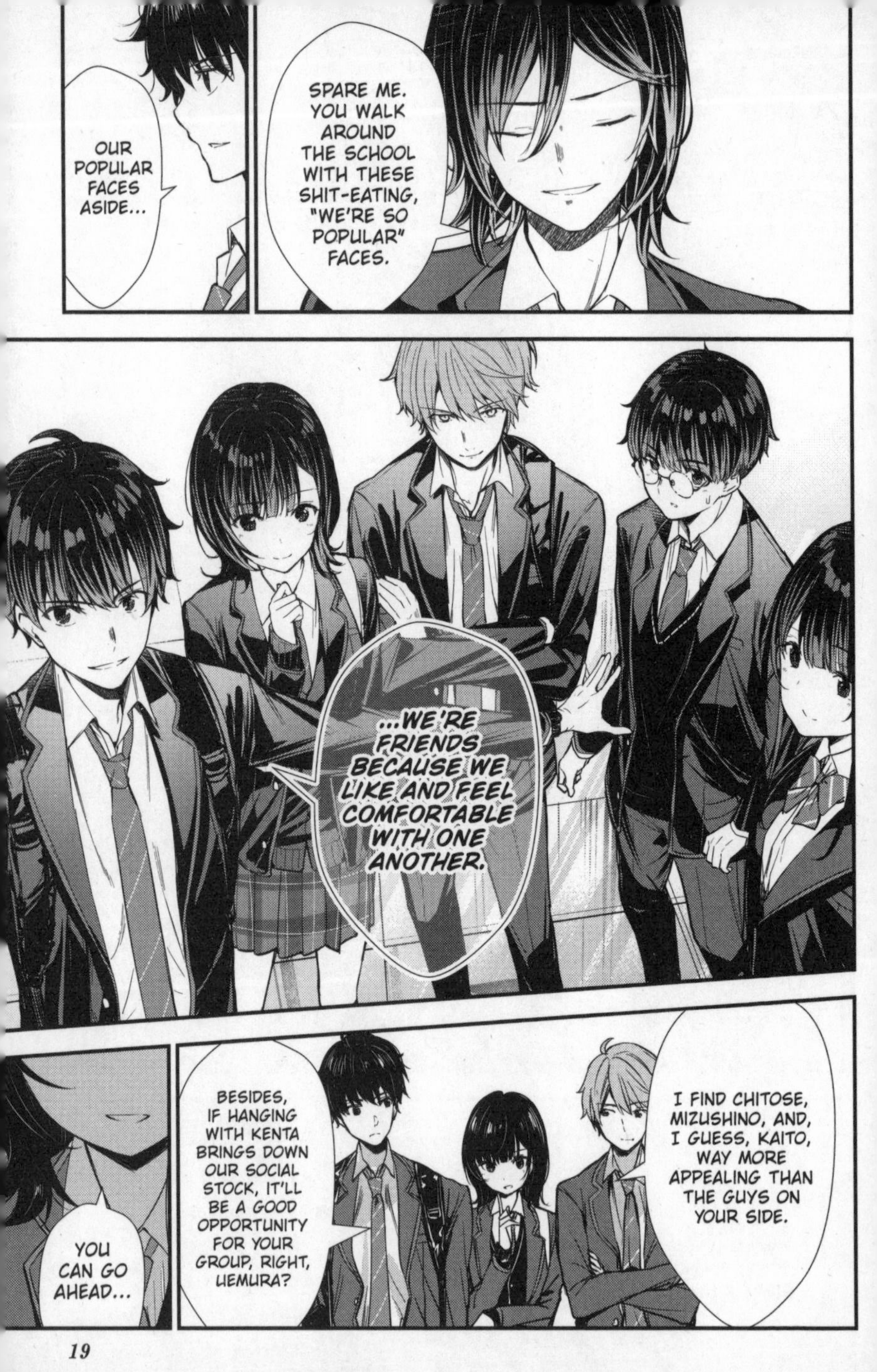

SPARE ME. YOU WALK AROUND THE SCHOOL WITH THESE SHIT-EATING, "WE'RE SO POPULAR" FACES.
OUR POPULAR FACES ASIDE...
...WE'RE FRIENDS BECAUSE WE LIKE AND FEEL COMFORTABLE WITH ONE ANOTHER.
I FIND CHITOSE, MIZUSHINO, AND, I GUESS, KAITO, WAY MORE APPEALING THAN THE GUYS ON YOUR SIDE.
BESIDES, IF HANGING WITH KENTA BRINGS DOWN OUR SOCIAL STOCK, IT'LL BE A GOOD OPPORTUNITY FOR YOUR GROUP, RIGHT, UEMURA?
YOU CAN GO AHEAD...

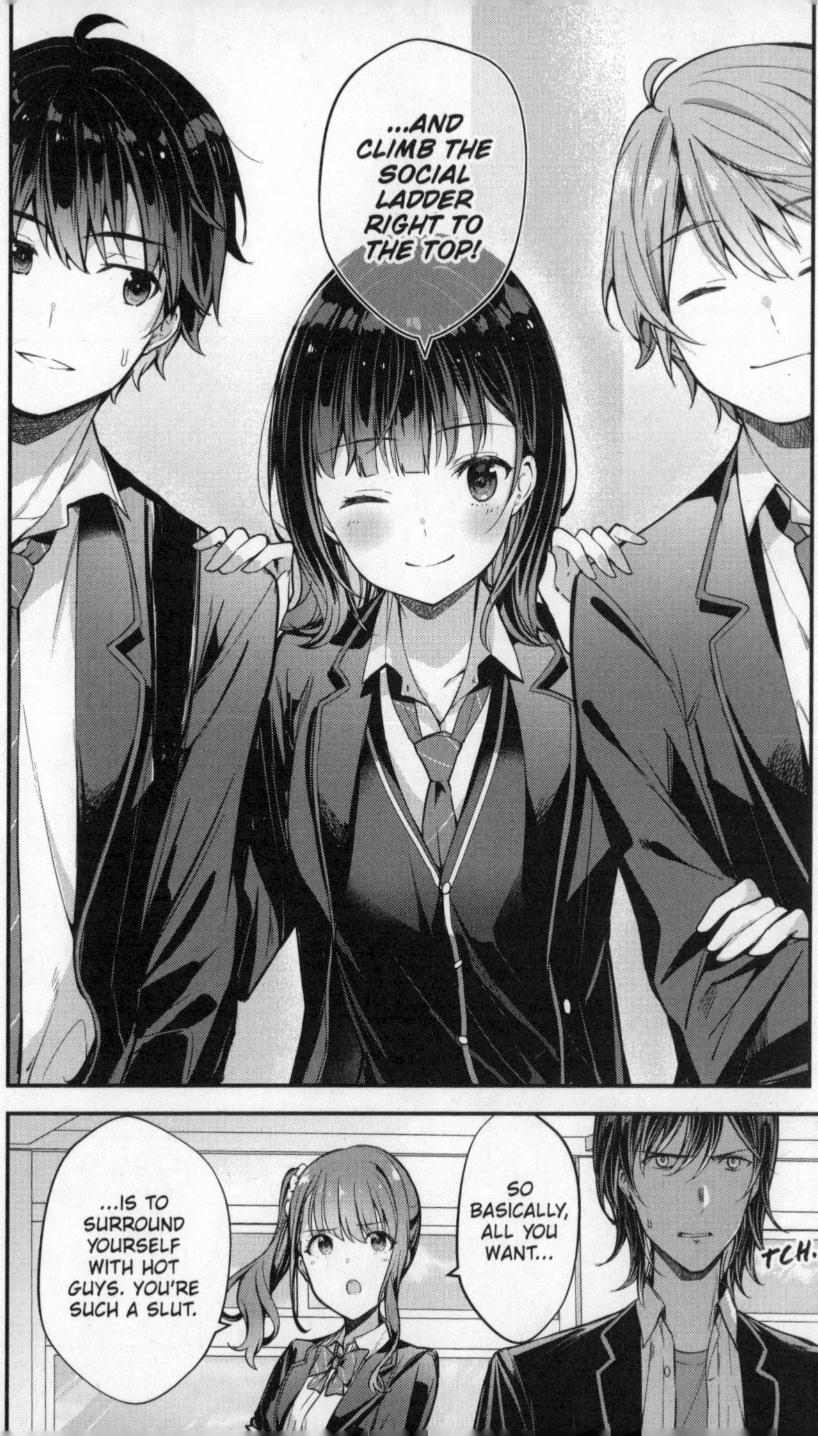
...AND CLIMB THE SOCIAL LADDER RIGHT TO THE TOP!
SO BASICALLY, ALL YOU WANT...
TCH.
...IS TO SURROUND YOURSELF WITH HOT GUYS. YOU'RE SUCH A SLUT.

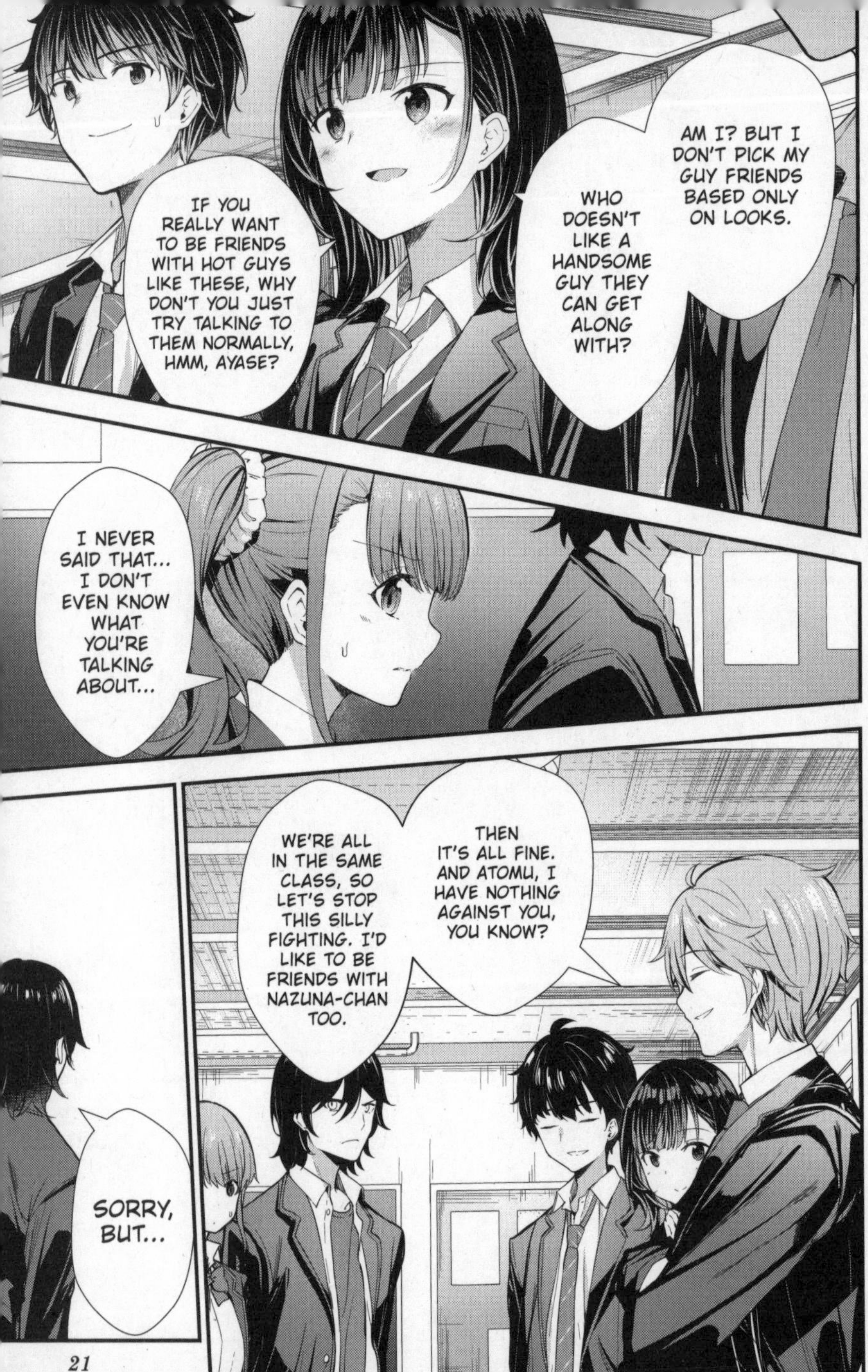
AM I? BUT I DON'T PICK MY GUY FRIENDS BASED ONLY ON LOOKS.
WHO DOESN'T LIKE A HANDSOME GUY THEY CAN GET ALONG WITH?
IF YOU REALLY WANT TO BE FRIENDS WITH HOT GUYS LIKE THESE, WHY DON'T YOU JUST TRY TALKING TO THEM NORMALLY, HMM, AYASE?
I NEVER SAID THAT... I DON'T EVEN KNOW WHAT YOU'RE TALKING ABOUT...
THEN IT'S ALL FINE. AND ATOMU, I HAVE NOTHING AGAINST YOU, YOU KNOW?
WE'RE ALL IN THE SAME CLASS, SO LET'S STOP THIS SILLY FIGHTING. I'D LIKE TO BE FRIENDS WITH NAZUNA-CHAN TOO.
SORRY, BUT...

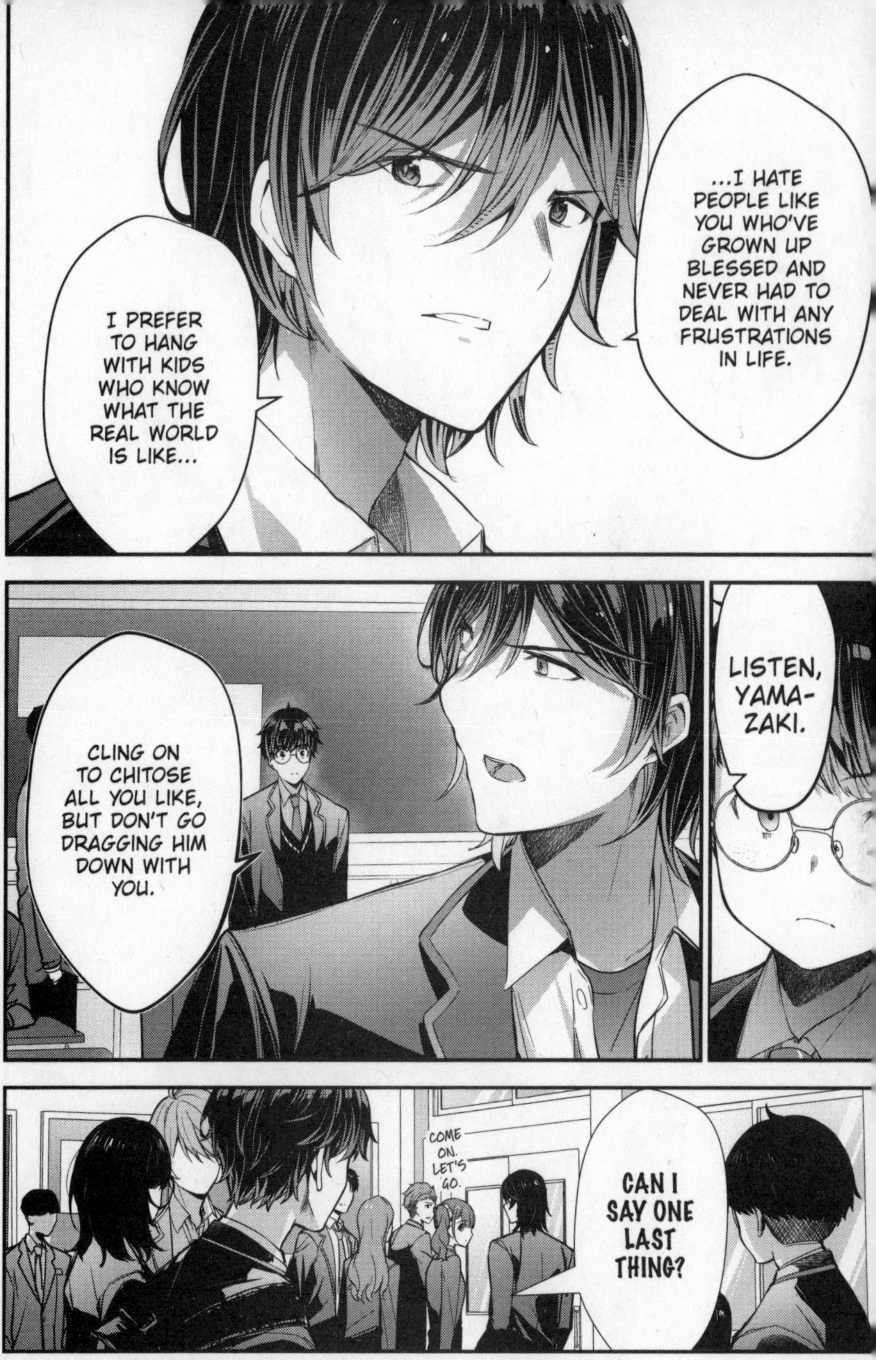
...I HATE PEOPLE LIKE YOU WHO'VE GROWN UP BLESSED AND NEVER HAD TO DEAL WITH ANY FRUSTRATIONS IN LIFE.
I PREFER TO HANG WITH KIDS WHO KNOW WHAT THE REAL WORLD IS LIKE...
LISTEN, YAMA-ZAKI.
CLING ON TO CHITOSE ALL YOU LIKE, BUT DON'T GO DRAGGING HIM DOWN WITH YOU.
CAN I SAY ONE LAST THING?
COME ON. LET'S GO.

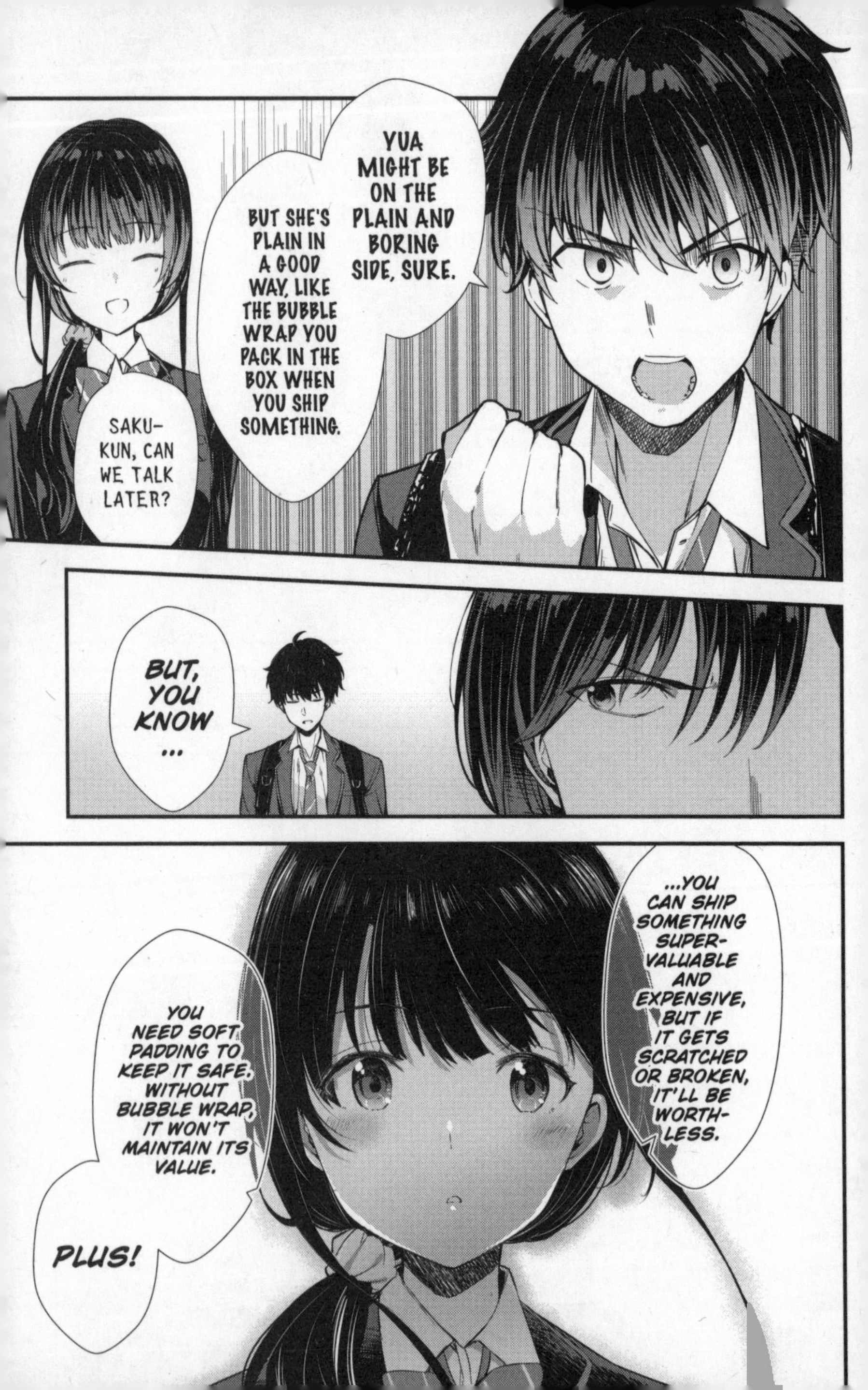
YUA MIGHT BE ON THE PLAIN AND BORING SIDE, SURE.
BUT SHE'S PLAIN IN A GOOD WAY, LIKE THE BUBBLE WRAP YOU PACK IN THE BOX WHEN YOU SHIP SOMETHING.
SAKU-KUN, CAN WE TALK LATER?
BUT, YOU KNOW ...
...YOU CAN SHIP SOMETHING SUPER-VALUABLE AND EXPENSIVE, BUT IF IT GETS SCRATCHED OR BROKEN, IT'LL BE WORTH-LESS.
YOU NEED SOFT PADDING TO KEEP IT SAFE. WITHOUT BUBBLE WRAP, IT WON'T MAINTAIN ITS VALUE.
PLUS!

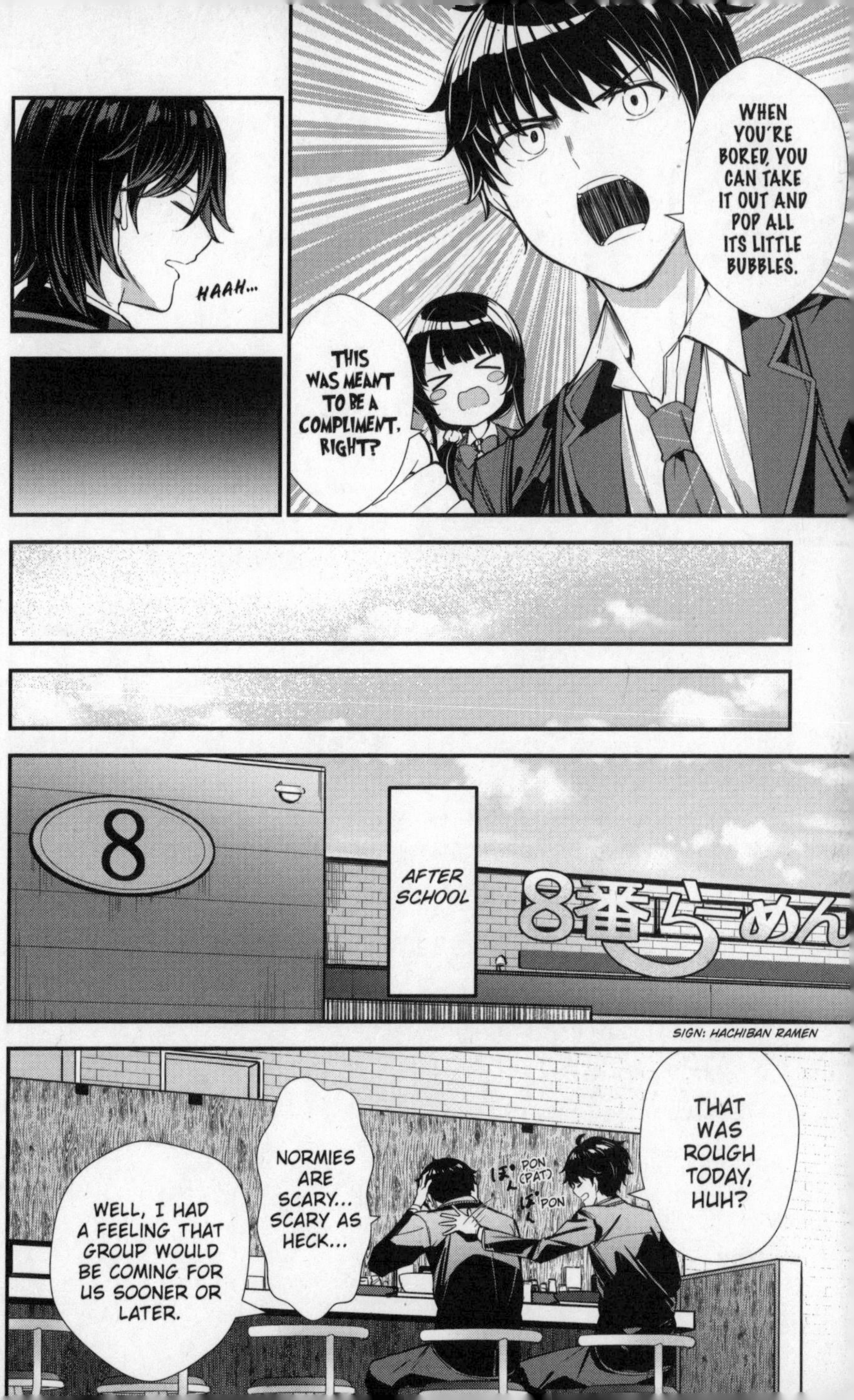
WHEN YOU'RE BORED, YOU CAN TAKE IT OUT AND POP ALL ITS LITTLE BUBBLES.
THIS WAS MEANT TO BE A COMPLIMENT, RIGHT?
HAAH...
AFTER SCHOOL
8番らーめん
SIGN: HACHIBAN RAMEN
THAT WAS ROUGH TODAY, HUH?
ぽん PON (PAT)
ぽん PON
NORMIES ARE SCARY... SCARY AS HECK...
WELL, I HAD A FEELING THAT GROUP WOULD BE COMING FOR US SOONER OR LATER.

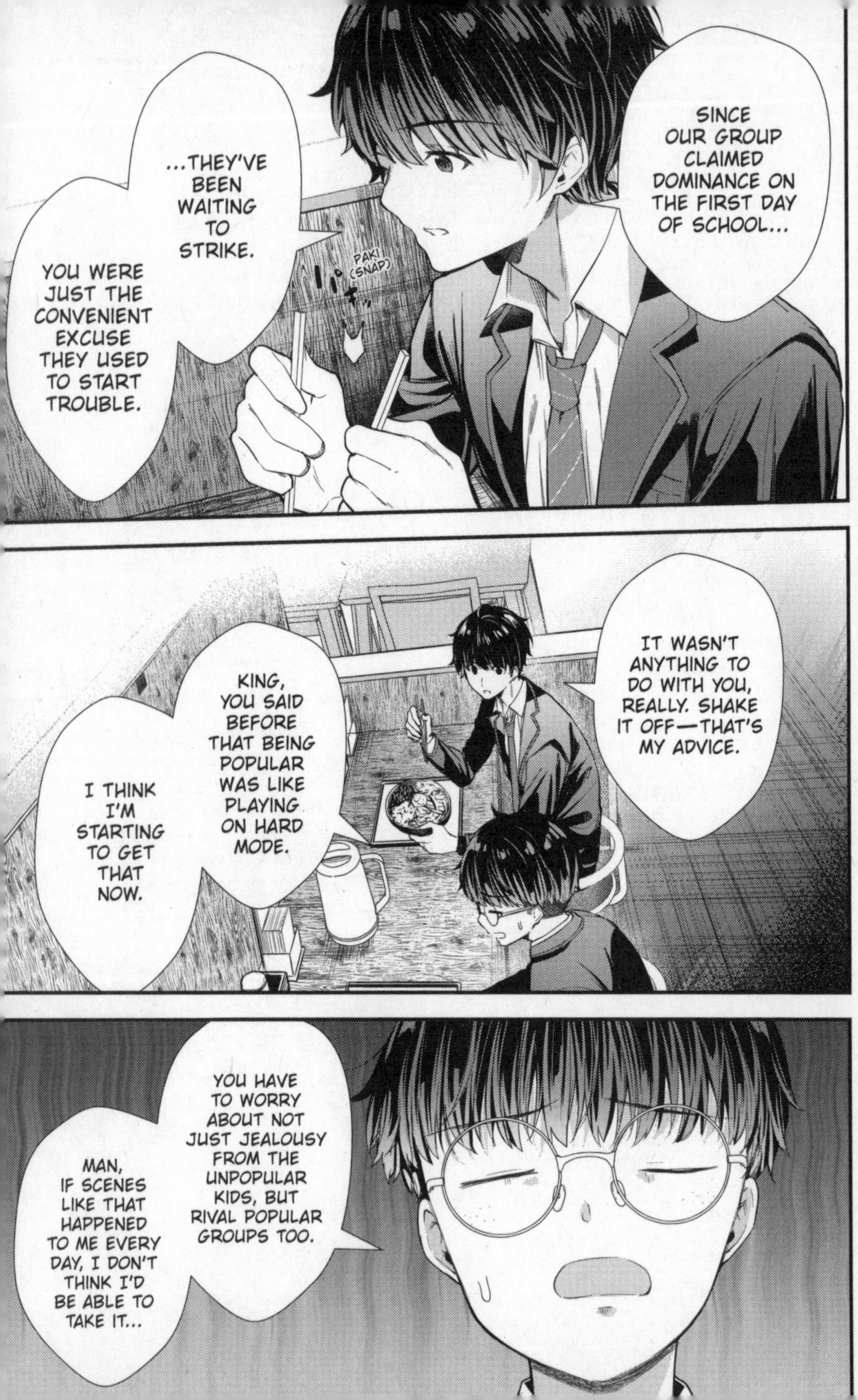
SINCE OUR GROUP CLAIMED DOMINANCE ON THE FIRST DAY OF SCHOOL...
...THEY'VE BEEN WAITING TO STRIKE.
PAKI (SNAP)
YOU WERE JUST THE CONVENIENT EXCUSE THEY USED TO START TROUBLE.
IT WASN'T ANYTHING TO DO WITH YOU, REALLY. SHAKE IT OFF—THAT'S MY ADVICE.
KING, YOU SAID BEFORE THAT BEING POPULAR WAS LIKE PLAYING ON HARD MODE.
I THINK I'M STARTING TO GET THAT NOW.
YOU HAVE TO WORRY ABOUT NOT JUST JEALOUSY FROM THE UNPOPULAR KIDS, BUT RIVAL POPULAR GROUPS TOO.
MAN, IF SCENES LIKE THAT HAPPENED TO ME EVERY DAY, I DON'T THINK I'D BE ABLE TO TAKE IT...

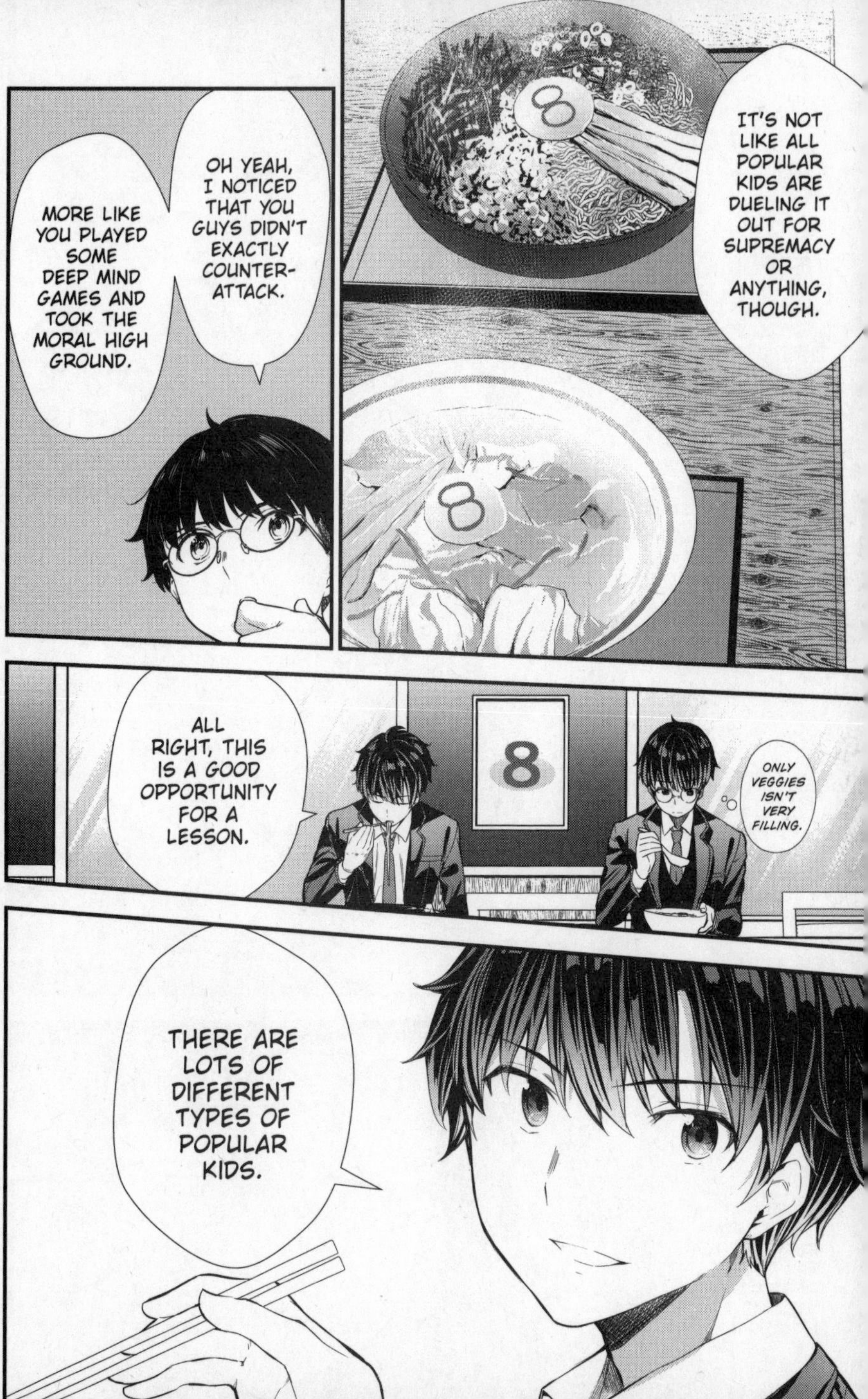
IT'S NOT LIKE ALL POPULAR KIDS ARE DUELING IT OUT FOR SUPREMACY OR ANYTHING, THOUGH.
OH YEAH, I NOTICED THAT YOU GUYS DIDN'T EXACTLY COUNTER-ATTACK.
MORE LIKE YOU PLAYED SOME DEEP MIND GAMES AND TOOK THE MORAL HIGH GROUND.
8
ONLY VEGGIES ISN'T VERY FILLING.
ALL RIGHT, THIS IS A GOOD OPPORTUNITY FOR A LESSON.
THERE ARE LOTS OF DIFFERENT TYPES OF POPULAR KIDS.

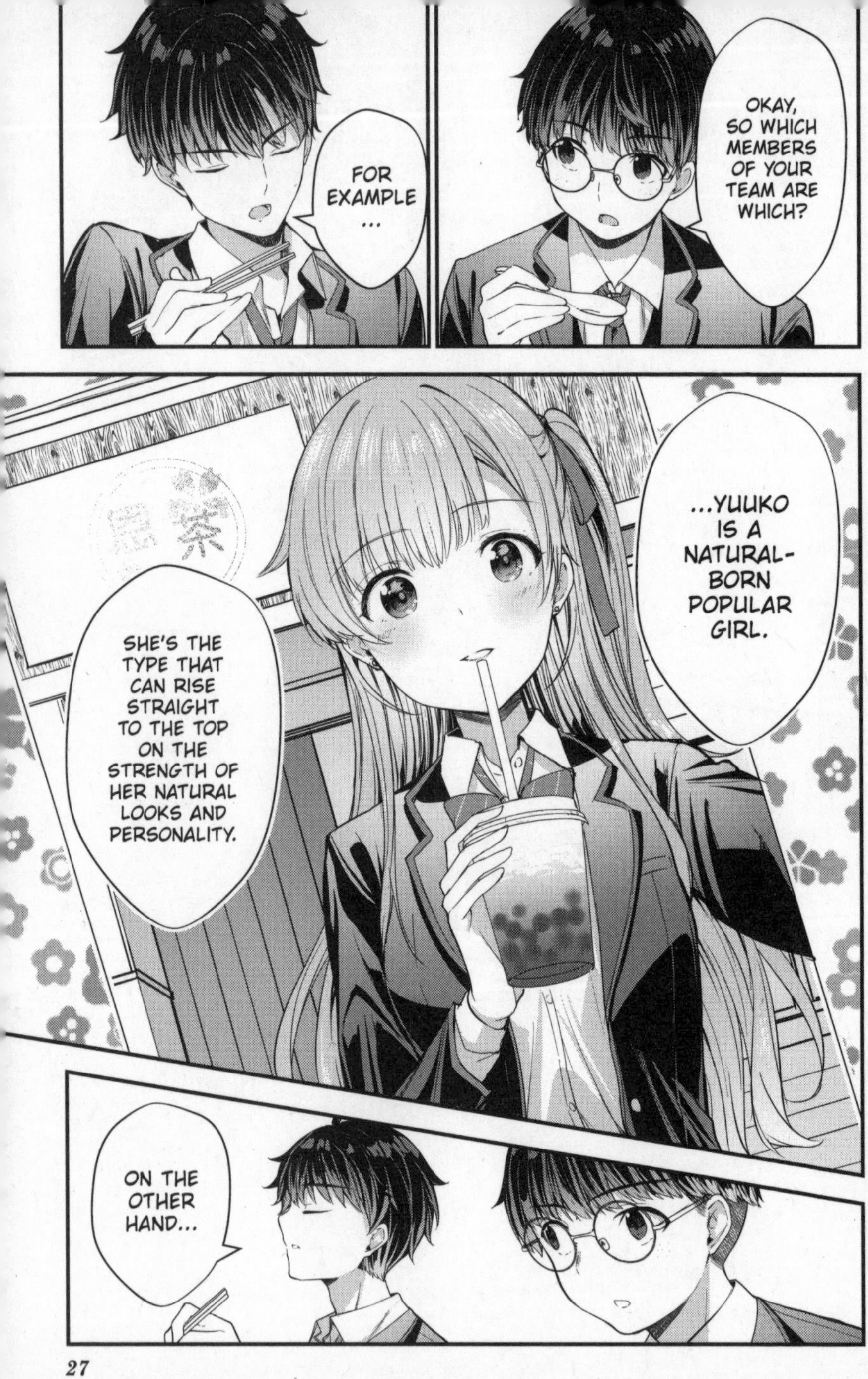
OKAY, SO WHICH MEMBERS OF YOUR TEAM ARE WHICH?
FOR EXAMPLE...
...YUUKO IS A NATURAL-BORN POPULAR GIRL.
SHE'S THE TYPE THAT CAN RISE STRAIGHT TO THE TOP ON THE STRENGTH OF HER NATURAL LOOKS AND PERSONALITY.
ON THE OTHER HAND...

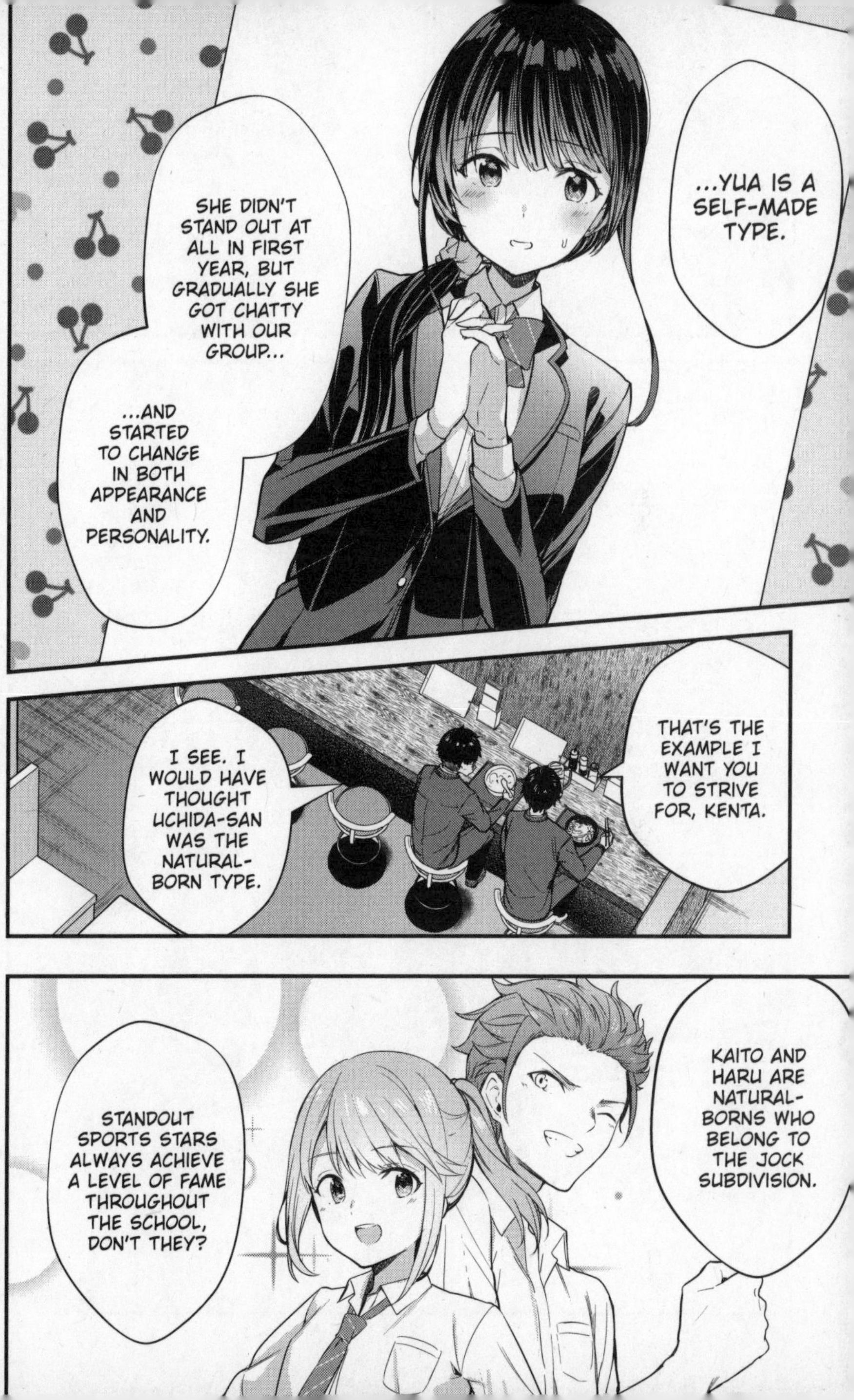
...YUA IS A SELF-MADE TYPE.
SHE DIDN'T STAND OUT AT ALL IN FIRST YEAR, BUT GRADUALLY SHE GOT CHATTY WITH OUR GROUP...
...AND STARTED TO CHANGE IN BOTH APPEARANCE AND PERSONALITY.
THAT'S THE EXAMPLE I WANT YOU TO STRIVE FOR, KENTA.
I SEE. I WOULD HAVE THOUGHT UCHIDA-SAN WAS THE NATURAL-BORN TYPE.
KAITO AND HARU ARE NATURAL-BORNS WHO BELONG TO THE JOCK SUBDIVISION.
STANDOUT SPORTS STARS ALWAYS ACHIEVE A LEVEL OF FAME THROUGHOUT THE SCHOOL, DON'T THEY?

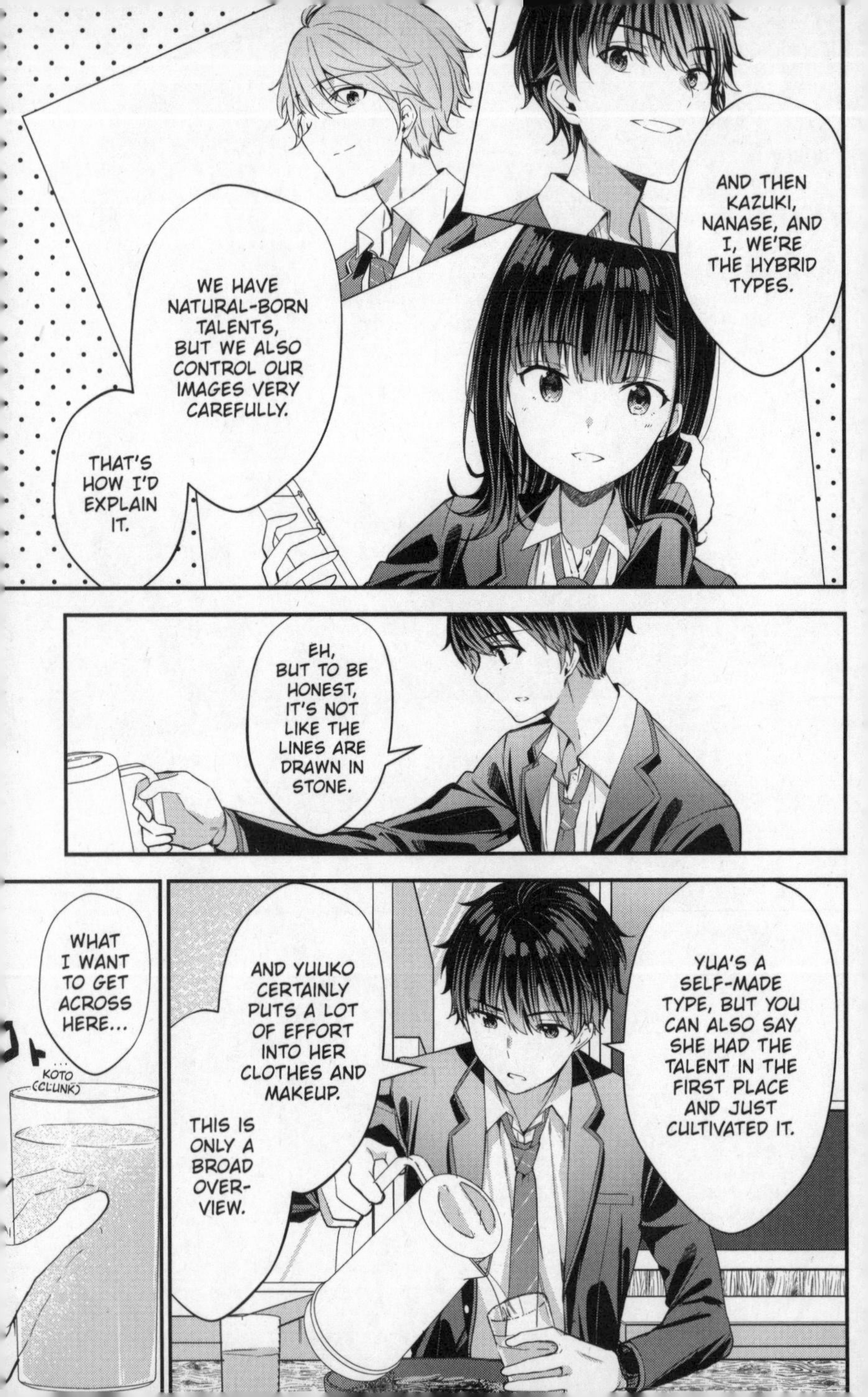
AND THEN KAZUKI, NANASE, AND I, WE'RE THE HYBRID TYPES.
WE HAVE NATURAL-BORN TALENTS, BUT WE ALSO CONTROL OUR IMAGES VERY CAREFULLY.
THAT'S HOW I'D EXPLAIN IT.
EH, BUT TO BE HONEST, IT'S NOT LIKE THE LINES ARE DRAWN IN STONE.
YUA'S A SELF-MADE TYPE, BUT YOU CAN ALSO SAY SHE HAD THE TALENT IN THE FIRST PLACE AND JUST CULTIVATED IT.
AND YUUKO CERTAINLY PUTS A LOT OF EFFORT INTO HER CLOTHES AND MAKEUP.
THIS IS ONLY A BROAD OVER-VIEW.
WHAT I WANT TO GET ACROSS HERE...
KOTO (CLUNK)

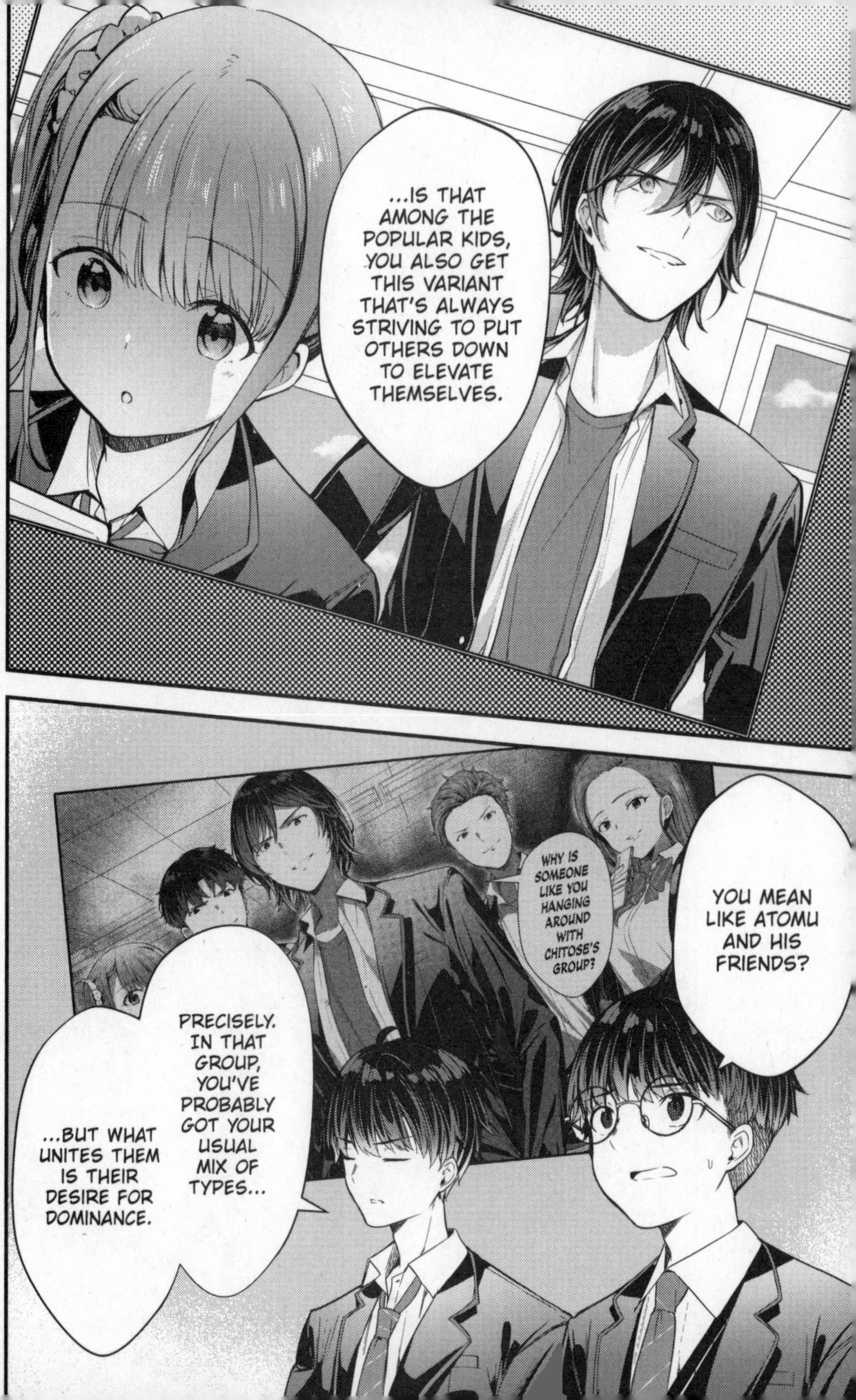
...IS THAT AMONG THE POPULAR KIDS, YOU ALSO GET THIS VARIANT THAT'S ALWAYS STRIVING TO PUT OTHERS DOWN TO ELEVATE THEMSELVES.
YOU MEAN LIKE ATOMU AND HIS FRIENDS?
WHY IS SOMEONE LIKE YOU HANGING AROUND WITH CHITOSE'S GROUP?
PRECISELY. IN THAT GROUP, YOU'VE PROBABLY GOT YOUR USUAL MIX OF TYPES...
...BUT WHAT UNITES THEM IS THEIR DESIRE FOR DOMINANCE.

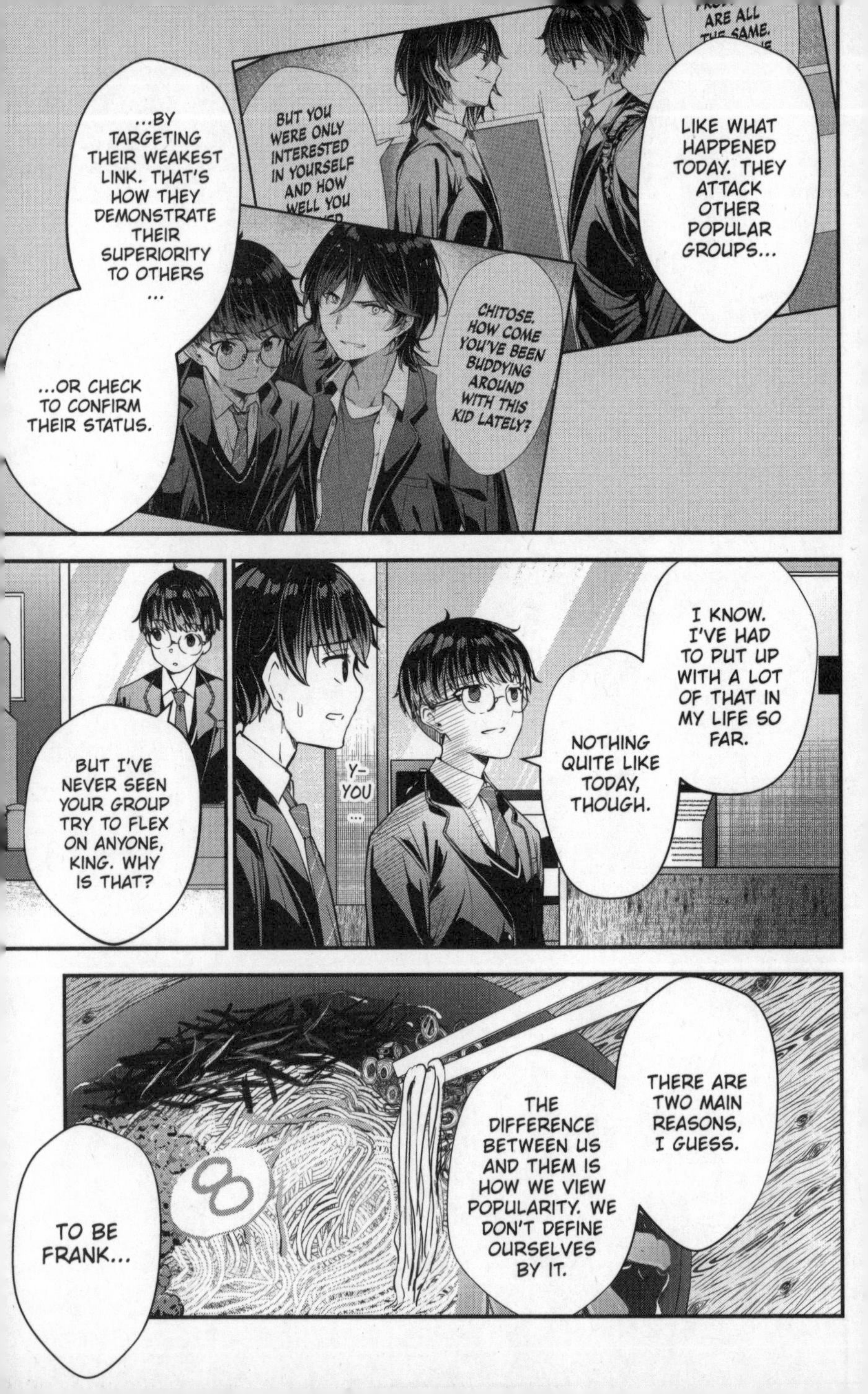
ARE ALL THE SAME.
LIKE WHAT HAPPENED TODAY. THEY ATTACK OTHER POPULAR GROUPS...
BUT YOU WERE ONLY INTERESTED IN YOURSELF AND HOW WELL YOU
...BY TARGETING THEIR WEAKEST LINK. THAT'S HOW THEY DEMONSTRATE THEIR SUPERIORITY TO OTHERS...
CHITOSE. HOW COME YOU'VE BEEN BUDDYING AROUND WITH THIS KID LATELY?
...OR CHECK TO CONFIRM THEIR STATUS.
I KNOW. I'VE HAD TO PUT UP WITH A LOT OF THAT IN MY LIFE SO FAR.
NOTHING QUITE LIKE TODAY, THOUGH.
Y-YOU...
BUT I'VE NEVER SEEN YOUR GROUP TRY TO FLEX ON ANYONE, KING. WHY IS THAT?
THERE ARE TWO MAIN REASONS, I GUESS.
THE DIFFERENCE BETWEEN US AND THEM IS HOW WE VIEW POPULARITY. WE DON'T DEFINE OURSELVES BY IT.
TO BE FRANK...

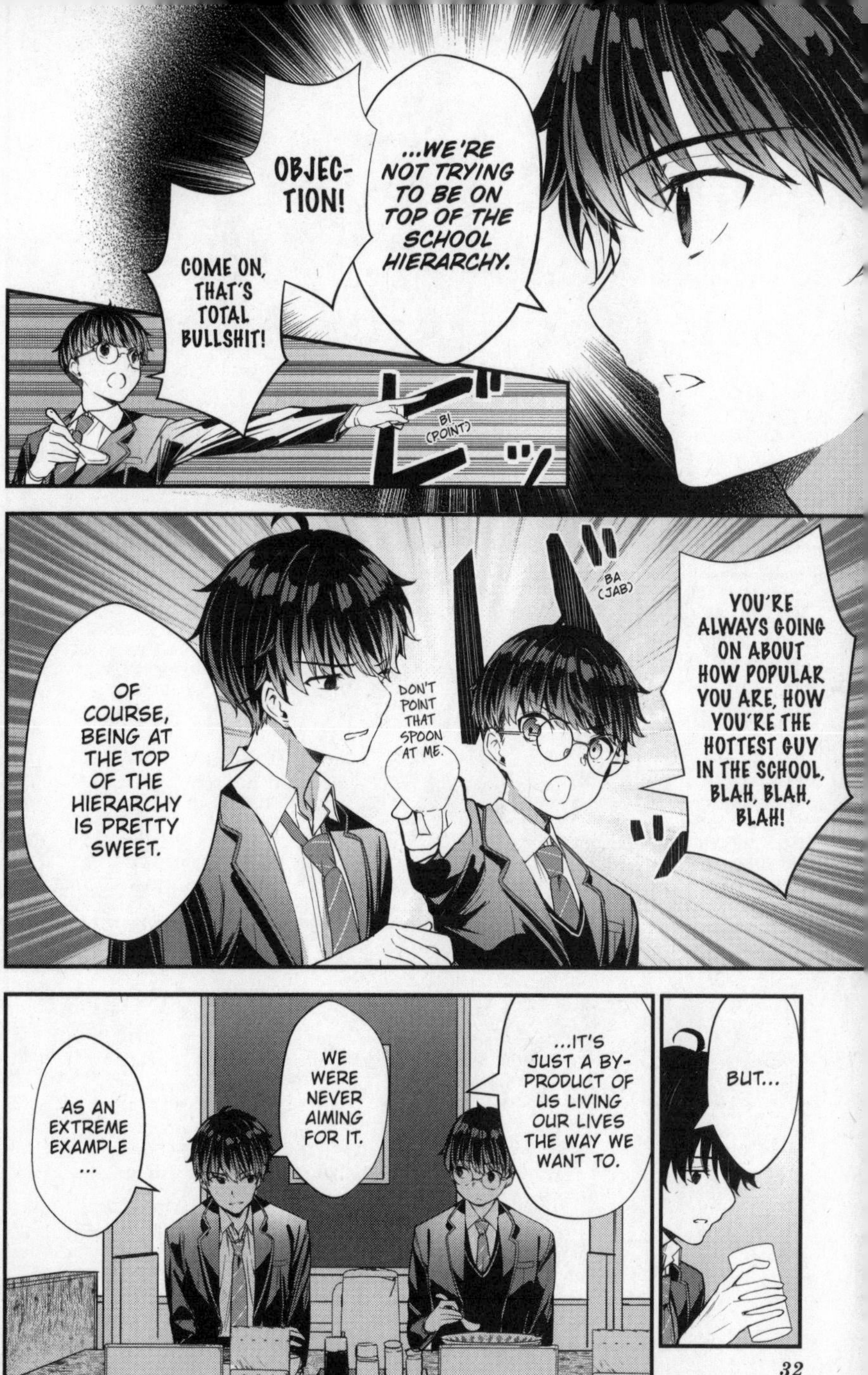

...WE'RE NOT TRYING TO BE ON TOP OF THE SCHOOL HIERARCHY.
OBJECTION!
COME ON, THAT'S TOTAL BULLSHIT!
BI (POINT)
BA (JAB)
YOU'RE ALWAYS GOING ON ABOUT HOW POPULAR YOU ARE, HOW YOU'RE THE HOTTEST GUY IN THE SCHOOL, BLAH, BLAH, BLAH!
DON'T POINT THAT SPOON AT ME.
OF COURSE, BEING AT THE TOP OF THE HIERARCHY IS PRETTY SWEET.
BUT...
...IT'S JUST A BY-PRODUCT OF US LIVING OUR LIVES THE WAY WE WANT TO.
WE WERE NEVER AIMING FOR IT.
AS AN EXTREME EXAMPLE ...

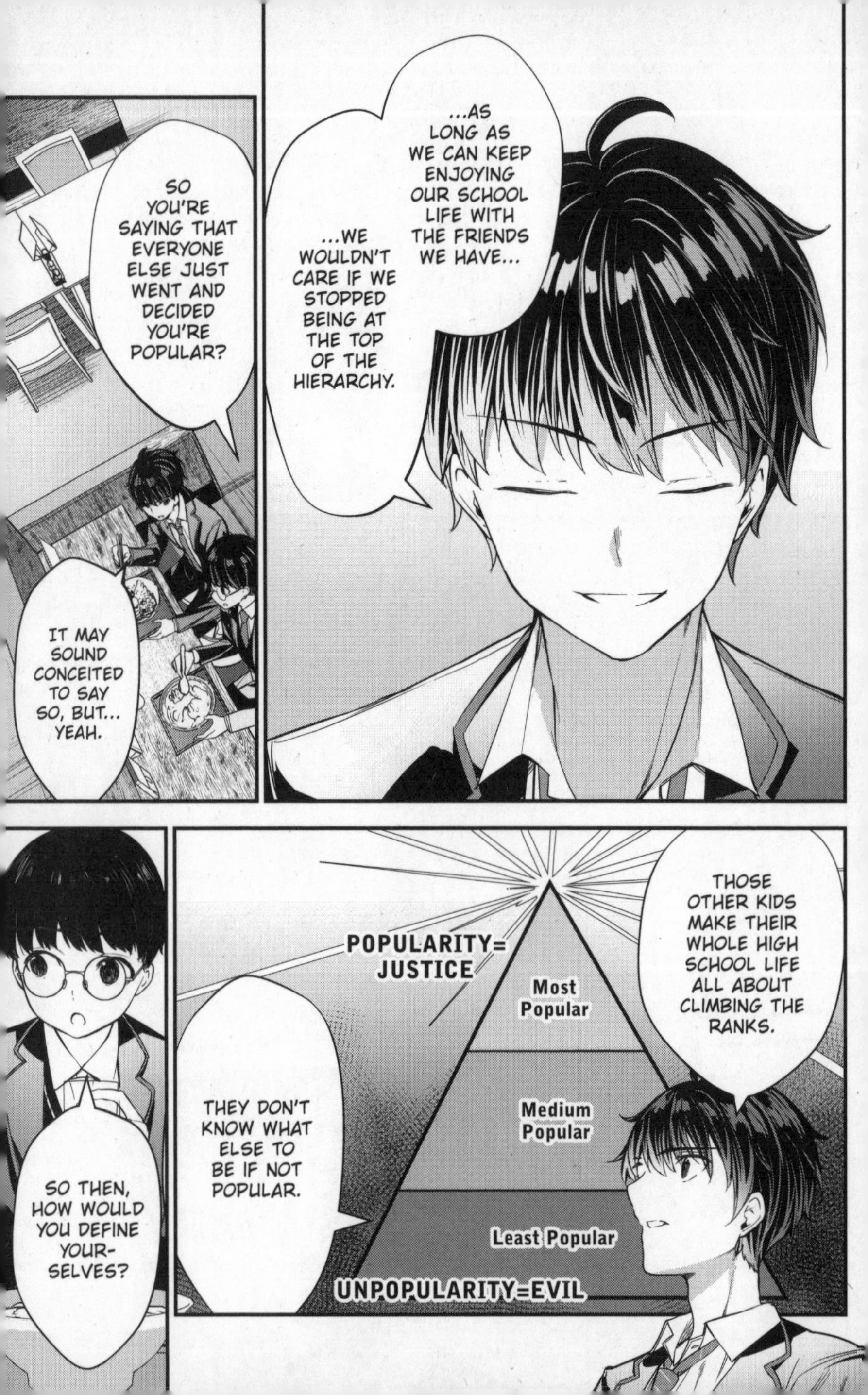
...AS LONG AS WE CAN KEEP ENJOYING OUR SCHOOL LIFE WITH THE FRIENDS WE HAVE...
...WE WOULDN'T CARE IF WE STOPPED BEING AT THE TOP OF THE HIERARCHY.
SO YOU'RE SAYING THAT EVERYONE ELSE JUST WENT AND DECIDED YOU'RE POPULAR?
IT MAY SOUND CONCEITED TO SAY SO, BUT... YEAH.
THOSE OTHER KIDS MAKE THEIR WHOLE HIGH SCHOOL LIFE ALL ABOUT CLIMBING THE RANKS.
POPULARITY= JUSTICE
Most Popular
Medium Popular
Least Popular
UNPOPULARITY=EVIL
THEY DON'T KNOW WHAT ELSE TO BE IF NOT POPULAR.
SO THEN, HOW WOULD YOU DEFINE YOUR-SELVES?

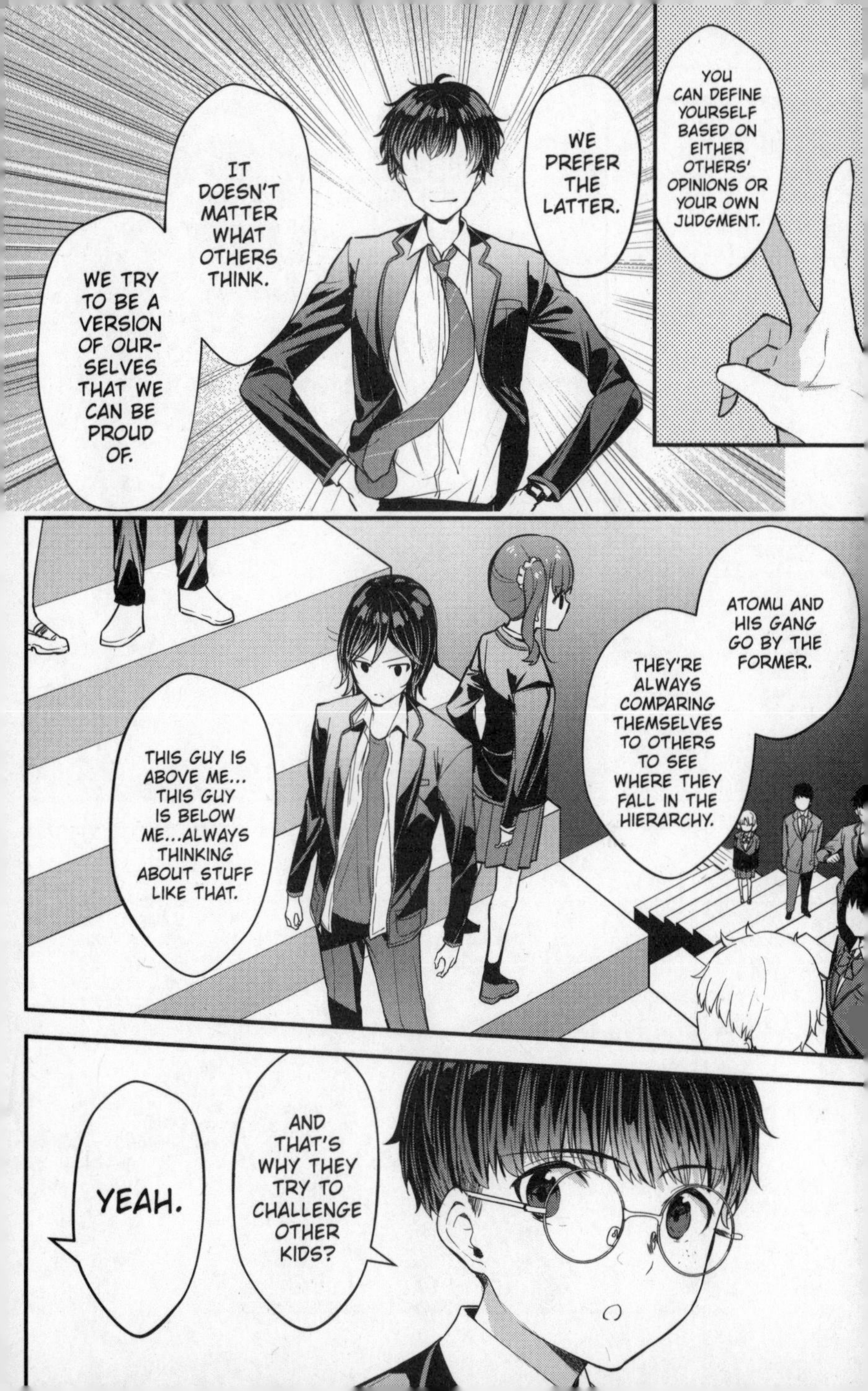
YOU CAN DEFINE YOURSELF BASED ON EITHER OTHERS' OPINIONS OR YOUR OWN JUDGMENT.
WE PREFER THE LATTER.
IT DOESN'T MATTER WHAT OTHERS THINK.
WE TRY TO BE A VERSION OF OUR-SELVES THAT WE CAN BE PROUD OF.
ATOMU AND HIS GANG GO BY THE FORMER.
THEY'RE ALWAYS COMPARING THEMSELVES TO OTHERS TO SEE WHERE THEY FALL IN THE HIERARCHY.
THIS GUY IS ABOVE ME... THIS GUY IS BELOW ME...ALWAYS THINKING ABOUT STUFF LIKE THAT.
AND THAT'S WHY THEY TRY TO CHALLENGE OTHER KIDS?
YEAH.

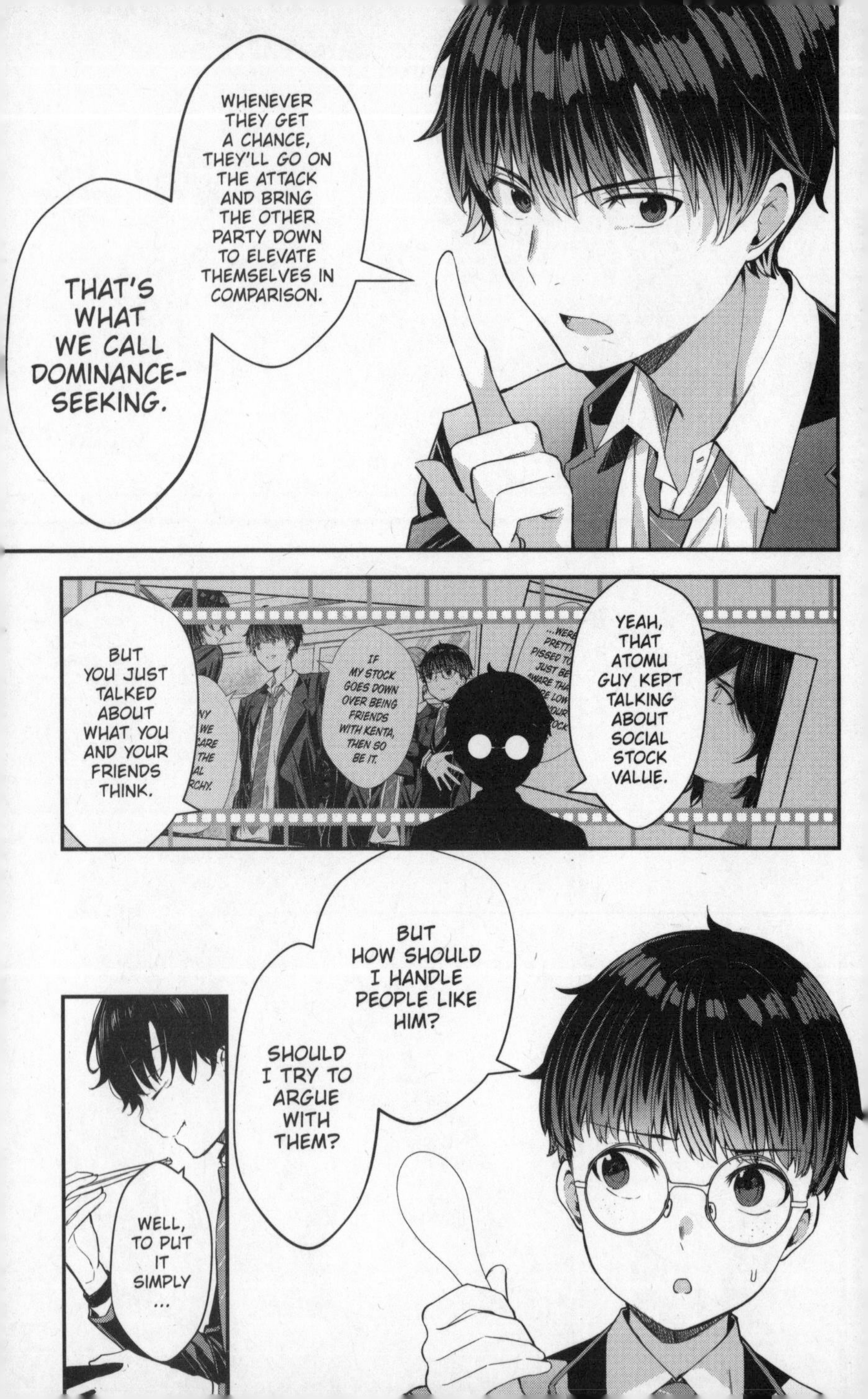
WHENEVER THEY GET A CHANCE, THEY'LL GO ON THE ATTACK AND BRING THE OTHER PARTY DOWN TO ELEVATE THEMSELVES IN COMPARISON.
THAT'S WHAT WE CALL DOMINANCE-SEEKING.
YEAH, THAT ATOMU GUY KEPT TALKING ABOUT SOCIAL STOCK VALUE.
IF MY STOCK GOES DOWN OVER BEING FRIENDS WITH KENTA, THEN SO BE IT.
BUT YOU JUST TALKED ABOUT WHAT YOU AND YOUR FRIENDS THINK.
BUT HOW SHOULD I HANDLE PEOPLE LIKE HIM?
SHOULD I TRY TO ARGUE WITH THEM?
WELL, TO PUT IT SIMPLY ...

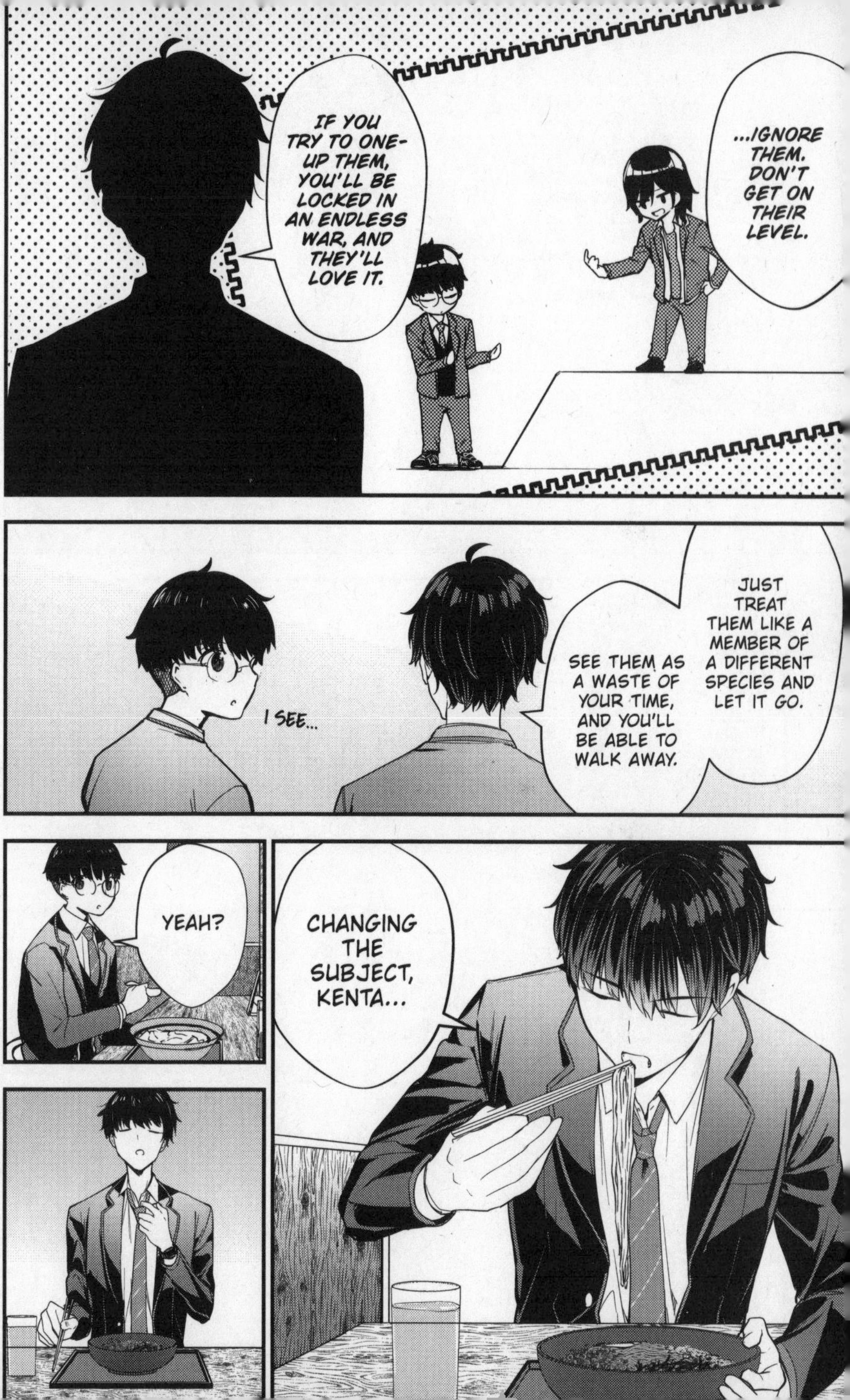
...IGNORE THEM. DON'T GET ON THEIR LEVEL.
IF YOU TRY TO ONE-UP THEM, YOU'LL BE LOCKED IN AN ENDLESS WAR, AND THEY'LL LOVE IT.
JUST TREAT THEM LIKE A MEMBER OF A DIFFERENT SPECIES AND LET IT GO.
SEE THEM AS A WASTE OF YOUR TIME, AND YOU'LL BE ABLE TO WALK AWAY.
I SEE...
CHANGING THE SUBJECT, KENTA...
YEAH?

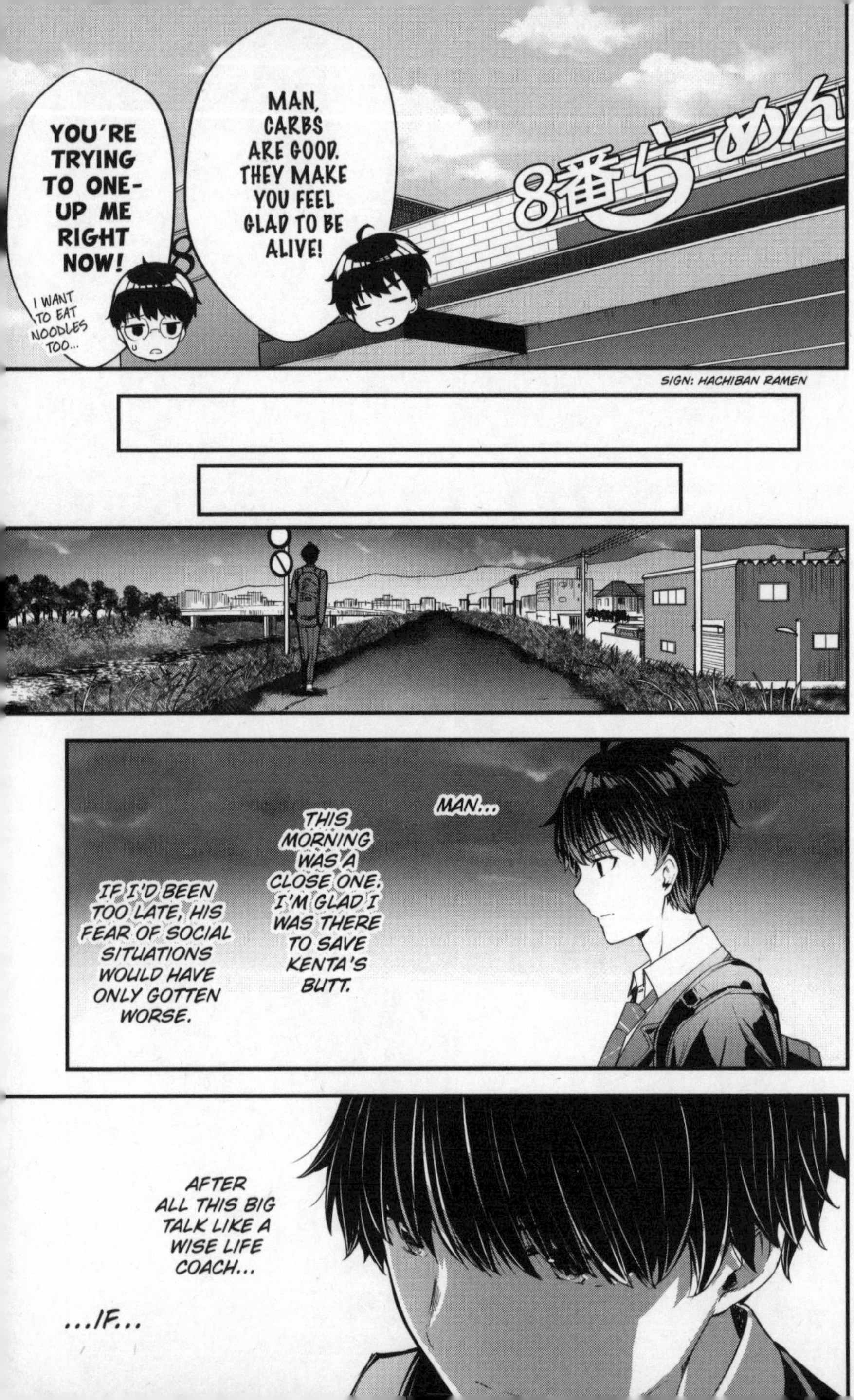
8番らーめん
MAN, CARBS ARE GOOD. THEY MAKE YOU FEEL GLAD TO BE ALIVE!
YOU'RE TRYING TO ONE-UP ME RIGHT NOW!
I WANT TO EAT NOODLES TOO...
SIGN: HACHIBAN RAMEN
MAN...
THIS MORNING WAS A CLOSE ONE. I'M GLAD I WAS THERE TO SAVE KENTA'S BUTT.
IF I'D BEEN TOO LATE, HIS FEAR OF SOCIAL SITUATIONS WOULD HAVE ONLY GOTTEN WORSE.
AFTER ALL THIS BIG TALK LIKE A WISE LIFE COACH...
...IF...

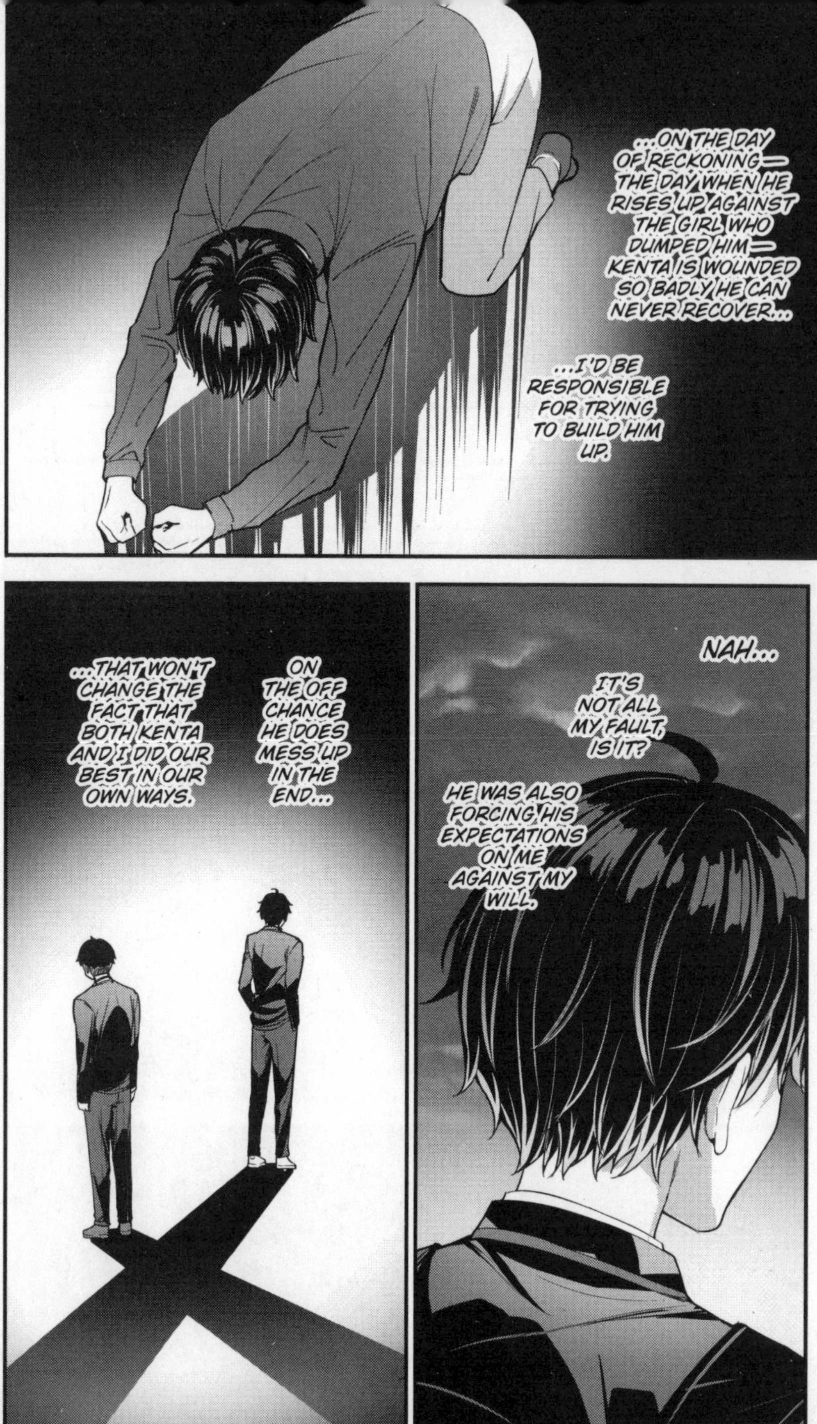
...ON THE DAY OF RECKONING—THE DAY WHEN HE RISES UP AGAINST THE GIRL WHO DUMPED HIM—KENTA IS WOUNDED SO BADLY HE CAN NEVER RECOVER...
...I'D BE RESPONSIBLE FOR TRYING TO BUILD HIM UP.
NAH...
IT'S NOT ALL MY FAULT, IS IT?
HE WAS ALSO FORCING HIS EXPECTATIONS ON ME AGAINST MY WILL.
ON THE OFF CHANCE HE DOES MESS UP IN THE END...
...THAT WON'T CHANGE THE FACT THAT BOTH KENTA AND I DID OUR BEST IN OUR OWN WAYS.

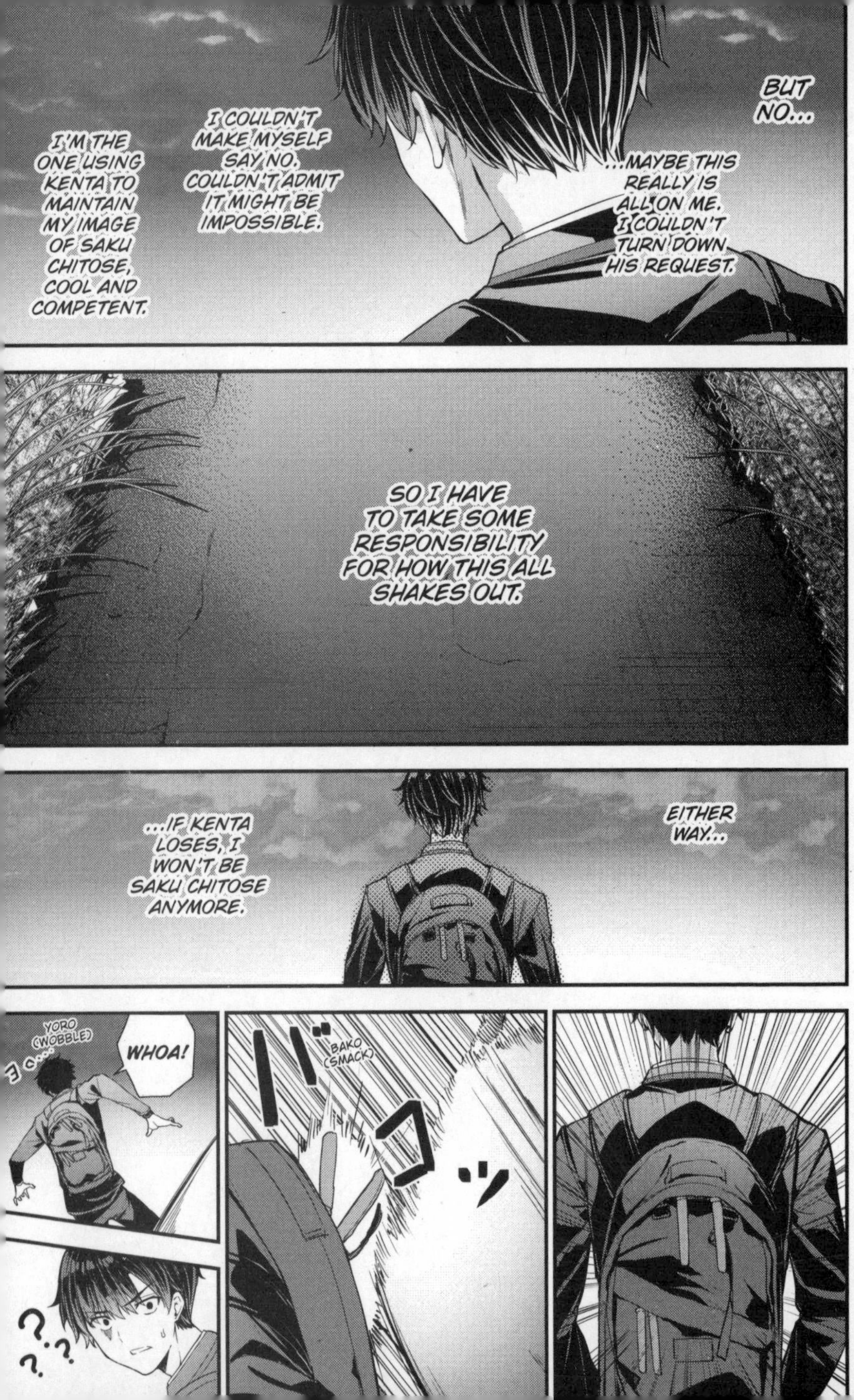
BUT NO...
...MAYBE THIS REALLY IS ALL ON ME. I COULDN'T TURN DOWN HIS REQUEST.
I COULDN'T MAKE MYSELF SAY NO. COULDN'T ADMIT IT MIGHT BE IMPOSSIBLE.
I'M THE ONE USING KENTA TO MAINTAIN MY IMAGE OF SAKU CHITOSE, COOL AND COMPETENT.
SO I HAVE TO TAKE SOME RESPONSIBILITY FOR HOW THIS ALL SHAKES OUT.
EITHER WAY...
...IF KENTA LOSES, I WON'T BE SAKU CHITOSE ANYMORE.
BAKO (SMACK)
YORO (WOBBLE)
WHOA!

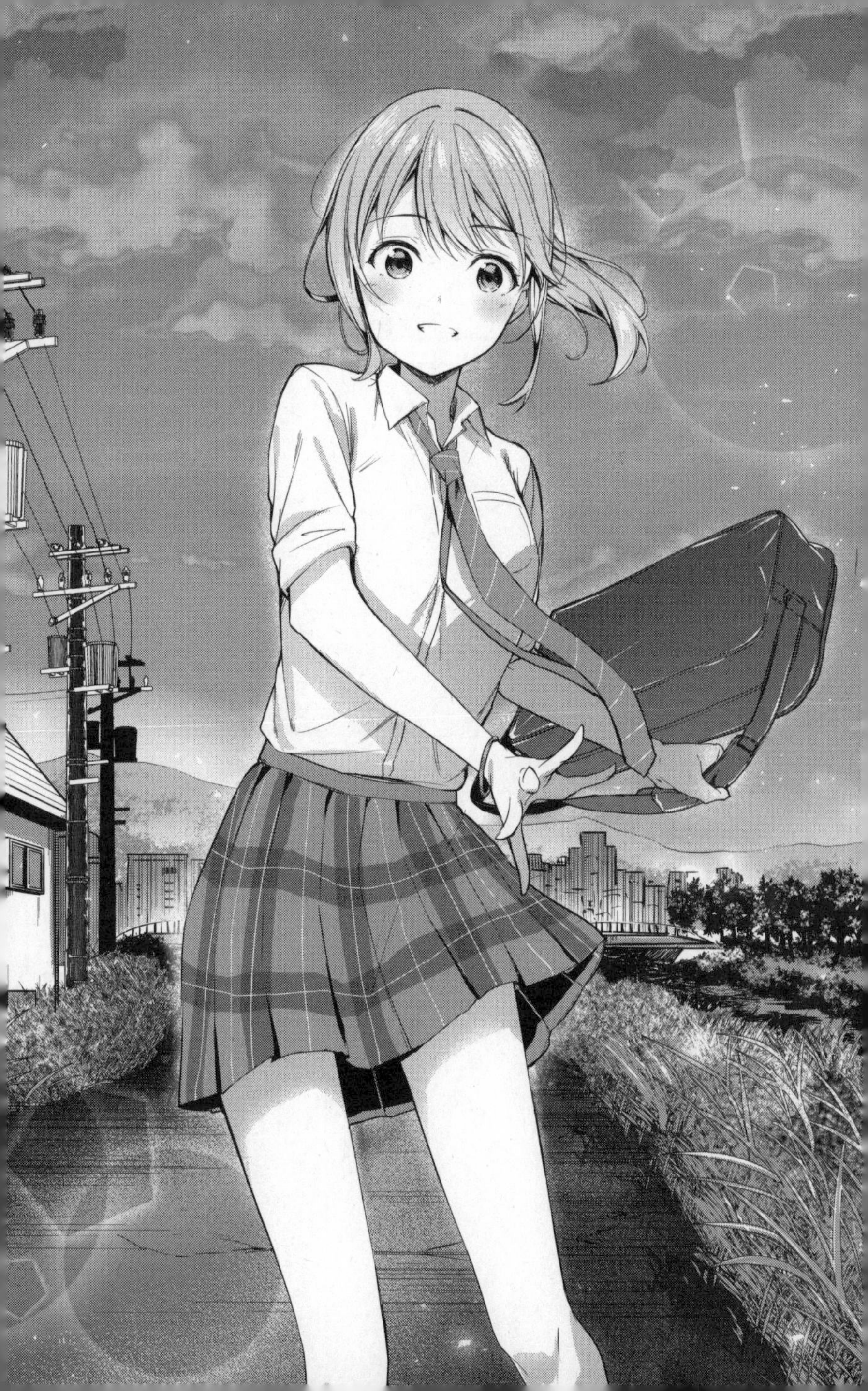

Chitose Is in the Ramune Bottle

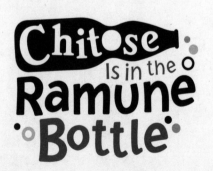

CHARACTER PROFILE

Kaito Asano

Age: 16 years old

Height: 6’0” (183 cm)

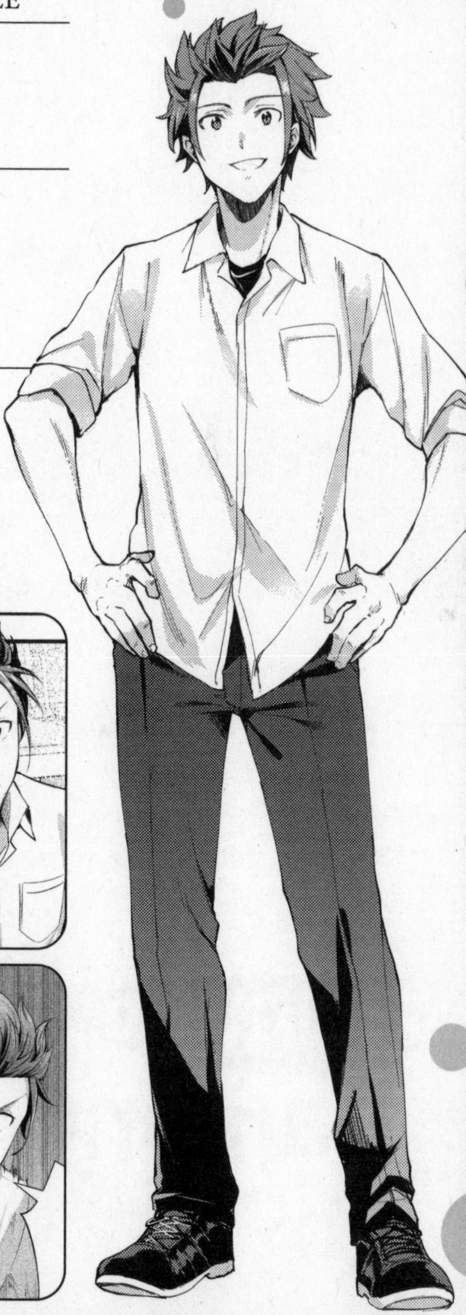

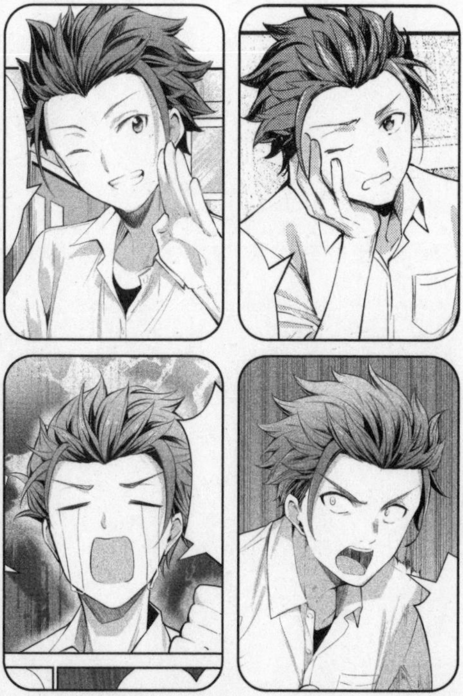

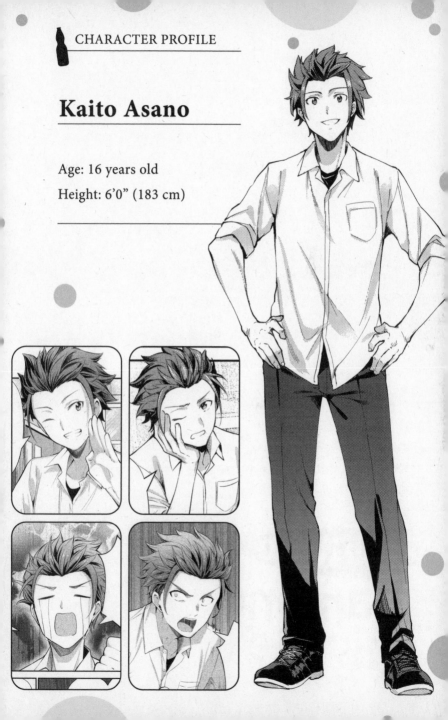

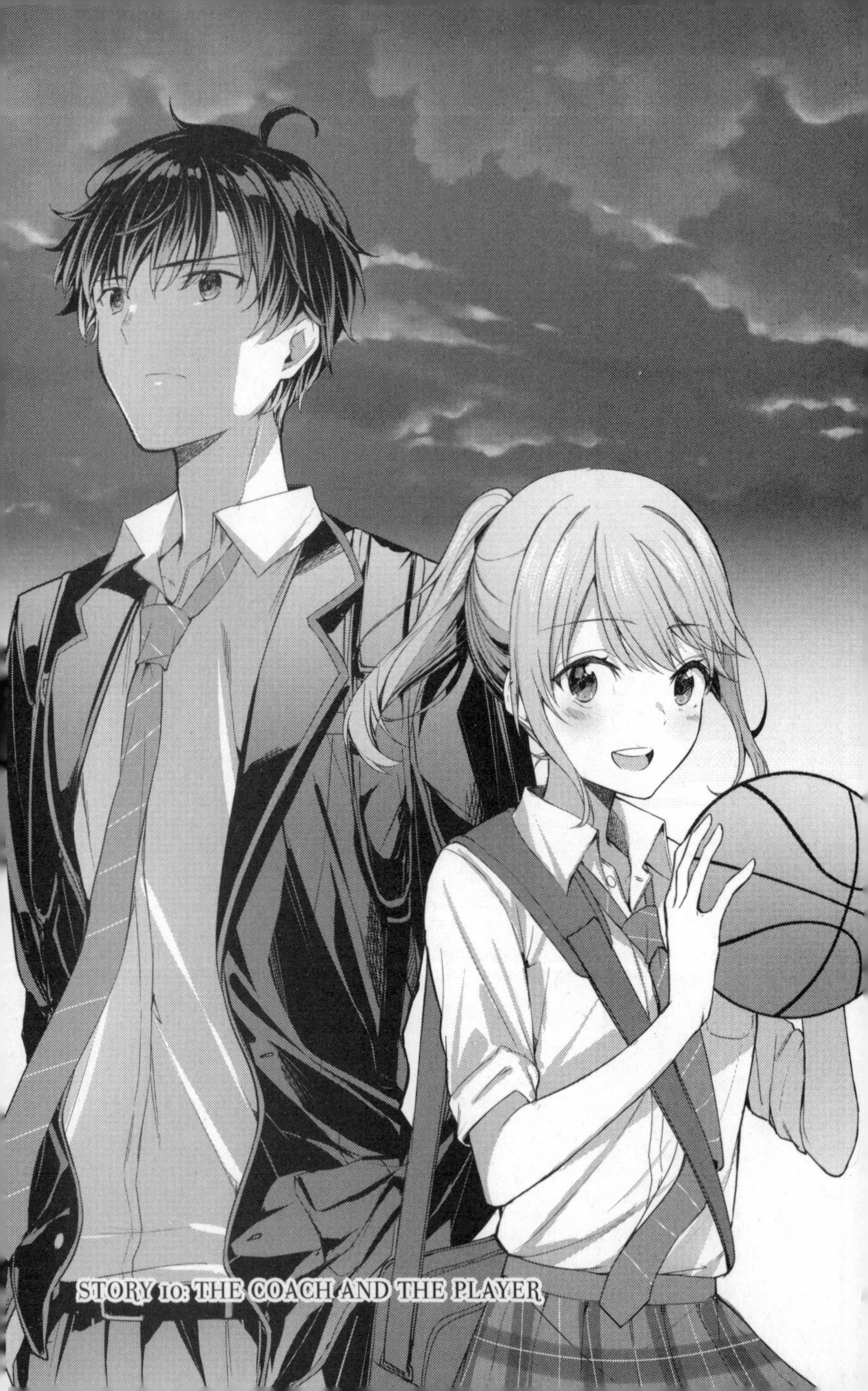
STORY 10: THE COACH AND THE PLAYER

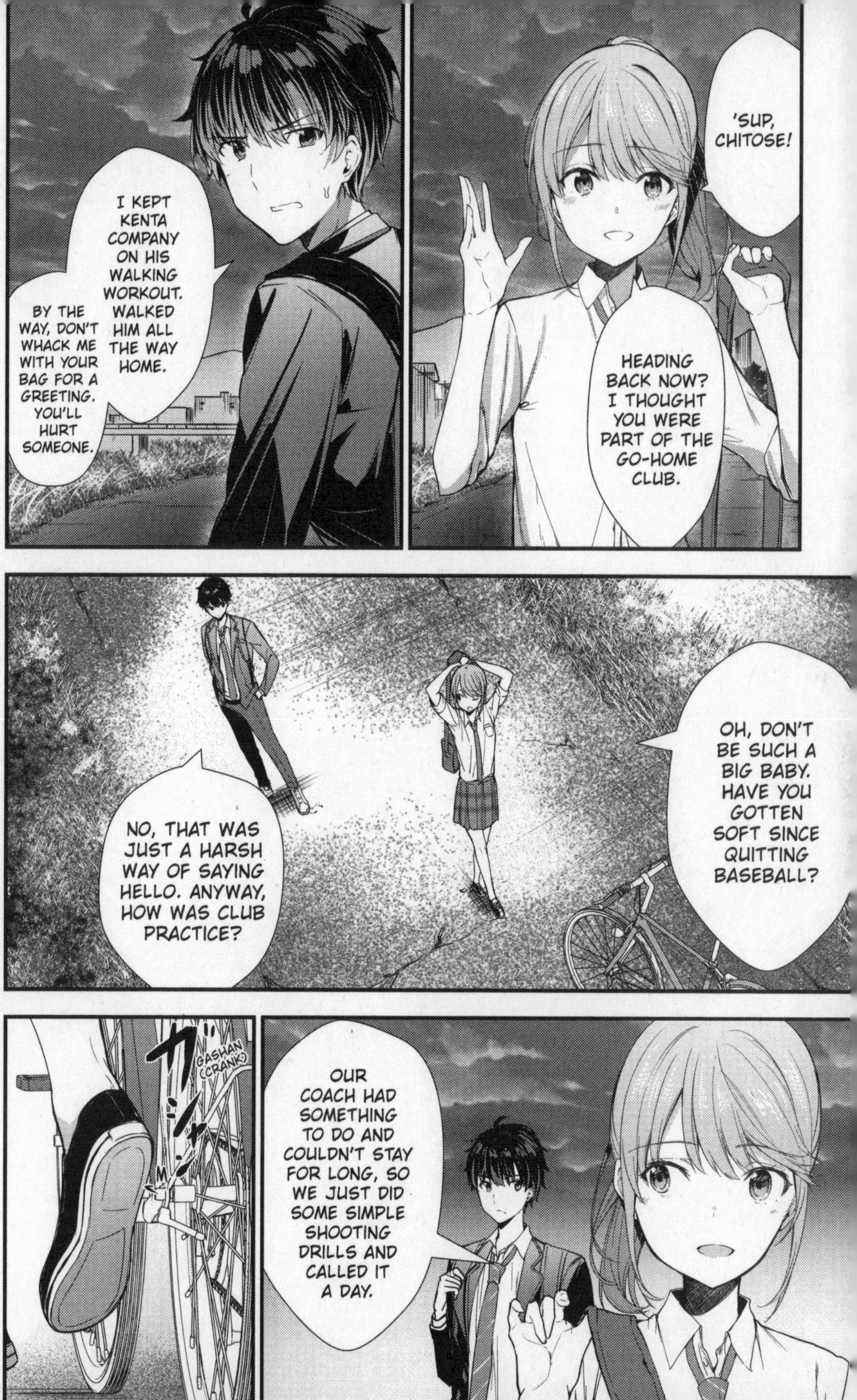
'SUP, CHITOSE!
HEADING BACK NOW? I THOUGHT YOU WERE PART OF THE GO-HOME CLUB.
I KEPT KENTA COMPANY ON HIS WALKING WORKOUT. WALKED HIM ALL THE WAY HOME.
BY THE WAY, DON'T WHACK ME WITH YOUR BAG FOR A GREETING. YOU'LL HURT SOMEONE.
OH, DON'T BE SUCH A BIG BABY. HAVE YOU GOTTEN SOFT SINCE QUITTING BASEBALL?
NO, THAT WAS JUST A HARSH WAY OF SAYING HELLO. ANYWAY, HOW WAS CLUB PRACTICE?
OUR COACH HAD SOMETHING TO DO AND COULDN'T STAY FOR LONG, SO WE JUST DID SOME SIMPLE SHOOTING DRILLS AND CALLED IT A DAY.
GASHAN (CRANK)

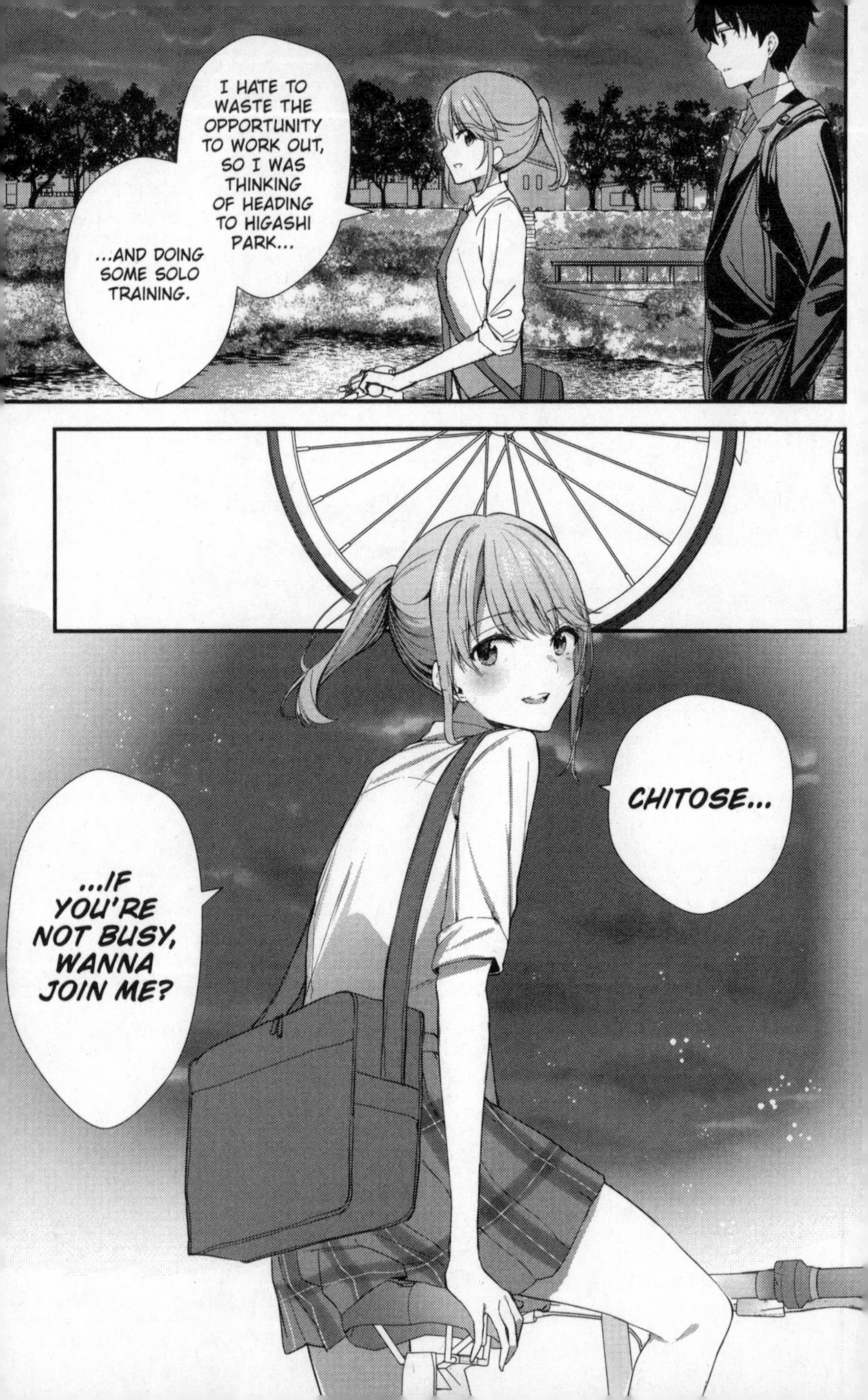
I HATE TO WASTE THE OPPORTUNITY TO WORK OUT, SO I WAS THINKING OF HEADING TO HIGASHI PARK...
...AND DOING SOME SOLO TRAINING.
CHITOSE...
...IF YOU'RE NOT BUSY, WANNA JOIN ME?

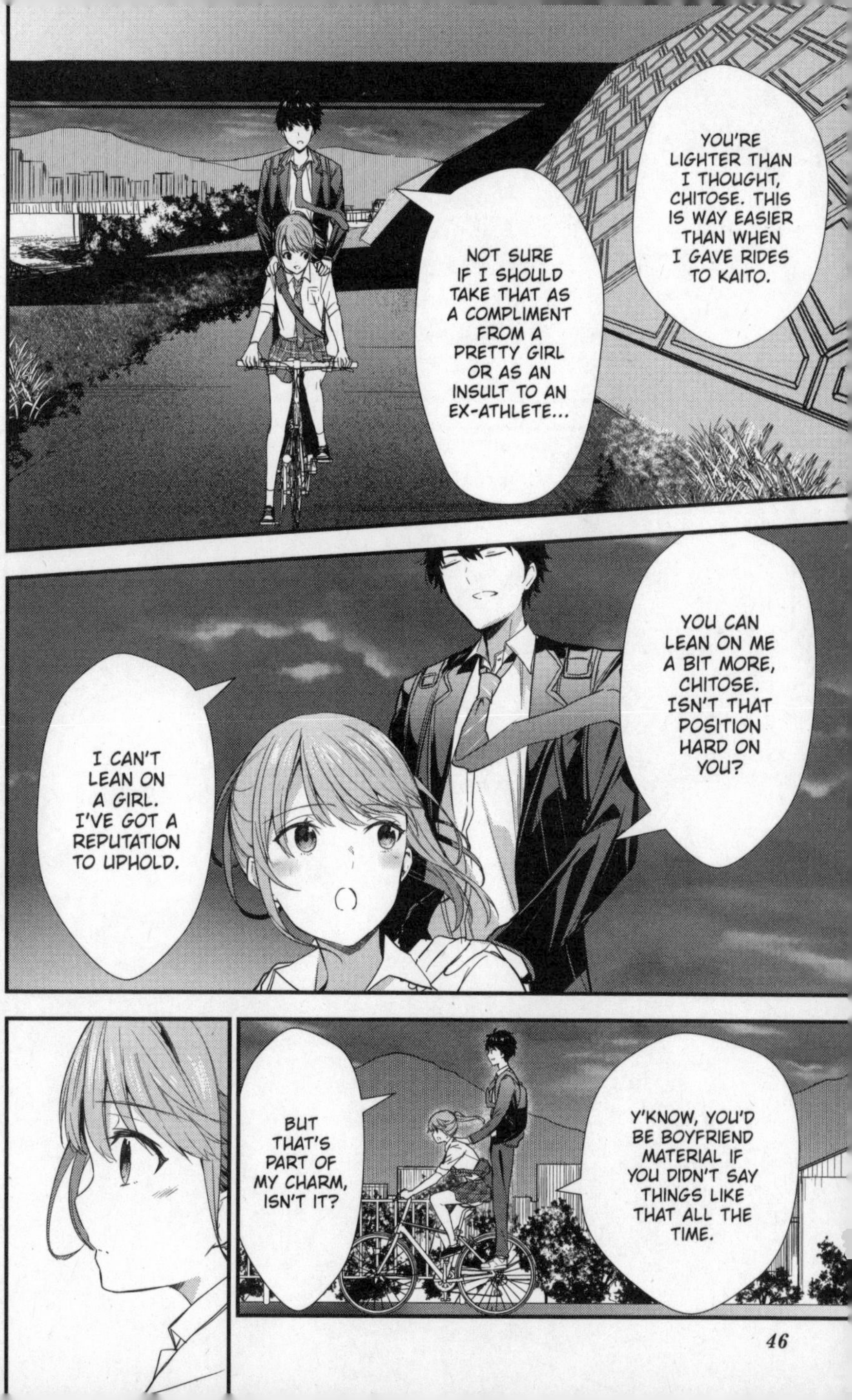
YOU'RE LIGHTER THAN I THOUGHT, CHITOSE. THIS IS WAY EASIER THAN WHEN I GAVE RIDES TO KAITO.
NOT SURE IF I SHOULD TAKE THAT AS A COMPLIMENT FROM A PRETTY GIRL OR AS AN INSULT TO AN EX-ATHLETE...
YOU CAN LEAN ON ME A BIT MORE, CHITOSE. ISN'T THAT POSITION HARD ON YOU?
I CAN'T LEAN ON A GIRL. I'VE GOT A REPUTATION TO UPHOLD.
Y'KNOW, YOU'D BE BOYFRIEND MATERIAL IF YOU DIDN'T SAY THINGS LIKE THAT ALL THE TIME.
BUT THAT'S PART OF MY CHARM, ISN'T IT?

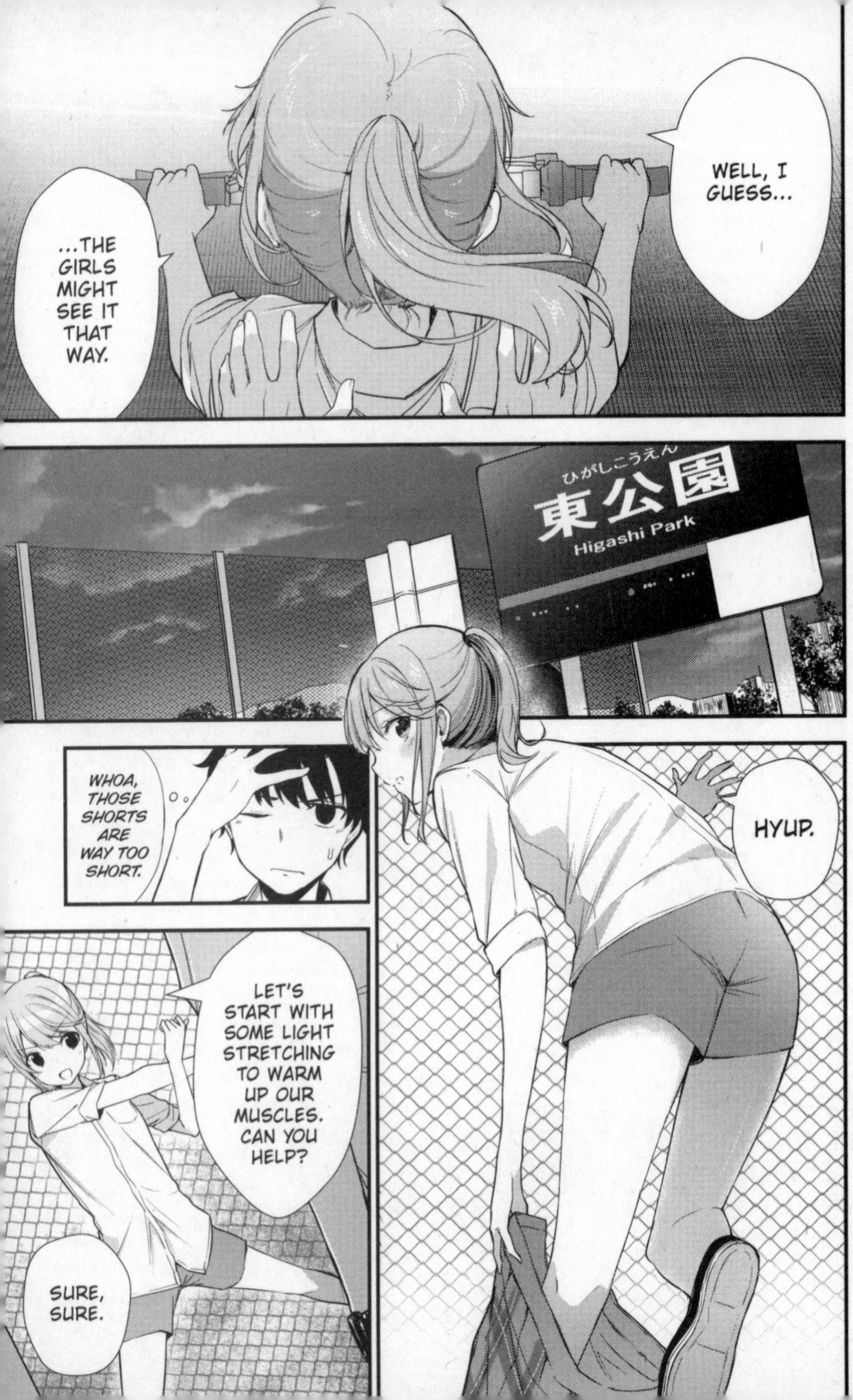
WELL, I GUESS...
...THE GIRLS MIGHT SEE IT THAT WAY.
ひがしこうえん
東公園
Higashi Park
HYUP.
WHOA, THOSE SHORTS ARE WAY TOO SHORT.
LET'S START WITH SOME LIGHT STRETCHING TO WARM UP OUR MUSCLES. CAN YOU HELP?
SURE, SURE.

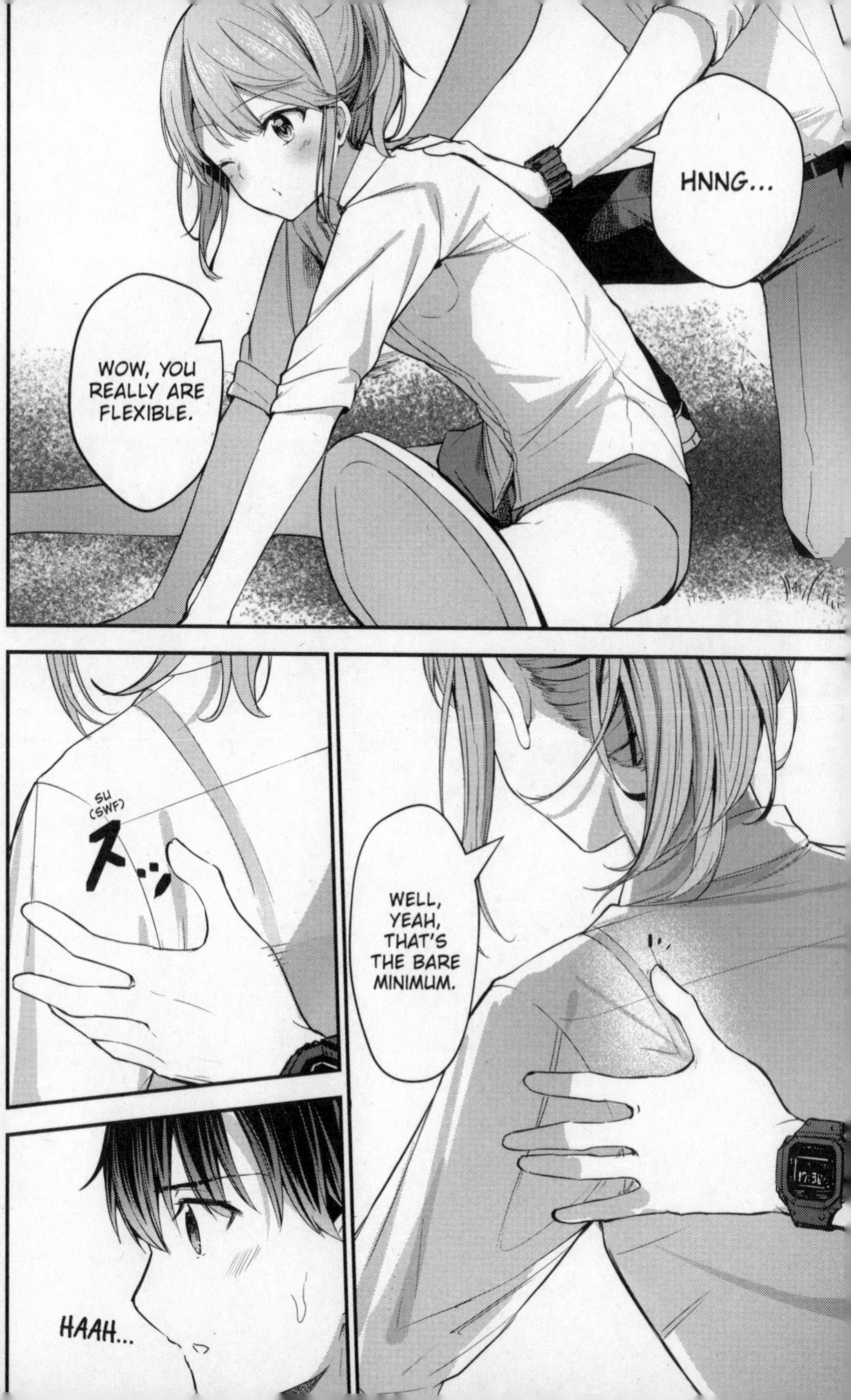
HNNG...
WOW, YOU REALLY ARE FLEXIBLE.
WELL, YEAH, THAT'S THE BARE MINIMUM.
SU (SWF)
HAAH...

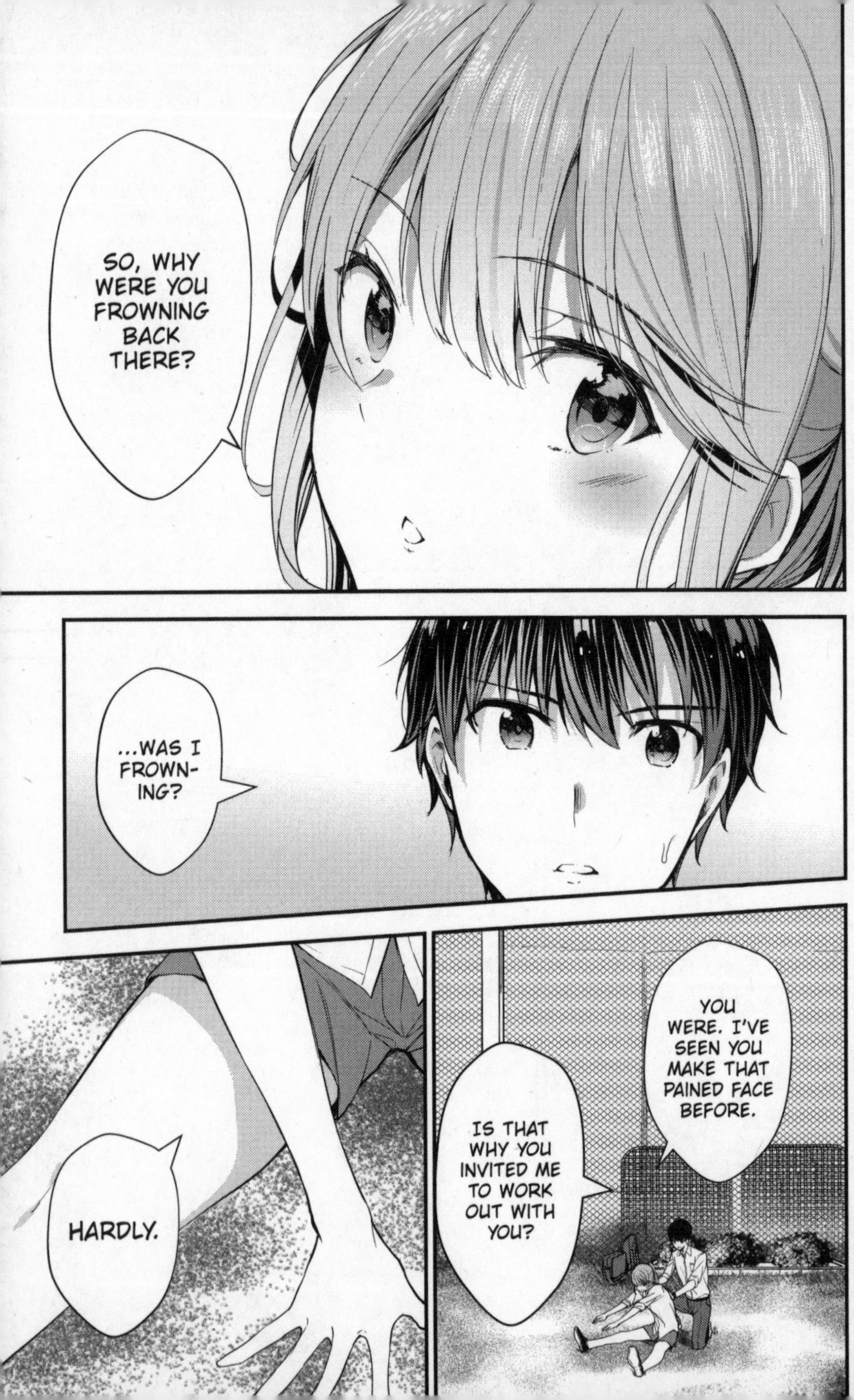
SO, WHY WERE YOU FROWNING BACK THERE?
...WAS I FROWNING?
YOU WERE. I'VE SEEN YOU MAKE THAT PAINED FACE BEFORE.
IS THAT WHY YOU INVITED ME TO WORK OUT WITH YOU?
HARDLY.

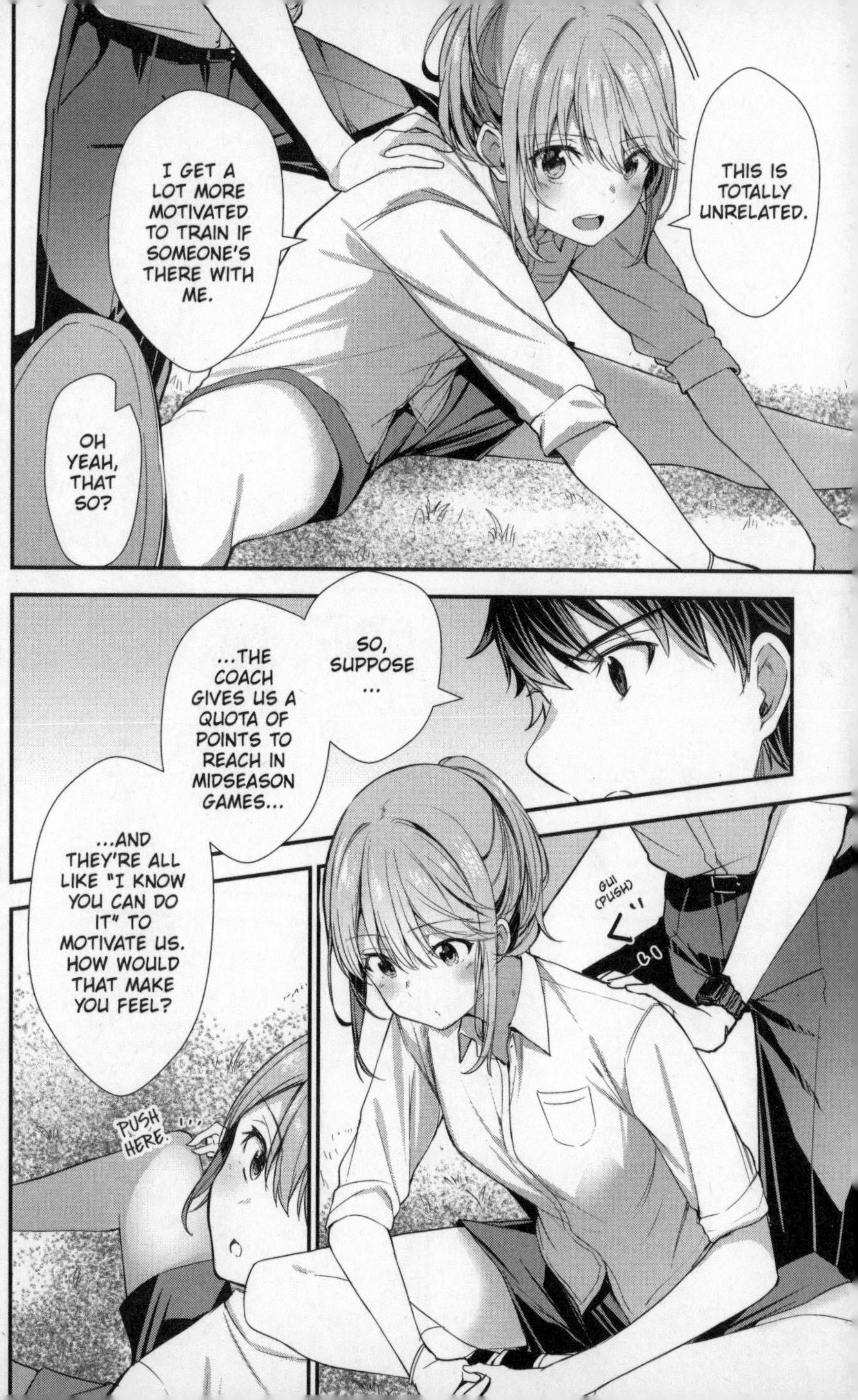
THIS IS TOTALLY UNRELATED.
I GET A LOT MORE MOTIVATED TO TRAIN IF SOMEONE'S THERE WITH ME.
OH YEAH, THAT SO?
SO, SUPPOSE...
...THE COACH GIVES US A QUOTA OF POINTS TO REACH IN MIDSEASON GAMES...
GUI (PUSH)
...AND THEY'RE ALL LIKE "I KNOW YOU CAN DO IT" TO MOTIVATE US. HOW WOULD THAT MAKE YOU FEEL?
PUSH HERE.

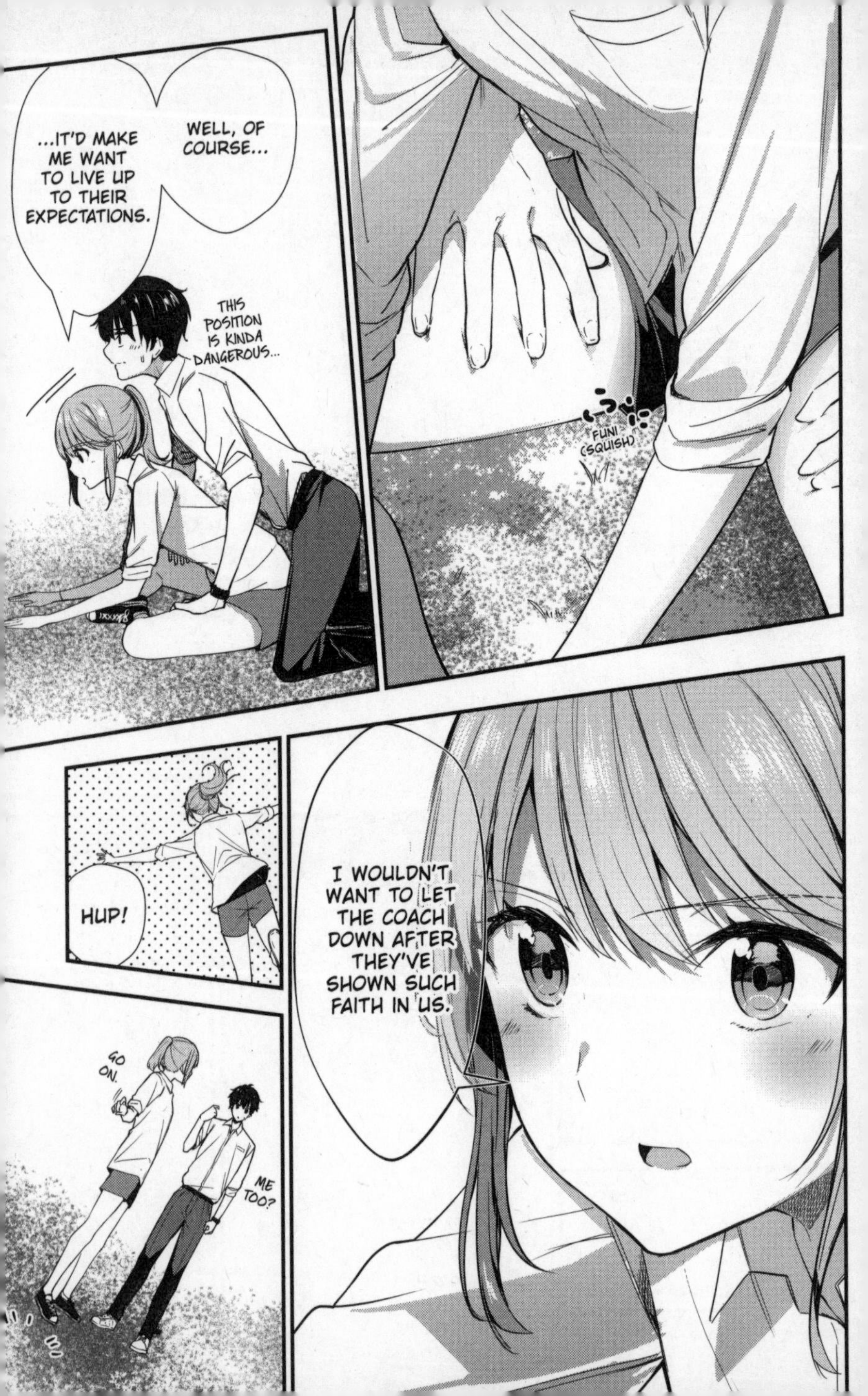
FUNI (SQUISH)
WELL, OF COURSE...
...IT'D MAKE ME WANT TO LIVE UP TO THEIR EXPECTATIONS.
THIS POSITION IS KINDA DANGEROUS...
I WOULDN'T WANT TO LET THE COACH DOWN AFTER THEY'VE SHOWN SUCH FAITH IN US.
HUP!
GO ON.
ME TOO?

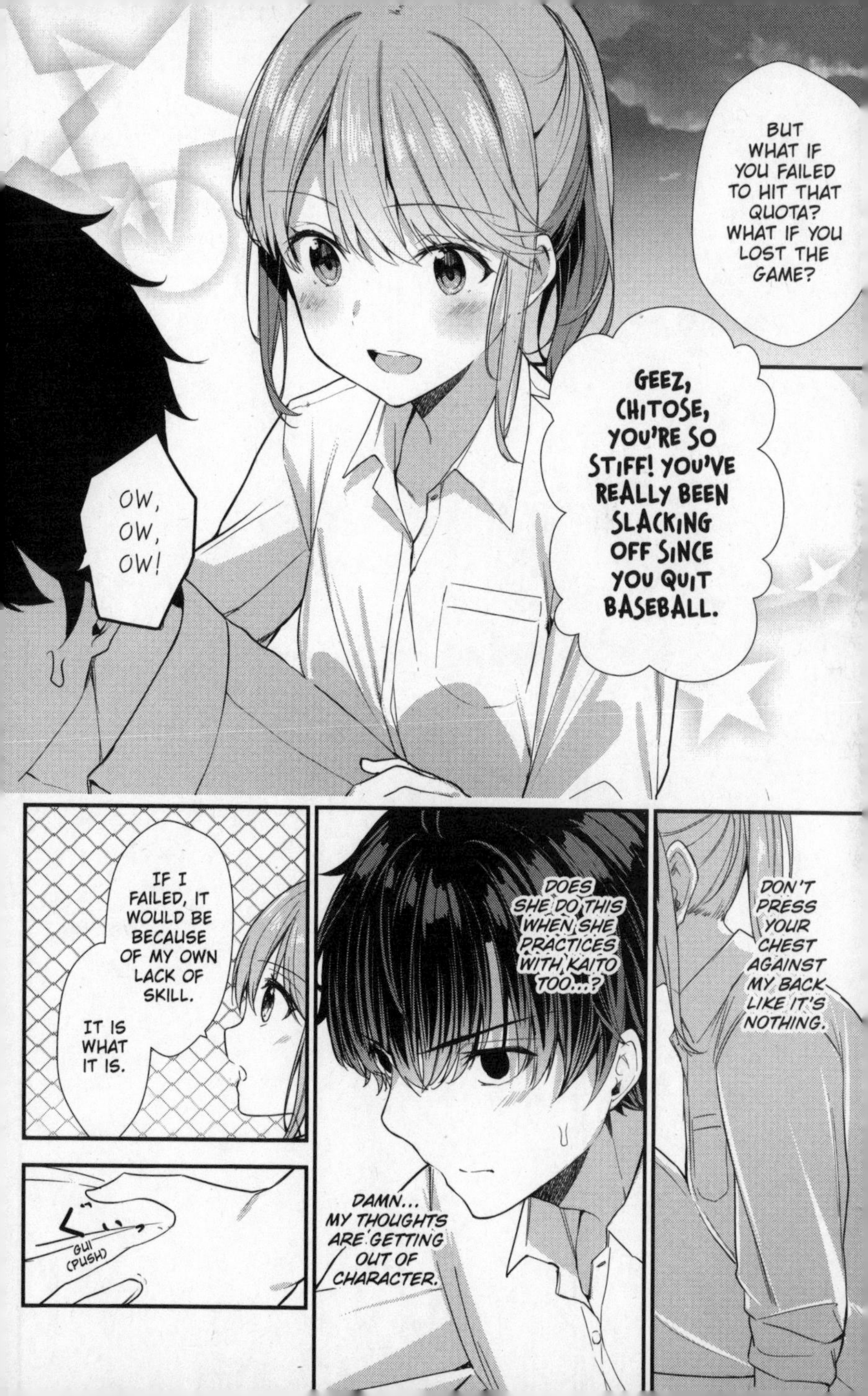
BUT WHAT IF YOU FAILED TO HIT THAT QUOTA? WHAT IF YOU LOST THE GAME?
GEEZ, CHITOSE, YOU'RE SO STIFF! YOU'VE REALLY BEEN SLACKING OFF SINCE YOU QUIT BASEBALL.
OW, OW, OW!
DON'T PRESS YOUR CHEST AGAINST MY BACK LIKE IT'S NOTHING.
DOES SHE DO THIS WHEN SHE PRACTICES WITH KAITO TOO...?
DAMN... MY THOUGHTS ARE GETTING OUT OF CHARACTER.
IF I FAILED, IT WOULD BE BECAUSE OF MY OWN LACK OF SKILL.
IT IS WHAT IT IS.
GUI (PUSH)

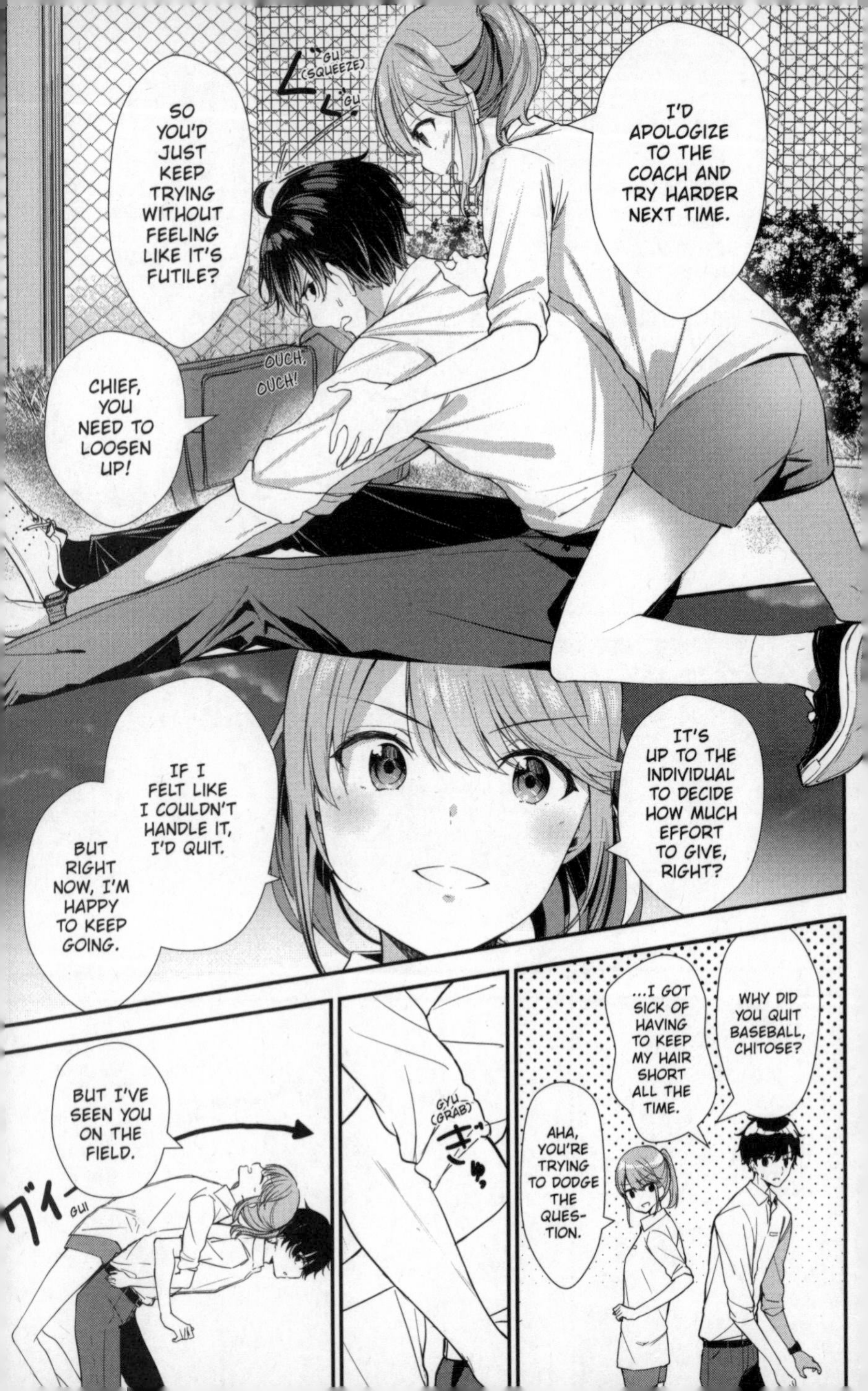
I'D APOLOGIZE TO THE COACH AND TRY HARDER NEXT TIME.
GUI (SQUEEZE)
GU
SO YOU'D JUST KEEP TRYING WITHOUT FEELING LIKE IT'S FUTILE?
OUCH, OUCH!
CHIEF, YOU NEED TO LOOSEN UP!
IT'S UP TO THE INDIVIDUAL TO DECIDE HOW MUCH EFFORT TO GIVE, RIGHT?
IF I FELT LIKE I COULDN'T HANDLE IT, I'D QUIT.
BUT RIGHT NOW, I'M HAPPY TO KEEP GOING.
WHY DID YOU QUIT BASEBALL, CHITOSE?
...I GOT SICK OF HAVING TO KEEP MY HAIR SHORT ALL THE TIME.
AHA, YOU'RE TRYING TO DODGE THE QUES-TION.
GYU (GRAB)
BUT I'VE SEEN YOU ON THE FIELD.
GUI

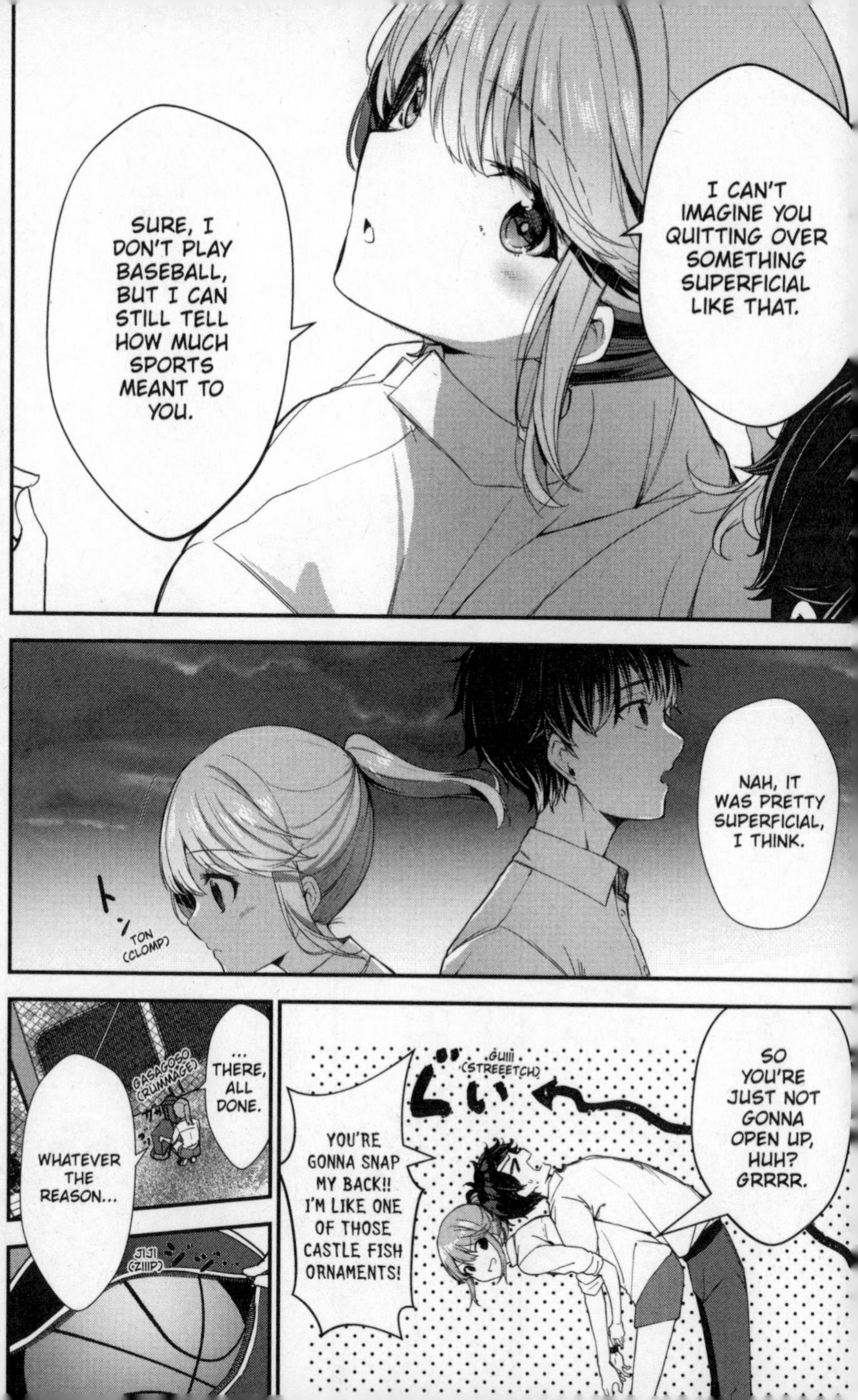
I CAN'T IMAGINE YOU QUITTING OVER SOMETHING SUPERFICIAL LIKE THAT.
SURE, I DON'T PLAY BASEBALL, BUT I CAN STILL TELL HOW MUCH SPORTS MEANT TO YOU.
NAH, IT WAS PRETTY SUPERFICIAL, I THINK.
TON (CLOMP)
SO YOU'RE JUST NOT GONNA OPEN UP, HUH? GRRRR.
GUIII (STREEETCH)
YOU'RE GONNA SNAP MY BACK!! I'M LIKE ONE OF THOSE CASTLE FISH ORNAMENTS!
... THERE, ALL DONE.
GASAGOSO (RUMMAGE)
WHATEVER THE REASON...
JIJI (ZIIIP)

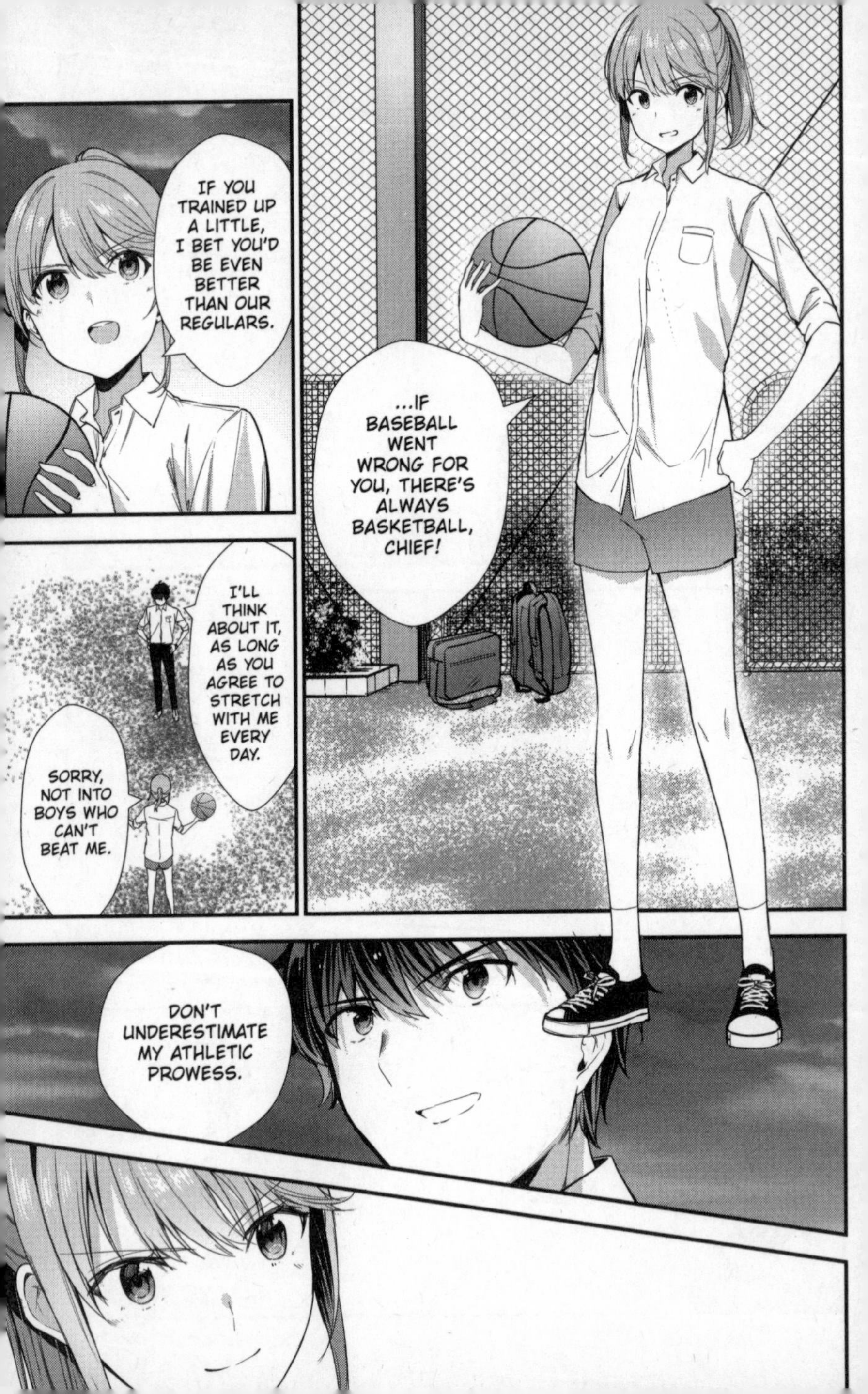
...IF BASEBALL WENT WRONG FOR YOU, THERE'S ALWAYS BASKETBALL, CHIEF!
IF YOU TRAINED UP A LITTLE, I BET YOU'D BE EVEN BETTER THAN OUR REGULARS.
I'LL THINK ABOUT IT, AS LONG AS YOU AGREE TO STRETCH WITH ME EVERY DAY.
SORRY, NOT INTO BOYS WHO CAN'T BEAT ME.
DON'T UNDERESTIMATE MY ATHLETIC PROWESS.

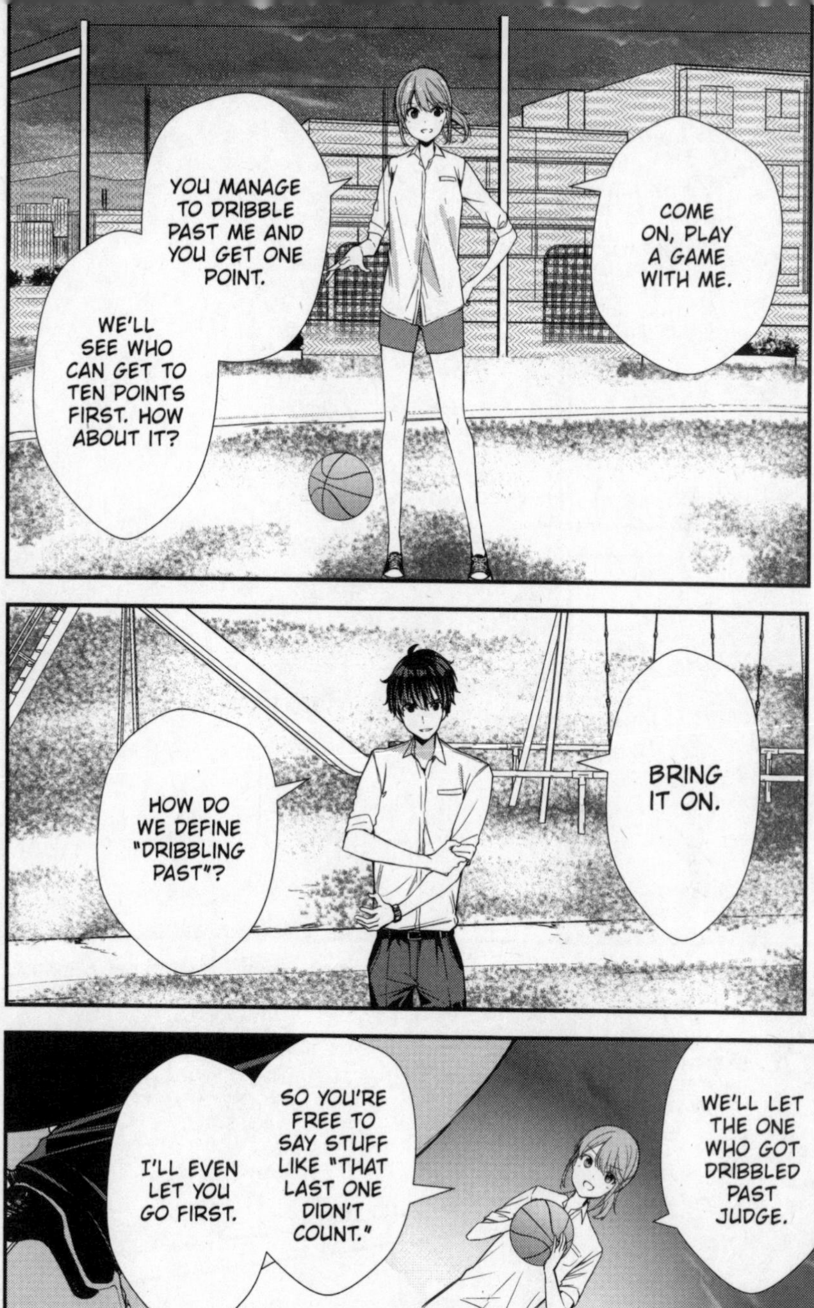
COME ON, PLAY A GAME WITH ME.
YOU MANAGE TO DRIBBLE PAST ME AND YOU GET ONE POINT.
WE'LL SEE WHO CAN GET TO TEN POINTS FIRST. HOW ABOUT IT?
BRING IT ON.
HOW DO WE DEFINE "DRIBBLING PAST"?
WE'LL LET THE ONE WHO GOT DRIBBLED PAST JUDGE.
SO YOU'RE FREE TO SAY STUFF LIKE "THAT LAST ONE DIDN'T COUNT."
I'LL EVEN LET YOU GO FIRST.

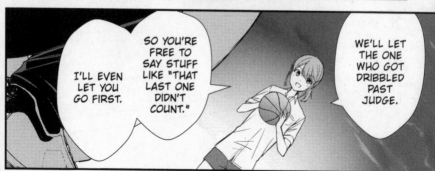

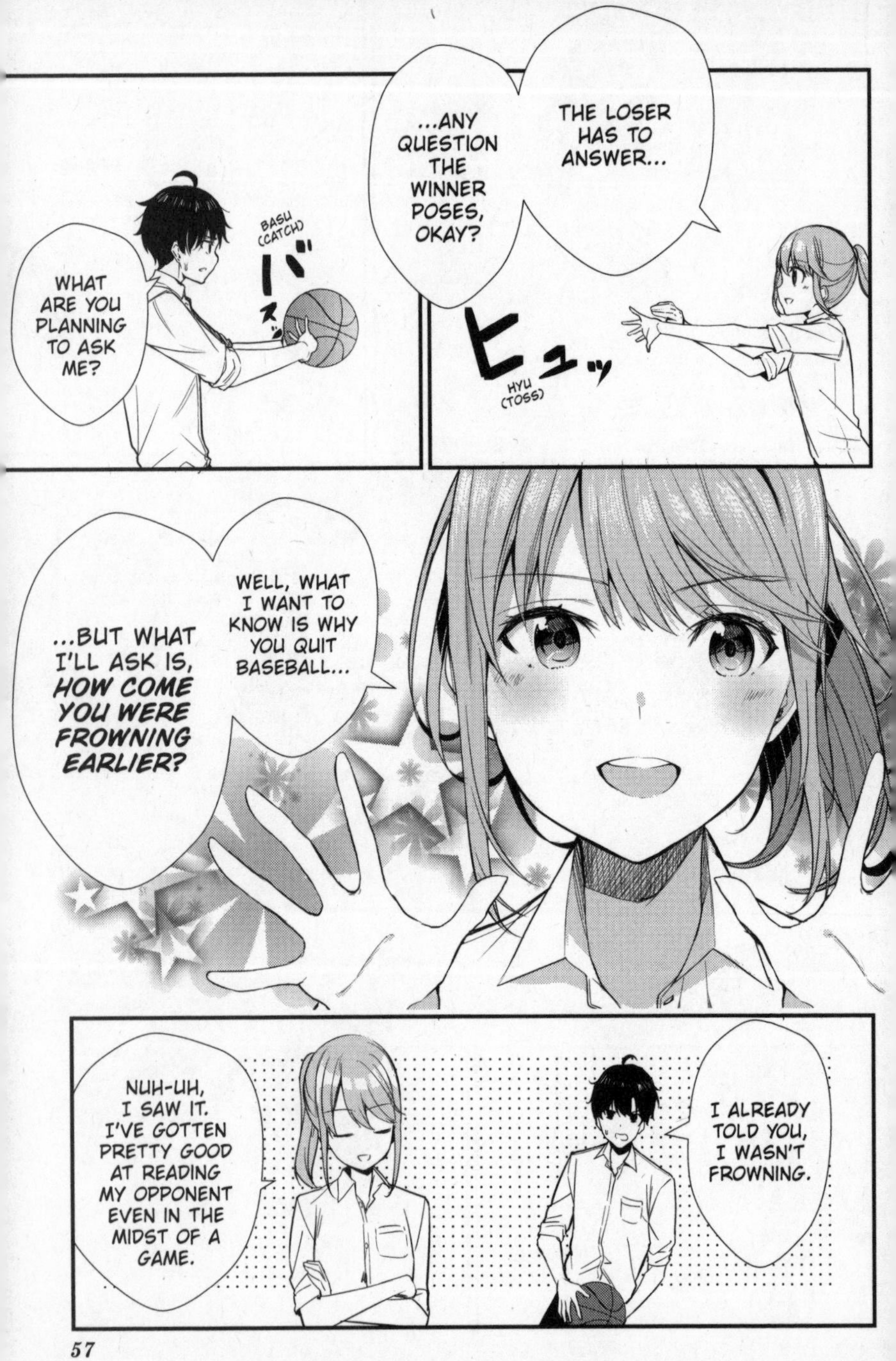
THE LOSER HAS TO ANSWER...
...ANY QUESTION THE WINNER POSES, OKAY?
HYU (TOSS)
BASU (CATCH)
WHAT ARE YOU PLANNING TO ASK ME?
WELL, WHAT I WANT TO KNOW IS WHY YOU QUIT BASEBALL...
...BUT WHAT I'LL ASK IS, *HOW COME YOU WERE FROWNING EARLIER?*
I ALREADY TOLD YOU, I WASN'T FROWNING.
NUH-UH, I SAW IT. I'VE GOTTEN PRETTY GOOD AT READING MY OPPONENT EVEN IN THE MIDST OF A GAME.

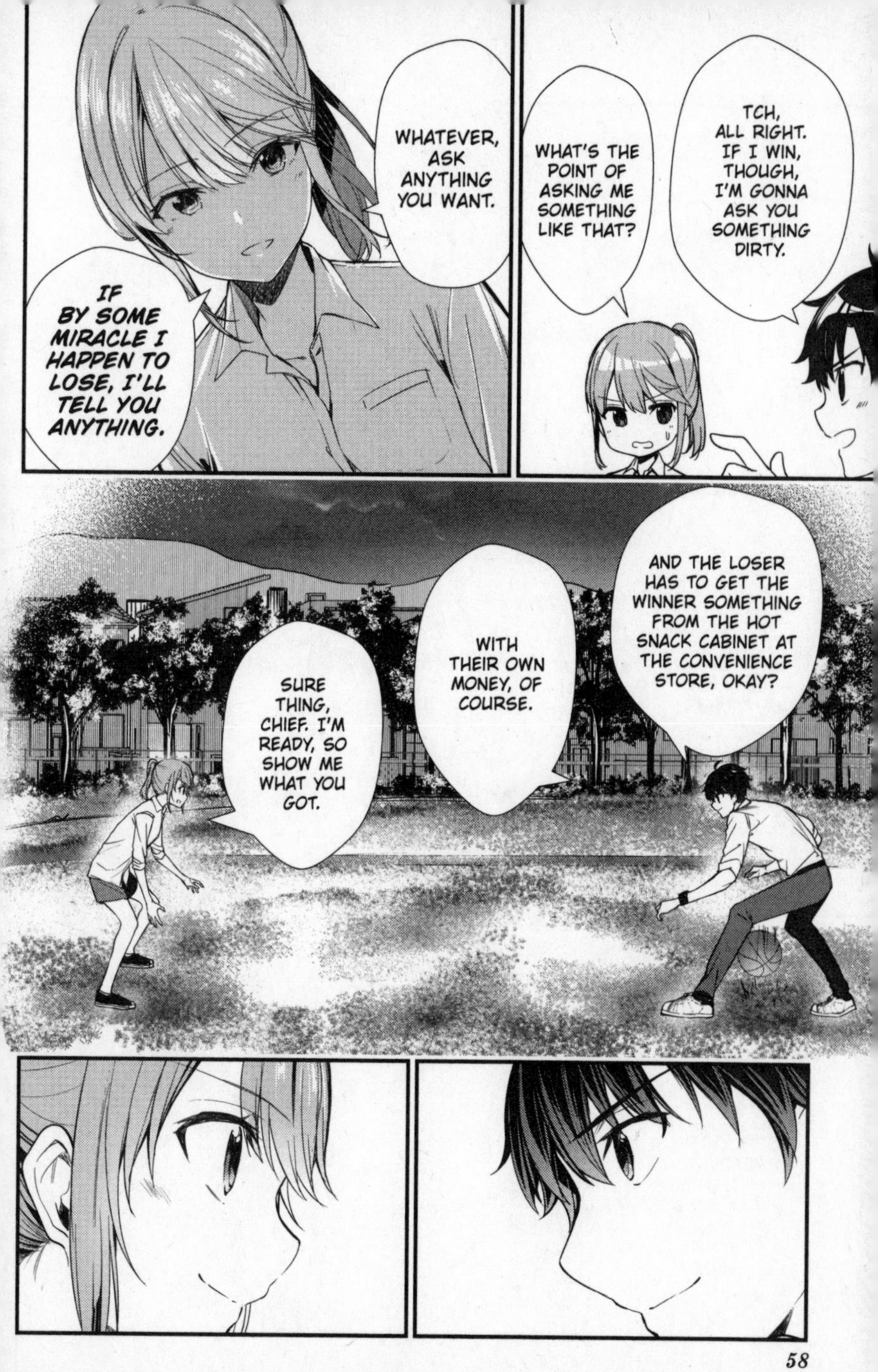
TCH, ALL RIGHT. IF I WIN, THOUGH, I'M GONNA ASK YOU SOMETHING DIRTY.
WHAT'S THE POINT OF ASKING ME SOMETHING LIKE THAT?
WHATEVER, ASK ANYTHING YOU WANT.
IF BY SOME MIRACLE I HAPPEN TO LOSE, I'LL TELL YOU ANYTHING.
AND THE LOSER HAS TO GET THE WINNER SOMETHING FROM THE HOT SNACK CABINET AT THE CONVENIENCE STORE, OKAY?
WITH THEIR OWN MONEY, OF COURSE.
SURE THING, CHIEF. I'M READY, SO SHOW ME WHAT YOU GOT.

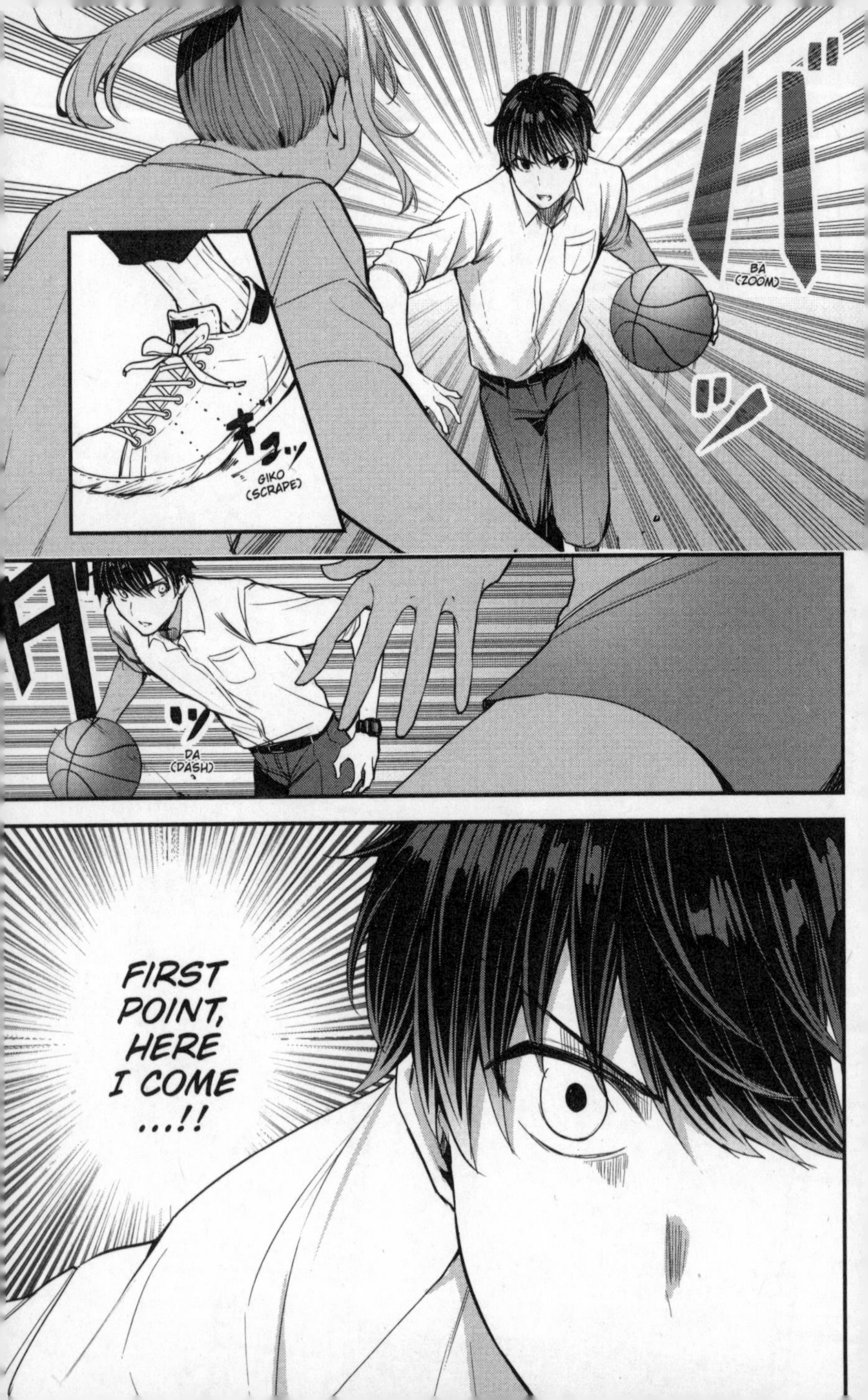
BA (ZOOM)
GIKO (SCRAPE)
DA (DASH)
FIRST POINT, HERE I COME ...!!

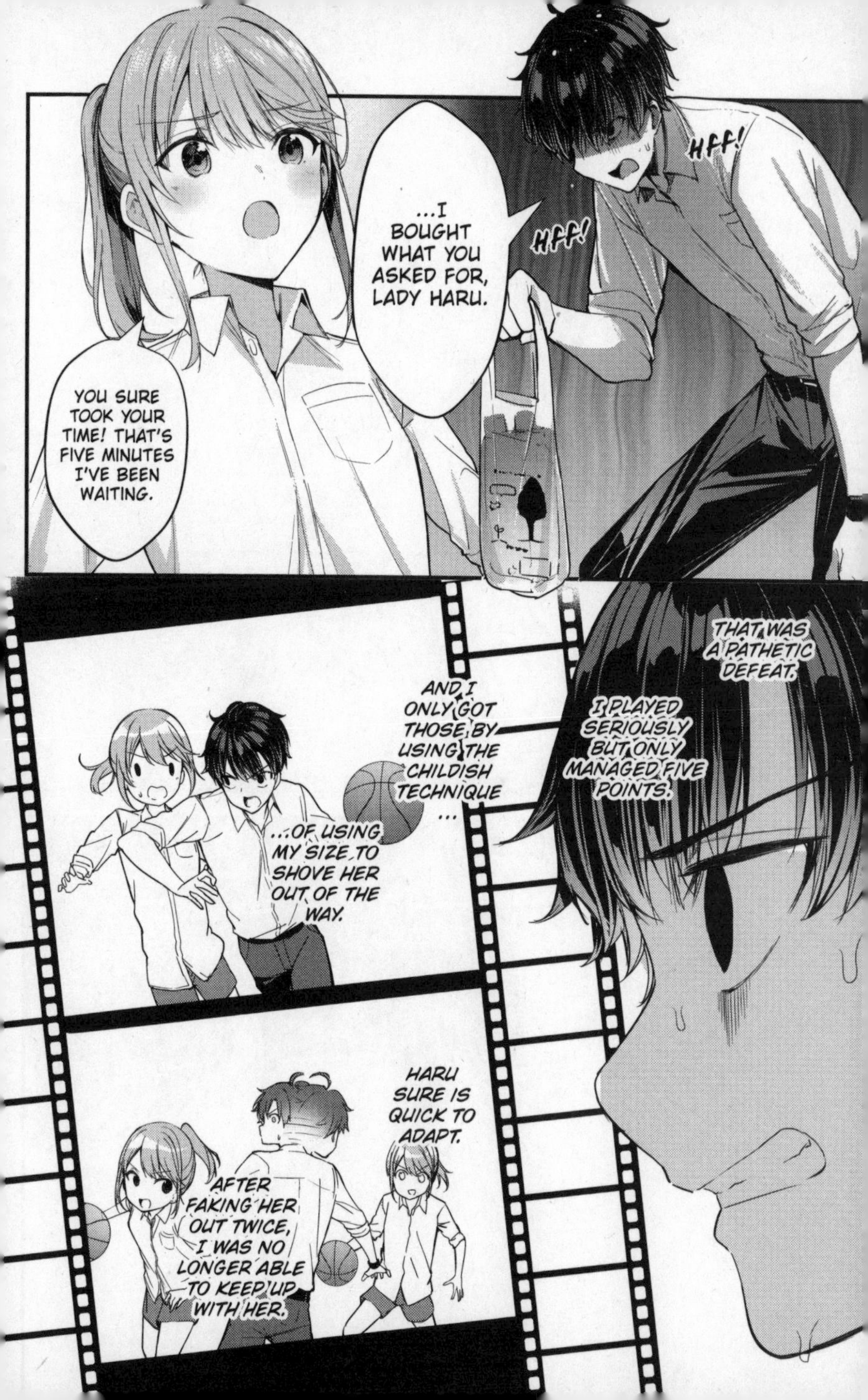
HFF!
HFF!
...I BOUGHT WHAT YOU ASKED FOR, LADY HARU.
YOU SURE TOOK YOUR TIME! THAT'S FIVE MINUTES I'VE BEEN WAITING.
THAT WAS A PATHETIC DEFEAT.
I PLAYED SERIOUSLY BUT ONLY MANAGED FIVE POINTS.
AND I ONLY GOT THOSE BY USING THE CHILDISH TECHNIQUE ...
...OF USING MY SIZE TO SHOVE HER OUT OF THE WAY.
HARU SURE IS QUICK TO ADAPT.
AFTER FAKING HER OUT TWICE, I WAS NO LONGER ABLE TO KEEP UP WITH HER.

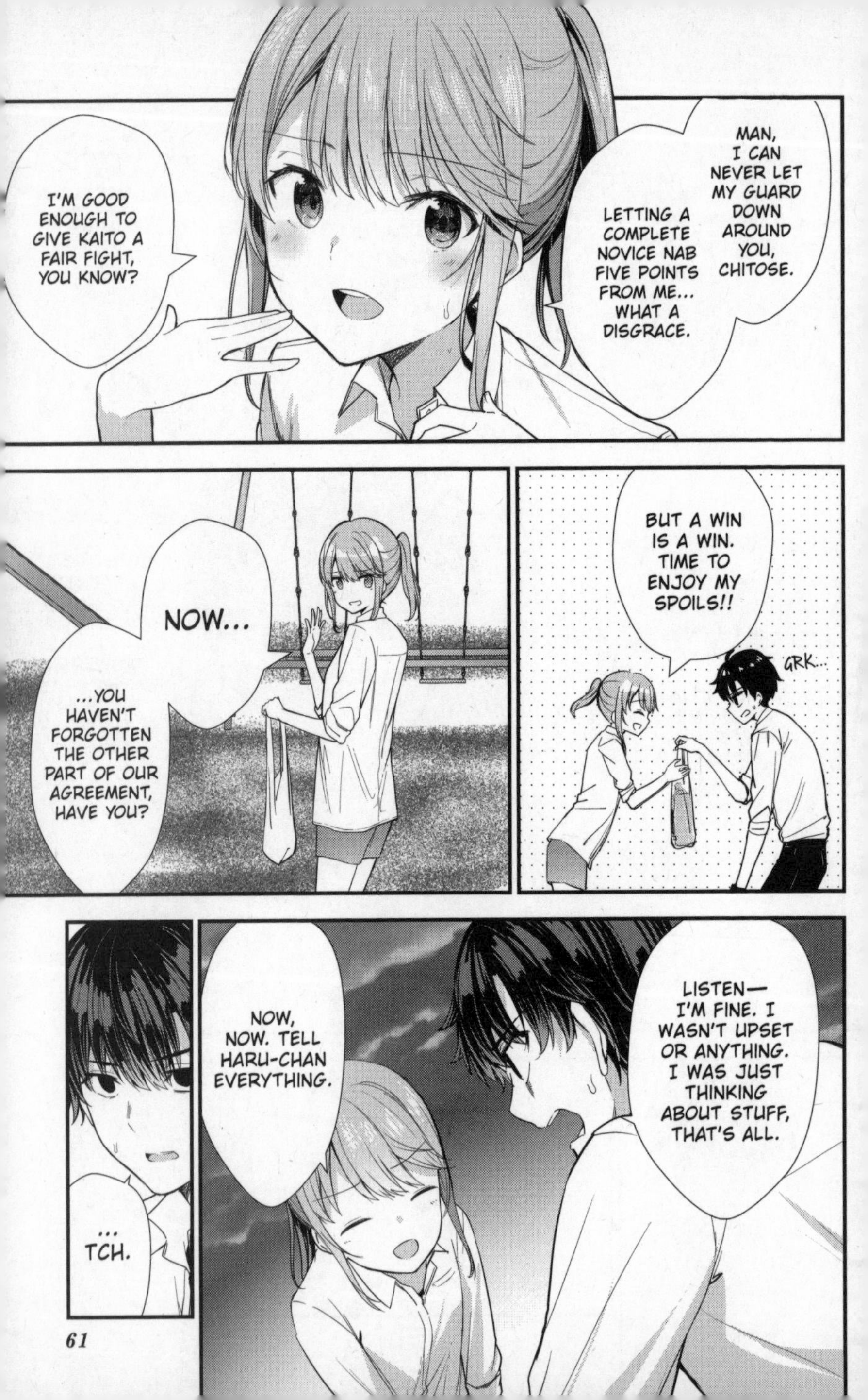
MAN, I CAN NEVER LET MY GUARD DOWN AROUND YOU, CHITOSE.
LETTING A COMPLETE NOVICE NAB FIVE POINTS FROM ME... WHAT A DISGRACE.
I'M GOOD ENOUGH TO GIVE KAITO A FAIR FIGHT, YOU KNOW?
BUT A WIN IS A WIN. TIME TO ENJOY MY SPOILS!!
GRK...
NOW...
...YOU HAVEN'T FORGOTTEN THE OTHER PART OF OUR AGREEMENT, HAVE YOU?
LISTEN— I'M FINE. I WASN'T UPSET OR ANYTHING. I WAS JUST THINKING ABOUT STUFF, THAT'S ALL.
NOW, NOW. TELL HARU-CHAN EVERYTHING.
... TCH.

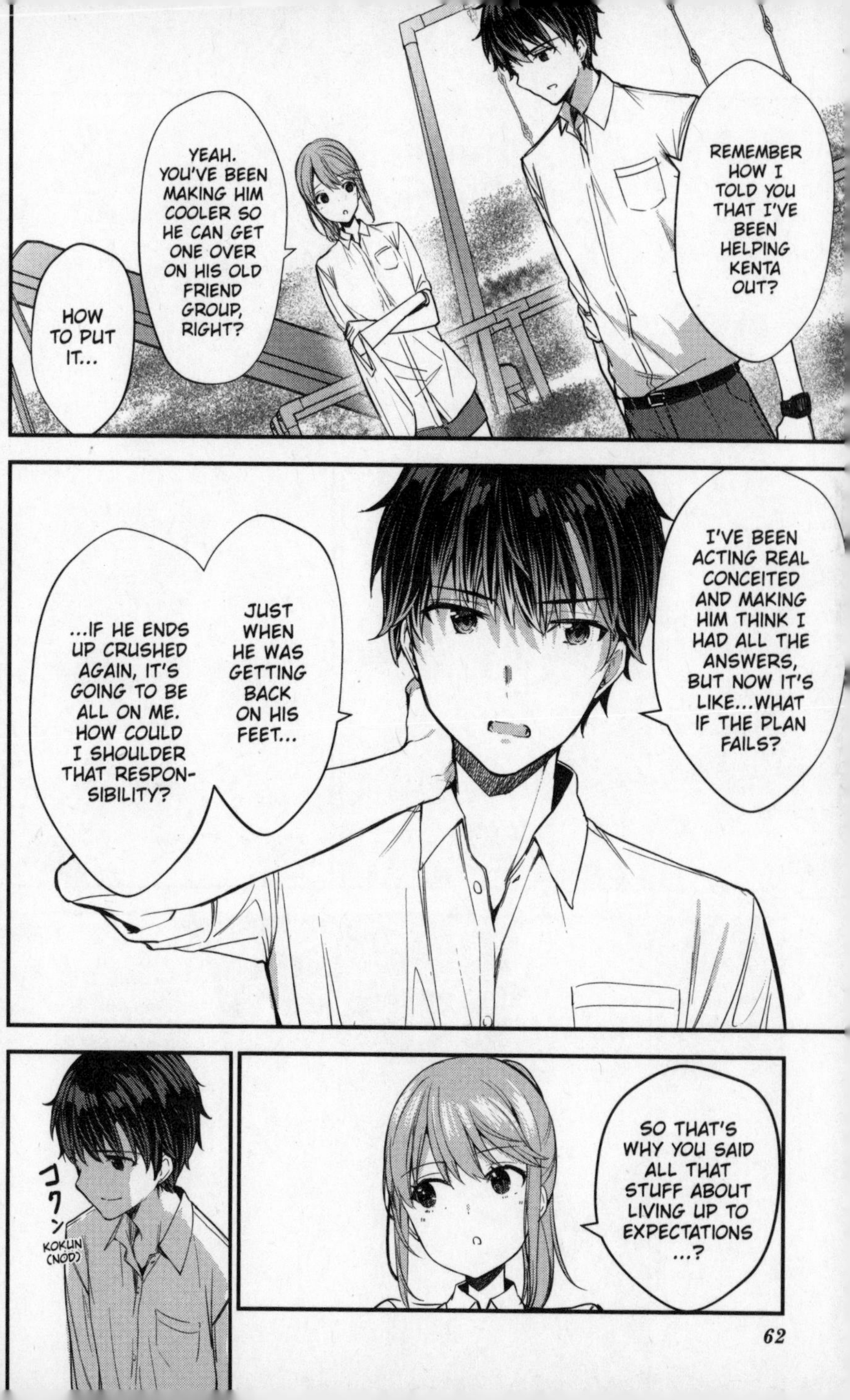
REMEMBER HOW I TOLD YOU THAT I'VE BEEN HELPING KENTA OUT?
YEAH. YOU'VE BEEN MAKING HIM COOLER SO HE CAN GET ONE OVER ON HIS OLD FRIEND GROUP, RIGHT?
HOW TO PUT IT...
I'VE BEEN ACTING REAL CONCEITED AND MAKING HIM THINK I HAD ALL THE ANSWERS, BUT NOW IT'S LIKE...WHAT IF THE PLAN FAILS?
JUST WHEN HE WAS GETTING BACK ON HIS FEET...
...IF HE ENDS UP CRUSHED AGAIN, IT'S GOING TO BE ALL ON ME. HOW COULD I SHOULDER THAT RESPON-SIBILITY?
SO THAT'S WHY YOU SAID ALL THAT STUFF ABOUT LIVING UP TO EXPECTATIONS ...?
コクン
KOKUN (NOD)

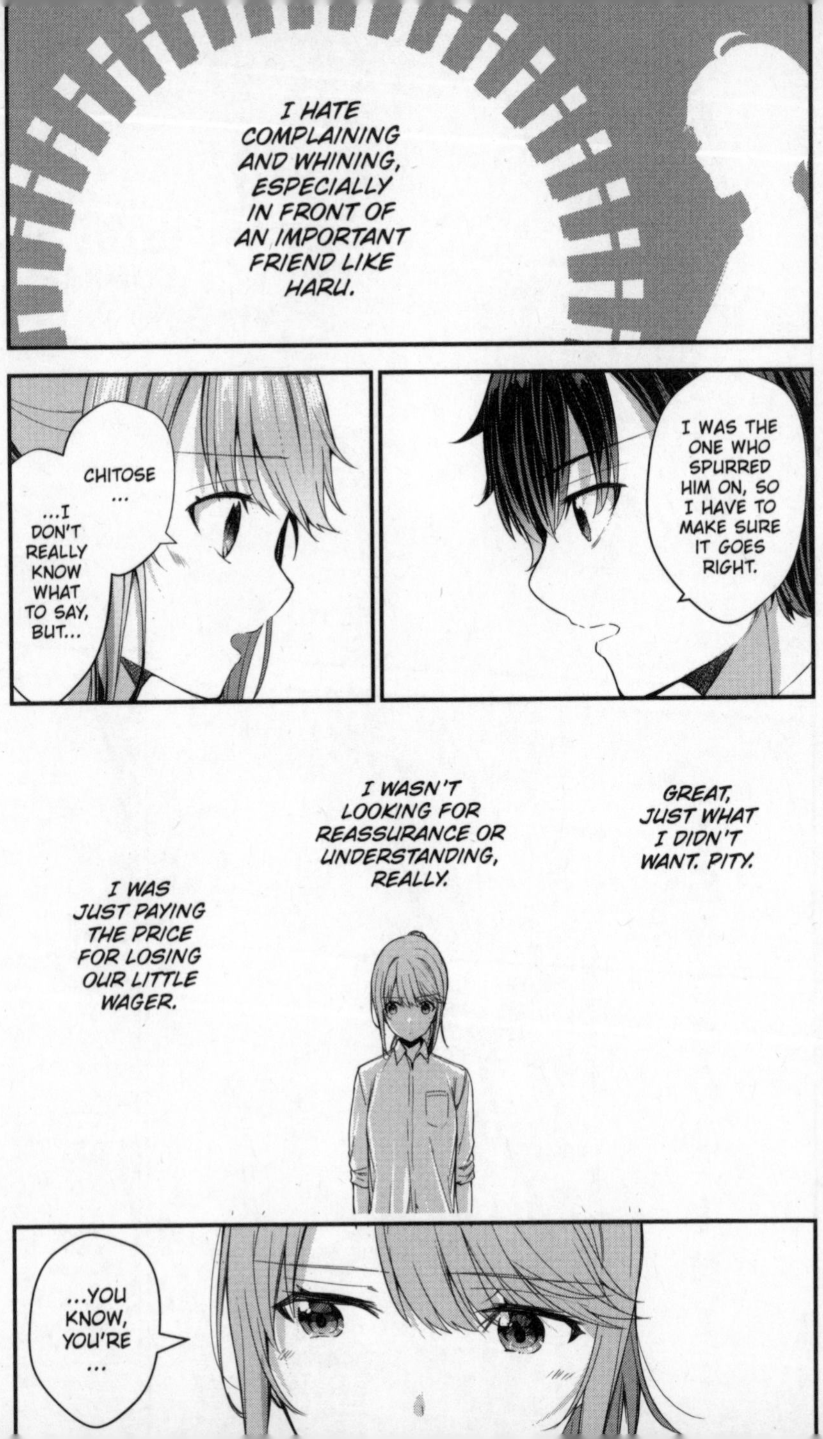
I HATE COMPLAINING AND WHINING, ESPECIALLY IN FRONT OF AN IMPORTANT FRIEND LIKE HARU.
I WAS THE ONE WHO SPURRED HIM ON, SO I HAVE TO MAKE SURE IT GOES RIGHT.
CHITOSE ...
...I DON'T REALLY KNOW WHAT TO SAY, BUT...
GREAT, JUST WHAT I DIDN'T WANT. PITY.
I WASN'T LOOKING FOR REASSURANCE OR UNDERSTANDING, REALLY.
I WAS JUST PAYING THE PRICE FOR LOSING OUR LITTLE WAGER.
...YOU KNOW, YOU'RE ...

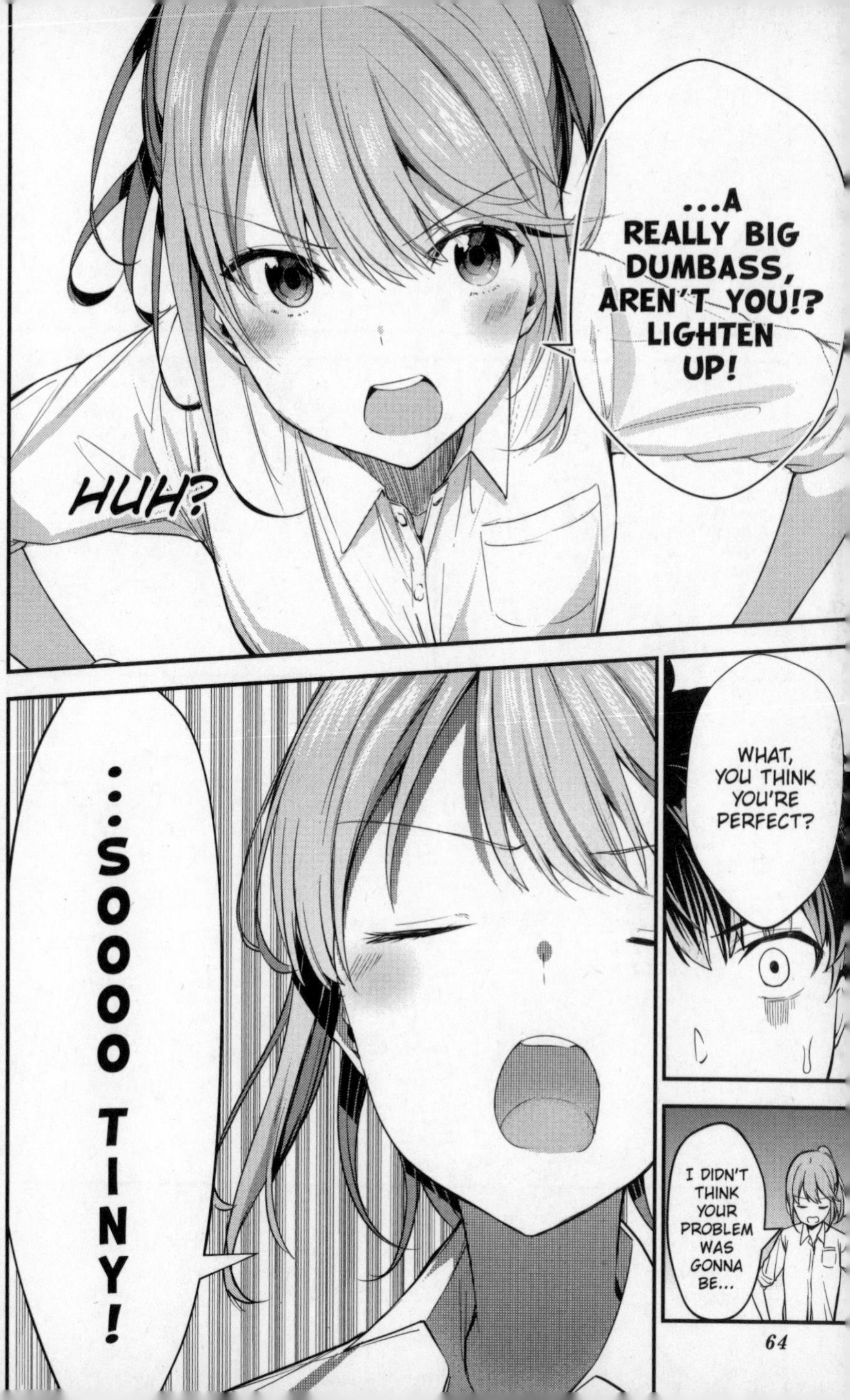

...A REALLY BIG DUMBASS, AREN'T YOU!? LIGHTEN UP!
HUH?
WHAT, YOU THINK YOU'RE PERFECT?
I DIDN'T THINK YOUR PROBLEM WAS GONNA BE...
...SOOOO TINY!

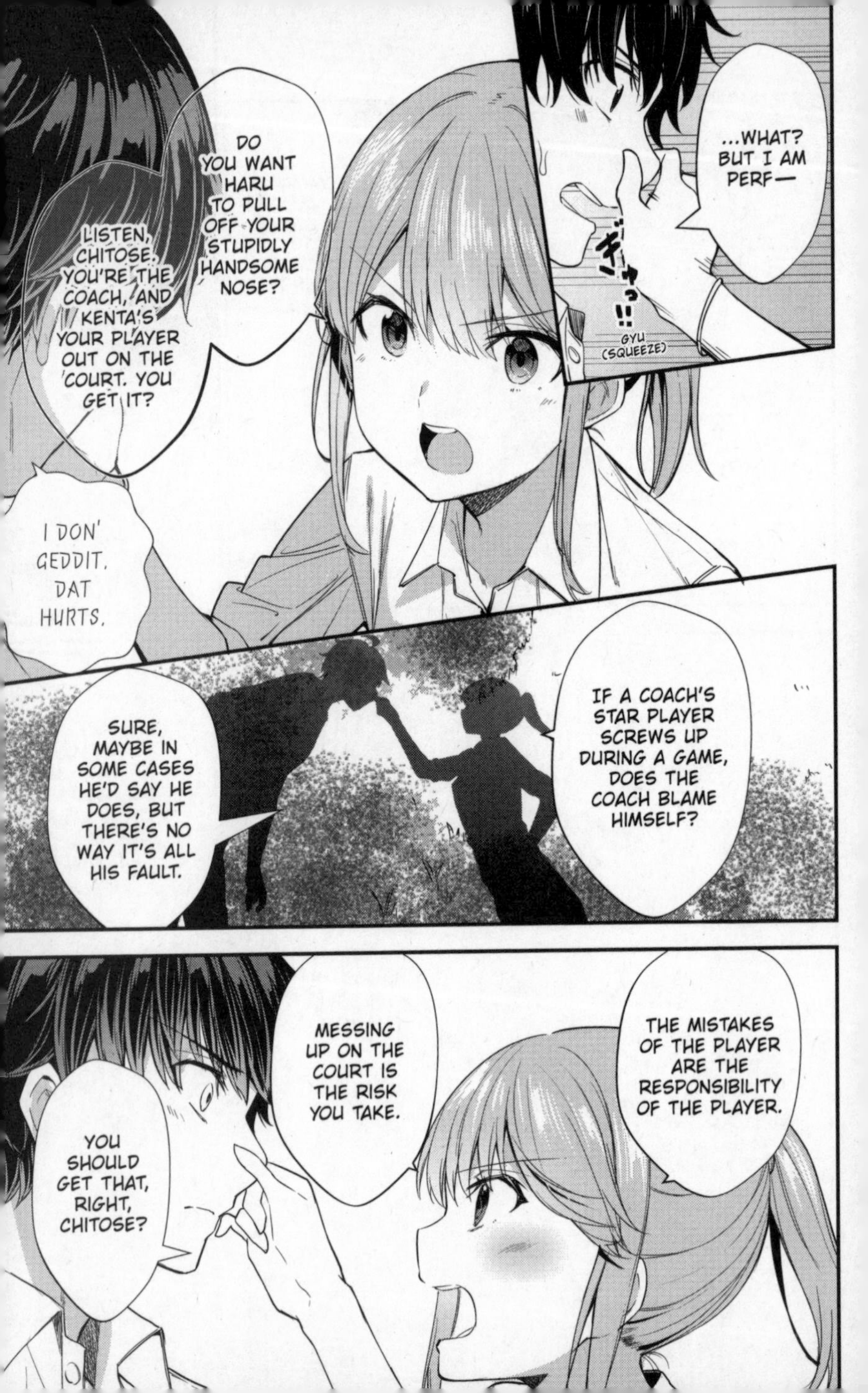
...WHAT? BUT I AM PERF—
ギュッ!!
GYU (SQUEEZE)
DO YOU WANT HARU TO PULL OFF YOUR STUPIDLY HANDSOME NOSE?
LISTEN, CHITOSE. YOU'RE THE COACH, AND KENTA'S YOUR PLAYER OUT ON THE COURT. YOU GET IT?
I DON' GEDDIT. DAT HURTS.
IF A COACH'S STAR PLAYER SCREWS UP DURING A GAME, DOES THE COACH BLAME HIMSELF?
SURE, MAYBE IN SOME CASES HE'D SAY HE DOES, BUT THERE'S NO WAY IT'S ALL HIS FAULT.
THE MISTAKES OF THE PLAYER ARE THE RESPONSIBILITY OF THE PLAYER.
MESSING UP ON THE COURT IS THE RISK YOU TAKE.
YOU SHOULD GET THAT, RIGHT, CHITOSE?

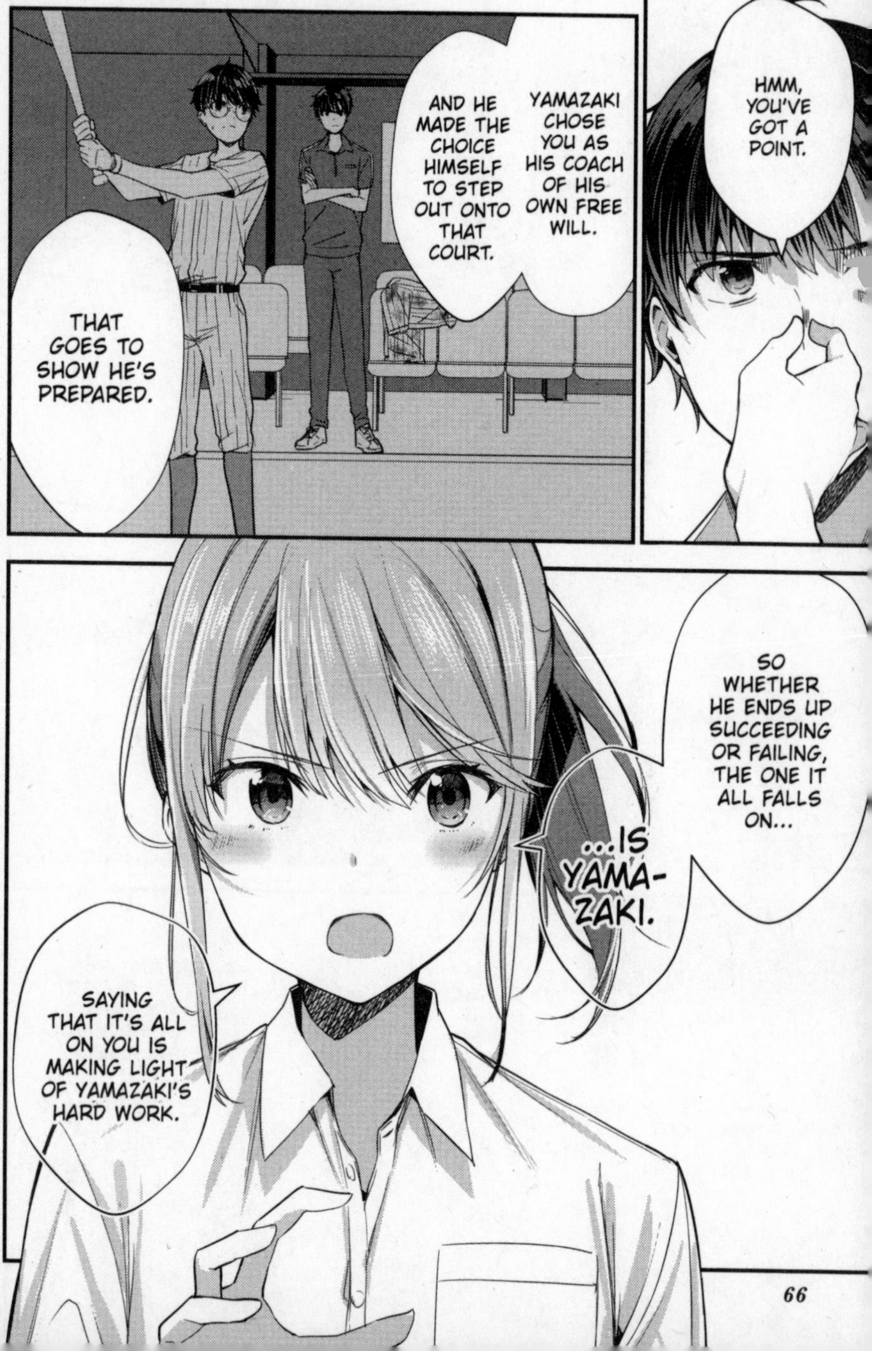
HMM, YOU'VE GOT A POINT.
YAMAZAKI CHOSE YOU AS HIS COACH OF HIS OWN FREE WILL.
AND HE MADE THE CHOICE HIMSELF TO STEP OUT ONTO THAT COURT.
THAT GOES TO SHOW HE'S PREPARED.
SO WHETHER HE ENDS UP SUCCEEDING OR FAILING, THE ONE IT ALL FALLS ON...
...IS YAMA-ZAKI.
SAYING THAT IT'S ALL ON YOU IS MAKING LIGHT OF YAMAZAKI'S HARD WORK.

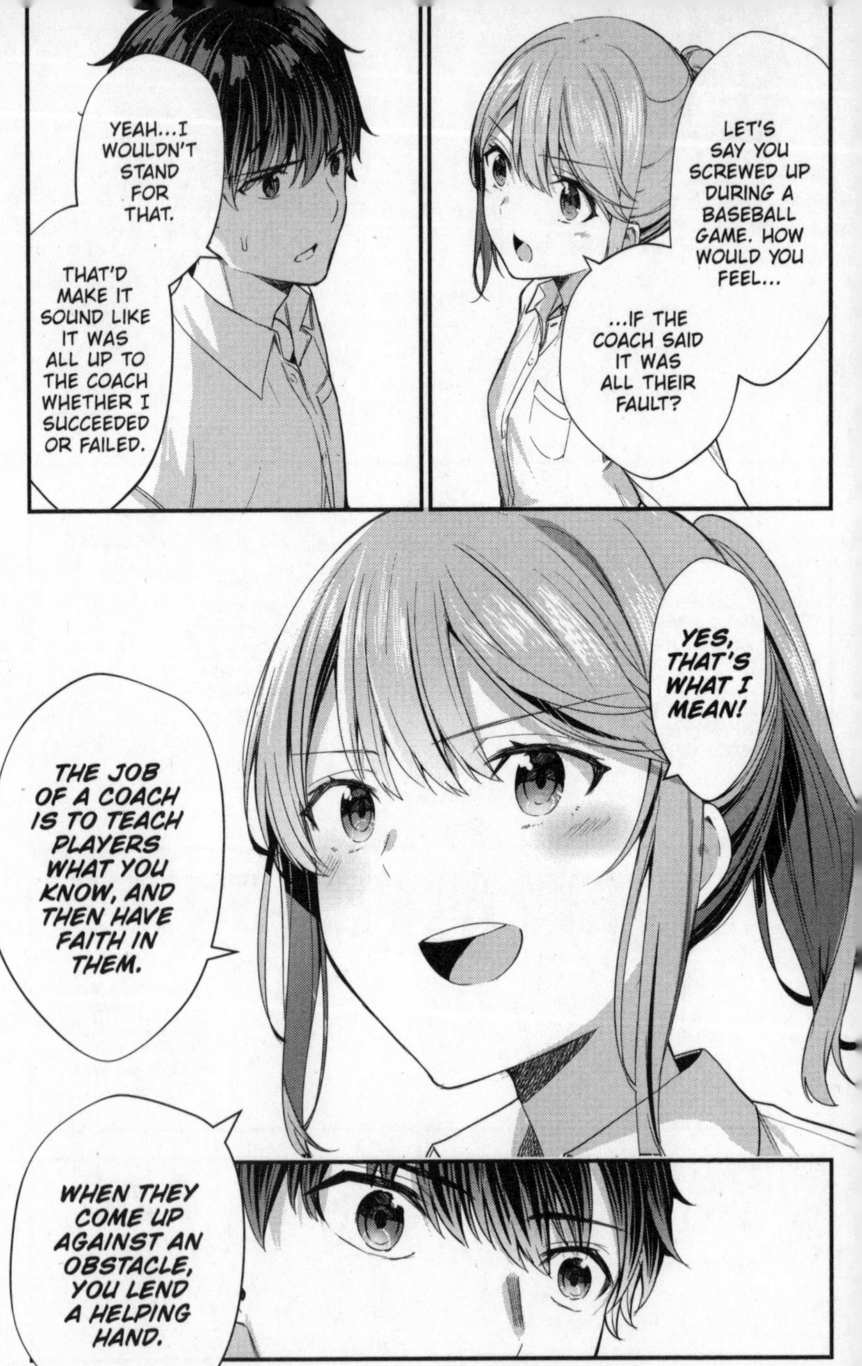
LET'S SAY YOU SCREWED UP DURING A BASEBALL GAME. HOW WOULD YOU FEEL...
...IF THE COACH SAID IT WAS ALL THEIR FAULT?
YEAH...I WOULDN'T STAND FOR THAT.
THAT'D MAKE IT SOUND LIKE IT WAS ALL UP TO THE COACH WHETHER I SUCCEEDED OR FAILED.
YES, THAT'S WHAT I MEAN!
THE JOB OF A COACH IS TO TEACH PLAYERS WHAT YOU KNOW, AND THEN HAVE FAITH IN THEM.
WHEN THEY COME UP AGAINST AN OBSTACLE, YOU LEND A HELPING HAND.

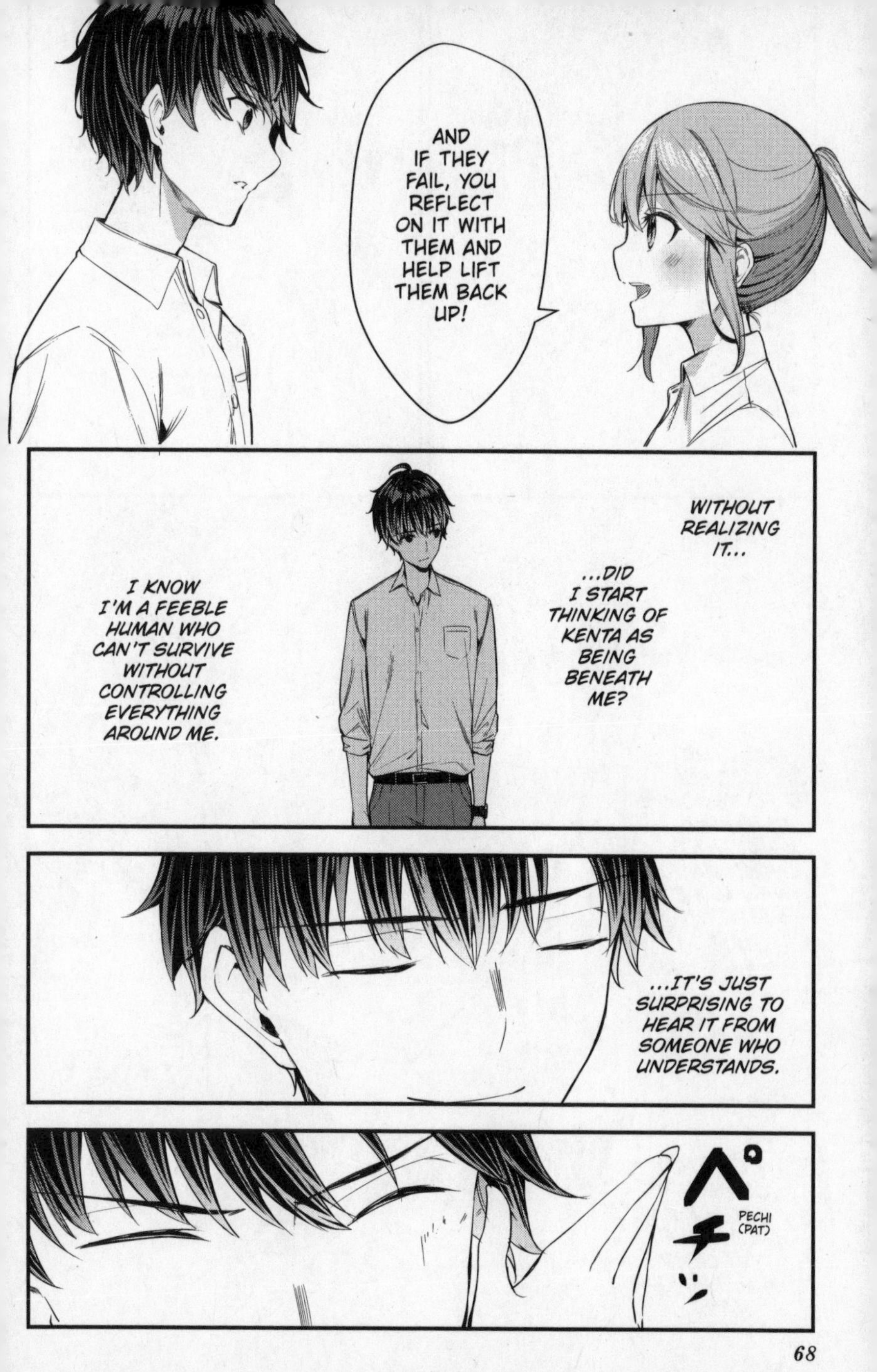
AND IF THEY FAIL, YOU REFLECT ON IT WITH THEM AND HELP LIFT THEM BACK UP!
WITHOUT REALIZING IT...
...DID I START THINKING OF KENTA AS BEING BENEATH ME?
I KNOW I'M A FEEBLE HUMAN WHO CAN'T SURVIVE WITHOUT CONTROLLING EVERYTHING AROUND ME.
...IT'S JUST SURPRISING TO HEAR IT FROM SOMEONE WHO UNDERSTANDS.
PECHI (PAT)

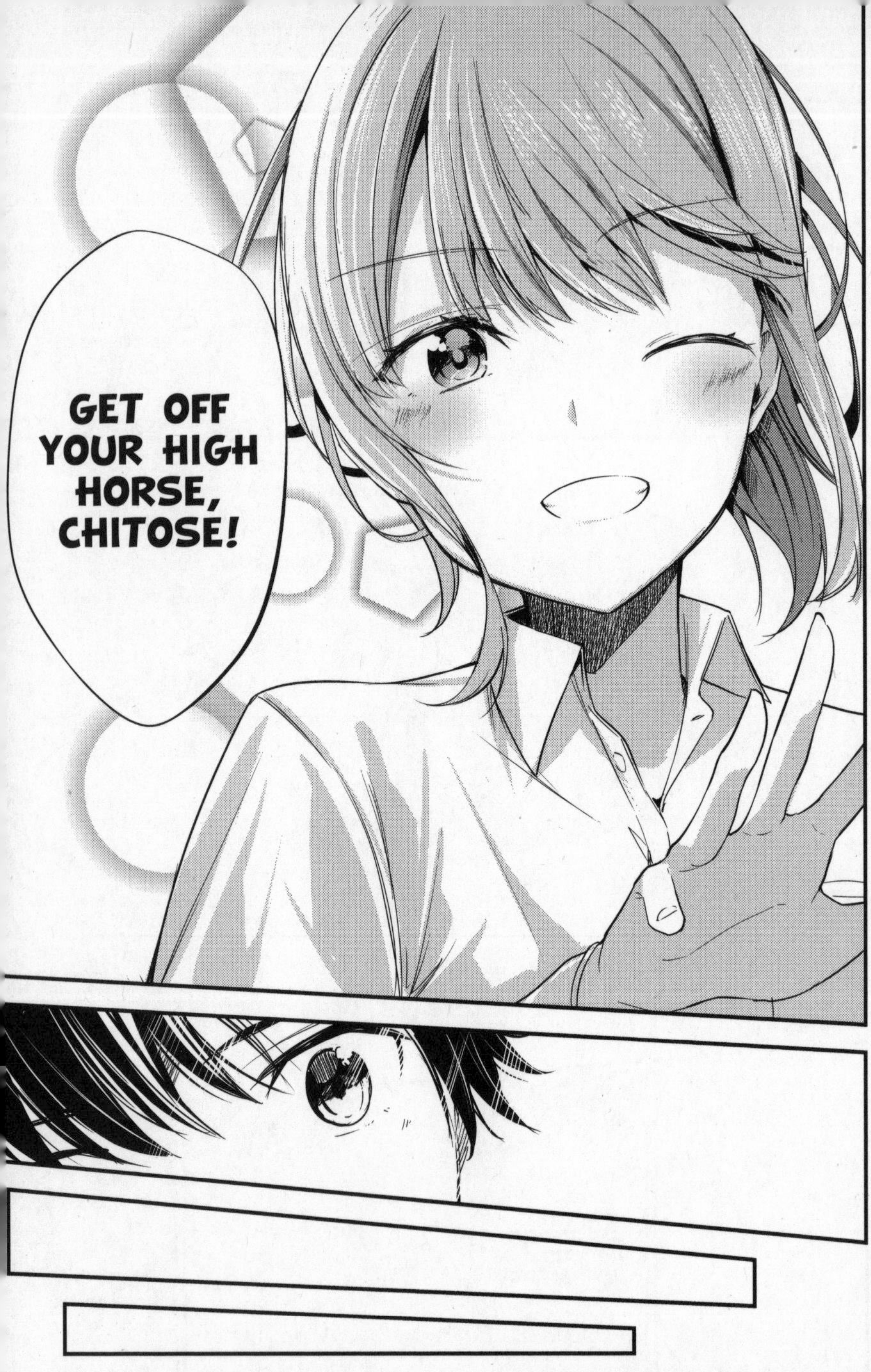
GET OFF YOUR HIGH HORSE, CHITOSE!

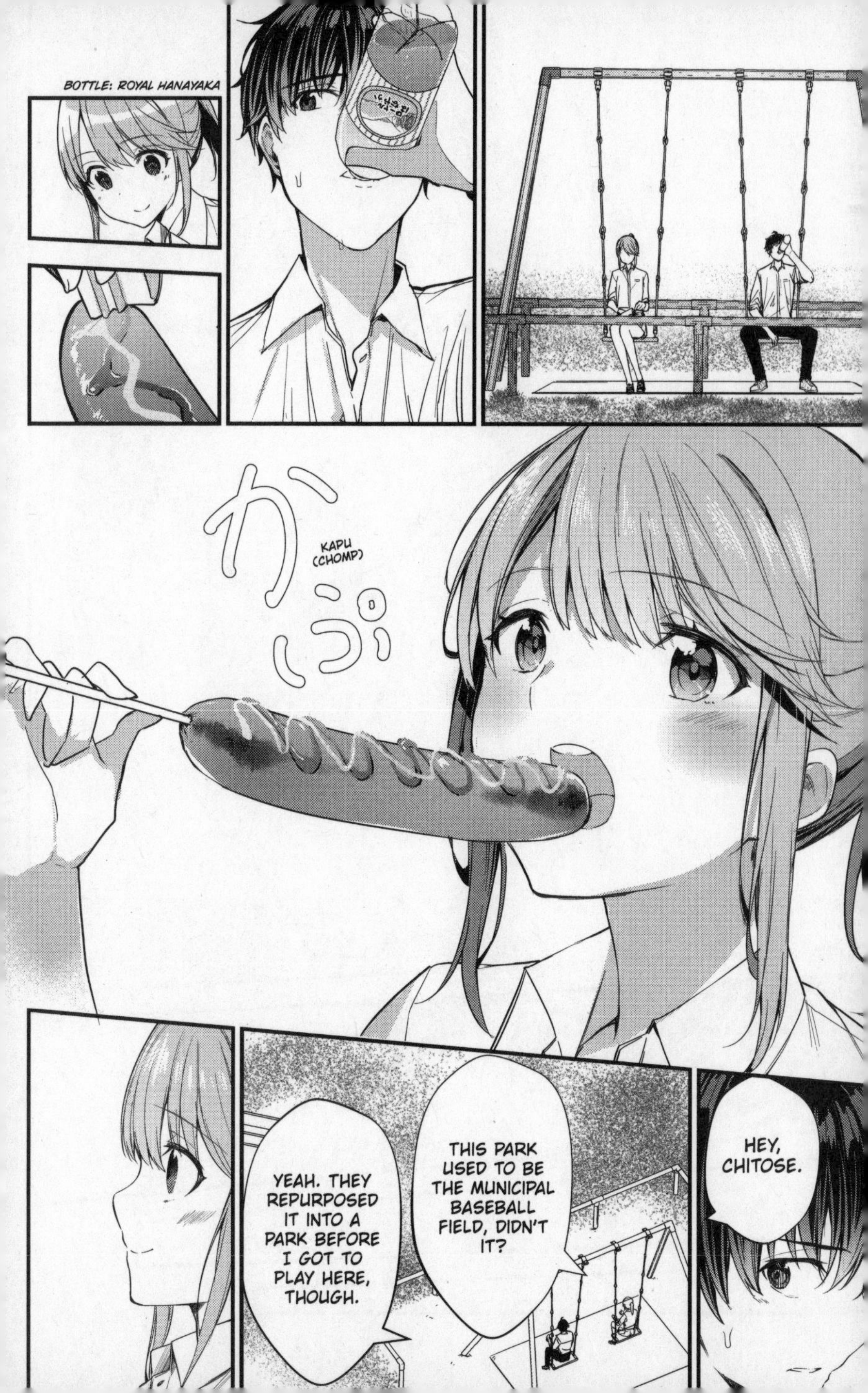
BOTTLE: ROYAL HANAYAKA
かぷっ
KAPU (CHOMP)
HEY, CHITOSE.
THIS PARK USED TO BE THE MUNICIPAL BASEBALL FIELD, DIDN'T IT?
YEAH. THEY REPURPOSED IT INTO A PARK BEFORE I GOT TO PLAY HERE, THOUGH.

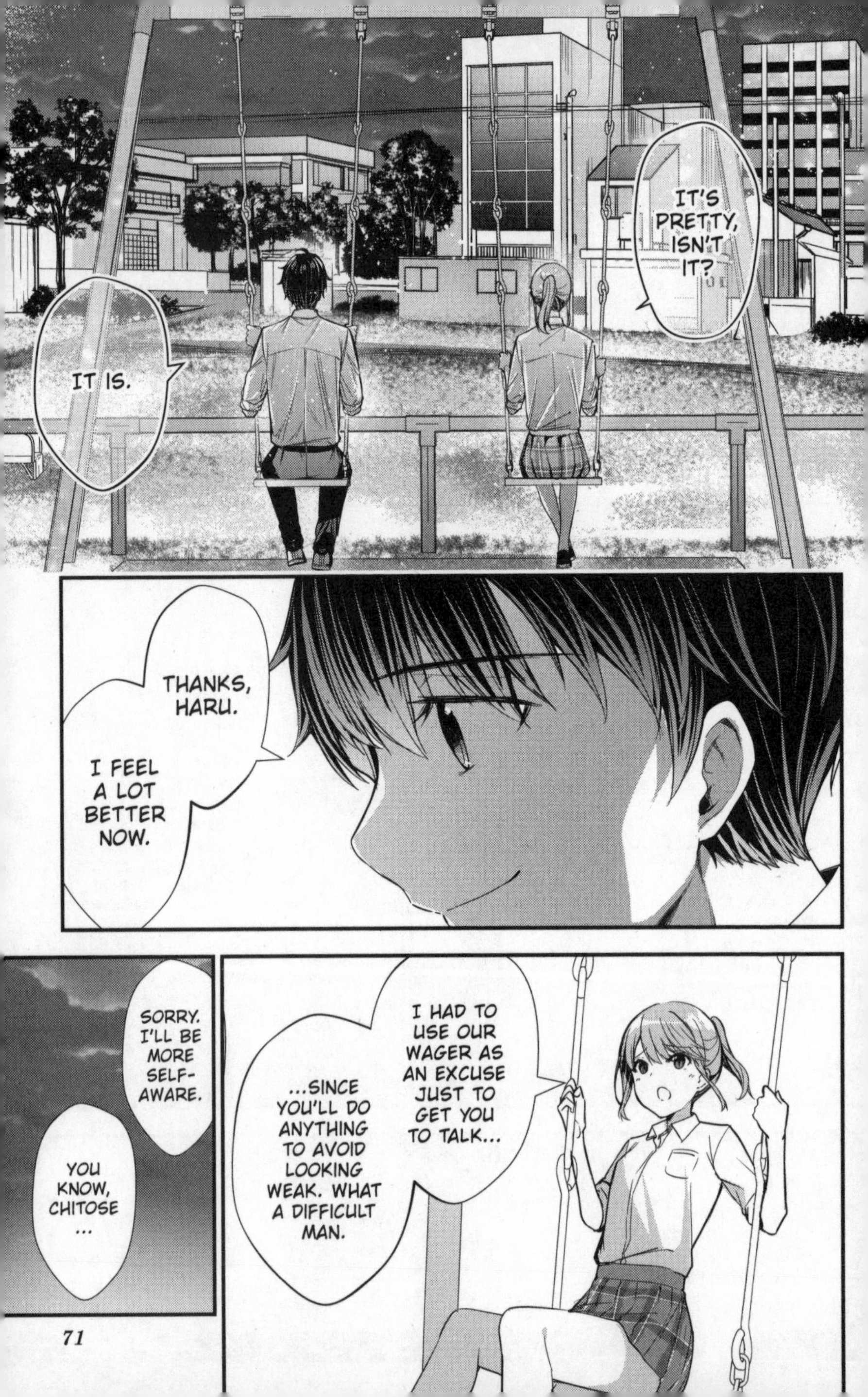
IT'S PRETTY, ISN'T IT?
IT IS.
THANKS, HARU.
I FEEL A LOT BETTER NOW.
I HAD TO USE OUR WAGER AS AN EXCUSE JUST TO GET YOU TO TALK...
...SINCE YOU'LL DO ANYTHING TO AVOID LOOKING WEAK. WHAT A DIFFICULT MAN.
SORRY. I'LL BE MORE SELF-AWARE.
YOU KNOW, CHITOSE...

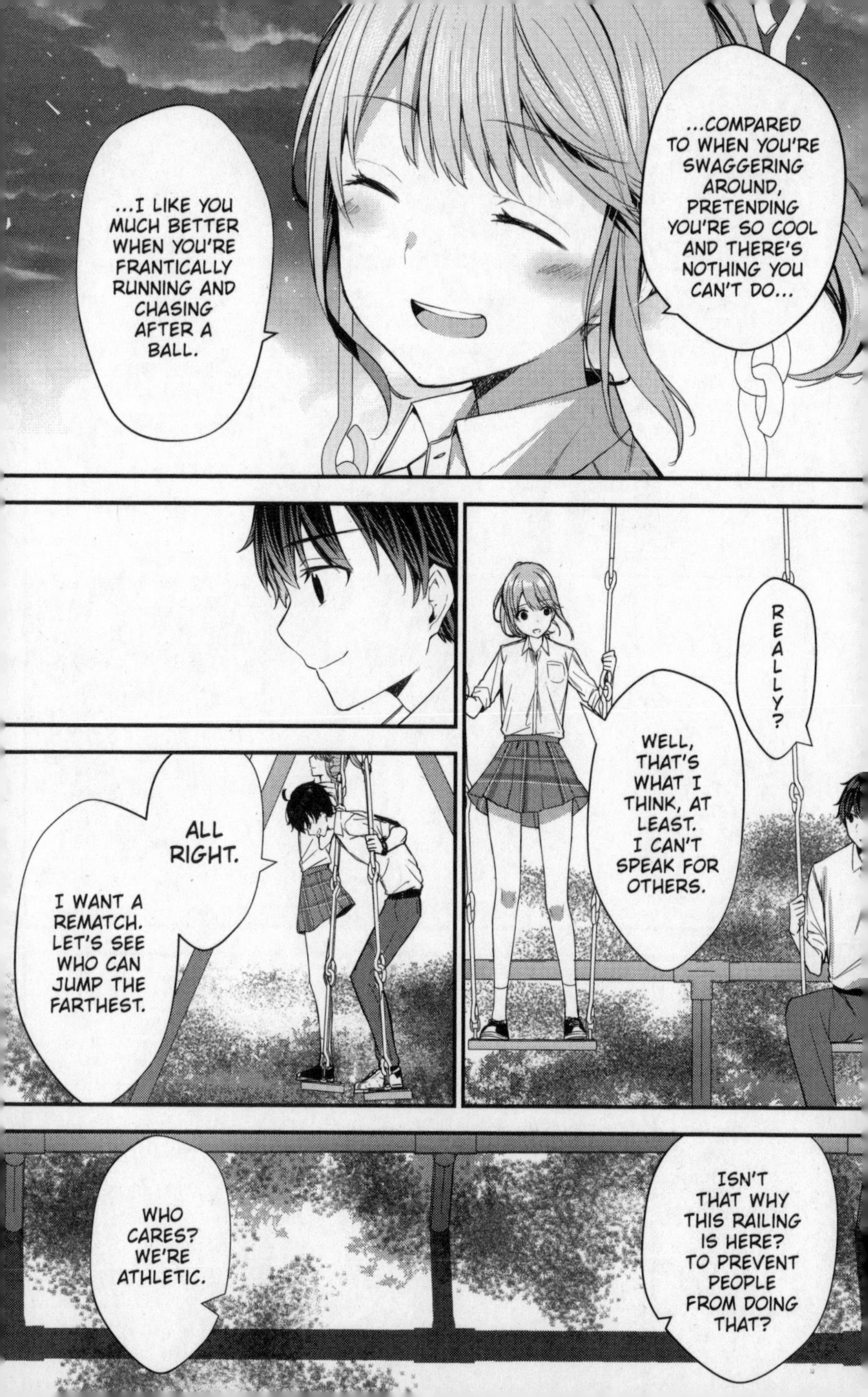
...COMPARED TO WHEN YOU'RE SWAGGERING AROUND, PRETENDING YOU'RE SO COOL AND THERE'S NOTHING YOU CAN'T DO...
...I LIKE YOU MUCH BETTER WHEN YOU'RE FRANTICALLY RUNNING AND CHASING AFTER A BALL.
REALLY?
WELL, THAT'S WHAT I THINK, AT LEAST. I CAN'T SPEAK FOR OTHERS.
ALL RIGHT.
I WANT A REMATCH. LET'S SEE WHO CAN JUMP THE FARTHEST.
ISN'T THAT WHY THIS RAILING IS HERE? TO PREVENT PEOPLE FROM DOING THAT?
WHO CARES? WE'RE ATHLETIC.

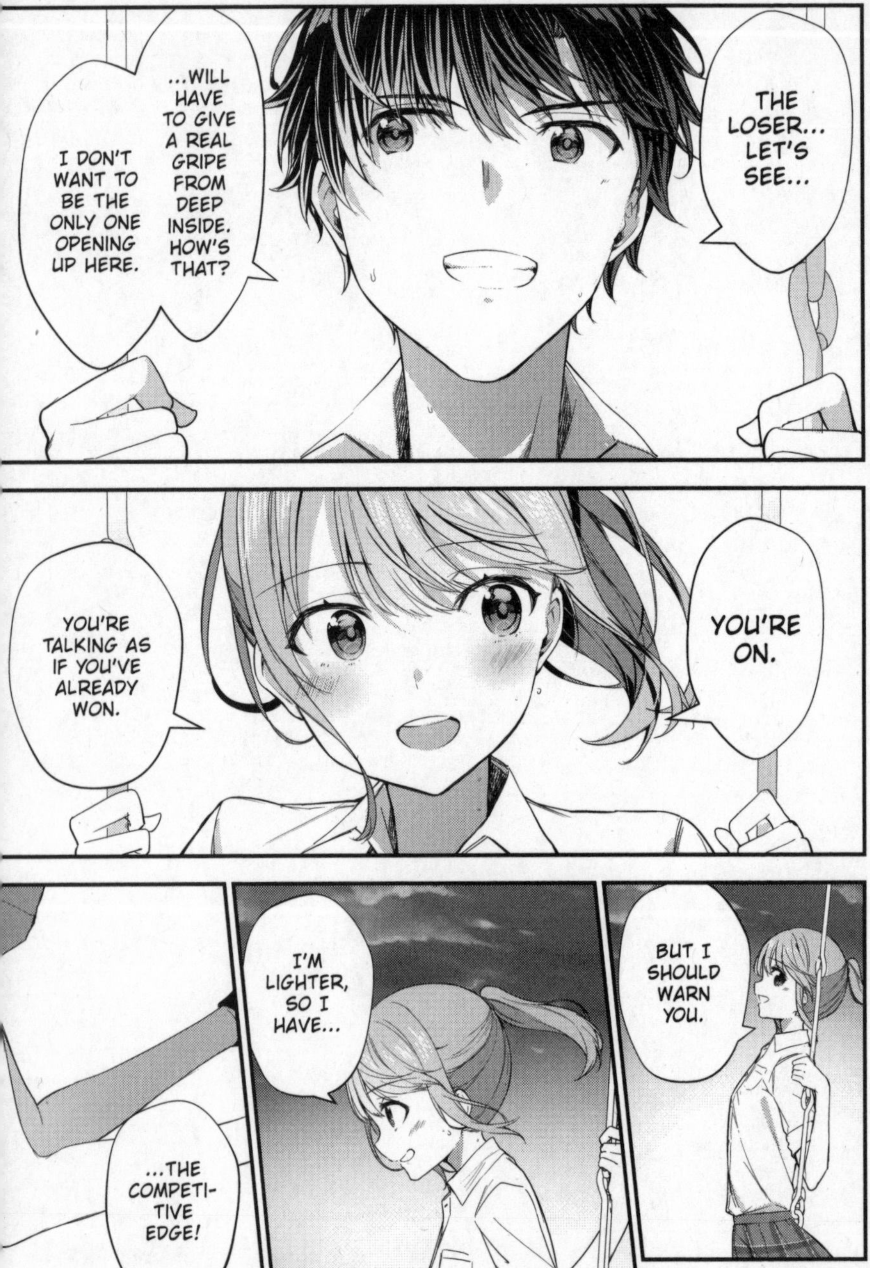
THE LOSER... LET'S SEE...
...WILL HAVE TO GIVE A REAL GRIPE FROM DEEP INSIDE. HOW'S THAT?
I DON'T WANT TO BE THE ONLY ONE OPENING UP HERE.
YOU'RE ON.
YOU'RE TALKING AS IF YOU'VE ALREADY WON.
BUT I SHOULD WARN YOU.
I'M LIGHTER, SO I HAVE...
...THE COMPETITIVE EDGE!

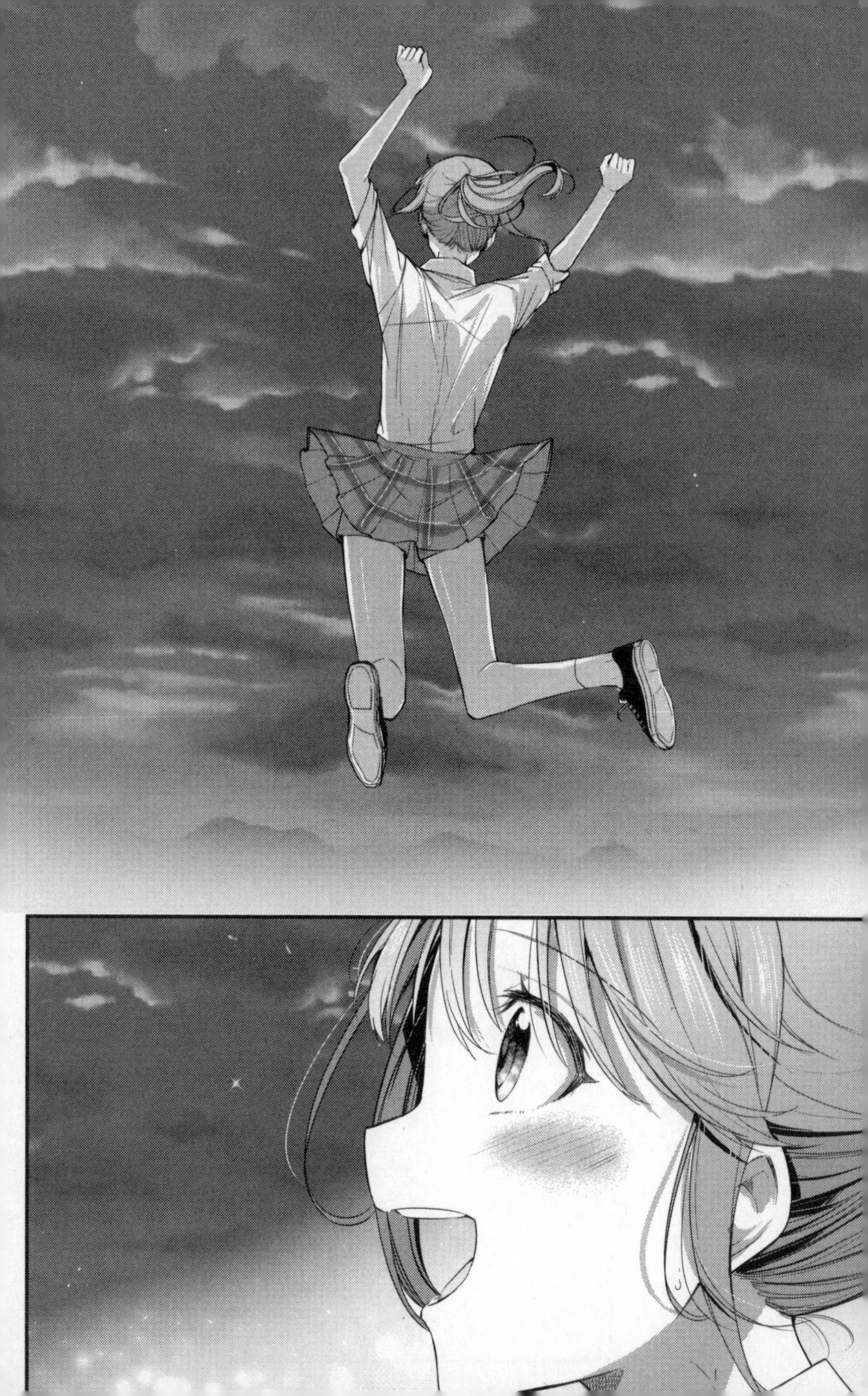

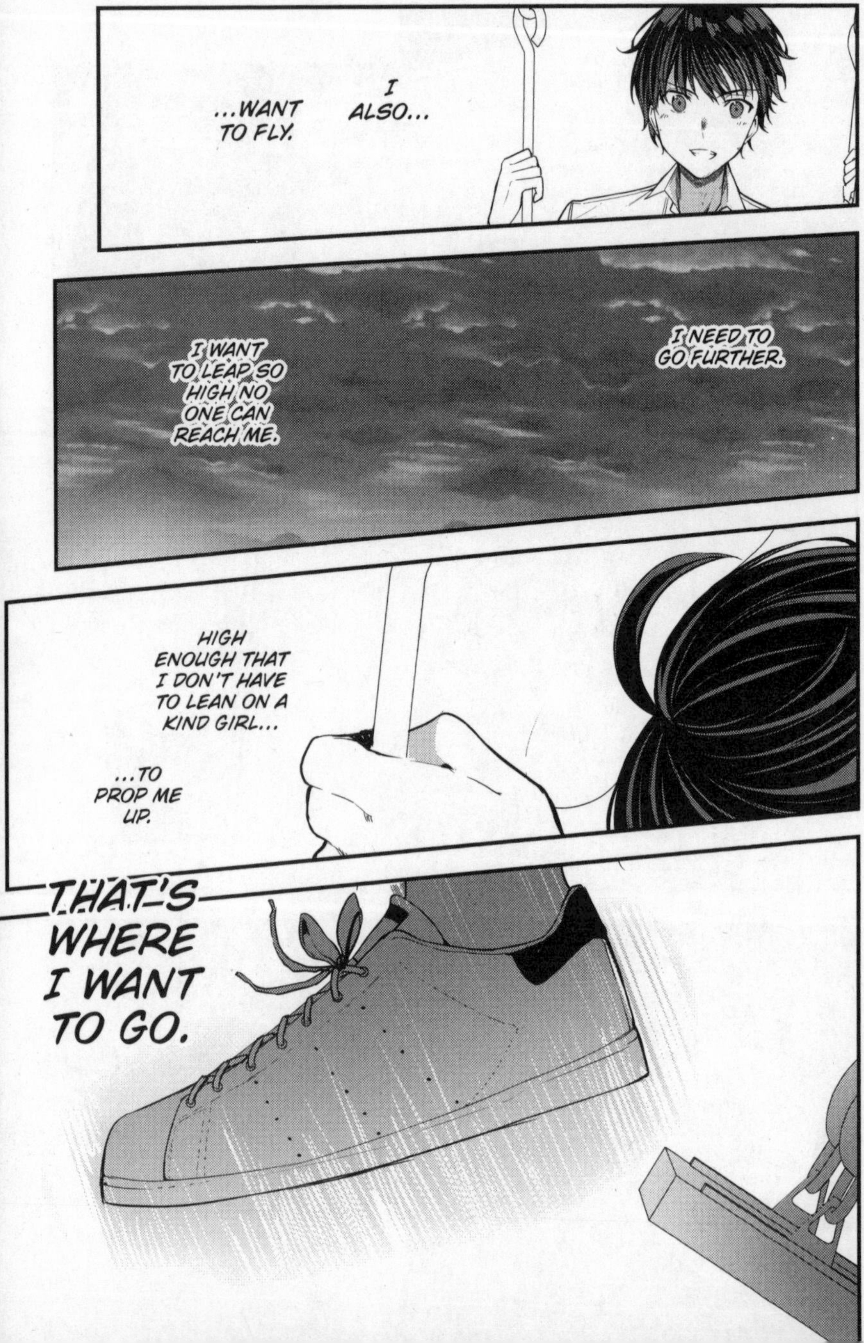
I ALSO...
...WANT TO FLY.
I NEED TO GO FURTHER.
I WANT TO LEAP SO HIGH NO ONE CAN REACH ME.
HIGH ENOUGH THAT I DON'T HAVE TO LEAN ON A KIND GIRL...
...TO PROP ME UP.
THAT'S WHERE I WANT TO GO.

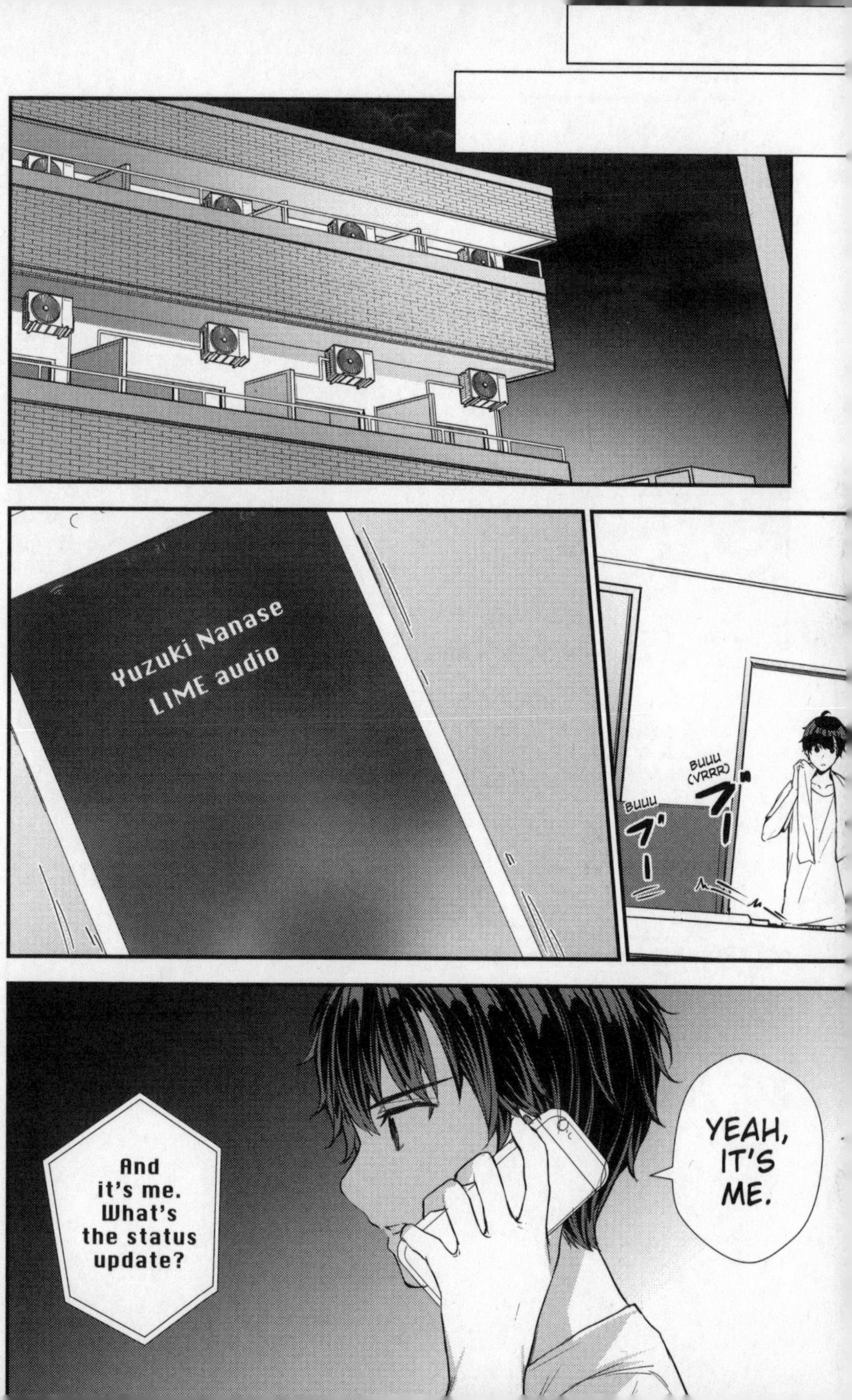
Yuzuki Nanase
LIME audio
BUUU (VRRR)
BUUU
YEAH, IT'S ME.
And it's me. What's the status update?

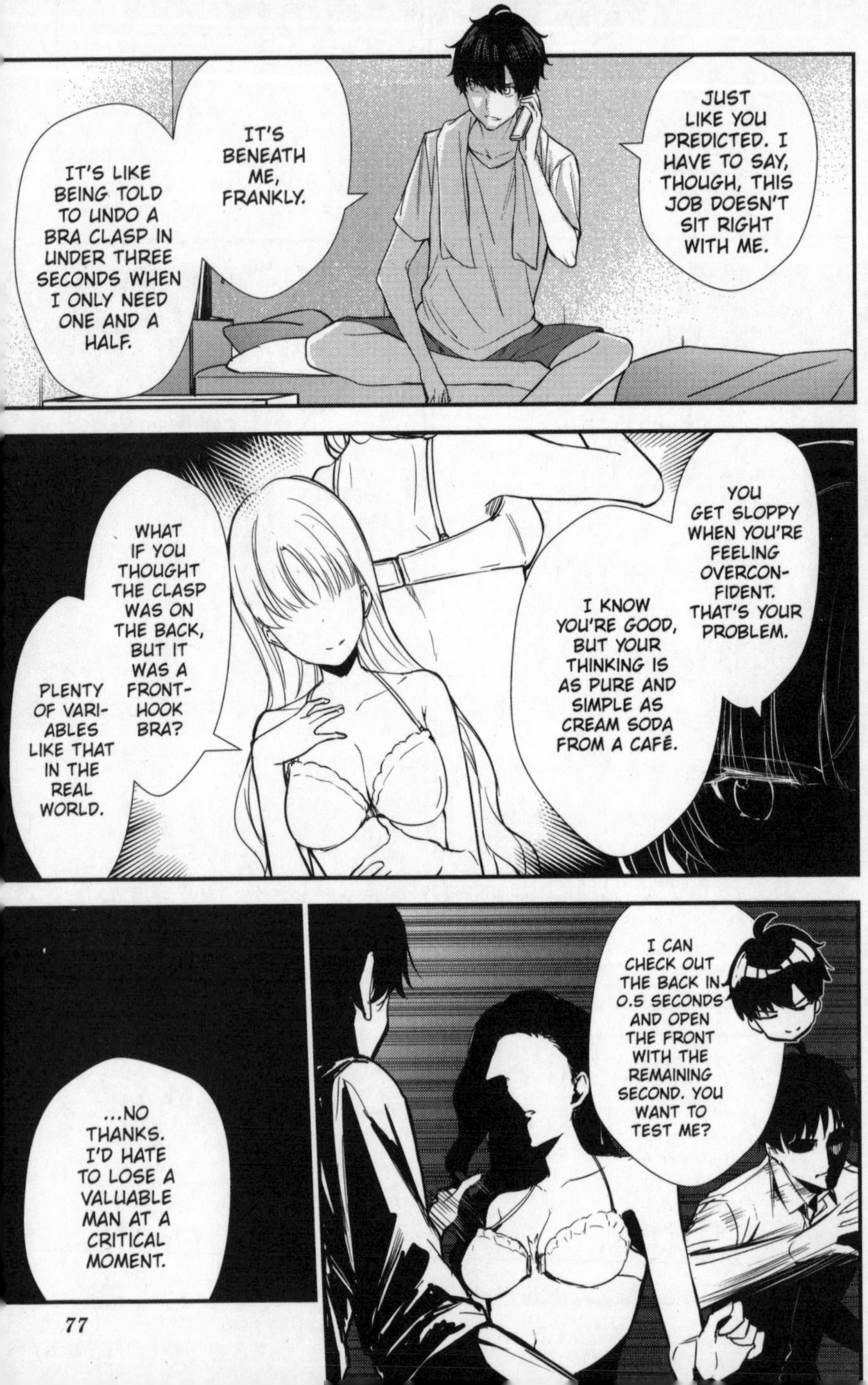
JUST LIKE YOU PREDICTED. I HAVE TO SAY, THOUGH, THIS JOB DOESN'T SIT RIGHT WITH ME.
IT'S BENEATH ME, FRANKLY.
IT'S LIKE BEING TOLD TO UNDO A BRA CLASP IN UNDER THREE SECONDS WHEN I ONLY NEED ONE AND A HALF.
YOU GET SLOPPY WHEN YOU'RE FEELING OVERCON-FIDENT. THAT'S YOUR PROBLEM.
I KNOW YOU'RE GOOD, BUT YOUR THINKING IS AS PURE AND SIMPLE AS CREAM SODA FROM A CAFÉ.
WHAT IF YOU THOUGHT THE CLASP WAS ON THE BACK, BUT IT WAS A FRONT-HOOK BRA?
PLENTY OF VARI-ABLES LIKE THAT IN THE REAL WORLD.
I CAN CHECK OUT THE BACK IN 0.5 SECONDS AND OPEN THE FRONT WITH THE REMAINING SECOND. YOU WANT TO TEST ME?
...NO THANKS. I'D HATE TO LOSE A VALUABLE MAN AT A CRITICAL MOMENT.

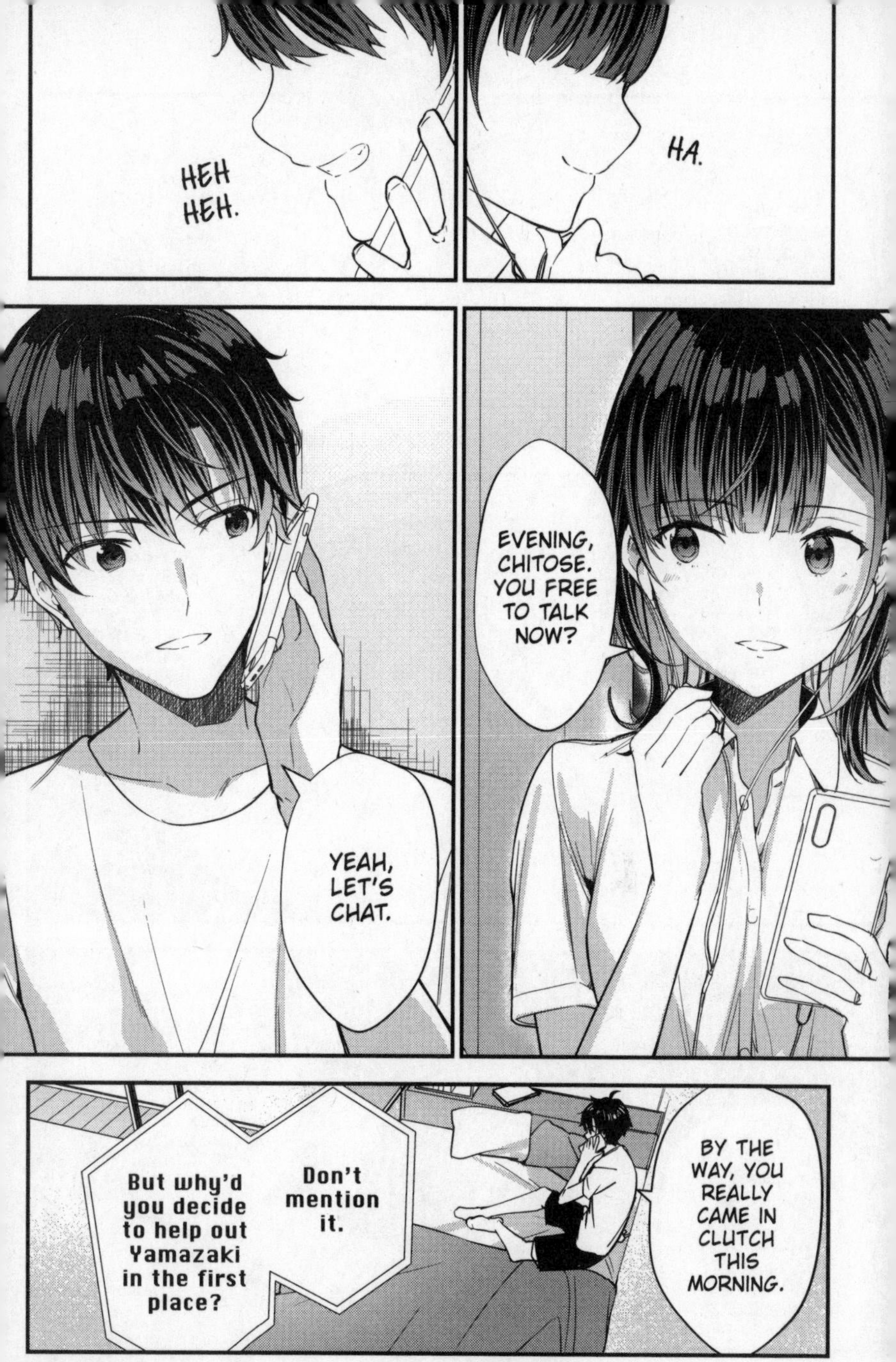
HA.
HEH HEH.
EVENING, CHITOSE. YOU FREE TO TALK NOW?
YEAH, LET'S CHAT.
BY THE WAY, YOU REALLY CAME IN CLUTCH THIS MORNING.
Don't mention it.
But why'd you decide to help out Yamazaki in the first place?

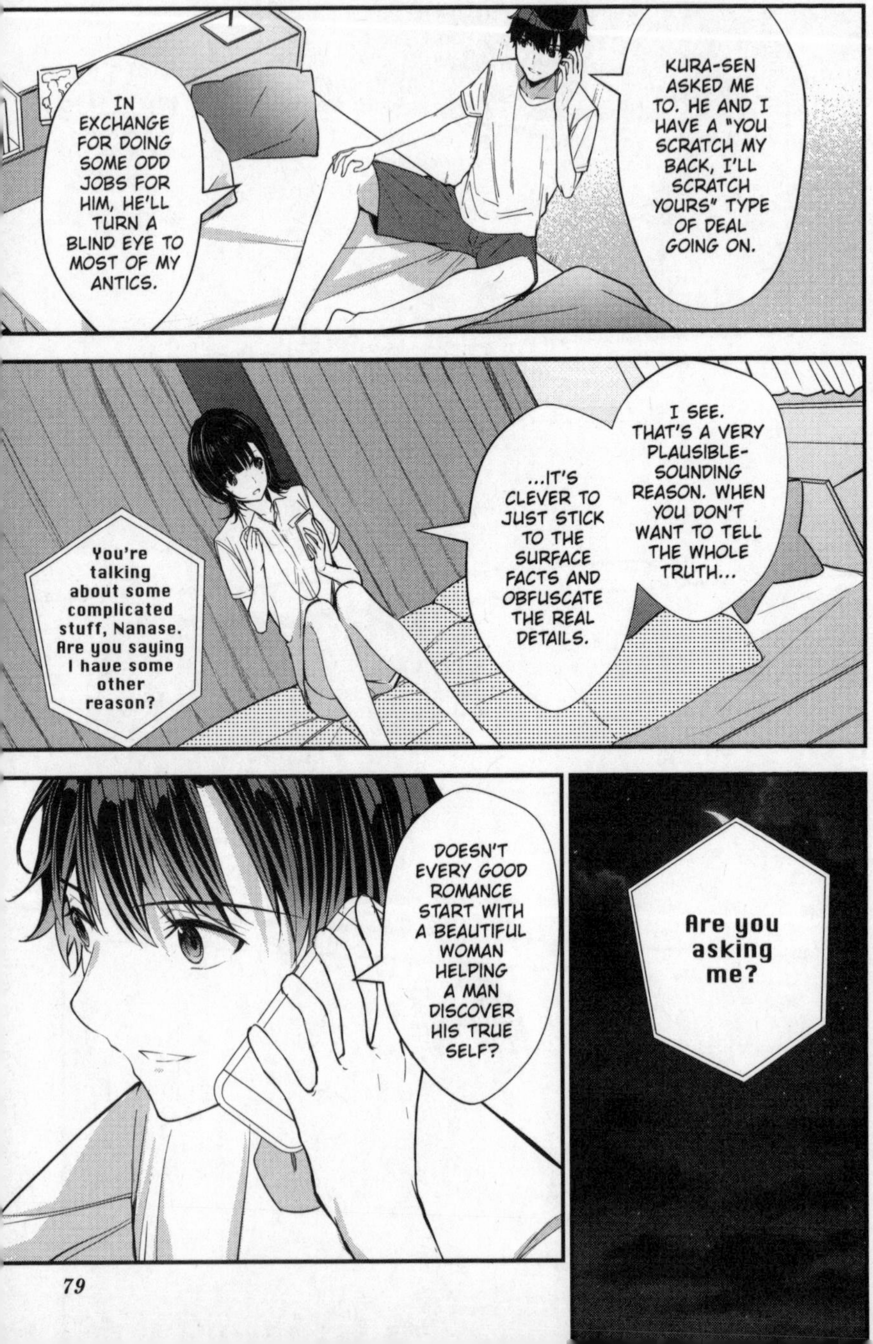
KURA-SEN ASKED ME TO. HE AND I HAVE A "YOU SCRATCH MY BACK, I'LL SCRATCH YOURS" TYPE OF DEAL GOING ON.
IN EXCHANGE FOR DOING SOME ODD JOBS FOR HIM, HE'LL TURN A BLIND EYE TO MOST OF MY ANTICS.
I SEE. THAT'S A VERY PLAUSIBLE-SOUNDING REASON. WHEN YOU DON'T WANT TO TELL THE WHOLE TRUTH...
...IT'S CLEVER TO JUST STICK TO THE SURFACE FACTS AND OBFUSCATE THE REAL DETAILS.
You're talking about some complicated stuff, Nanase. Are you saying I have some other reason?
Are you asking me?
DOESN'T EVERY GOOD ROMANCE START WITH A BEAUTIFUL WOMAN HELPING A MAN DISCOVER HIS TRUE SELF?

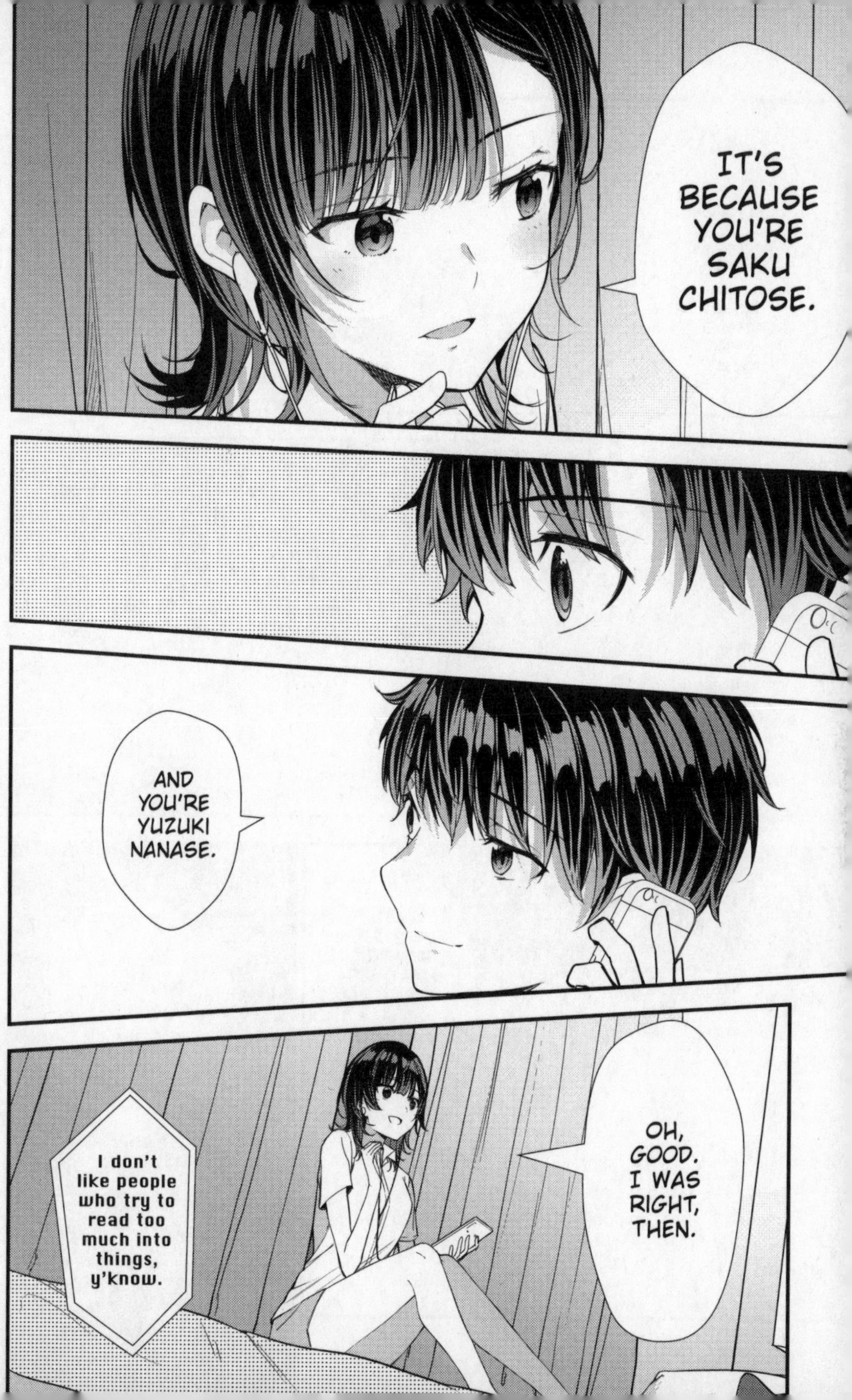
IT'S BECAUSE YOU'RE SAKU CHITOSE.
AND YOU'RE YUZUKI NANASE.
OH, GOOD. I WAS RIGHT, THEN.
I don't like people who try to read too much into things, y'know.

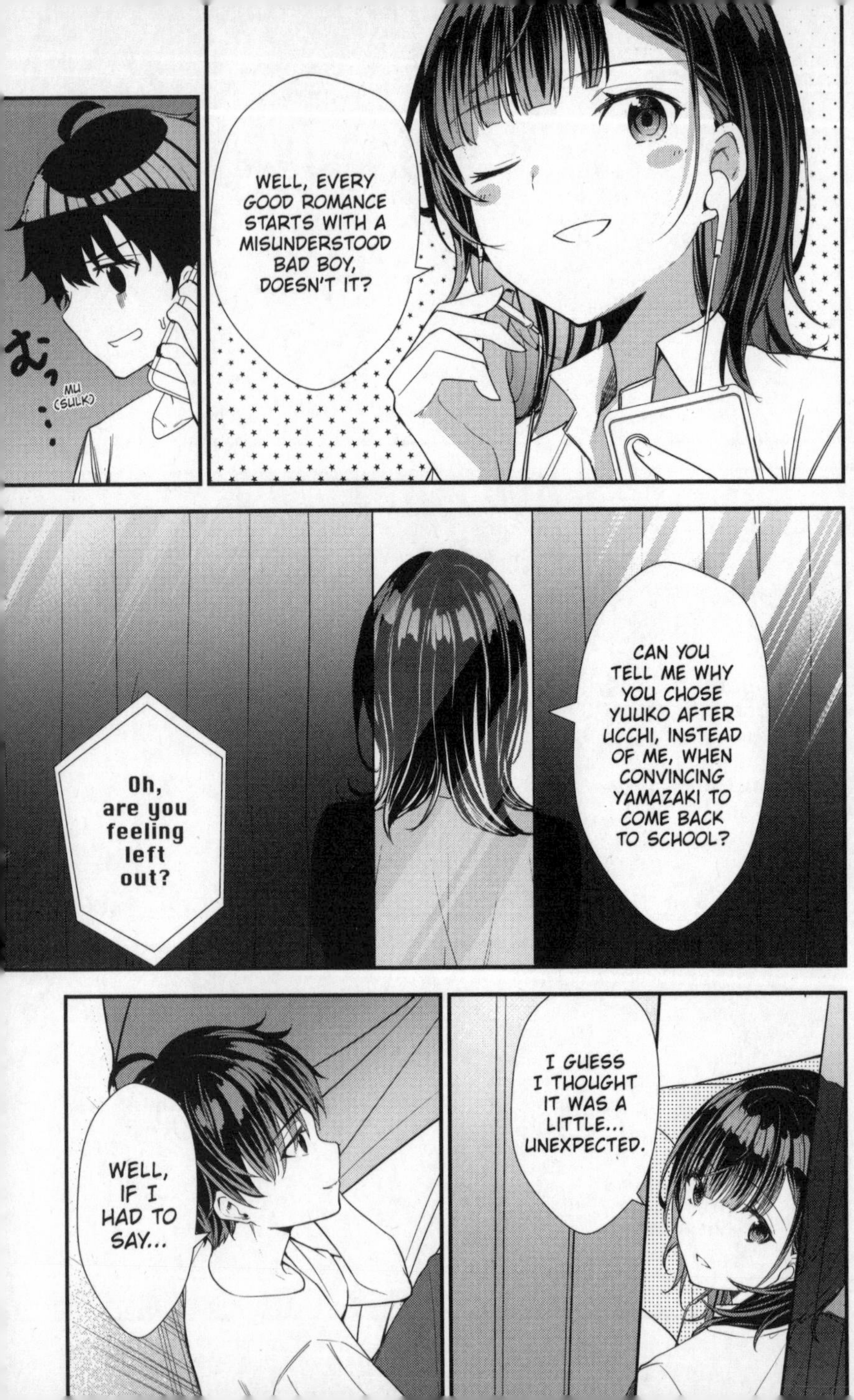
WELL, EVERY GOOD ROMANCE STARTS WITH A MISUNDERSTOOD BAD BOY, DOESN'T IT?
むっ
MU (SULK)
CAN YOU TELL ME WHY YOU CHOSE YUUKO AFTER UCCHI, INSTEAD OF ME, WHEN CONVINCING YAMAZAKI TO COME BACK TO SCHOOL?
Oh, are you feeling left out?
I GUESS I THOUGHT IT WAS A LITTLE... UNEXPECTED.
WELL, IF I HAD TO SAY...

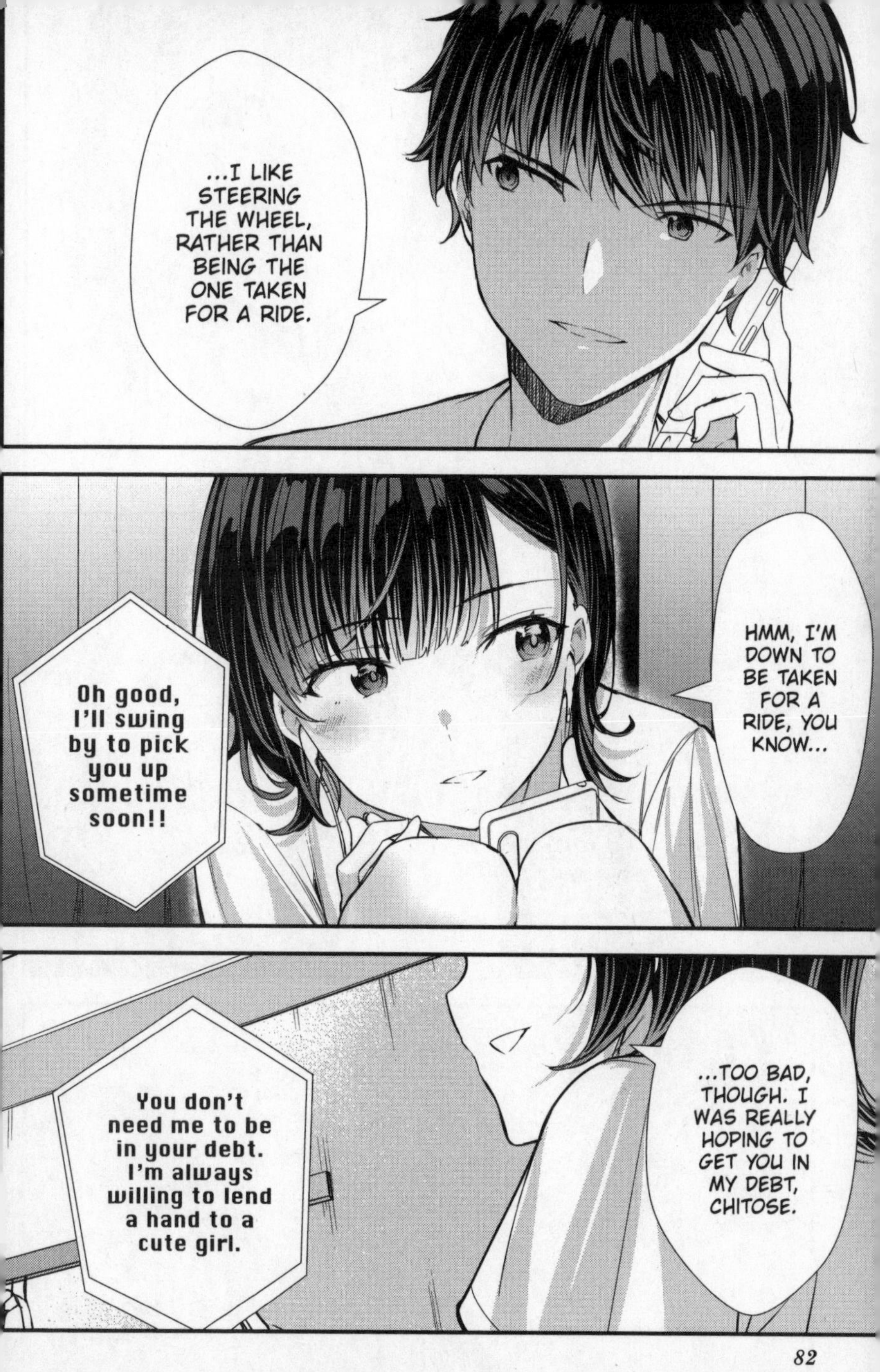
...I LIKE STEERING THE WHEEL, RATHER THAN BEING THE ONE TAKEN FOR A RIDE.
HMM, I'M DOWN TO BE TAKEN FOR A RIDE, YOU KNOW...
Oh good, I'll swing by to pick you up sometime soon!!
...TOO BAD, THOUGH. I WAS REALLY HOPING TO GET YOU IN MY DEBT, CHITOSE.
You don't need me to be in your debt. I'm always willing to lend a hand to a cute girl.

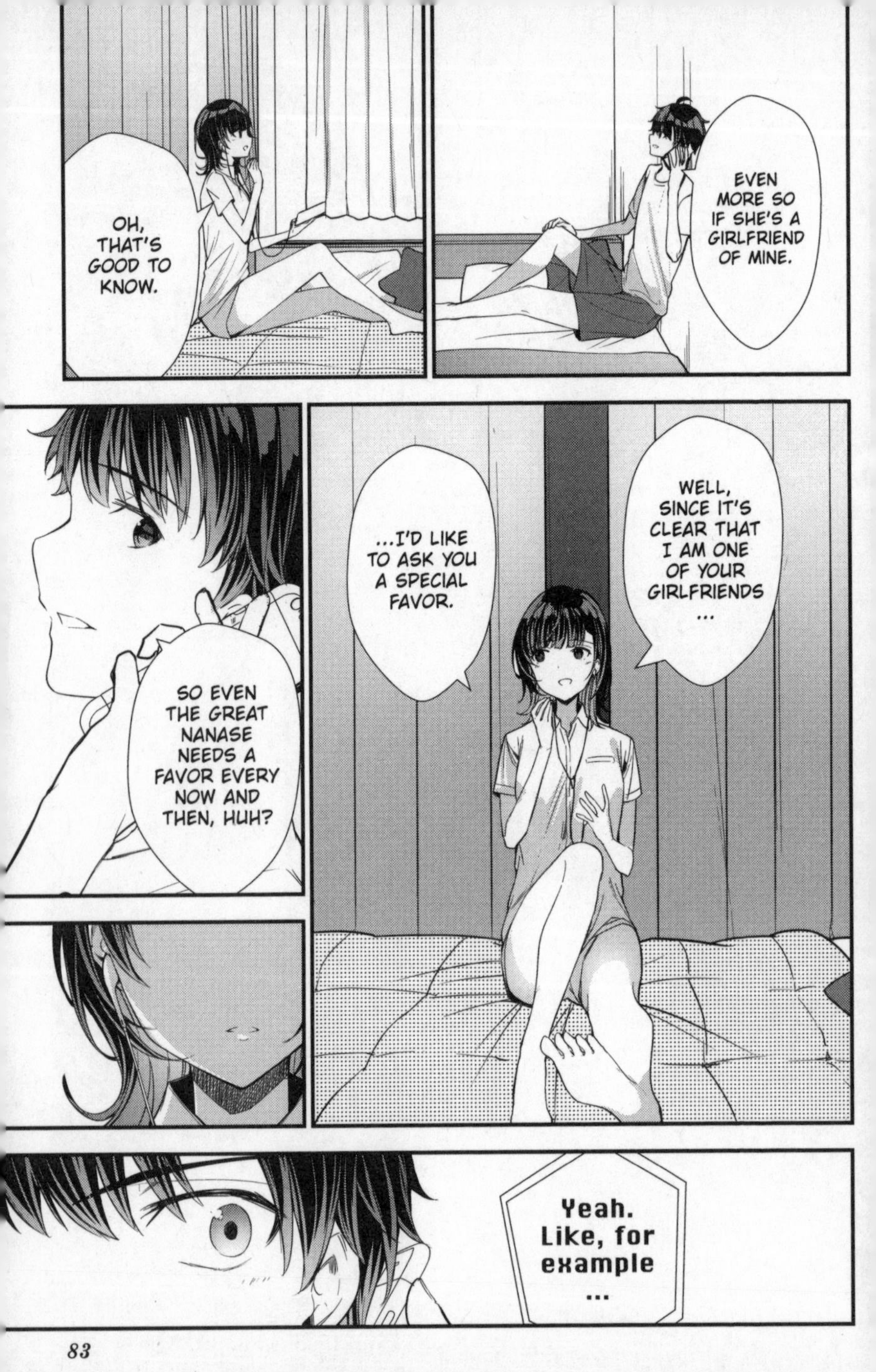
EVEN MORE SO IF SHE'S A GIRLFRIEND OF MINE.
OH, THAT'S GOOD TO KNOW.
WELL, SINCE IT'S CLEAR THAT I AM ONE OF YOUR GIRLFRIENDS ...
...I'D LIKE TO ASK YOU A SPECIAL FAVOR.
SO EVEN THE GREAT NANASE NEEDS A FAVOR EVERY NOW AND THEN, HUH?
Yeah. Like, for example ...

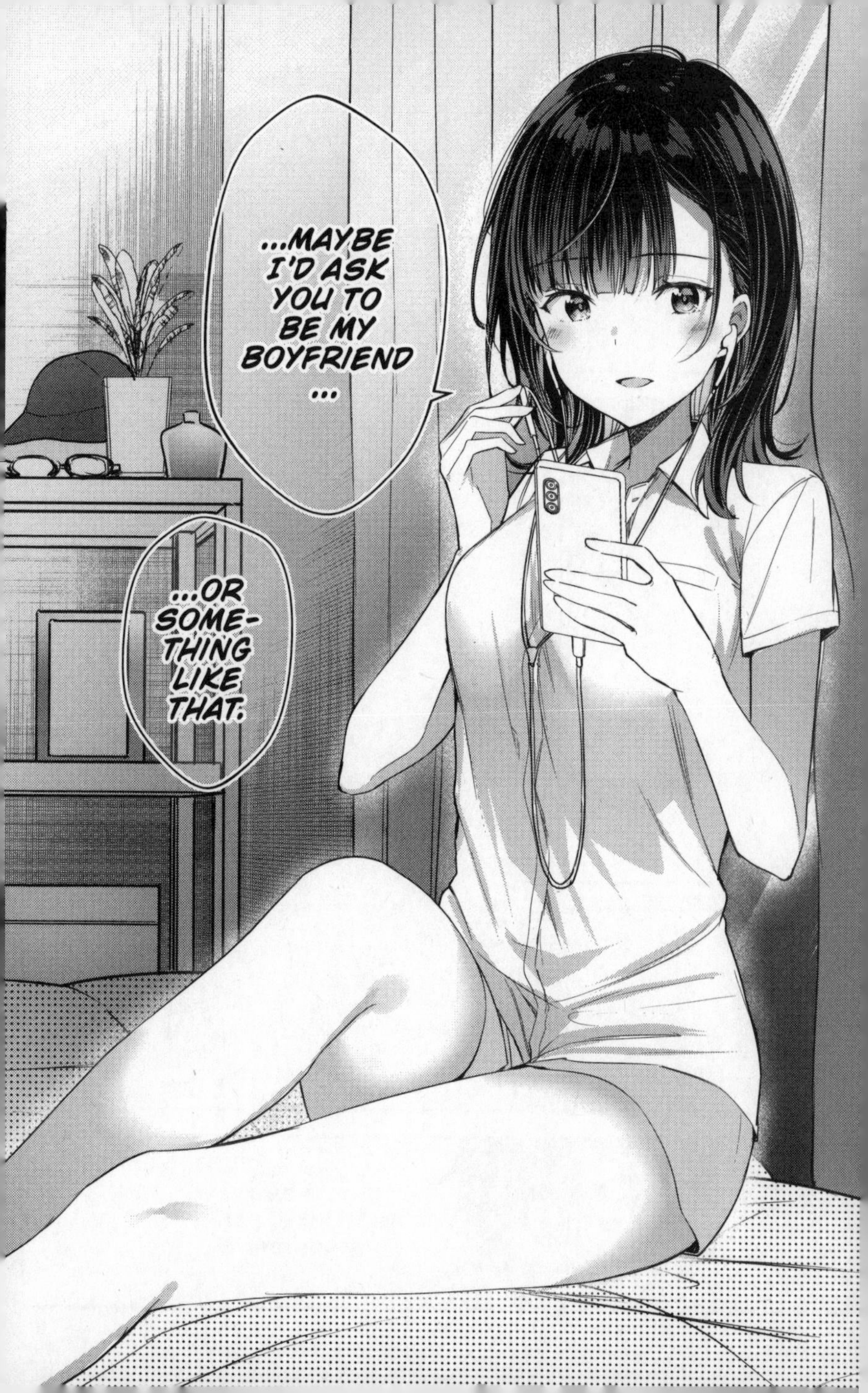
...MAYBE I'D ASK YOU TO BE MY BOYFRIEND ...
...OR SOME-THING LIKE THAT.

Chitose Is in the Ramune Bottle

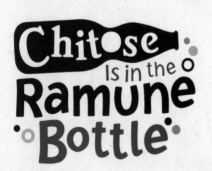

CHARACTER PROFILE

Kazuki Mizushino

Age: 16 years old

Height: 5’9” (176 cm)

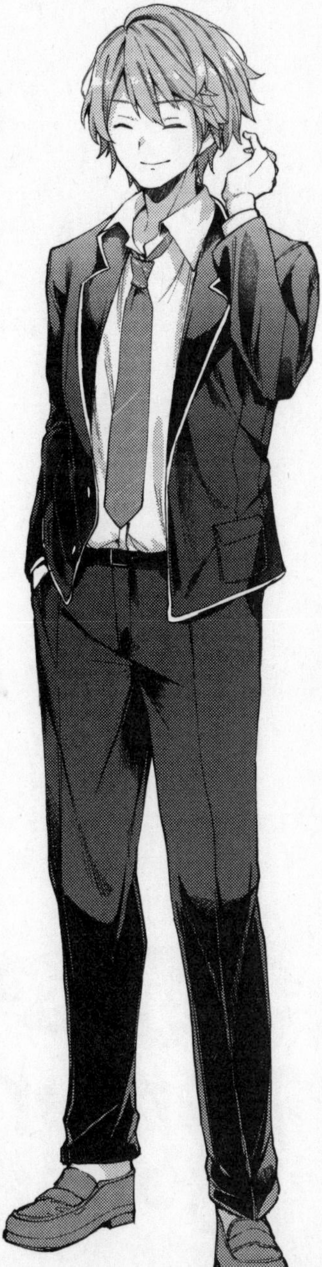

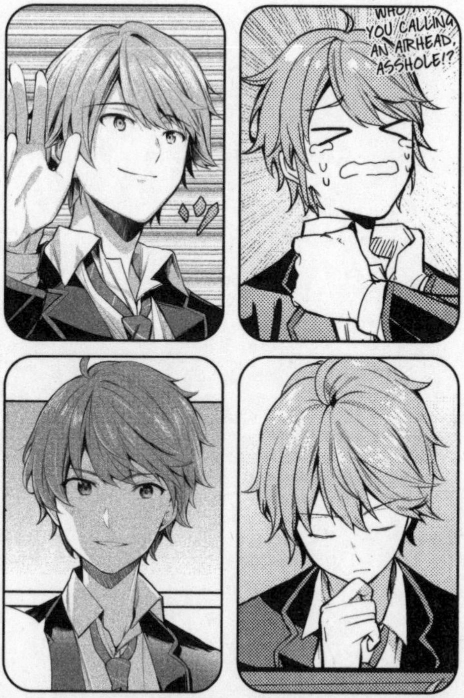
WHO
YOU CALLING AN AIRHEAD, ASSHOLE!?

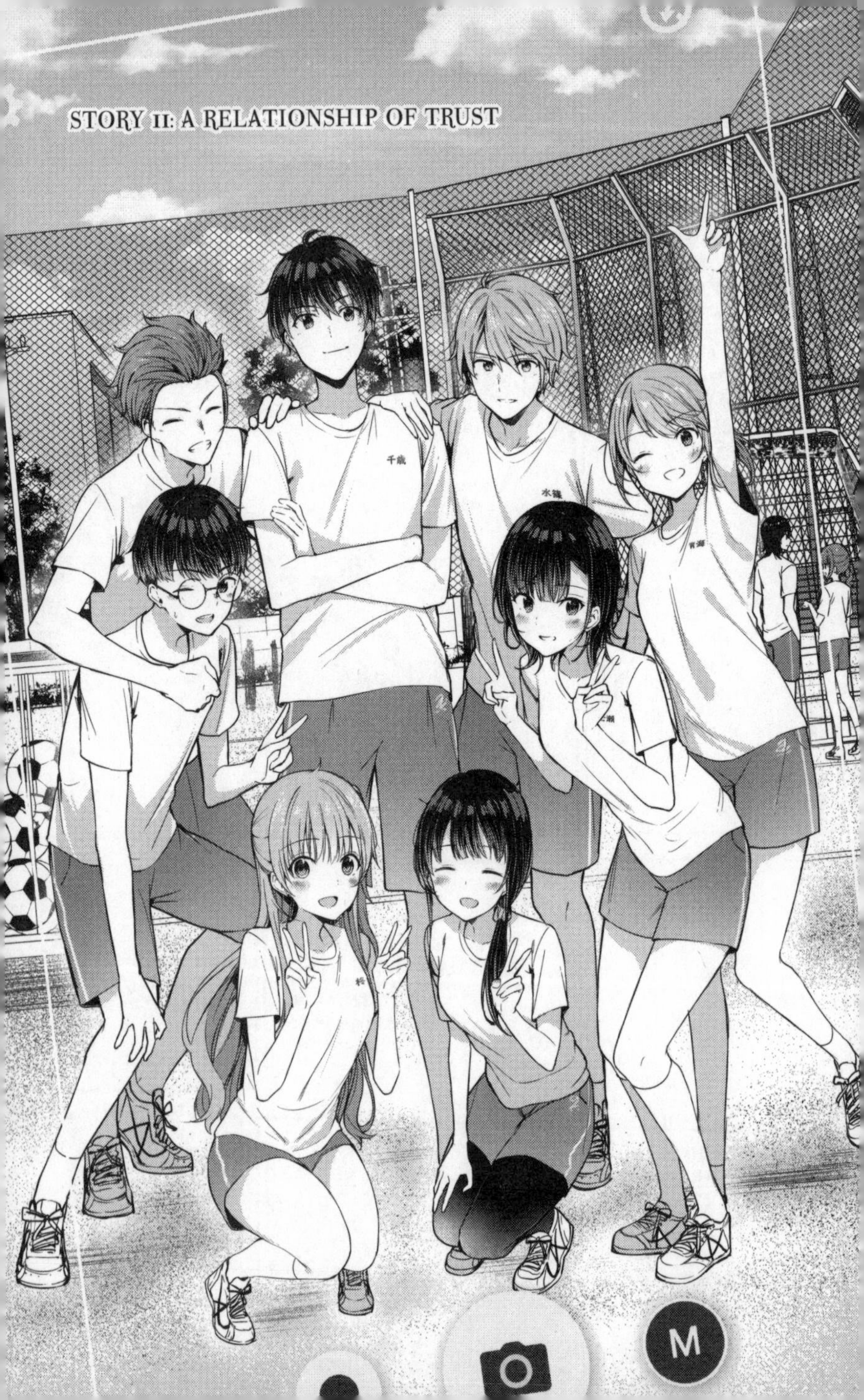
STORY 11: A RELATIONSHIP OF TRUST
M

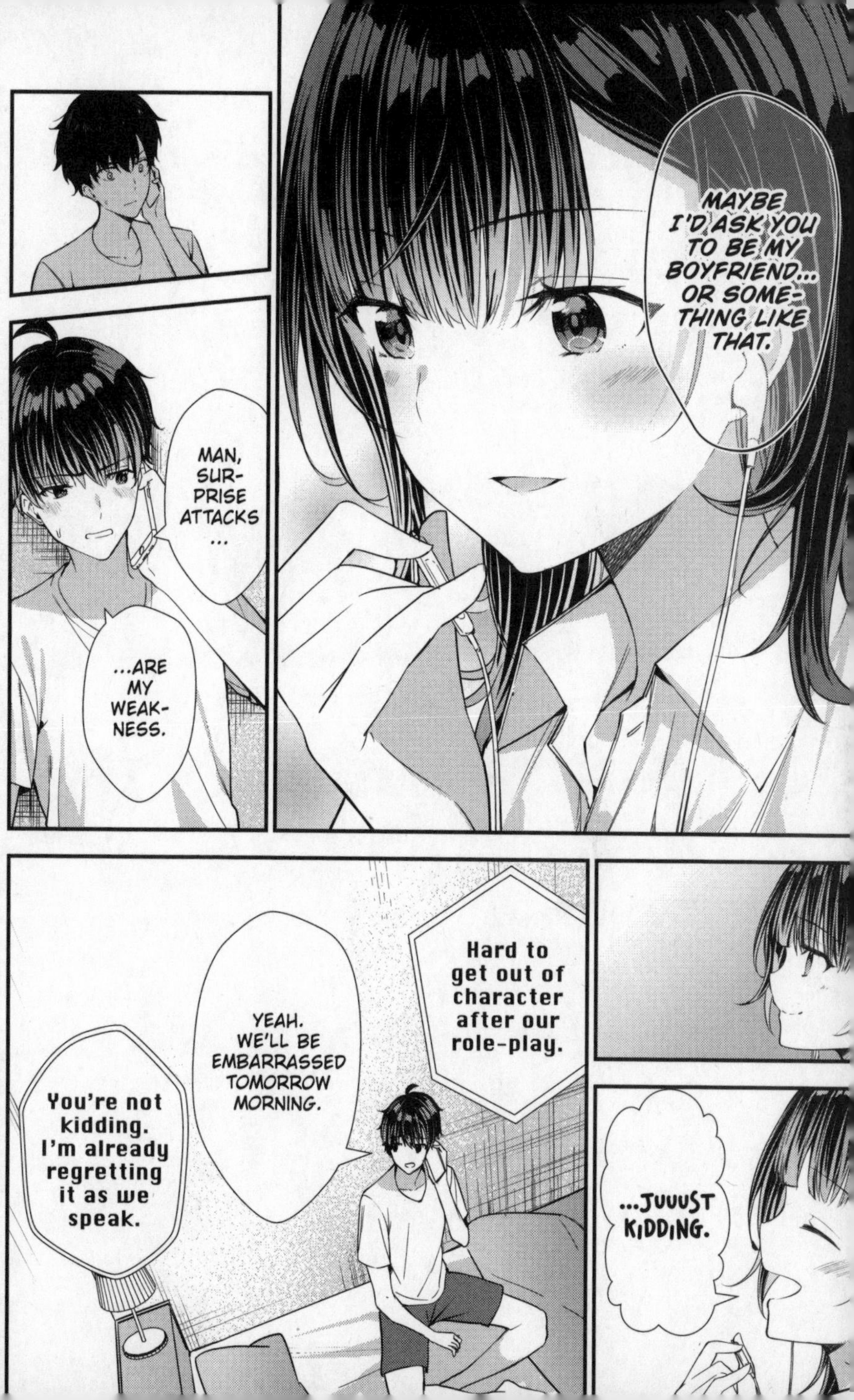
MAYBE I'D ASK YOU TO BE MY BOYFRIEND... OR SOMETHING LIKE THAT.
MAN, SURPRISE ATTACKS...
...ARE MY WEAKNESS.
...JUUUST KIDDING.
Hard to get out of character after our role-play.
YEAH. WE'LL BE EMBARRASSED TOMORROW MORNING.
You're not kidding. I'm already regretting it as we speak.

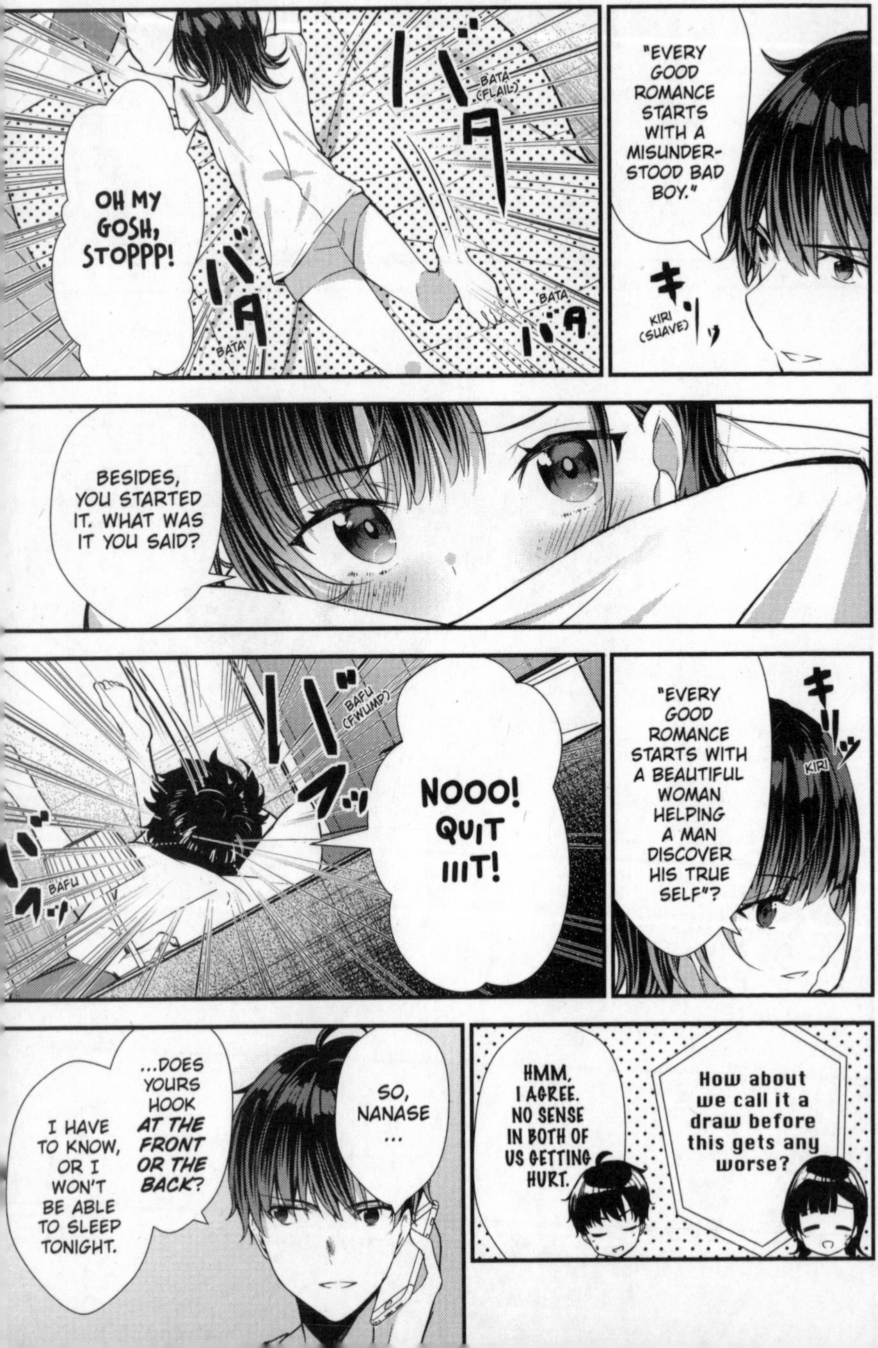
"EVERY GOOD ROMANCE STARTS WITH A MISUNDERSTOOD BAD BOY."
KIRI (SUAVE)
BATA (FLAIL)
OH MY GOSH, STOPPP!
BATA
BATA
BESIDES, YOU STARTED IT. WHAT WAS IT YOU SAID?
KIRI
"EVERY GOOD ROMANCE STARTS WITH A BEAUTIFUL WOMAN HELPING A MAN DISCOVER HIS TRUE SELF"?
BAFU (FWUMP)
NOOO! QUIT IIIT!
BAFU
How about we call it a draw before this gets any worse?
HMM, I AGREE. NO SENSE IN BOTH OF US GETTING HURT.
SO, NANASE...
...DOES YOURS HOOK AT THE FRONT OR THE BACK?
I HAVE TO KNOW, OR I WON'T BE ABLE TO SLEEP TONIGHT.

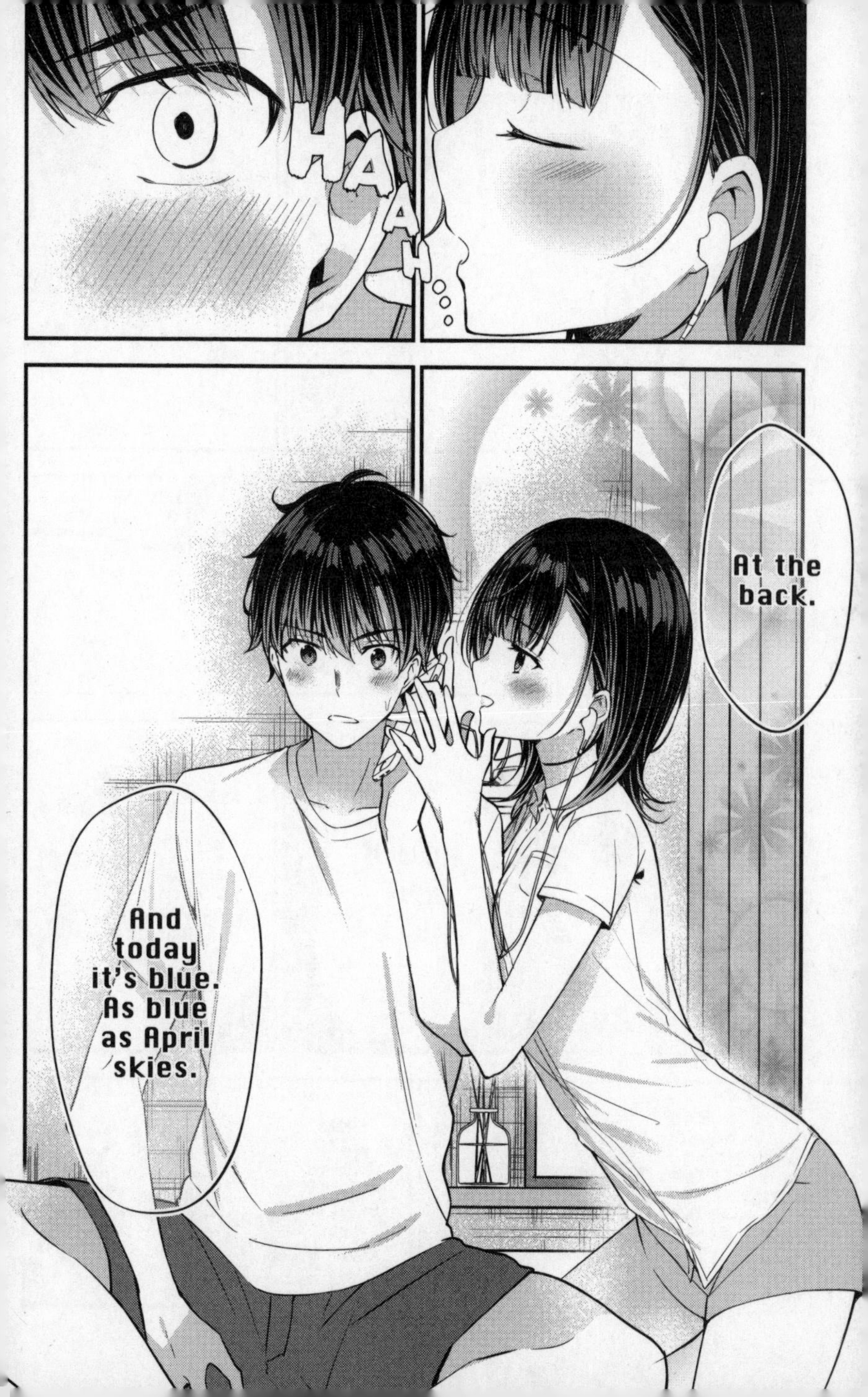
HAAH...
At the back.
And today it's blue. As blue as April skies.

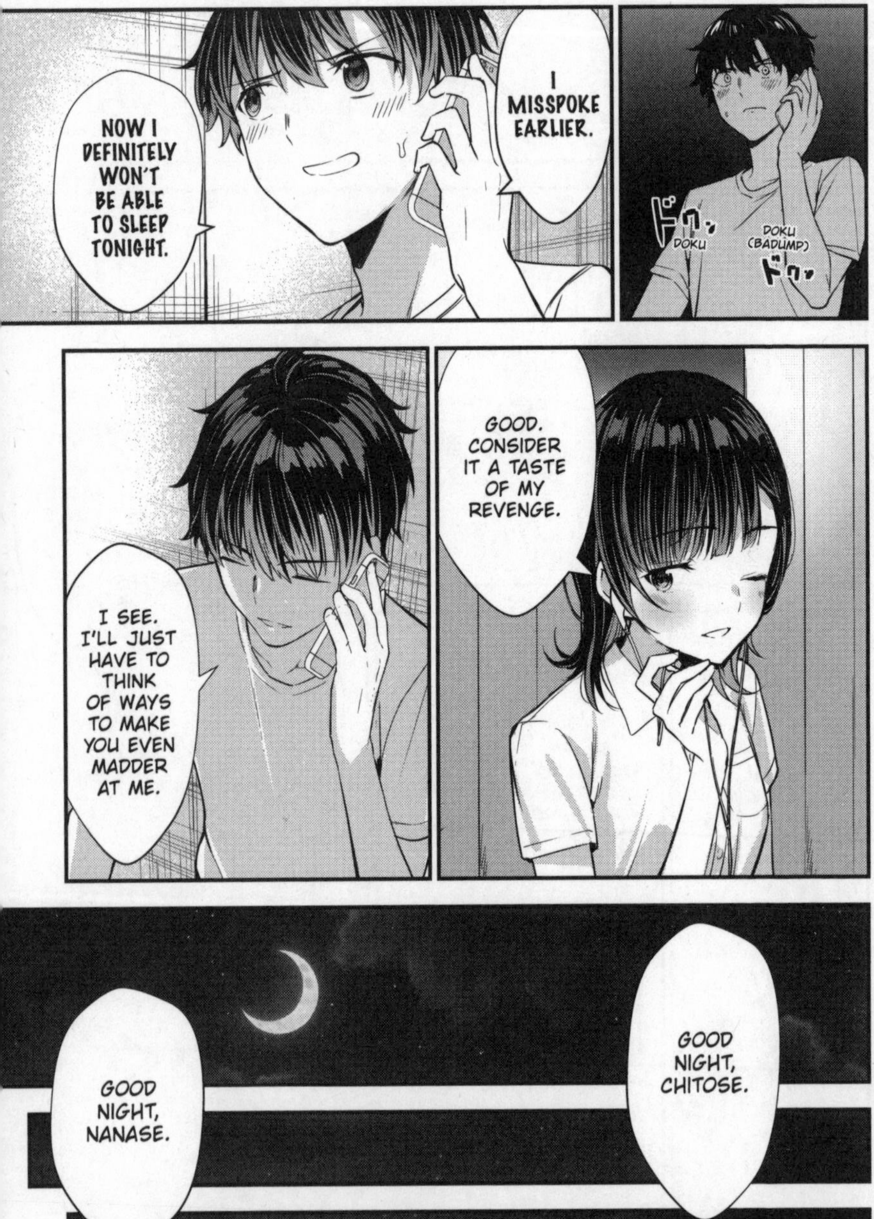
DOKU
DOKU (BADUMP)
I MISSPOKE EARLIER.
NOW I DEFINITELY WON'T BE ABLE TO SLEEP TONIGHT.
GOOD. CONSIDER IT A TASTE OF MY REVENGE.
I SEE. I'LL JUST HAVE TO THINK OF WAYS TO MAKE YOU EVEN MADDER AT ME.
GOOD NIGHT, CHITOSE.
GOOD NIGHT, NANASE.

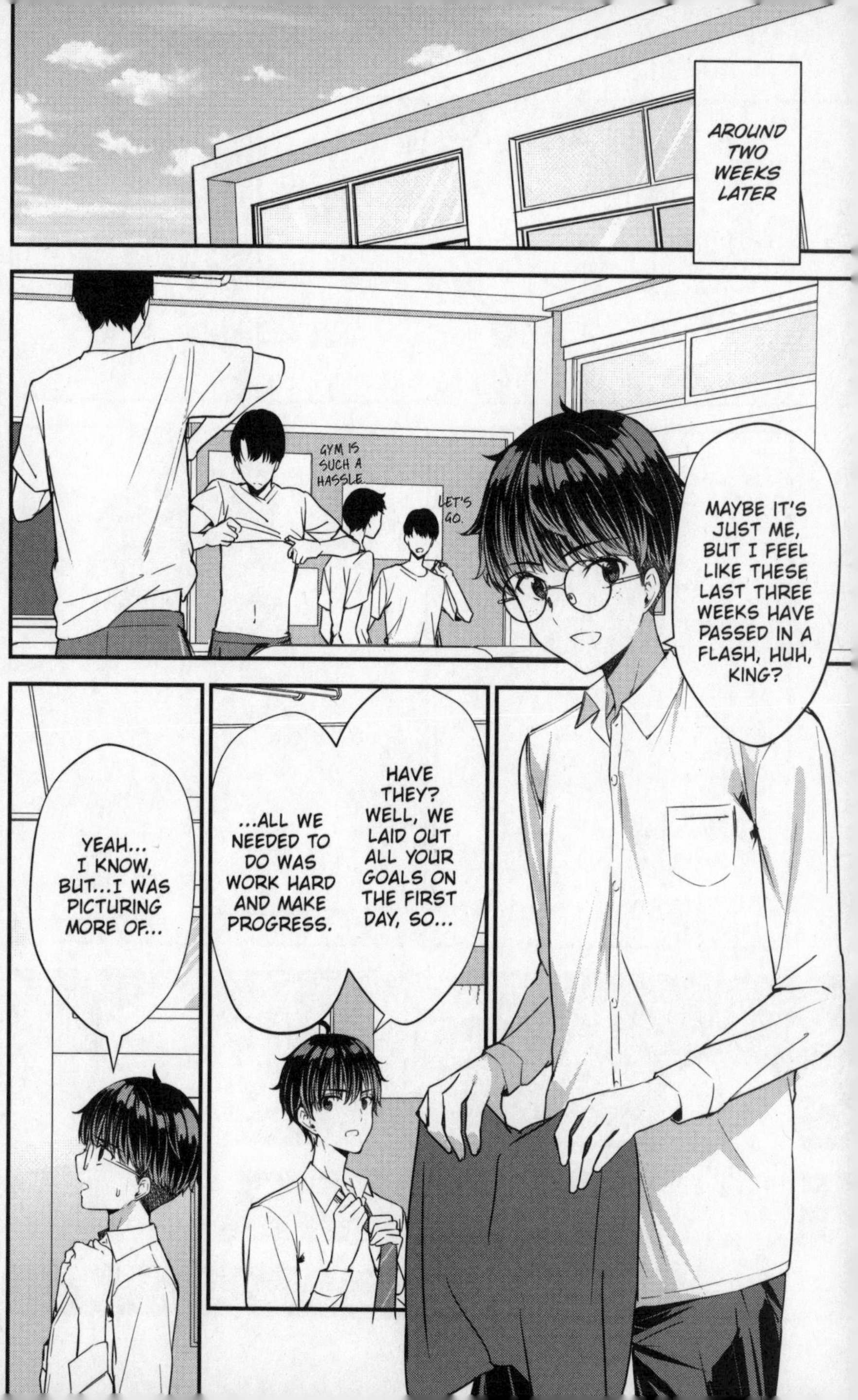
AROUND TWO WEEKS LATER
MAYBE IT'S JUST ME, BUT I FEEL LIKE THESE LAST THREE WEEKS HAVE PASSED IN A FLASH, HUH, KING?
LET'S GO.
GYM IS SUCH A HASSLE.
HAVE THEY? WELL, WE LAID OUT ALL YOUR GOALS ON THE FIRST DAY, SO...
...ALL WE NEEDED TO DO WAS WORK HARD AND MAKE PROGRESS.
YEAH... I KNOW, BUT...I WAS PICTURING MORE OF...

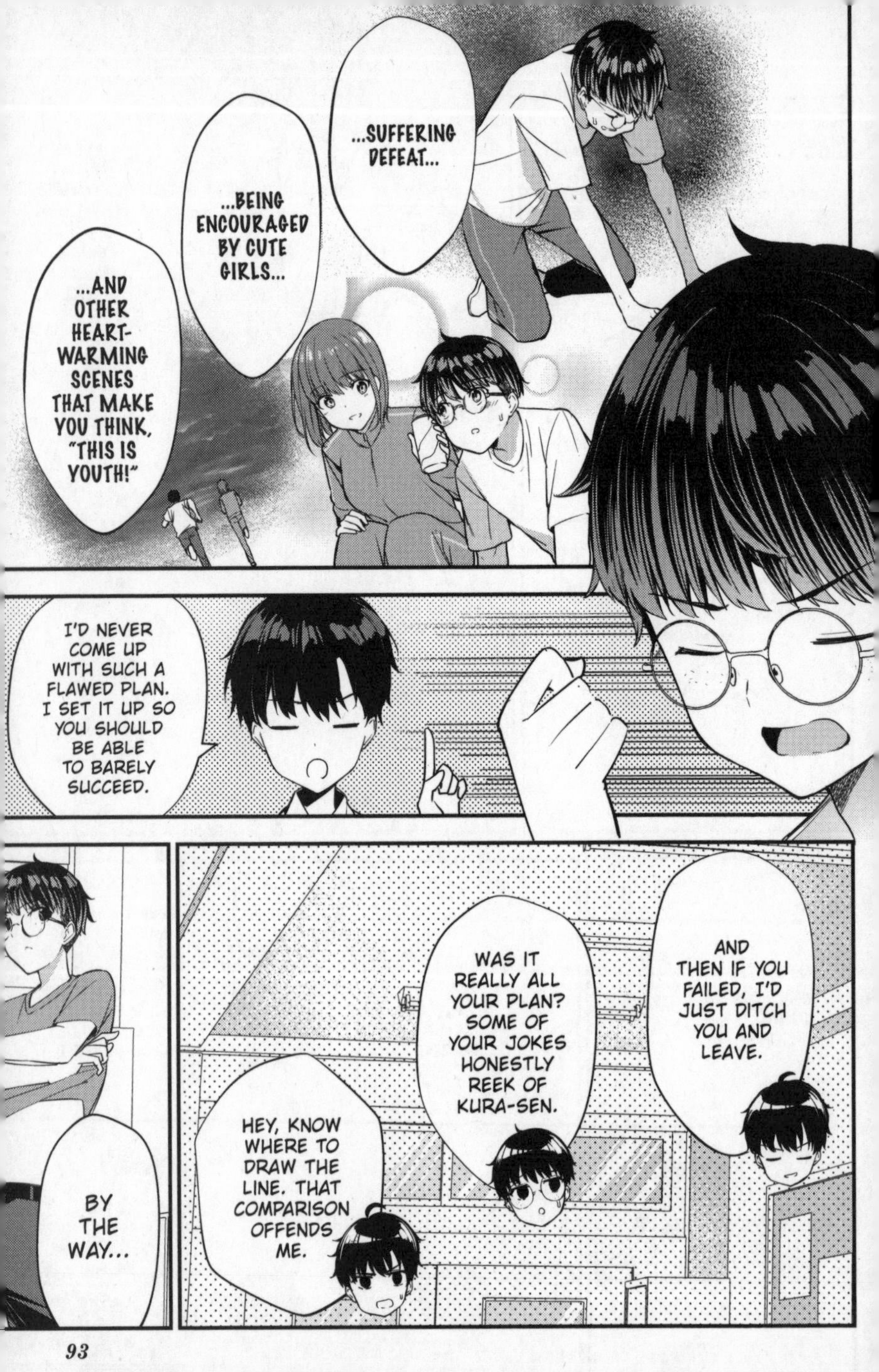
...SUFFERING DEFEAT...
...BEING ENCOURAGED BY CUTE GIRLS...
...AND OTHER HEART-WARMING SCENES THAT MAKE YOU THINK, "THIS IS YOUTH!"
I'D NEVER COME UP WITH SUCH A FLAWED PLAN. I SET IT UP SO YOU SHOULD BE ABLE TO BARELY SUCCEED.
AND THEN IF YOU FAILED, I'D JUST DITCH YOU AND LEAVE.
WAS IT REALLY ALL YOUR PLAN? SOME OF YOUR JOKES HONESTLY REEK OF KURA-SEN.
HEY, KNOW WHERE TO DRAW THE LINE. THAT COMPARISON OFFENDS ME.
BY THE WAY...

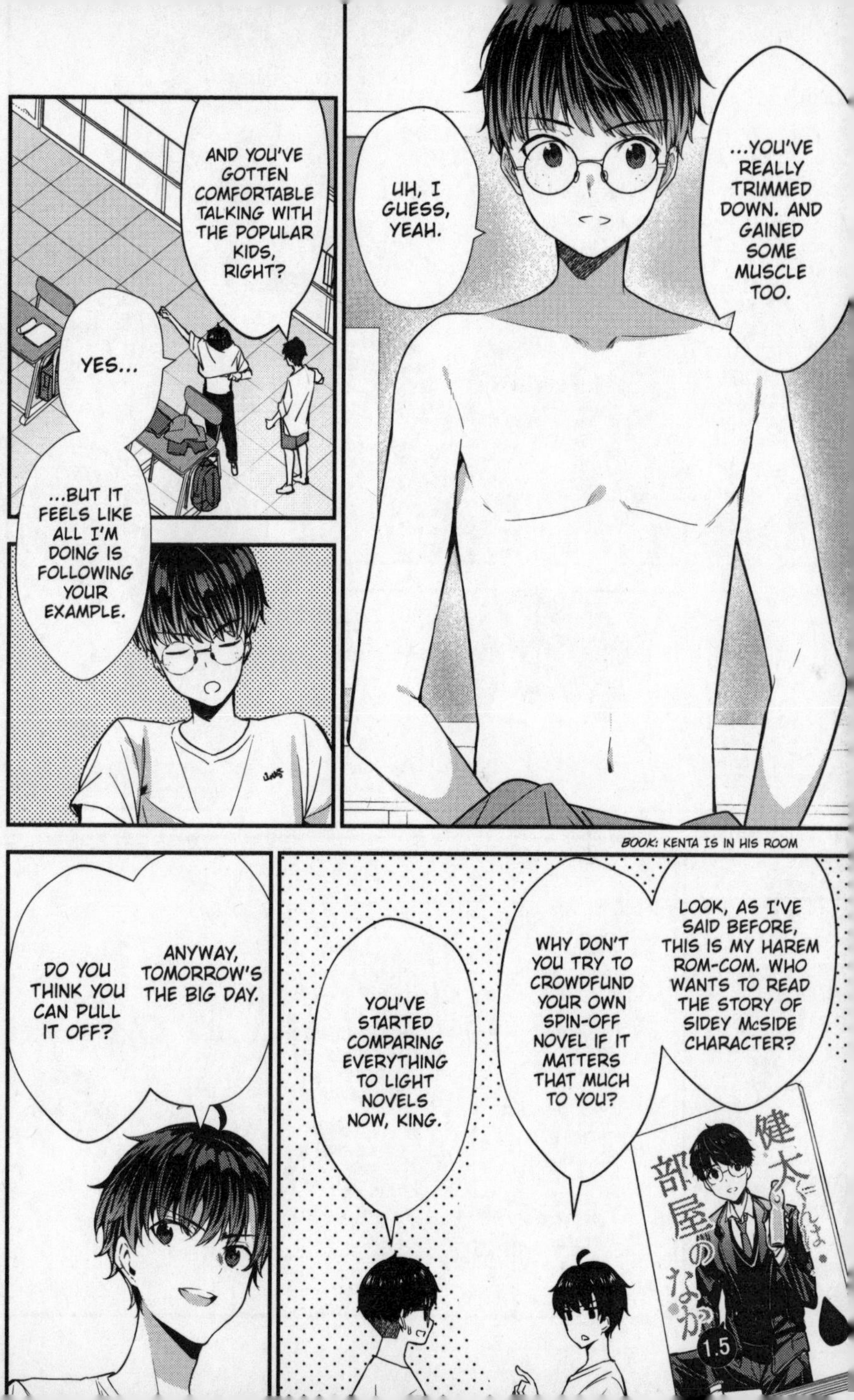
...YOU'VE REALLY TRIMMED DOWN. AND GAINED SOME MUSCLE TOO.
UH, I GUESS, YEAH.
AND YOU'VE GOTTEN COMFORTABLE TALKING WITH THE POPULAR KIDS, RIGHT?
YES...
...BUT IT FEELS LIKE ALL I'M DOING IS FOLLOWING YOUR EXAMPLE.
BOOK: KENTA IS IN HIS ROOM
LOOK, AS I'VE SAID BEFORE, THIS IS MY HAREM ROM-COM. WHO WANTS TO READ THE STORY OF SIDEY McSIDE CHARACTER?
WHY DON'T YOU TRY TO CROWDFUND YOUR OWN SPIN-OFF NOVEL IF IT MATTERS THAT MUCH TO YOU?
YOU'VE STARTED COMPARING EVERYTHING TO LIGHT NOVELS NOW, KING.
部屋のなか
1.5
ANYWAY, TOMORROW'S THE BIG DAY.
DO YOU THINK YOU CAN PULL IT OFF?

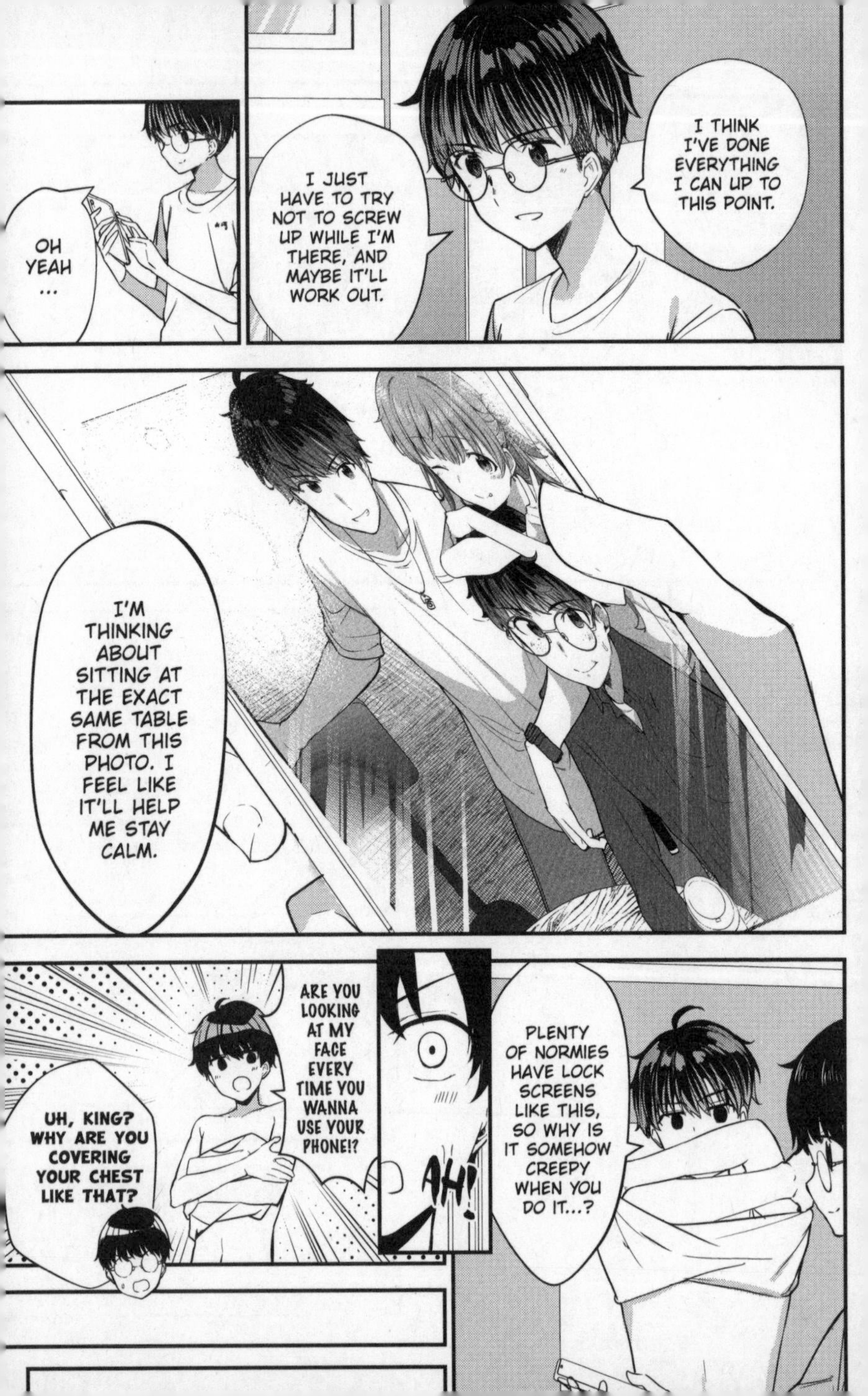
I THINK I'VE DONE EVERYTHING I CAN UP TO THIS POINT.
I JUST HAVE TO TRY NOT TO SCREW UP WHILE I'M THERE, AND MAYBE IT'LL WORK OUT.
OH YEAH ...
I'M THINKING ABOUT SITTING AT THE EXACT SAME TABLE FROM THIS PHOTO. I FEEL LIKE IT'LL HELP ME STAY CALM.
PLENTY OF NORMIES HAVE LOCK SCREENS LIKE THIS, SO WHY IS IT SOMEHOW CREEPY WHEN YOU DO IT...?
AH!
ARE YOU LOOKING AT MY FACE EVERY TIME YOU WANNA USE YOUR PHONE!?
UH, KING? WHY ARE YOU COVERING YOUR CHEST LIKE THAT?

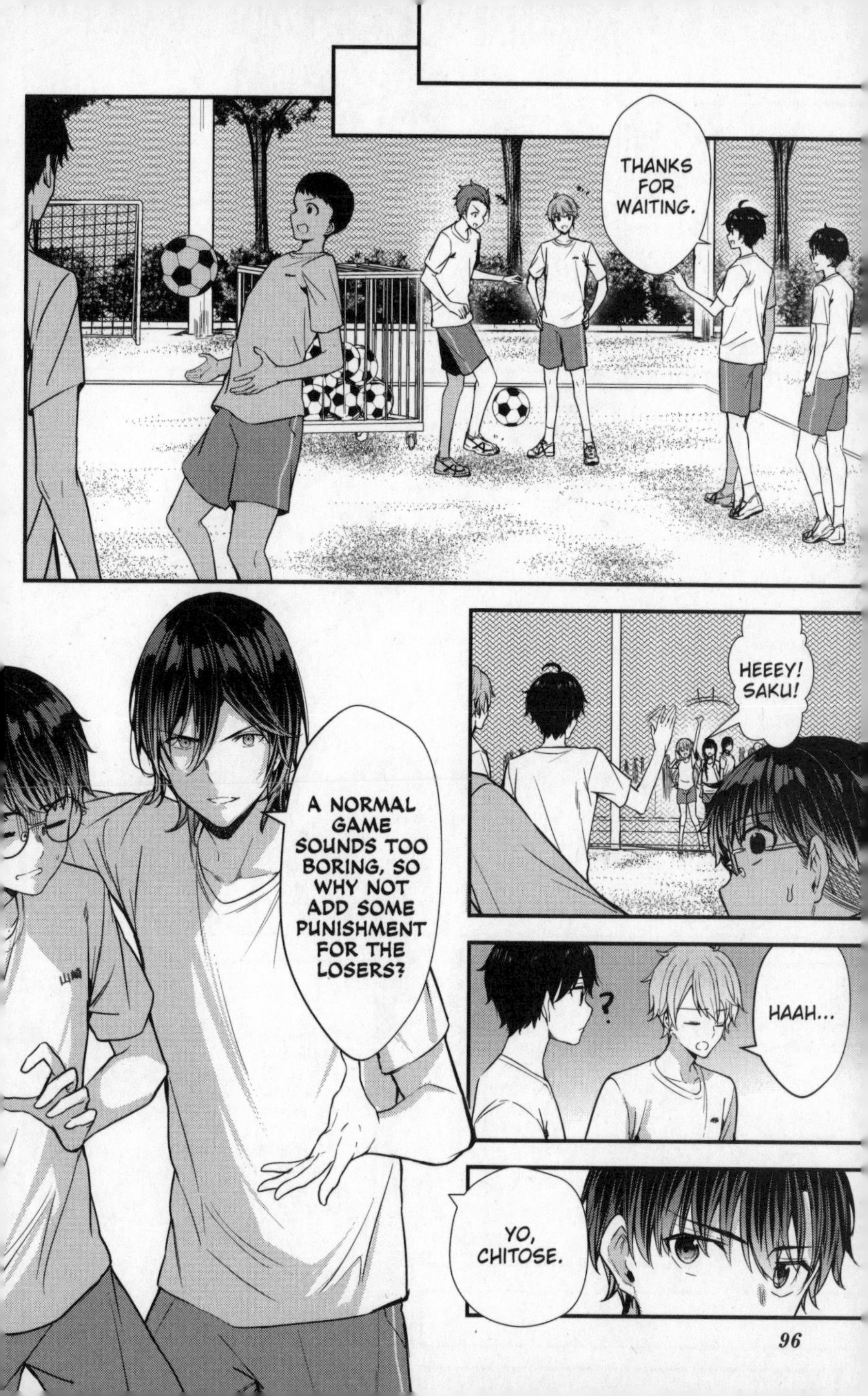
THANKS FOR WAITING.
HEEEY! SAKU!
HAAH...
YO, CHITOSE.
A NORMAL GAME SOUNDS TOO BORING, SO WHY NOT ADD SOME PUNISHMENT FOR THE LOSERS?

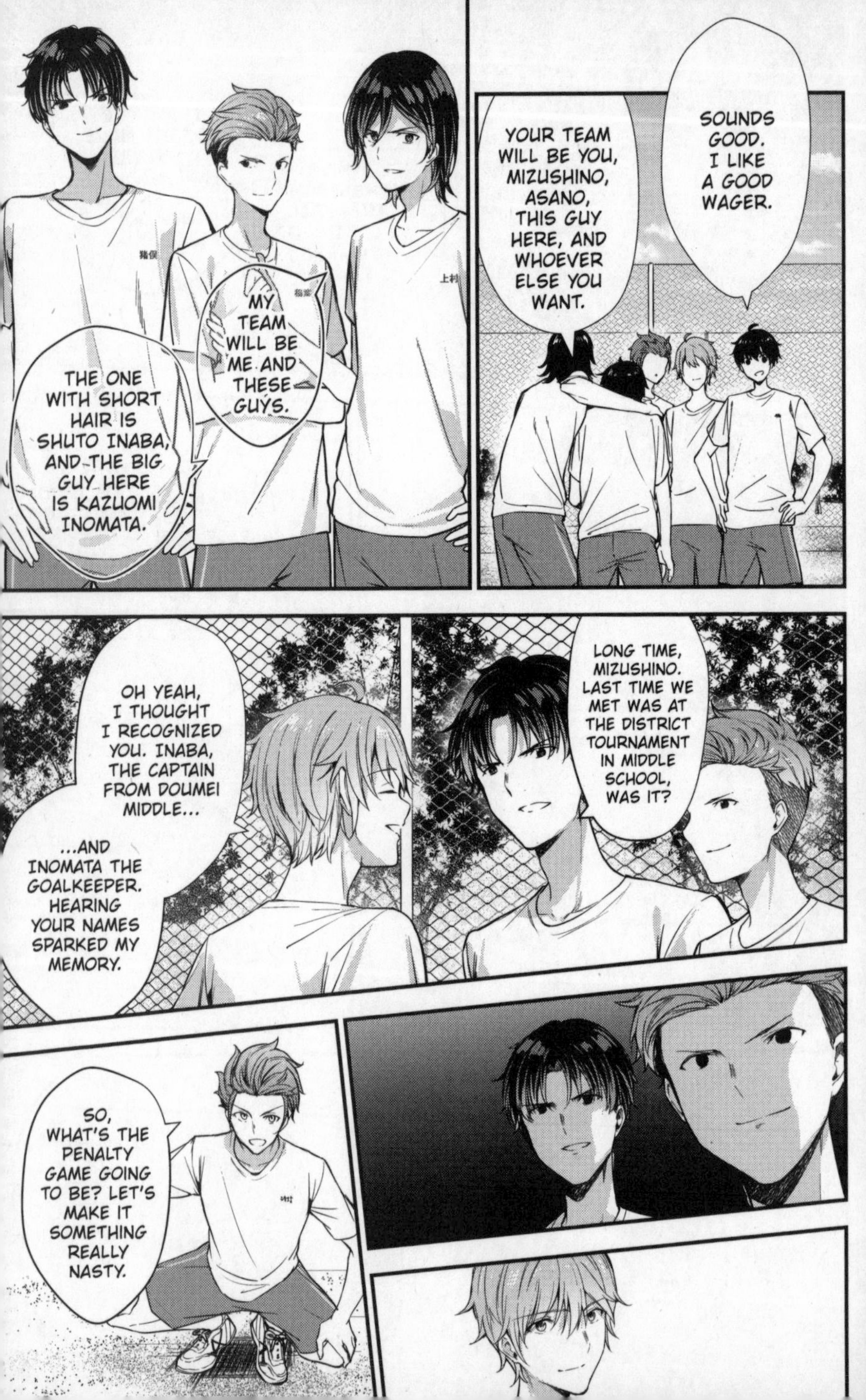
SOUNDS GOOD. I LIKE A GOOD WAGER.
YOUR TEAM WILL BE YOU, MIZUSHINO, ASANO, THIS GUY HERE, AND WHOEVER ELSE YOU WANT.
MY TEAM WILL BE ME AND THESE GUYS.
THE ONE WITH SHORT HAIR IS SHUTO INABA, AND THE BIG GUY HERE IS KAZUOMI INOMATA.
LONG TIME, MIZUSHINO. LAST TIME WE MET WAS AT THE DISTRICT TOURNAMENT IN MIDDLE SCHOOL, WAS IT?
OH YEAH, I THOUGHT I RECOGNIZED YOU. INABA, THE CAPTAIN FROM DOUMEI MIDDLE...
...AND INOMATA THE GOALKEEPER. HEARING YOUR NAMES SPARKED MY MEMORY.
SO, WHAT'S THE PENALTY GAME GOING TO BE? LET'S MAKE IT SOMETHING REALLY NASTY.

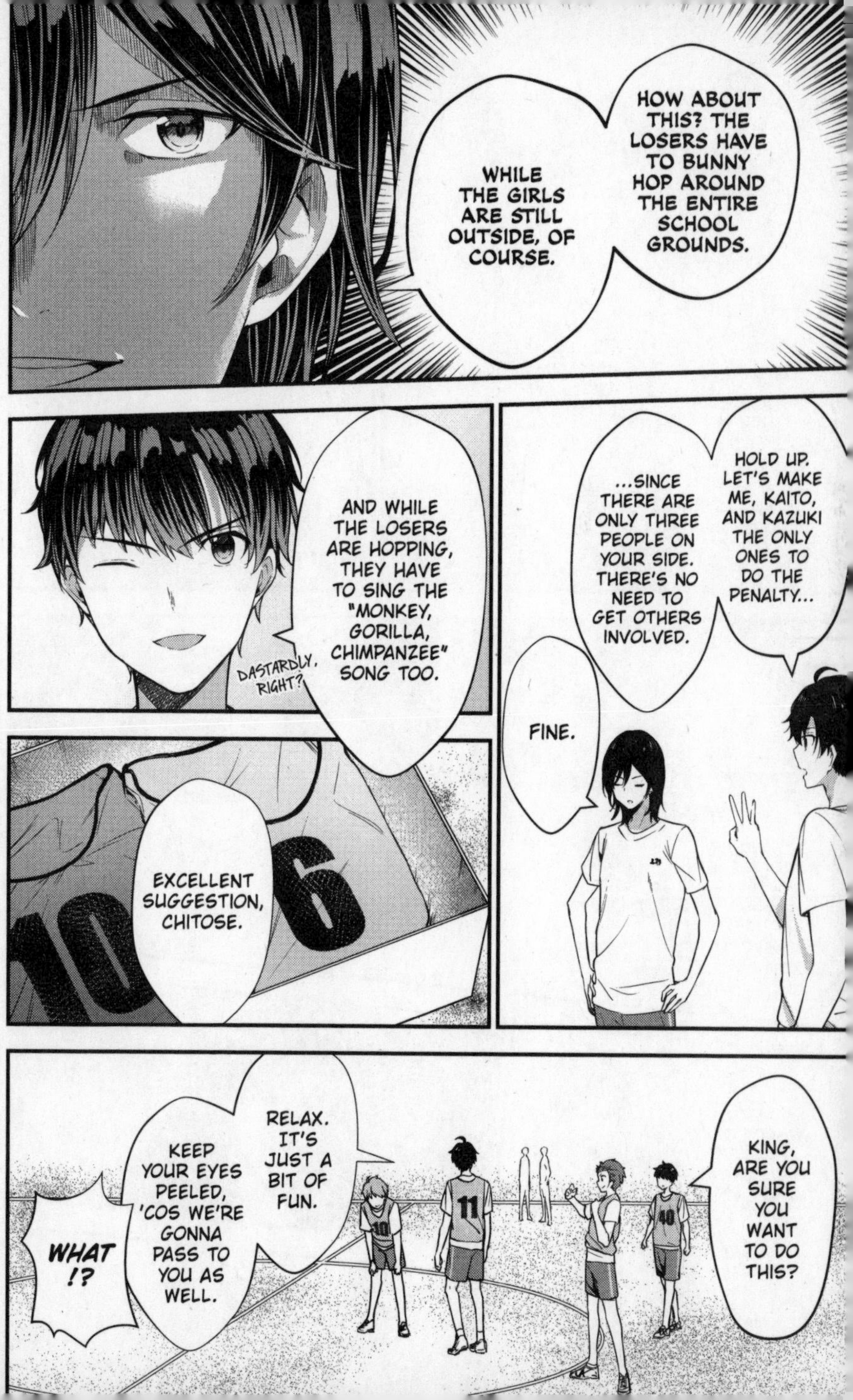
HOW ABOUT THIS? THE LOSERS HAVE TO BUNNY HOP AROUND THE ENTIRE SCHOOL GROUNDS.
WHILE THE GIRLS ARE STILL OUTSIDE, OF COURSE.
HOLD UP. LET'S MAKE ME, KAITO, AND KAZUKI THE ONLY ONES TO DO THE PENALTY...
...SINCE THERE ARE ONLY THREE PEOPLE ON YOUR SIDE. THERE'S NO NEED TO GET OTHERS INVOLVED.
FINE.
AND WHILE THE LOSERS ARE HOPPING, THEY HAVE TO SING THE "MONKEY, GORILLA, CHIMPANZEE" SONG TOO.
DASTARDLY, RIGHT?
EXCELLENT SUGGESTION, CHITOSE.
KING, ARE YOU SURE YOU WANT TO DO THIS?
RELAX. IT'S JUST A BIT OF FUN.
KEEP YOUR EYES PEELED, 'COS WE'RE GONNA PASS TO YOU AS WELL.
WHAT!?

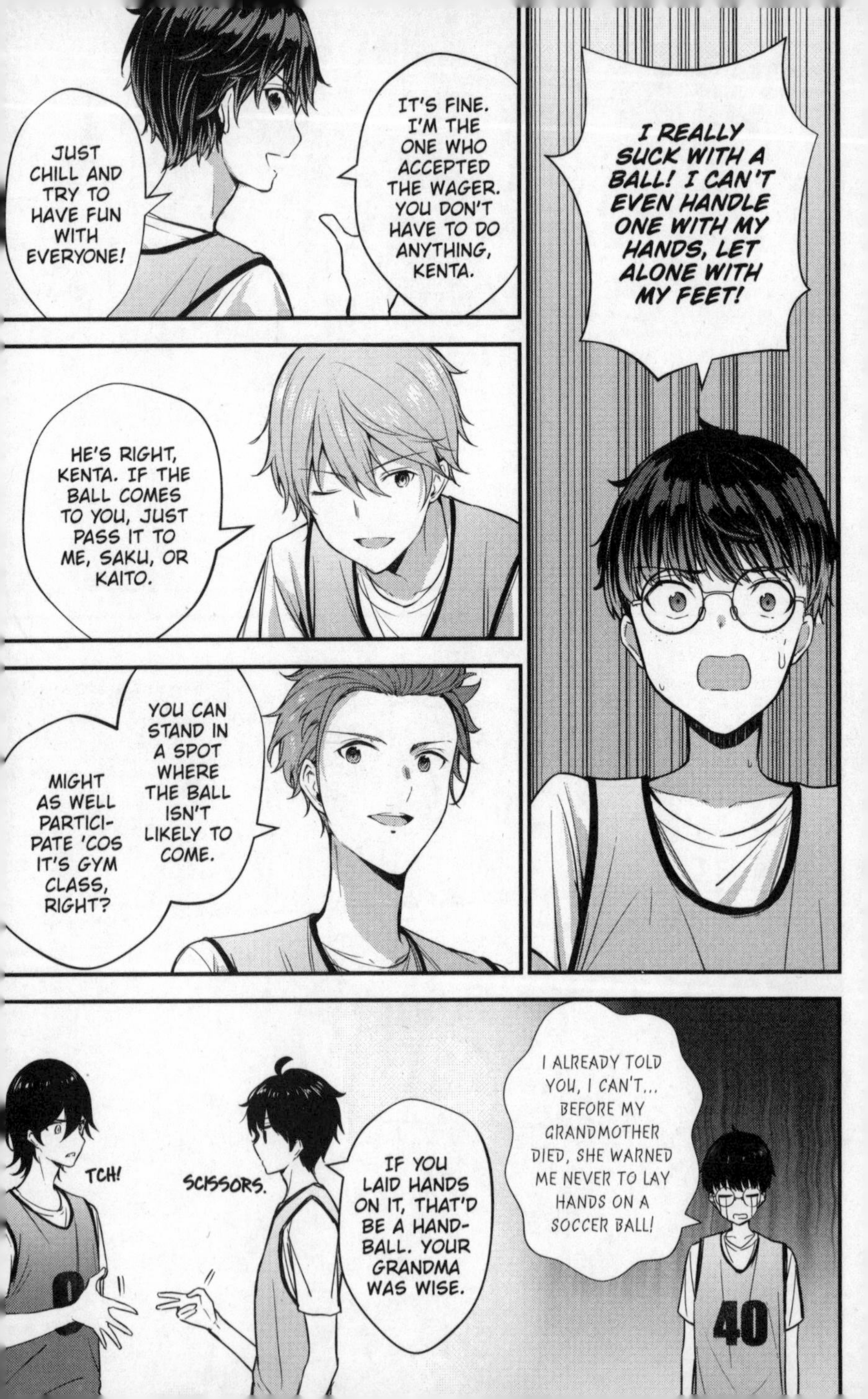
I REALLY SUCK WITH A BALL! I CAN'T EVEN HANDLE ONE WITH MY HANDS, LET ALONE WITH MY FEET!
IT'S FINE. I'M THE ONE WHO ACCEPTED THE WAGER. YOU DON'T HAVE TO DO ANYTHING, KENTA.
JUST CHILL AND TRY TO HAVE FUN WITH EVERYONE!
HE'S RIGHT, KENTA. IF THE BALL COMES TO YOU, JUST PASS IT TO ME, SAKU, OR KAITO.
YOU CAN STAND IN A SPOT WHERE THE BALL ISN'T LIKELY TO COME.
MIGHT AS WELL PARTICIPATE 'COS IT'S GYM CLASS, RIGHT?
I ALREADY TOLD YOU, I CAN'T... BEFORE MY GRANDMOTHER DIED, SHE WARNED ME NEVER TO LAY HANDS ON A SOCCER BALL!
IF YOU LAID HANDS ON IT, THAT'D BE A HANDBALL. YOUR GRANDMA WAS WISE.
SCISSORS.
TCH!

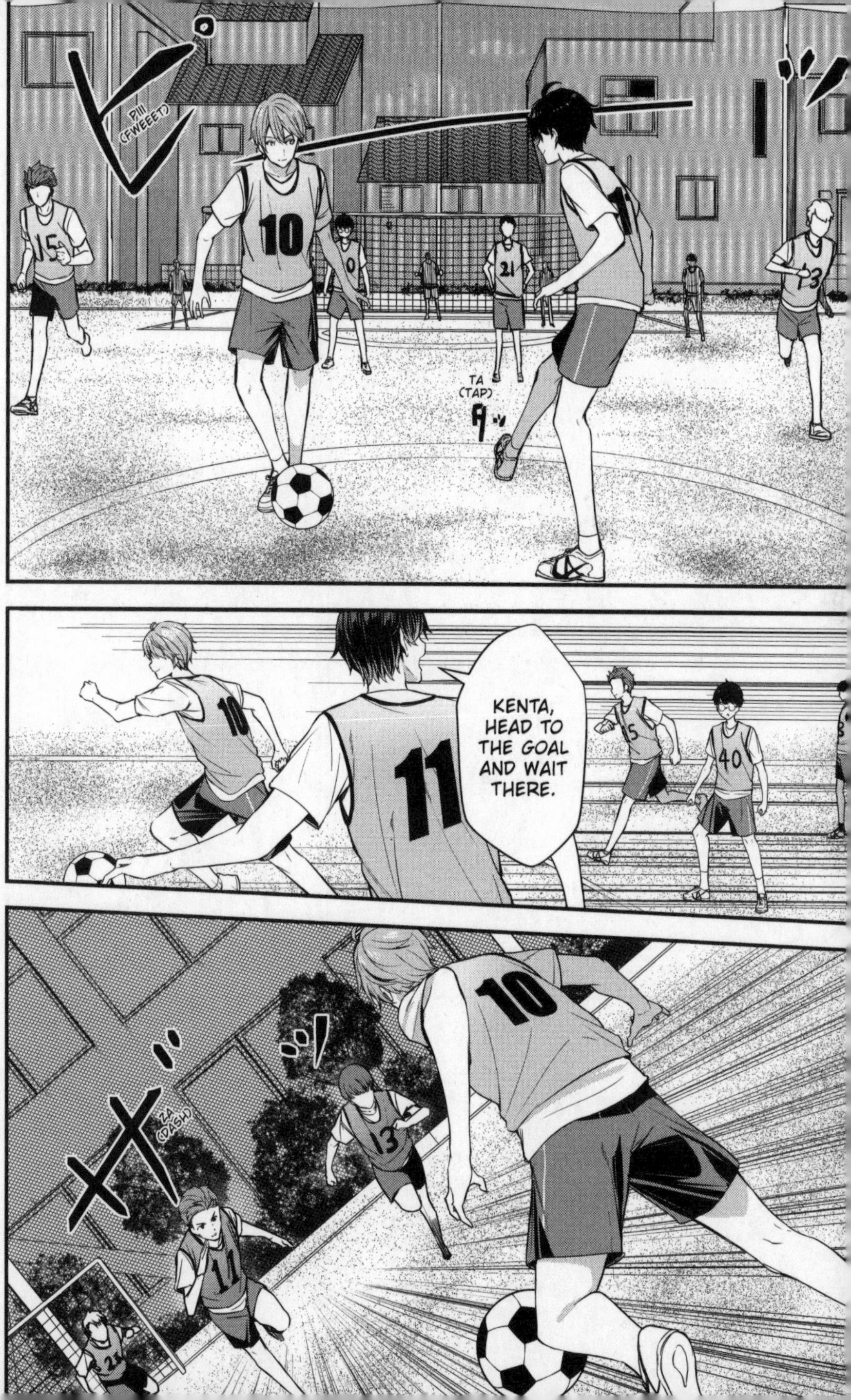
PIII (FWEEET)
TA (TAP)
KENTA, HEAD TO THE GOAL AND WAIT THERE.
ZA (DASH)

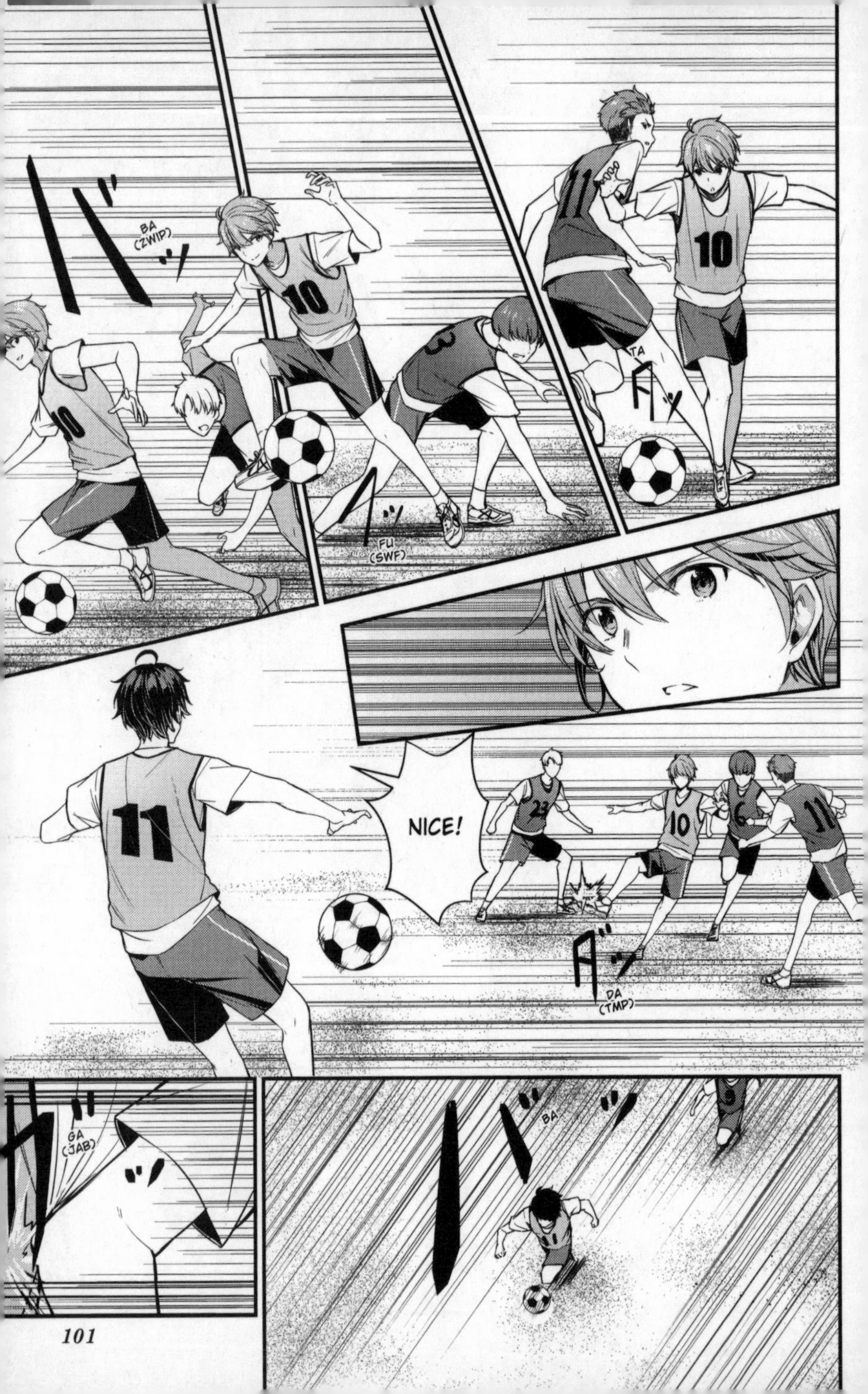
TA
FU
(SWF)
BA
(ZWIP)
NICE!
DA
(TMP)
BA
GA
(JAB)

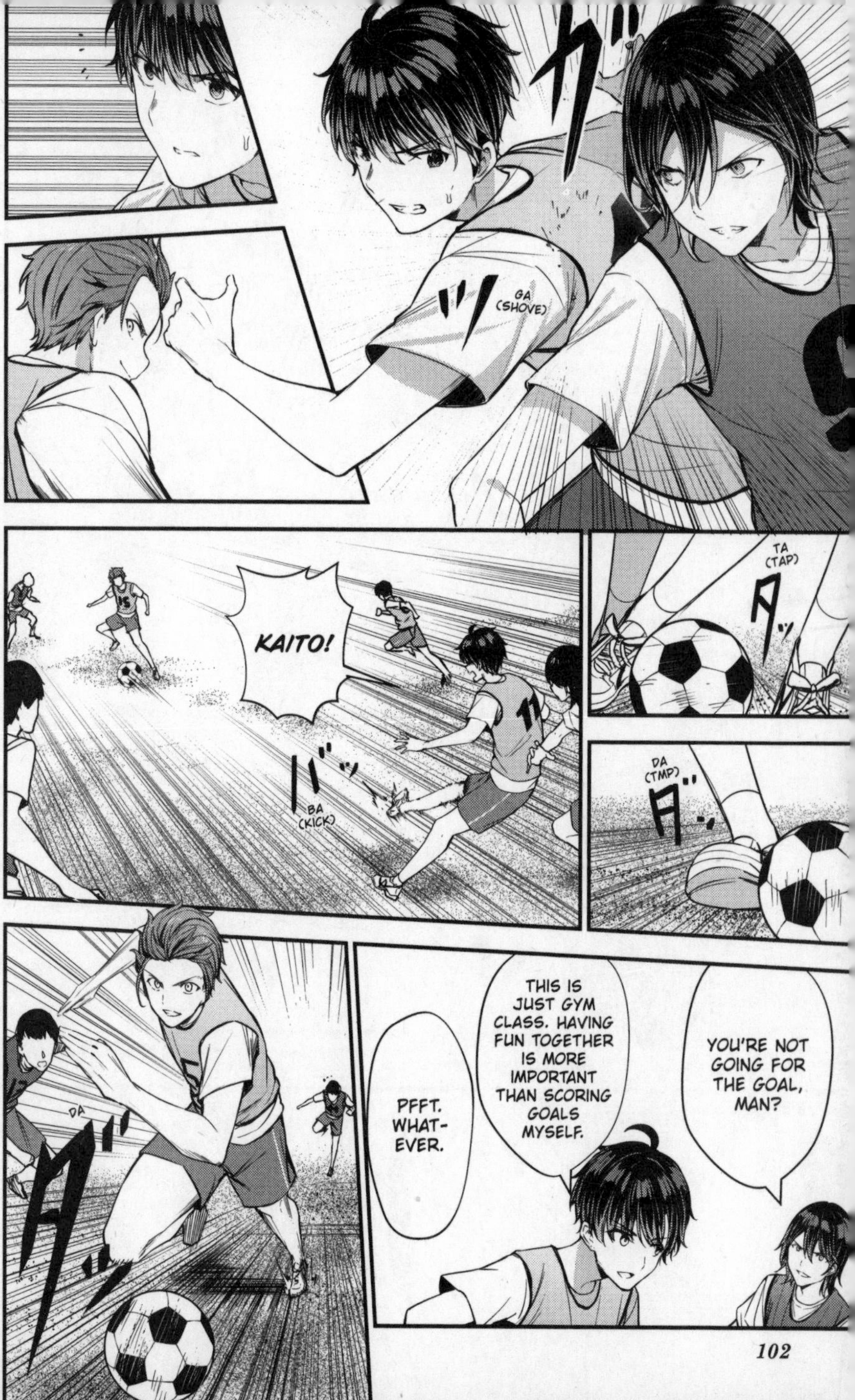
GA
(SHOVE)
TA
(TAP)
DA
(TMP)
KAITO!
BA
(KICK)
YOU'RE NOT GOING FOR THE GOAL, MAN?
THIS IS JUST GYM CLASS. HAVING FUN TOGETHER IS MORE IMPORTANT THAN SCORING GOALS MYSELF.
PFFT. WHAT-EVER.
DA

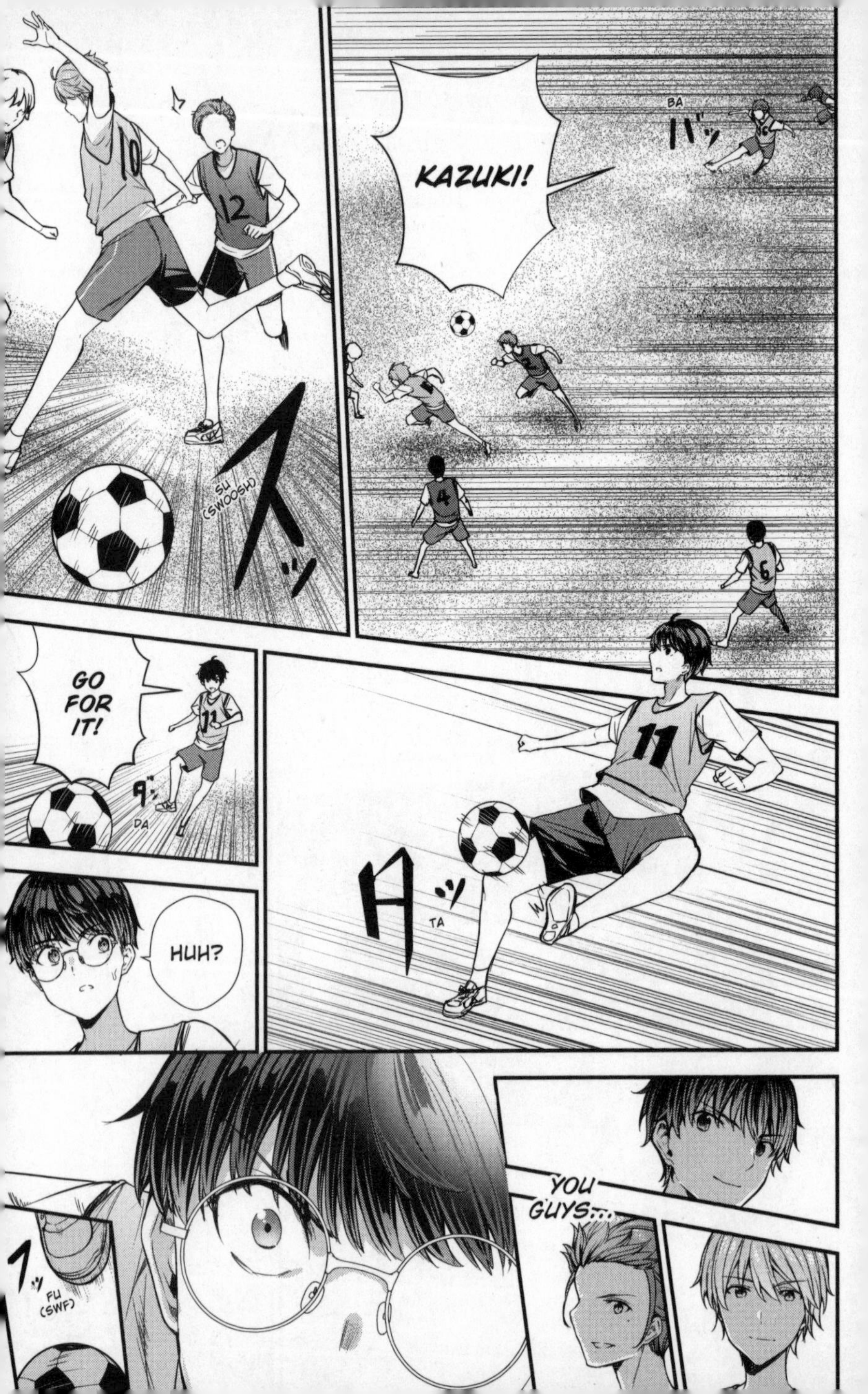
KAZUKI!
BA
バッ
スッ
SU (SWOOSH)
タッ
TA
GO FOR IT!
ダッ
DA
HUH?
YOU GUYS...
フッ
FU (SWF)

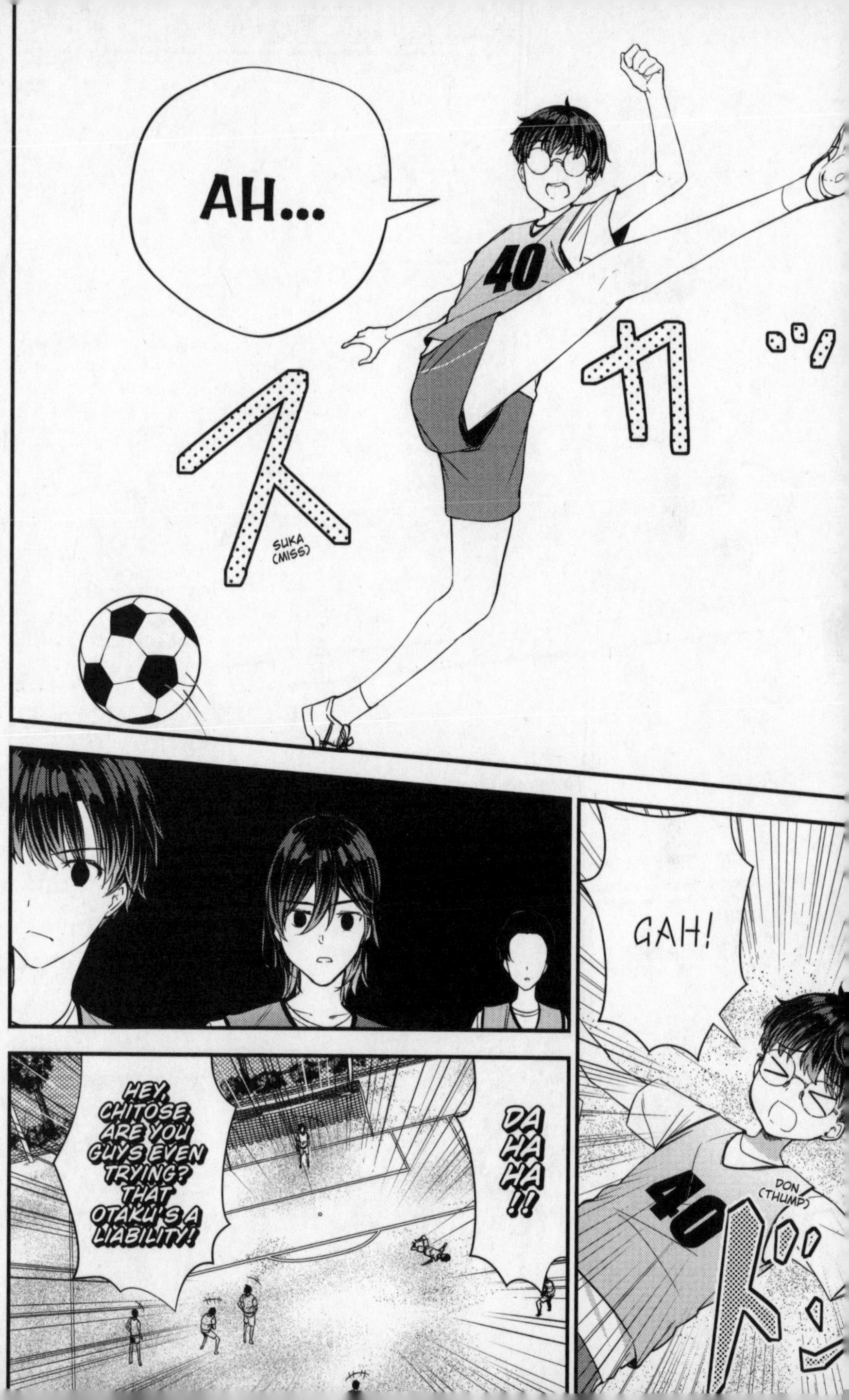
AH...
スカッ
SUKA (MISS)
GAH!
DON (THUMP)
DA HA HA!!
HEY, CHITOSE, ARE YOU GUYS EVEN TRYING? THAT OTAKU'S A LIABILITY!

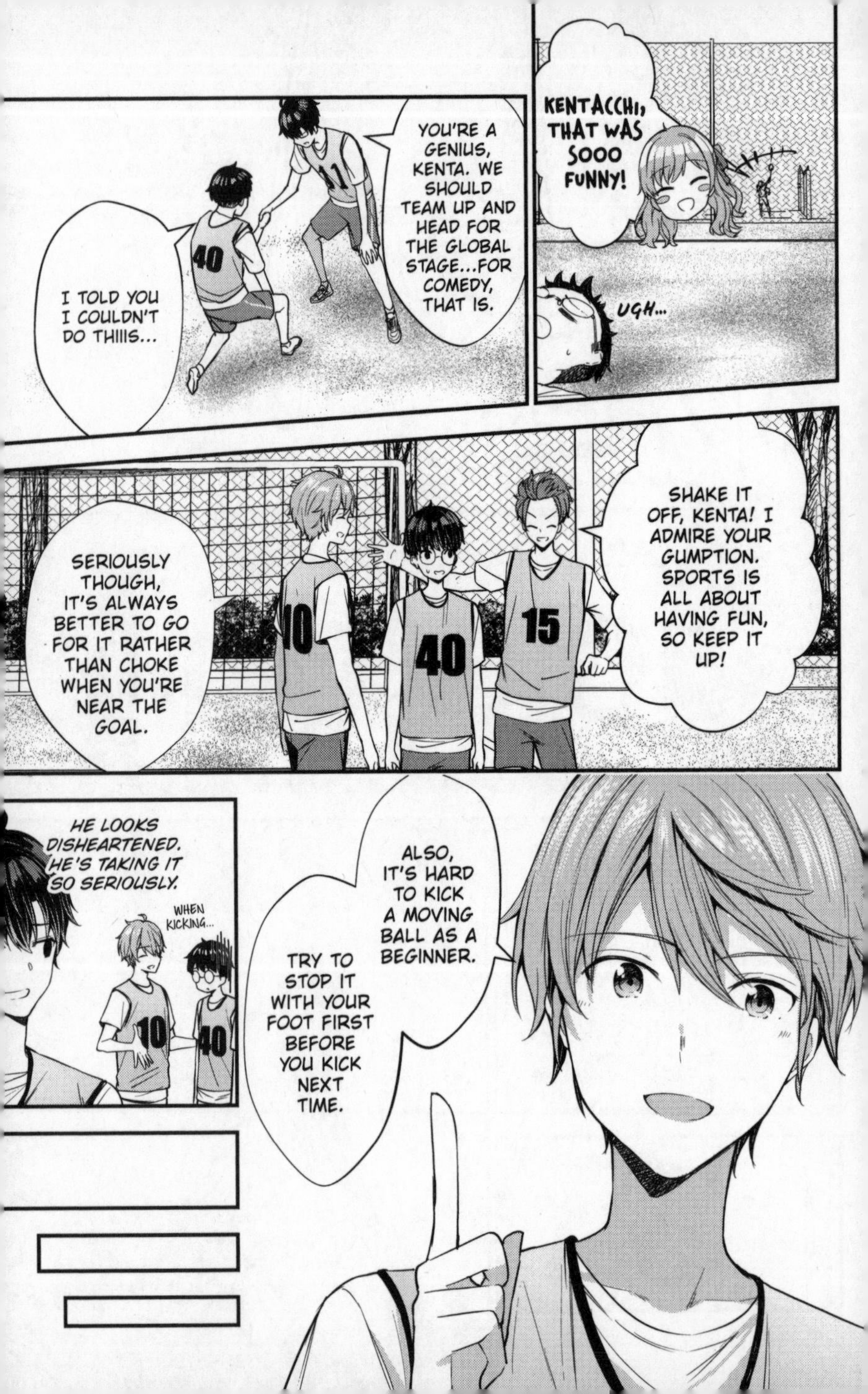
KENTACCHI, THAT WAS SOOO FUNNY!
UGH...
YOU'RE A GENIUS, KENTA. WE SHOULD TEAM UP AND HEAD FOR THE GLOBAL STAGE...FOR COMEDY, THAT IS.
I TOLD YOU I COULDN'T DO THIIIS...
SHAKE IT OFF, KENTA! I ADMIRE YOUR GUMPTION. SPORTS IS ALL ABOUT HAVING FUN, SO KEEP IT UP!
SERIOUSLY THOUGH, IT'S ALWAYS BETTER TO GO FOR IT RATHER THAN CHOKE WHEN YOU'RE NEAR THE GOAL.
ALSO, IT'S HARD TO KICK A MOVING BALL AS A BEGINNER.
TRY TO STOP IT WITH YOUR FOOT FIRST BEFORE YOU KICK NEXT TIME.
HE LOOKS DISHEARTENED. HE'S TAKING IT SO SERIOUSLY.
WHEN KICKING...

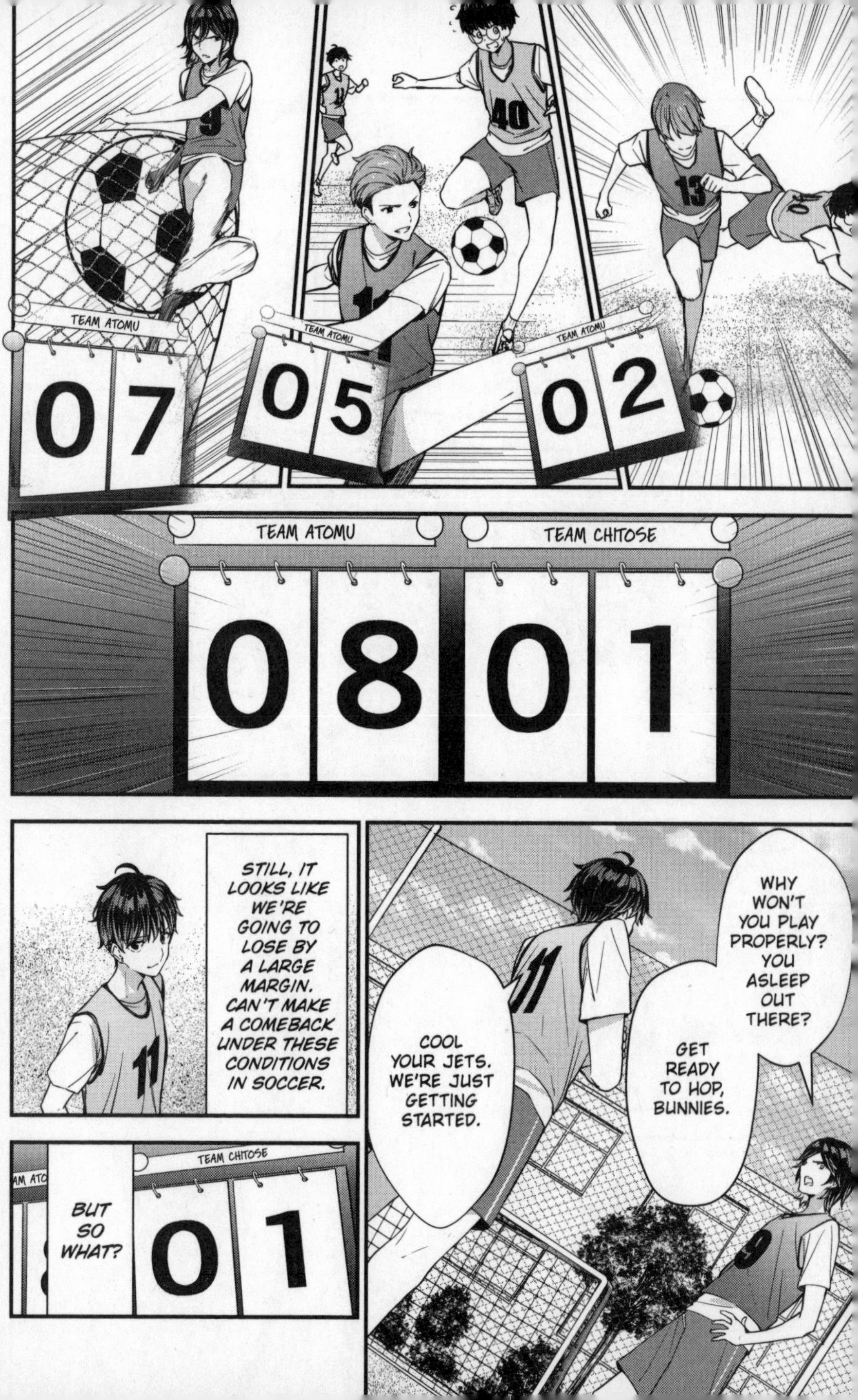
TEAM ATOMU
02
TEAM ATOMU
05
TEAM ATOMU
07
TEAM ATOMU
TEAM CHITOSE
08
01
WHY WON'T YOU PLAY PROPERLY? YOU ASLEEP OUT THERE?
GET READY TO HOP, BUNNIES.
COOL YOUR JETS. WE'RE JUST GETTING STARTED.
STILL, IT LOOKS LIKE WE'RE GOING TO LOSE BY A LARGE MARGIN. CAN'T MAKE A COMEBACK UNDER THESE CONDITIONS IN SOCCER.
TEAM CHITOSE
01
BUT SO WHAT?

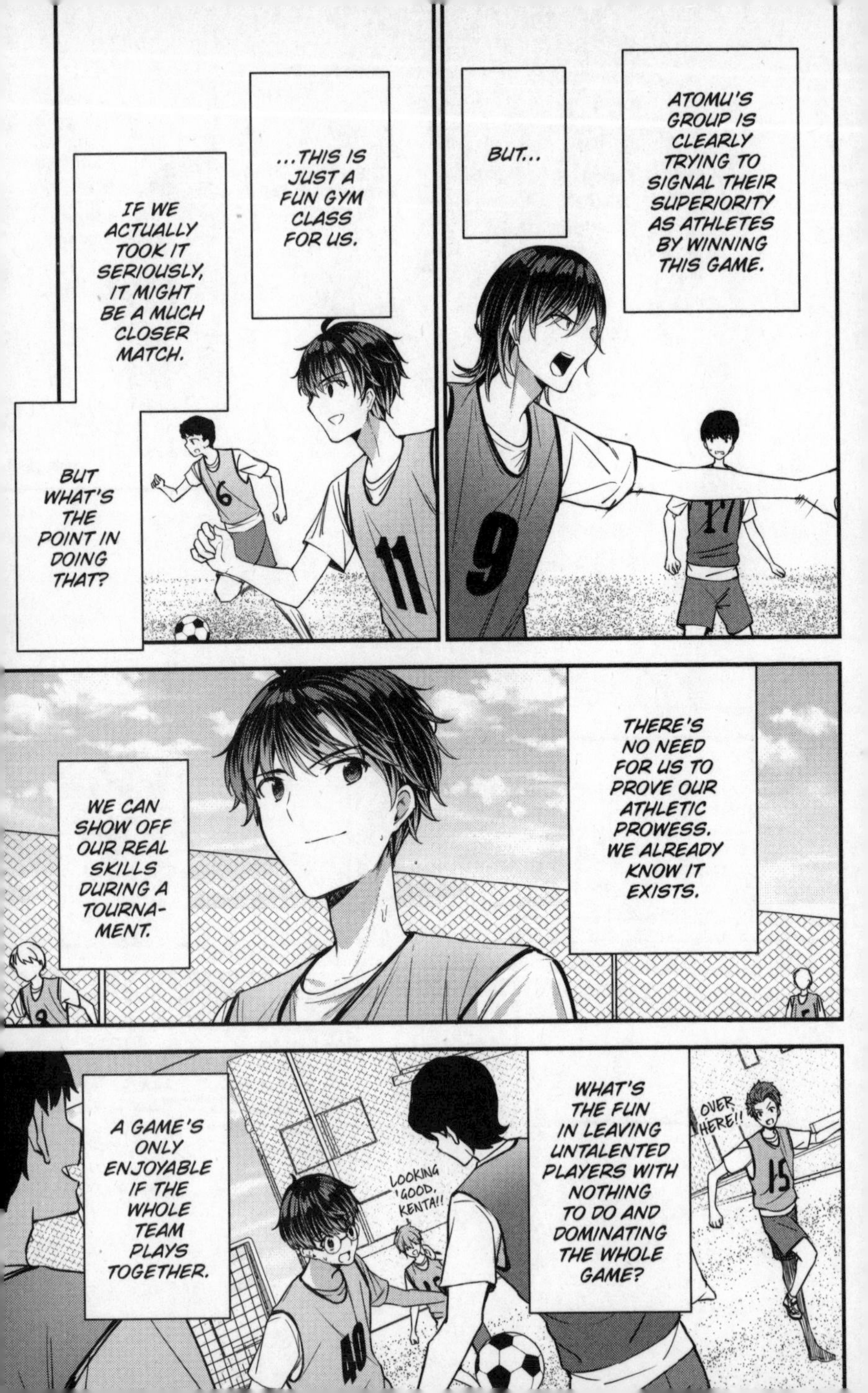
ATOMU'S GROUP IS CLEARLY TRYING TO SIGNAL THEIR SUPERIORITY AS ATHLETES BY WINNING THIS GAME.
BUT...
...THIS IS JUST A FUN GYM CLASS FOR US.
IF WE ACTUALLY TOOK IT SERIOUSLY, IT MIGHT BE A MUCH CLOSER MATCH.
BUT WHAT'S THE POINT IN DOING THAT?
THERE'S NO NEED FOR US TO PROVE OUR ATHLETIC PROWESS. WE ALREADY KNOW IT EXISTS.
WE CAN SHOW OFF OUR REAL SKILLS DURING A TOURNA-MENT.
OVER HERE!!
WHAT'S THE FUN IN LEAVING UNTALENTED PLAYERS WITH NOTHING TO DO AND DOMINATING THE WHOLE GAME?
LOOKING GOOD, KENTA!!
A GAME'S ONLY ENJOYABLE IF THE WHOLE TEAM PLAYS TOGETHER.

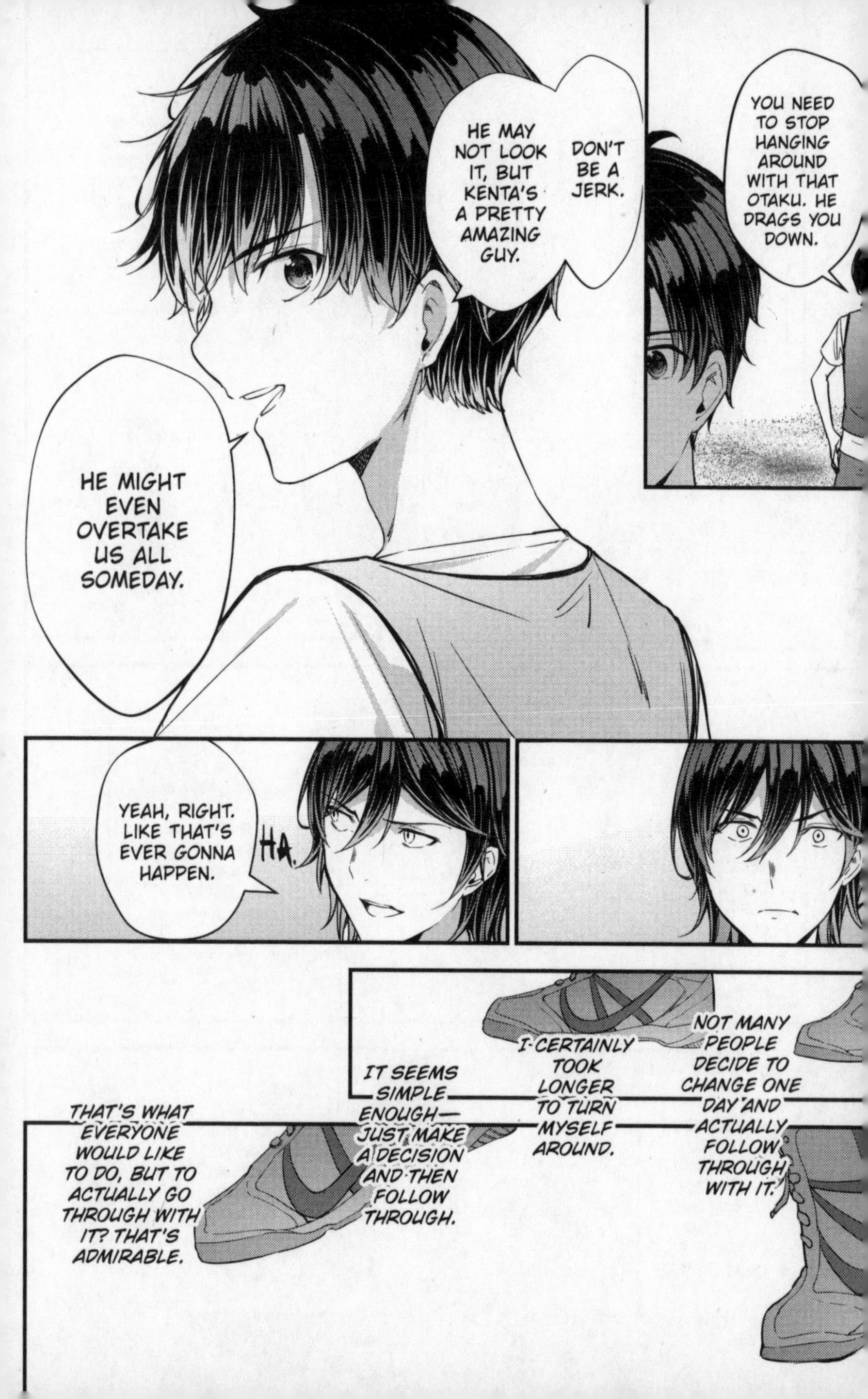
YOU NEED TO STOP HANGING AROUND WITH THAT OTAKU. HE DRAGS YOU DOWN.
DON'T BE A JERK.
HE MAY NOT LOOK IT, BUT KENTA'S A PRETTY AMAZING GUY.
HE MIGHT EVEN OVERTAKE US ALL SOMEDAY.
HA.
YEAH, RIGHT. LIKE THAT'S EVER GONNA HAPPEN.
NOT MANY PEOPLE DECIDE TO CHANGE ONE DAY AND ACTUALLY FOLLOW THROUGH WITH IT.
I CERTAINLY TOOK LONGER TO TURN MYSELF AROUND.
IT SEEMS SIMPLE ENOUGH—JUST MAKE A DECISION AND THEN FOLLOW THROUGH.
THAT'S WHAT EVERYONE WOULD LIKE TO DO, BUT TO ACTUALLY GO THROUGH WITH IT? THAT'S ADMIRABLE.

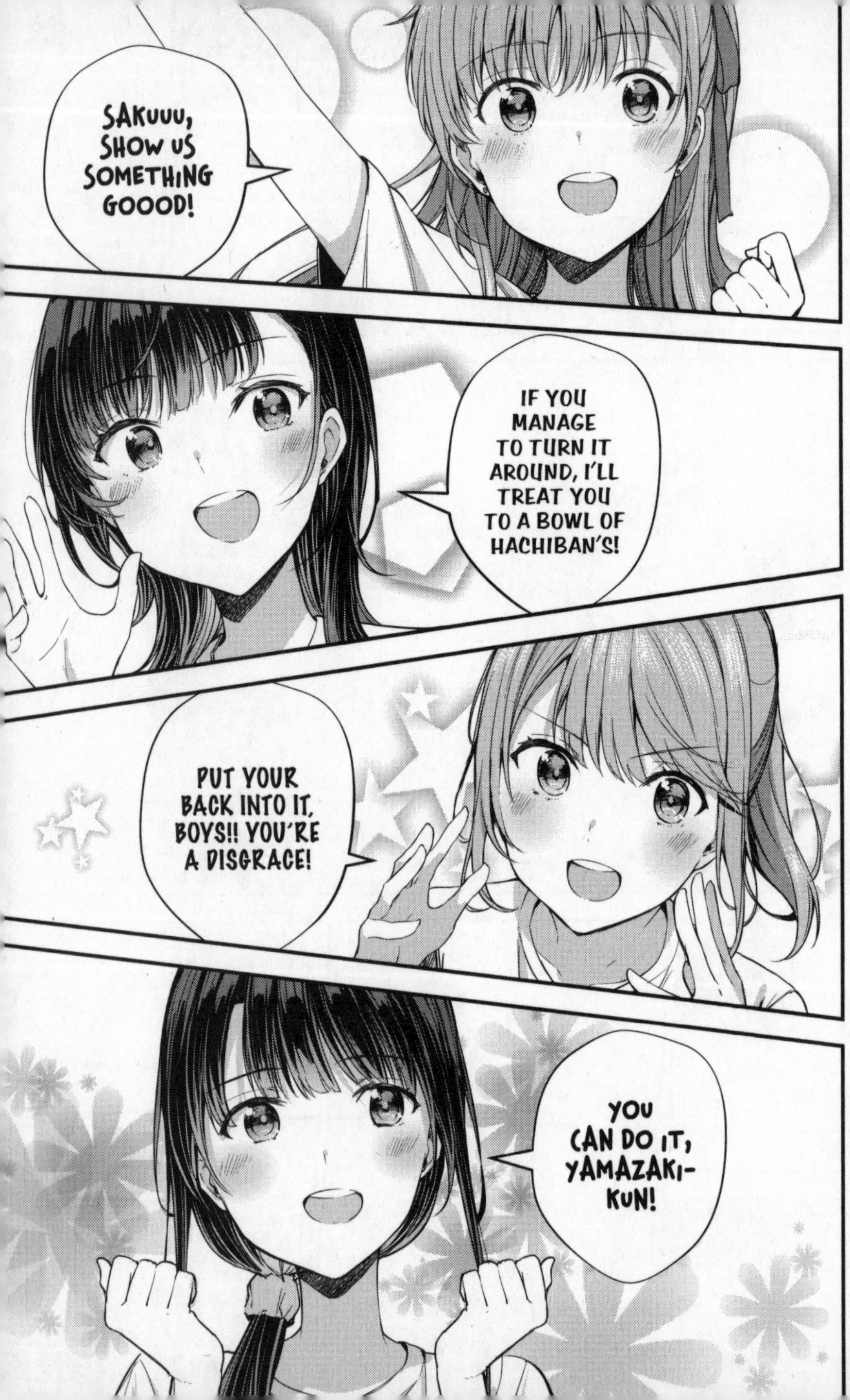
SAKUUU, SHOW US SOMETHING GOOOD!
IF YOU MANAGE TO TURN IT AROUND, I'LL TREAT YOU TO A BOWL OF HACHIBAN'S!
PUT YOUR BACK INTO IT, BOYS!! YOU'RE A DISGRACE!
YOU CAN DO IT, YAMAZAKI-KUN!

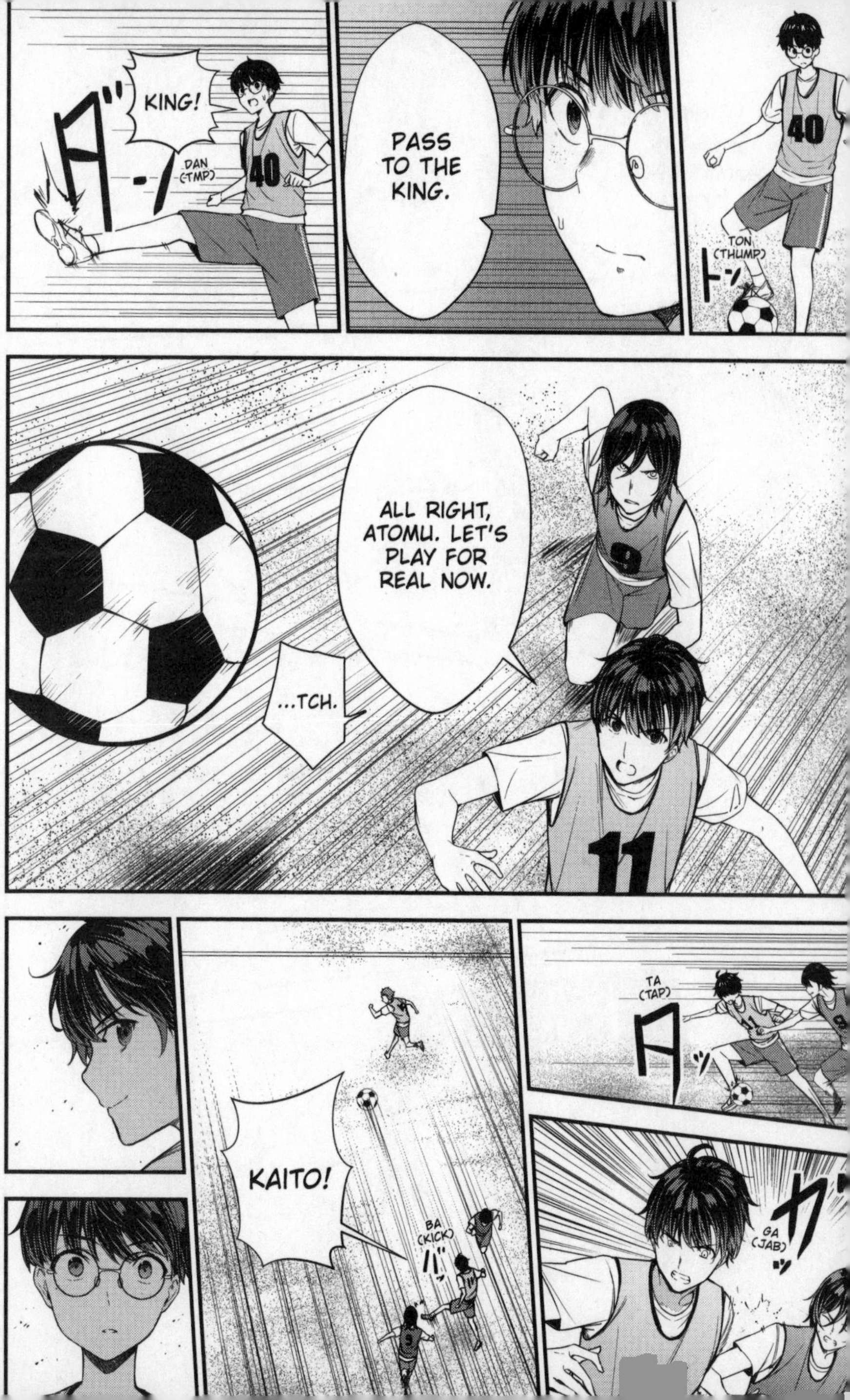
TON (THUMP)
PASS TO THE KING.
KING!
DAN (TMP)
ALL RIGHT, ATOMU. LET'S PLAY FOR REAL NOW.
...TCH.
TA (TAP)
GA (JAB)
KAITO!
BA (KICK)

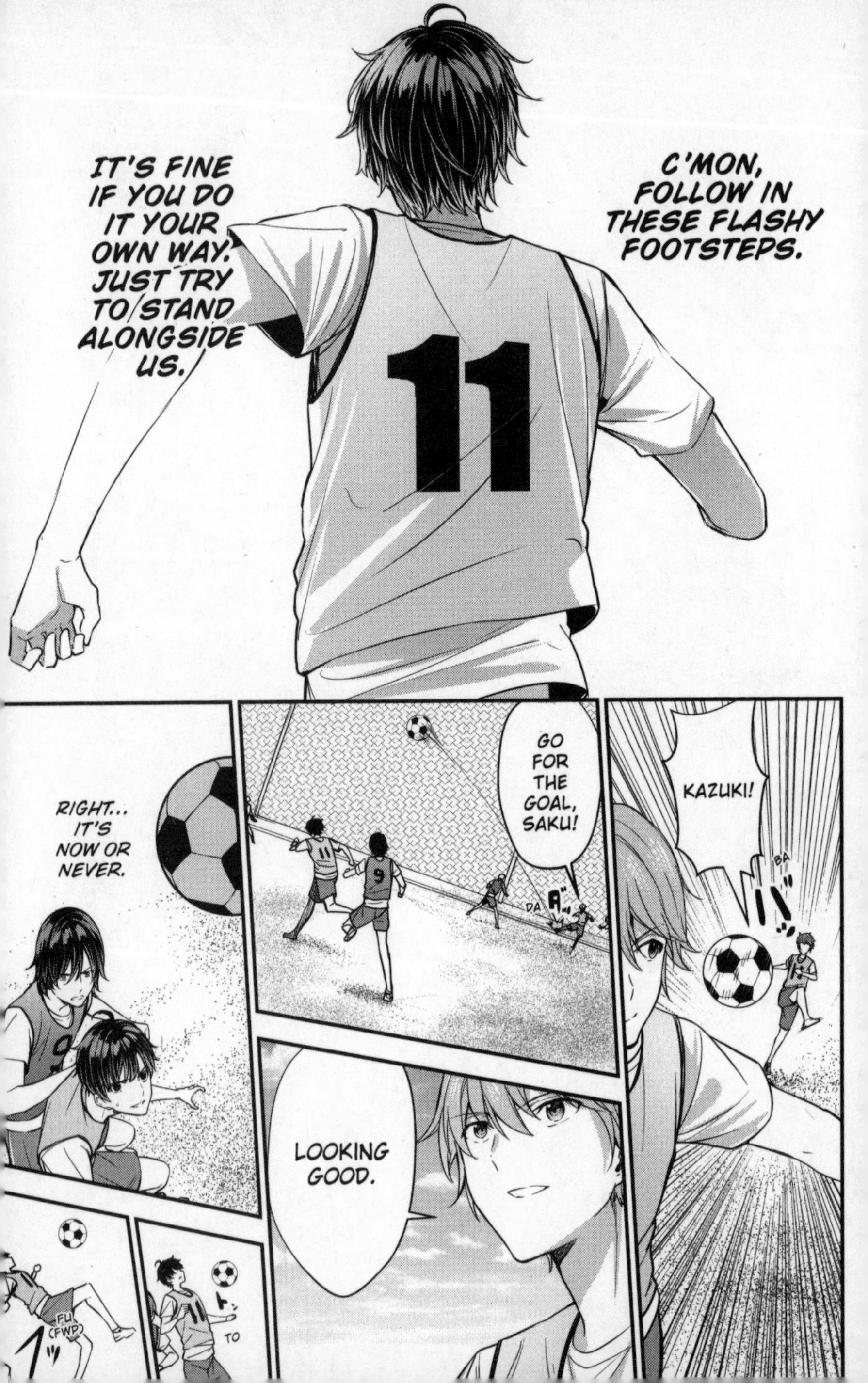
C'MON, FOLLOW IN THESE FLASHY FOOTSTEPS.
IT'S FINE IF YOU DO IT YOUR OWN WAY. JUST TRY TO STAND ALONGSIDE US.
KAZUKI!
BA
GO FOR THE GOAL, SAKU!
DA
RIGHT... IT'S NOW OR NEVER.
LOOKING GOOD.
TO
FU (FWP)

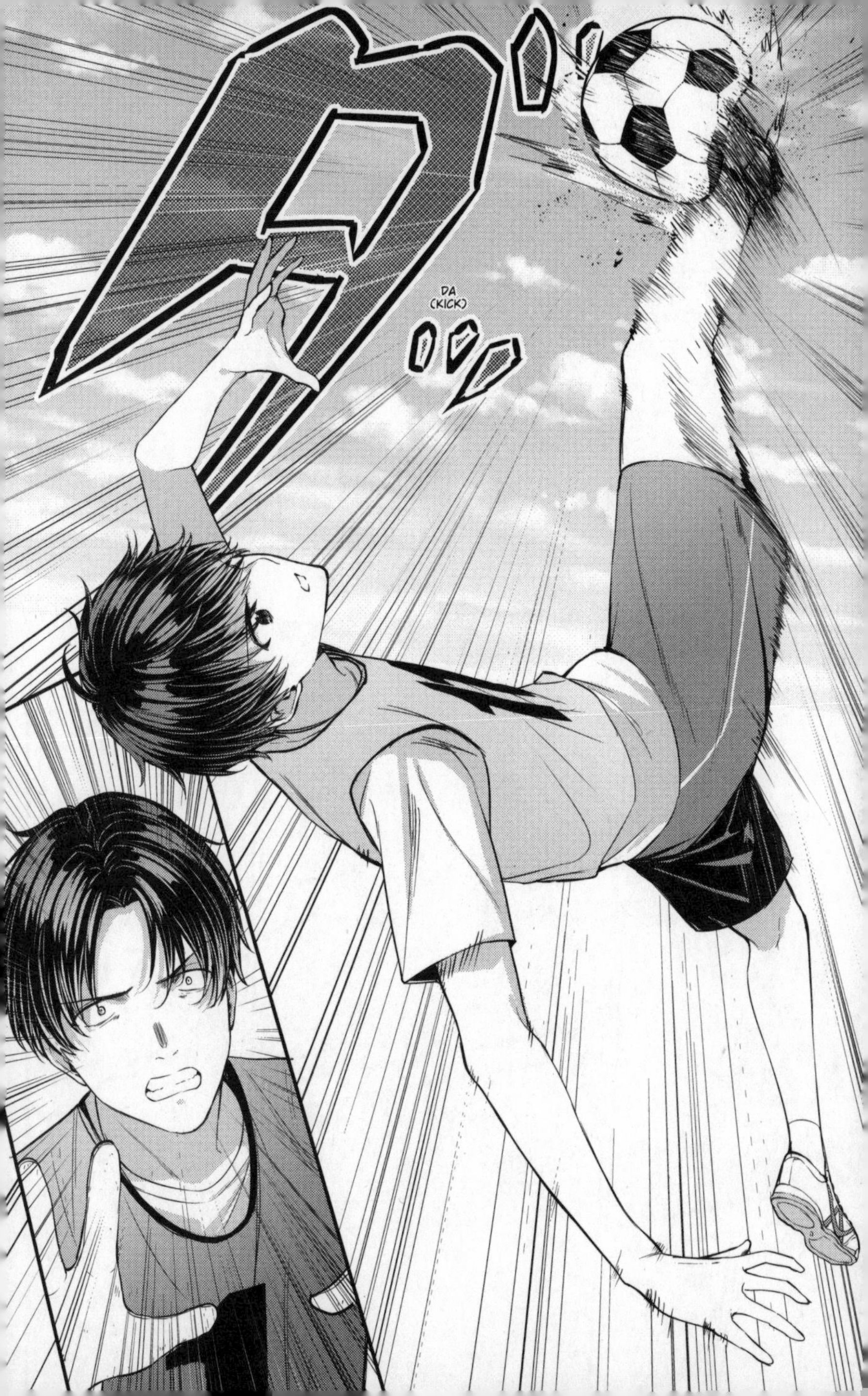
DA
(KICK)

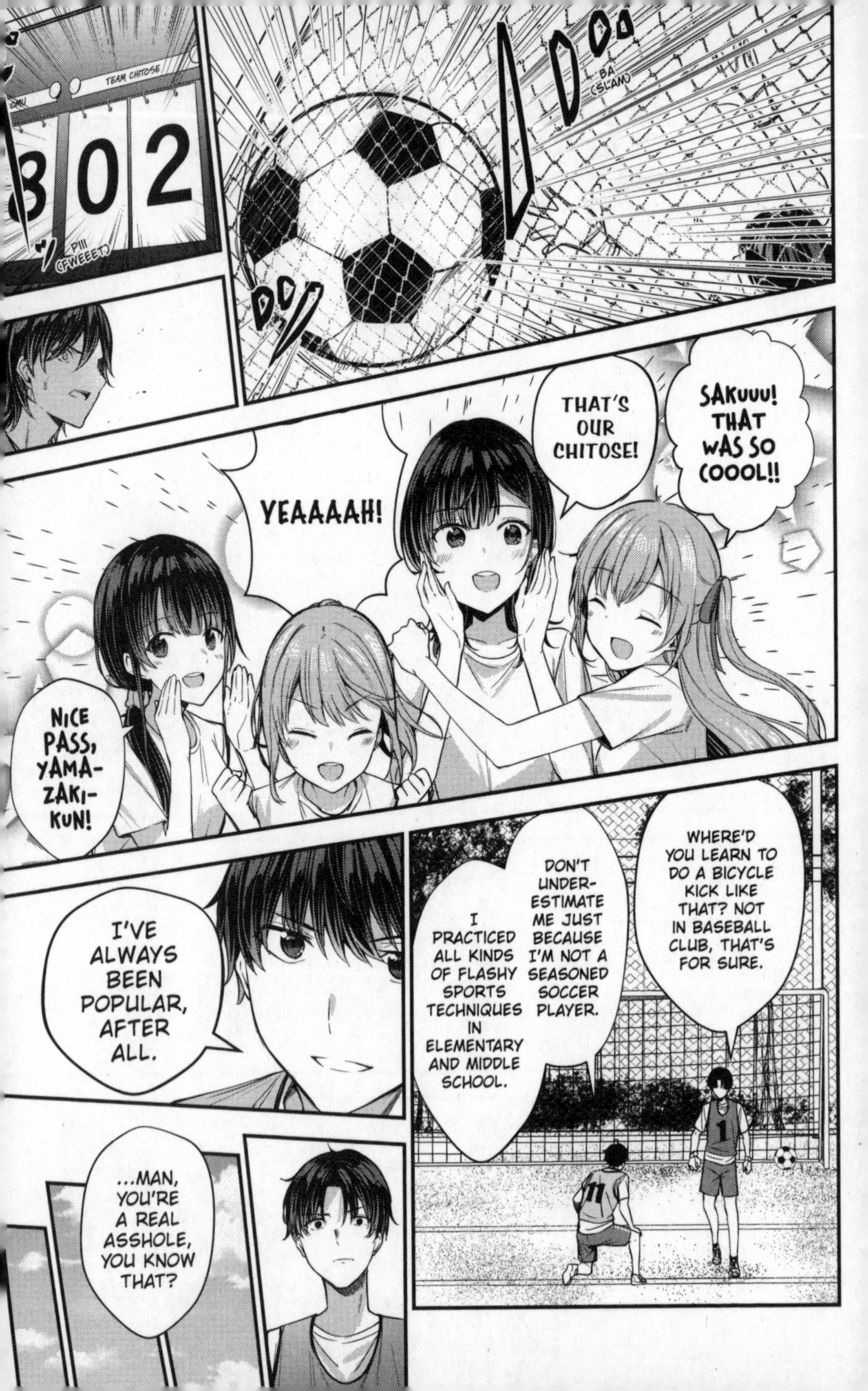
DO
DO
BA (SLAM)
DO
TEAM CHITOSE
3 0 2
PIII (FWEEET)
SAKUUU! THAT WAS SO COOOL!!
THAT'S OUR CHITOSE!
YEAAAAH!
NICE PASS, YAMA-ZAKI-KUN!
WHERE'D YOU LEARN TO DO A BICYCLE KICK LIKE THAT? NOT IN BASEBALL CLUB, THAT'S FOR SURE.
DON'T UNDER-ESTIMATE ME JUST BECAUSE I'M NOT A SEASONED SOCCER PLAYER.
I PRACTICED ALL KINDS OF FLASHY SPORTS TECHNIQUES IN ELEMENTARY AND MIDDLE SCHOOL.
I'VE ALWAYS BEEN POPULAR, AFTER ALL.
...MAN, YOU'RE A REAL ASSHOLE, YOU KNOW THAT?

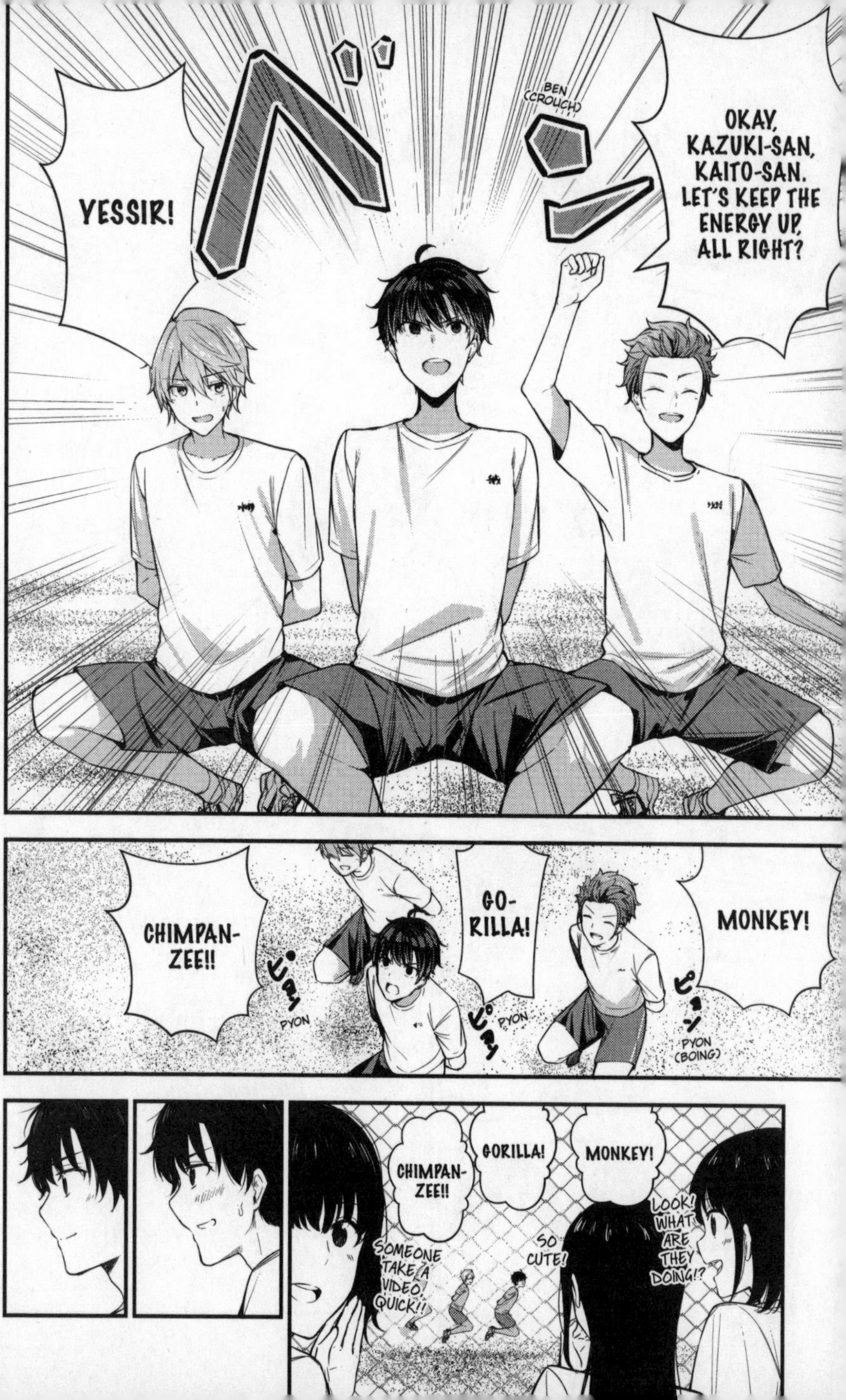
OKAY, KAZUKI-SAN, KAITO-SAN. LET'S KEEP THE ENERGY UP, ALL RIGHT?
BEN (CROUCH)
YESSIR!
MONKEY!
PYON (BOING)
GO-RILLA!
PYON
CHIMPAN-ZEE!!
PYON
LOOK! WHAT ARE THEY DOING!?
MONKEY!
GORILLA!
SO CUTE!
CHIMPAN-ZEE!!
SOMEONE TAKE A VIDEO, QUICK!!

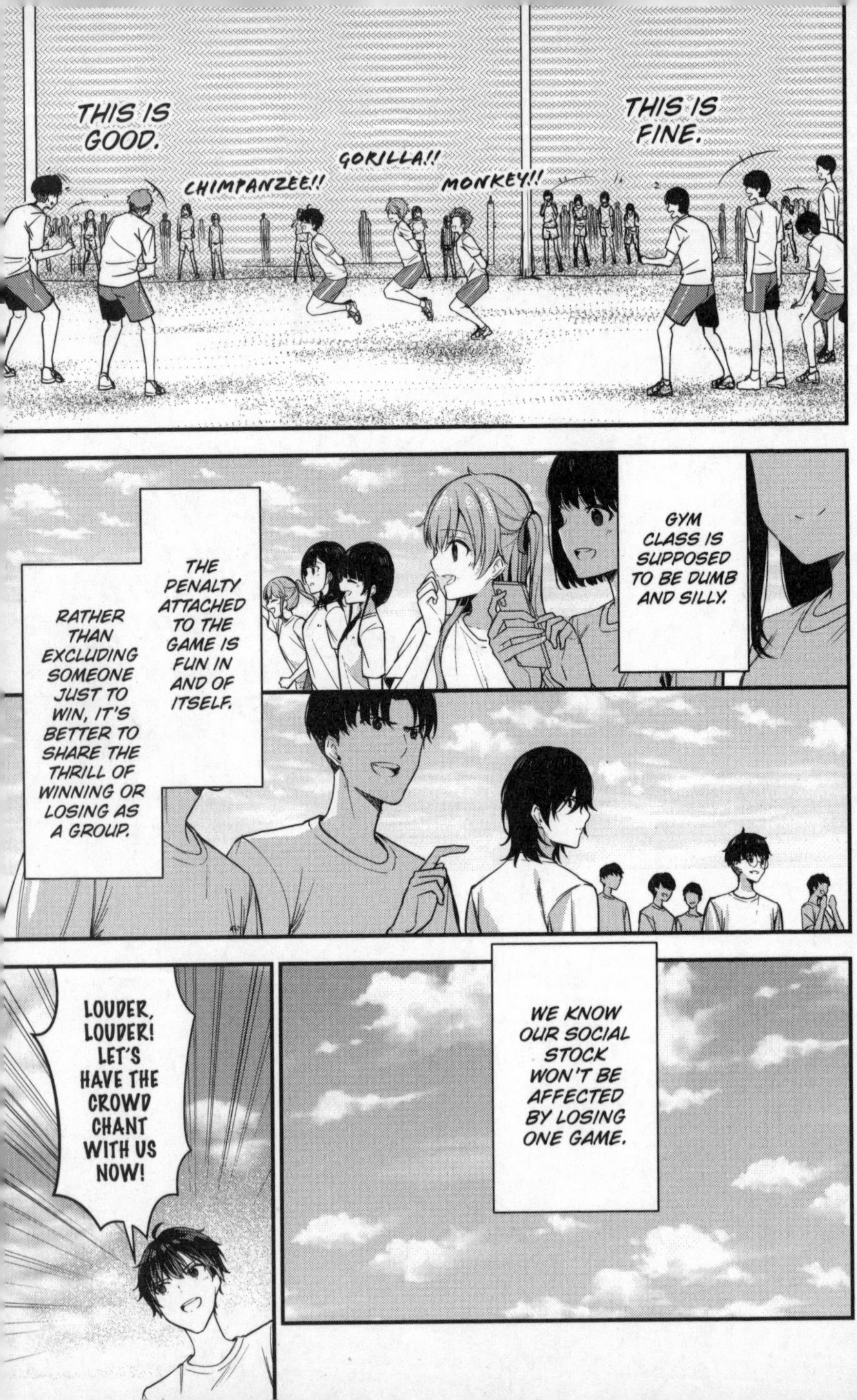
THIS IS FINE.
MONKEY!!
GORILLA!!
CHIMPANZEE!!
THIS IS GOOD.
GYM CLASS IS SUPPOSED TO BE DUMB AND SILLY.
THE PENALTY ATTACHED TO THE GAME IS FUN IN AND OF ITSELF.
RATHER THAN EXCLUDING SOMEONE JUST TO WIN, IT'S BETTER TO SHARE THE THRILL OF WINNING OR LOSING AS A GROUP.
WE KNOW OUR SOCIAL STOCK WON'T BE AFFECTED BY LOSING ONE GAME.
LOUDER, LOUDER! LET'S HAVE THE CROWD CHANT WITH US NOW!

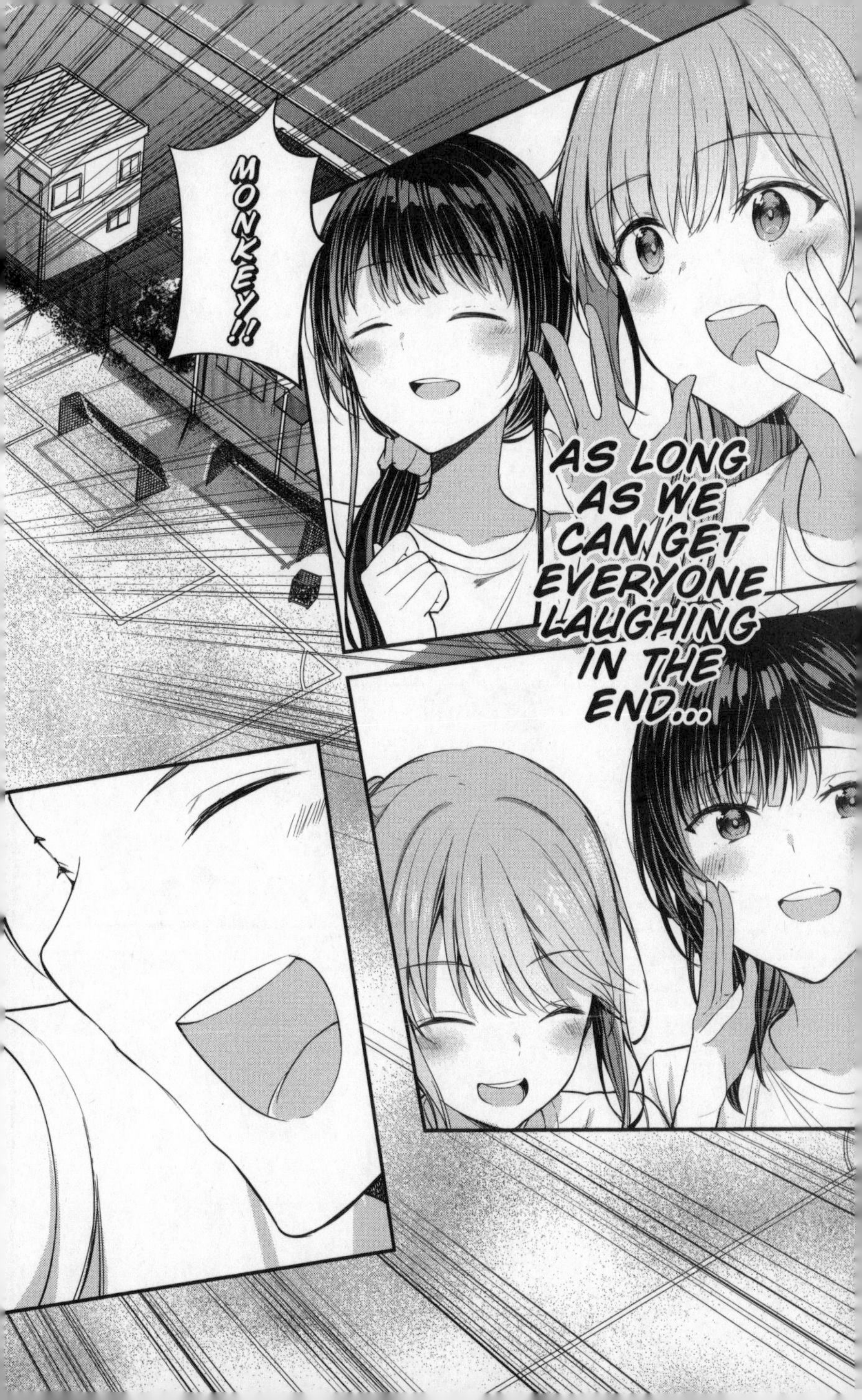
MONKEY!!
AS LONG AS WE CAN GET EVERYONE LAUGHING IN THE END...

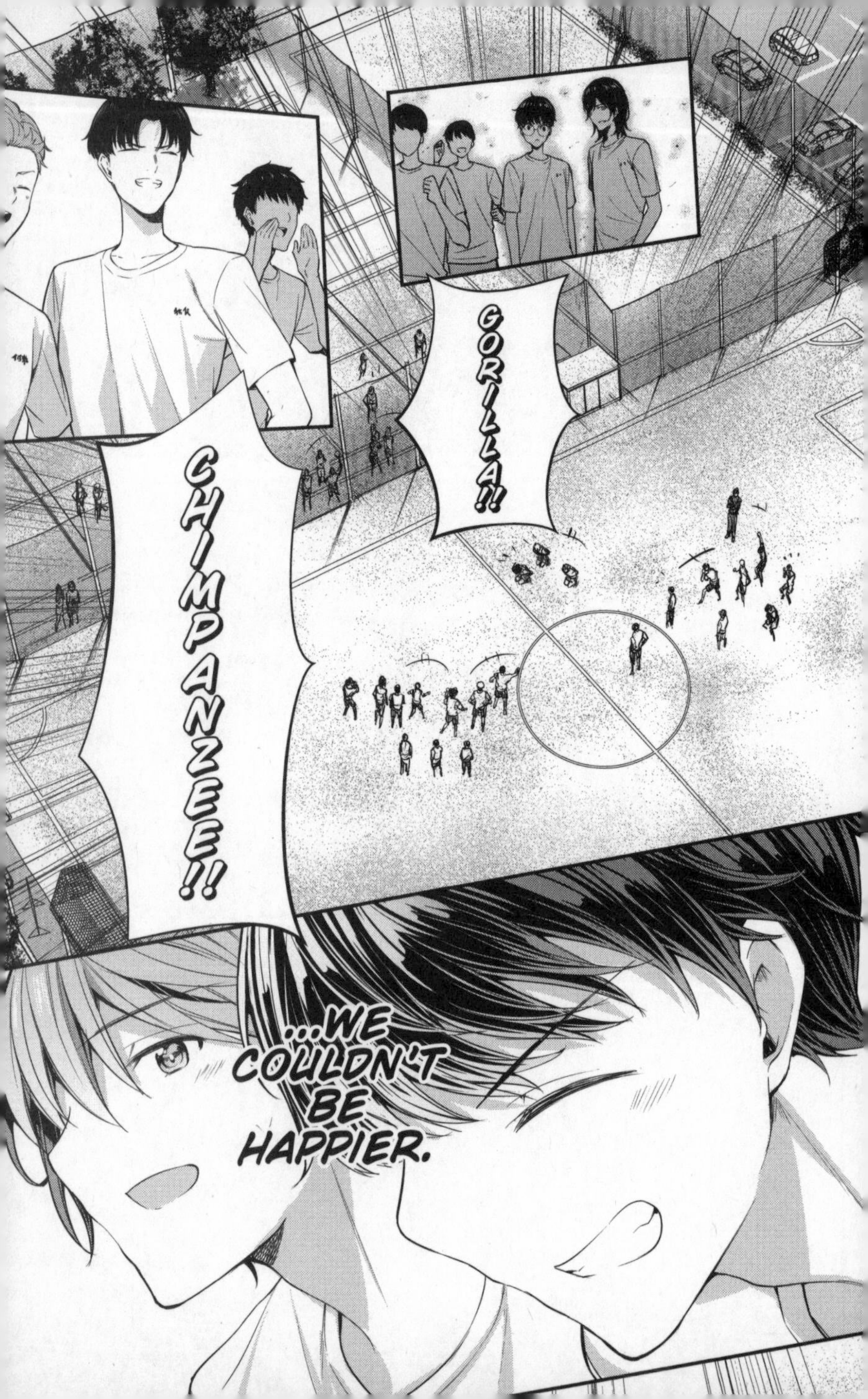
GORILLA!!
CHIMPANZEE!!
...WE COULDN'T BE HAPPIER.

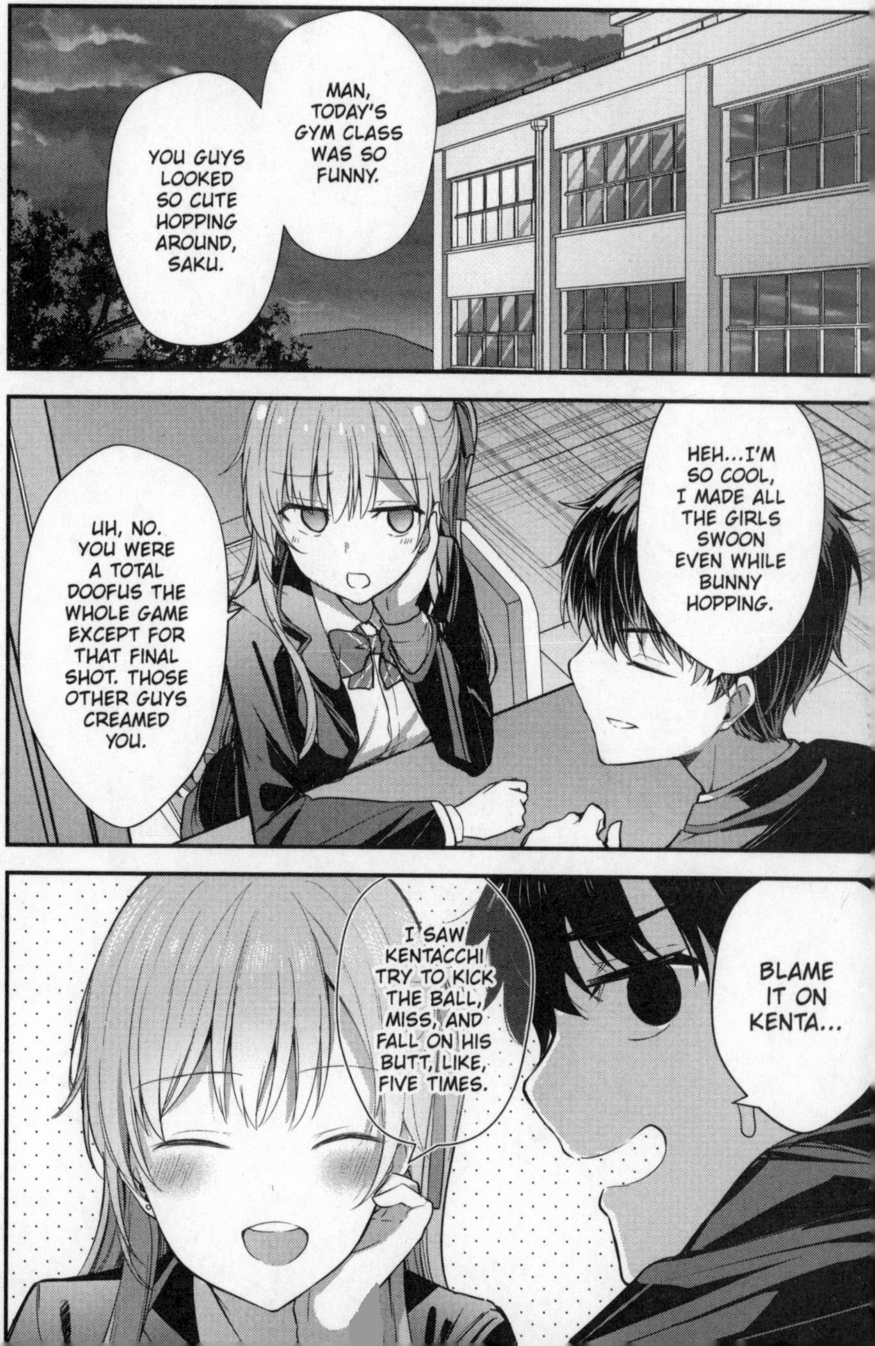
MAN, TODAY'S GYM CLASS WAS SO FUNNY.
YOU GUYS LOOKED SO CUTE HOPPING AROUND, SAKU.
HEH...I'M SO COOL, I MADE ALL THE GIRLS SWOON EVEN WHILE BUNNY HOPPING.
UH, NO. YOU WERE A TOTAL DOOFUS THE WHOLE GAME EXCEPT FOR THAT FINAL SHOT. THOSE OTHER GUYS CREAMED YOU.
BLAME IT ON KENTA...
I SAW KENTACCHI TRY TO KICK THE BALL, MISS, AND FALL ON HIS BUTT, LIKE, FIVE TIMES.

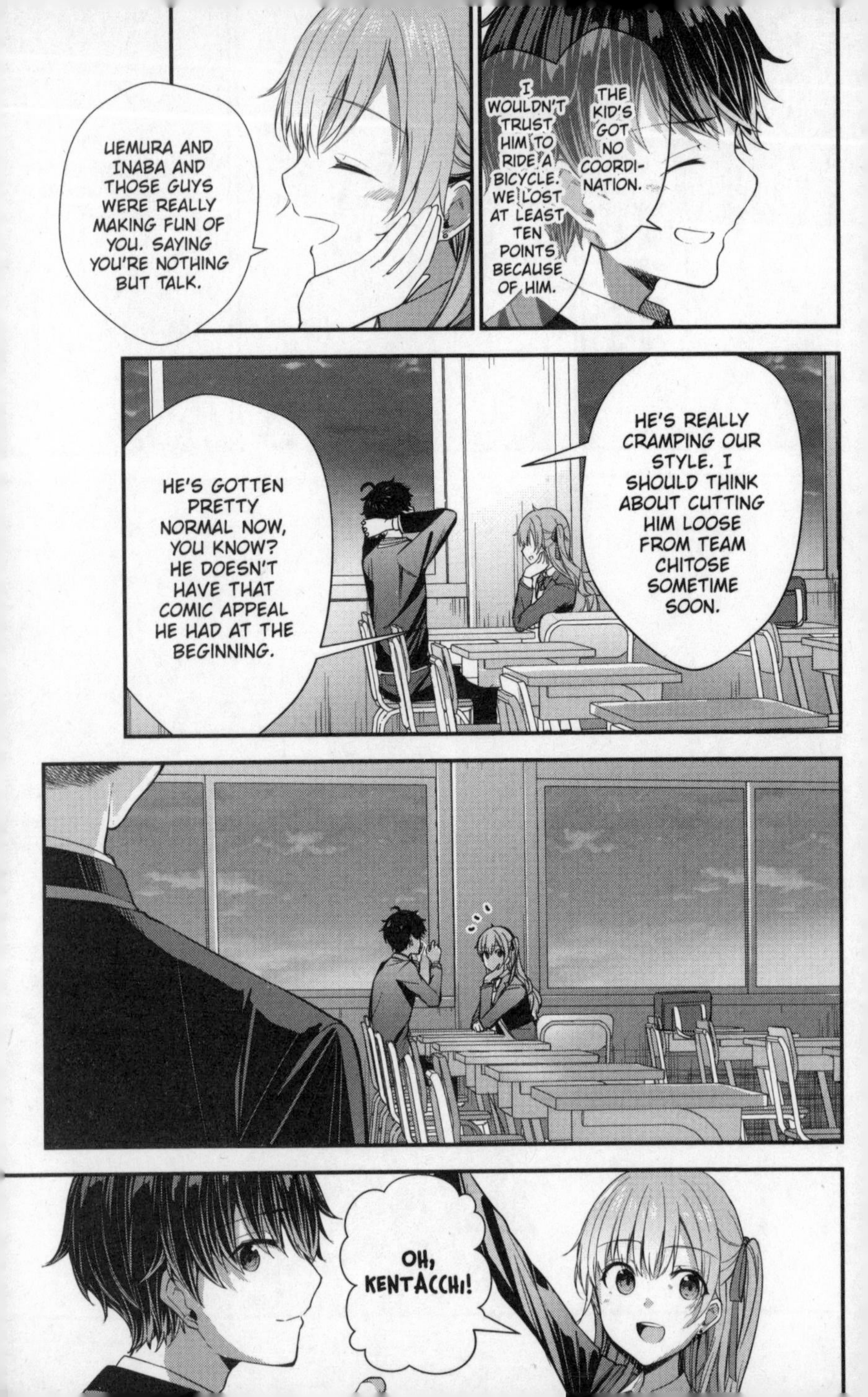
THE KID'S GOT NO COORDINATION.
I WOULDN'T TRUST HIM TO RIDE A BICYCLE. WE LOST AT LEAST TEN POINTS BECAUSE OF HIM.
UEMURA AND INABA AND THOSE GUYS WERE REALLY MAKING FUN OF YOU. SAYING YOU'RE NOTHING BUT TALK.
HE'S REALLY CRAMPING OUR STYLE. I SHOULD THINK ABOUT CUTTING HIM LOOSE FROM TEAM CHITOSE SOMETIME SOON.
HE'S GOTTEN PRETTY NORMAL NOW, YOU KNOW? HE DOESN'T HAVE THAT COMIC APPEAL HE HAD AT THE BEGINNING.
OH, KENTACCHI!

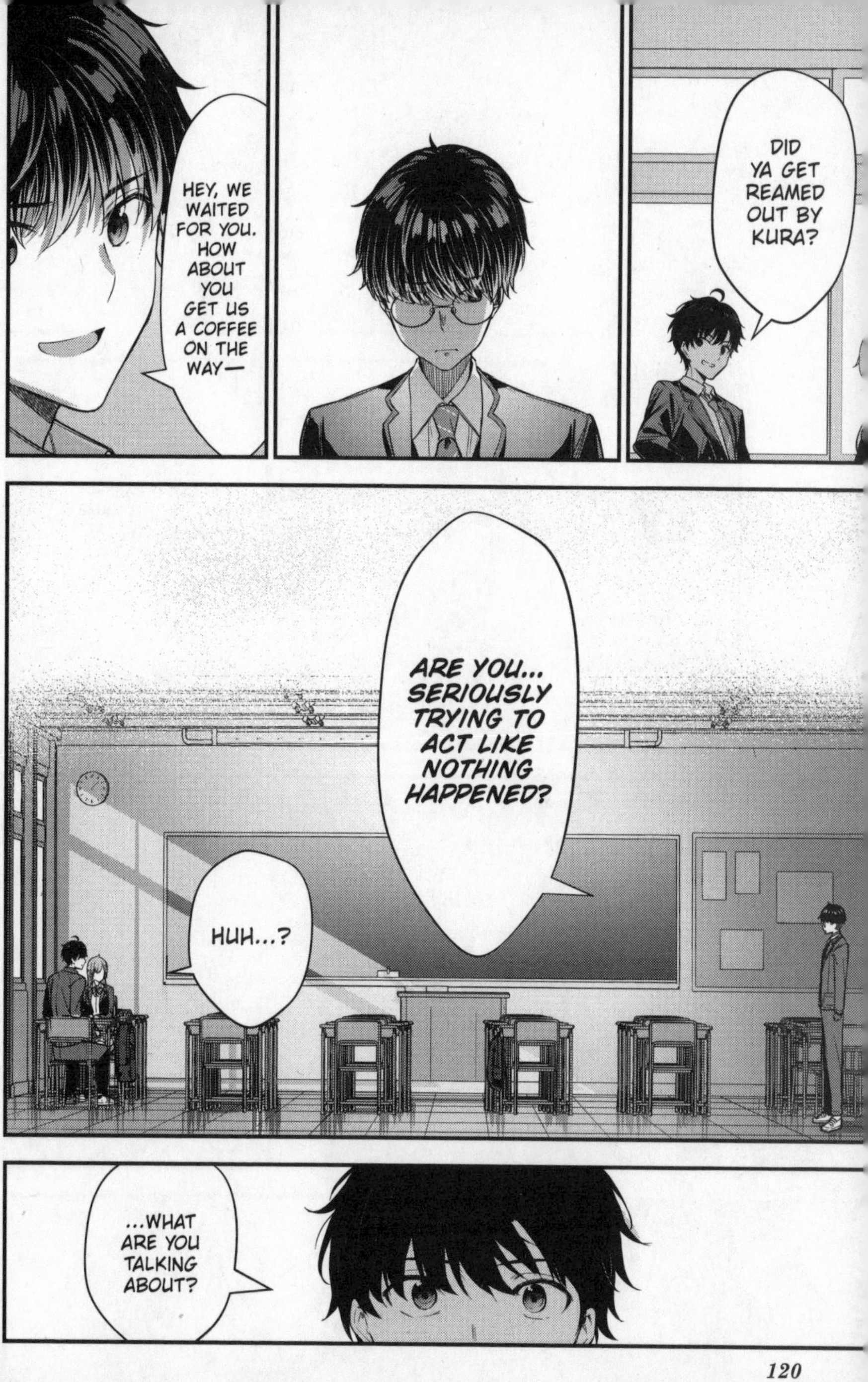
DID YA GET REAMED OUT BY KURA?
HEY, WE WAITED FOR YOU. HOW ABOUT YOU GET US A COFFEE ON THE WAY—
ARE YOU... SERIOUSLY TRYING TO ACT LIKE NOTHING HAPPENED?
HUH...?
...WHAT ARE YOU TALKING ABOUT?

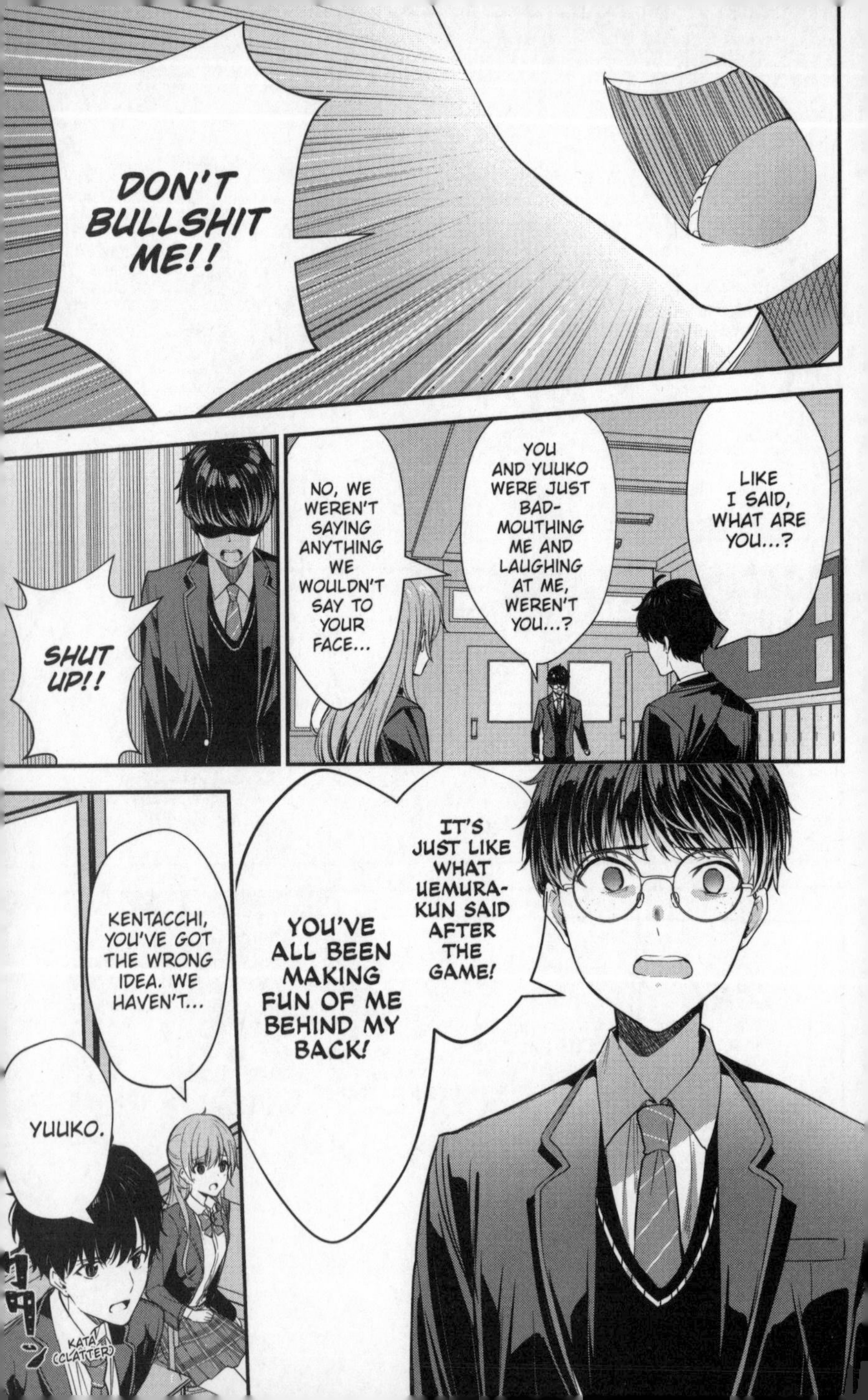
DON'T BULLSHIT ME!!
LIKE I SAID, WHAT ARE YOU...?
YOU AND YUUKO WERE JUST BAD-MOUTHING ME AND LAUGHING AT ME, WEREN'T YOU...?
NO, WE WEREN'T SAYING ANYTHING WE WOULDN'T SAY TO YOUR FACE...
SHUT UP!!
IT'S JUST LIKE WHAT UEMURA-KUN SAID AFTER THE GAME!
YOU'VE ALL BEEN MAKING FUN OF ME BEHIND MY BACK!
KENTACCHI, YOU'VE GOT THE WRONG IDEA. WE HAVEN'T...
YUUKO.
KATA (CLATTER)

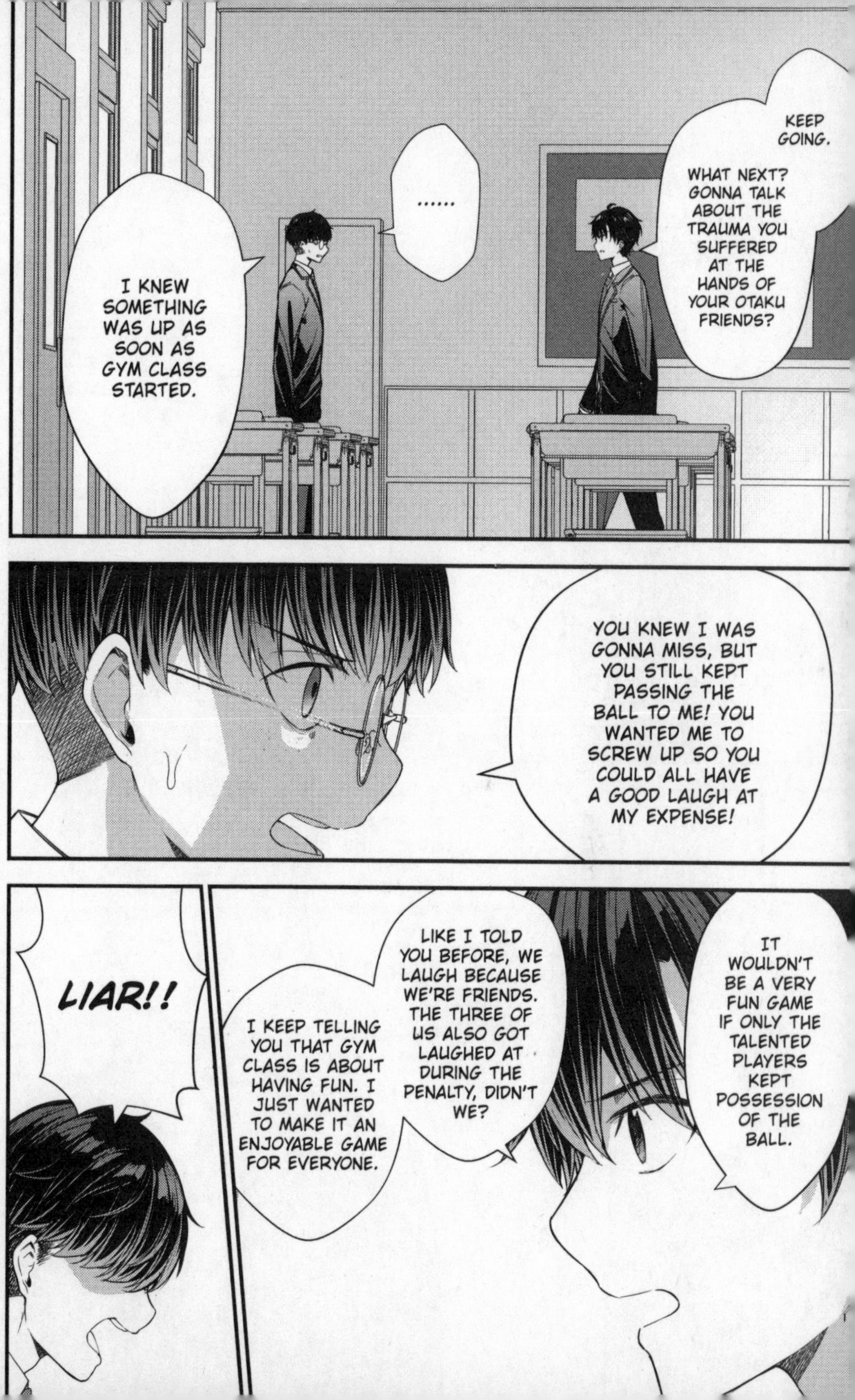
KEEP GOING.
WHAT NEXT? GONNA TALK ABOUT THE TRAUMA YOU SUFFERED AT THE HANDS OF YOUR OTAKU FRIENDS?
......
I KNEW SOMETHING WAS UP AS SOON AS GYM CLASS STARTED.
YOU KNEW I WAS GONNA MISS, BUT YOU STILL KEPT PASSING THE BALL TO ME! YOU WANTED ME TO SCREW UP SO YOU COULD ALL HAVE A GOOD LAUGH AT MY EXPENSE!
IT WOULDN'T BE A VERY FUN GAME IF ONLY THE TALENTED PLAYERS KEPT POSSESSION OF THE BALL.
LIKE I TOLD YOU BEFORE, WE LAUGH BECAUSE WE'RE FRIENDS. THE THREE OF US ALSO GOT LAUGHED AT DURING THE PENALTY, DIDN'T WE?
I KEEP TELLING YOU THAT GYM CLASS IS ABOUT HAVING FUN. I JUST WANTED TO MAKE IT AN ENJOYABLE GAME FOR EVERYONE.
LIAR!!

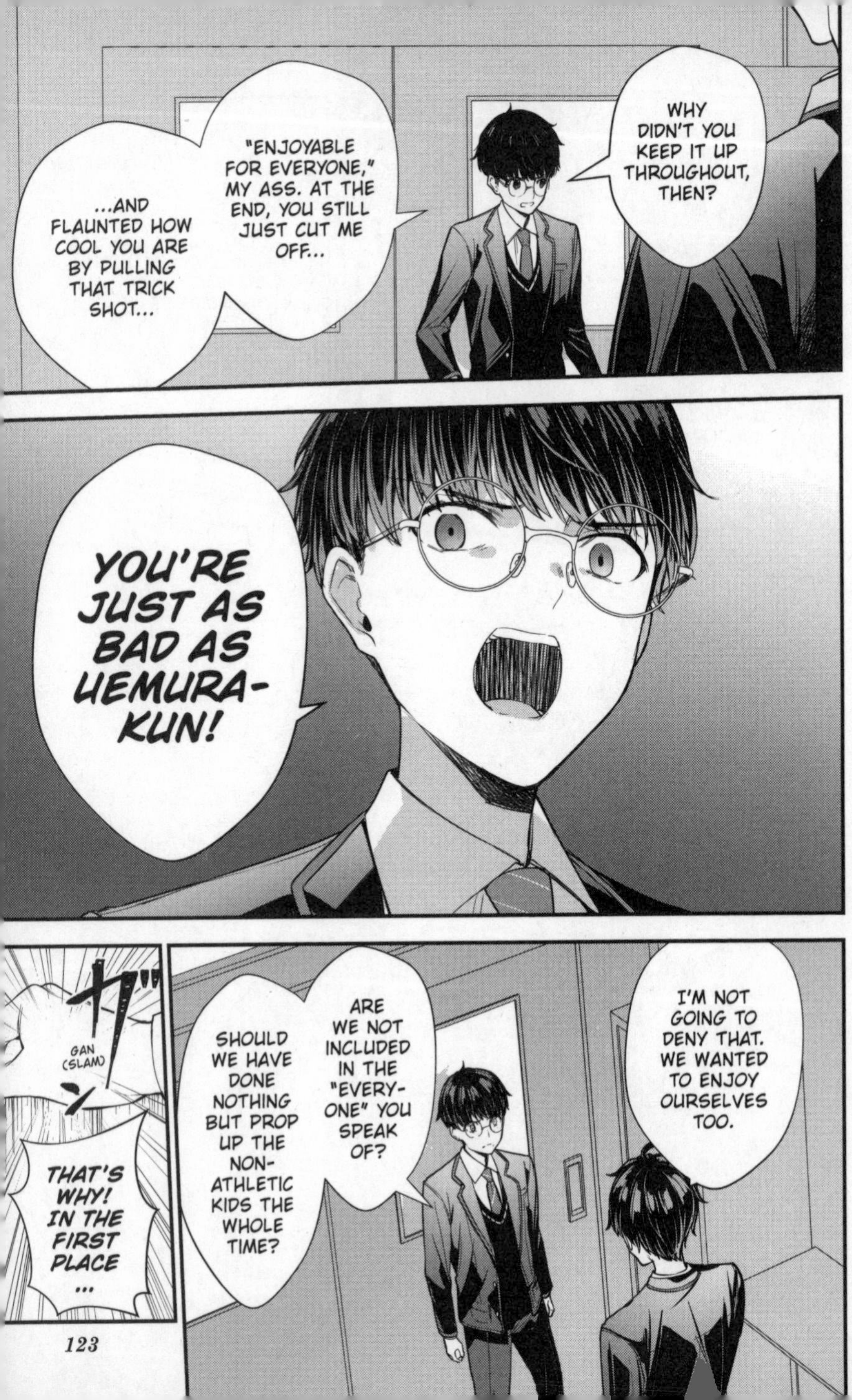
WHY DIDN'T YOU KEEP IT UP THROUGHOUT, THEN?
"ENJOYABLE FOR EVERYONE," MY ASS. AT THE END, YOU STILL JUST CUT ME OFF...
...AND FLAUNTED HOW COOL YOU ARE BY PULLING THAT TRICK SHOT...
YOU'RE JUST AS BAD AS UEMURA-KUN!
I'M NOT GOING TO DENY THAT. WE WANTED TO ENJOY OURSELVES TOO.
ARE WE NOT INCLUDED IN THE "EVERY-ONE" YOU SPEAK OF?
SHOULD WE HAVE DONE NOTHING BUT PROP UP THE NON-ATHLETIC KIDS THE WHOLE TIME?
GAN (SLAM)
THAT'S WHY! IN THE FIRST PLACE...

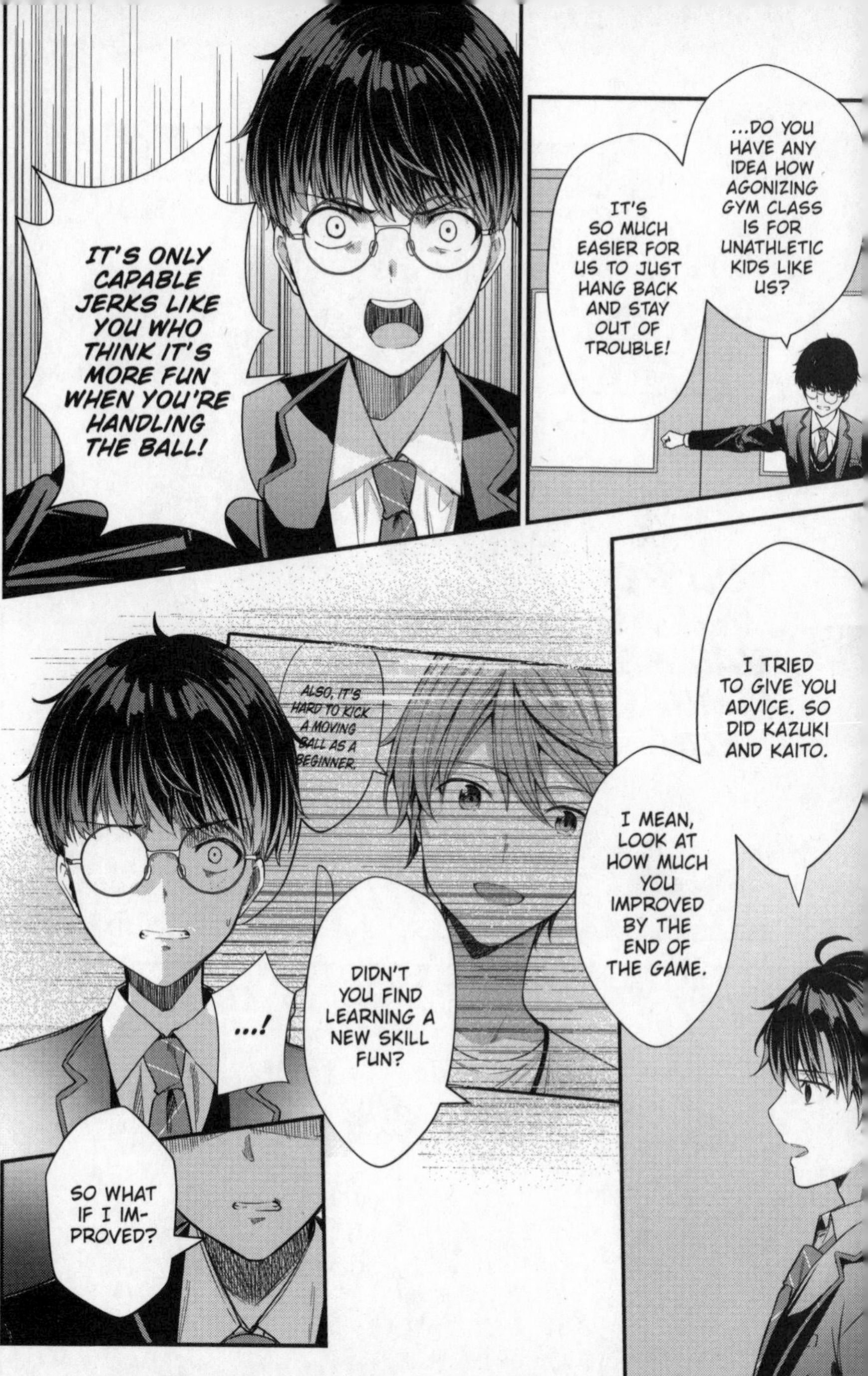
...DO YOU HAVE ANY IDEA HOW AGONIZING GYM CLASS IS FOR UNATHLETIC KIDS LIKE US?
IT'S SO MUCH EASIER FOR US TO JUST HANG BACK AND STAY OUT OF TROUBLE!
IT'S ONLY CAPABLE JERKS LIKE YOU WHO THINK IT'S MORE FUN WHEN YOU'RE HANDLING THE BALL!
I TRIED TO GIVE YOU ADVICE. SO DID KAZUKI AND KAITO.
I MEAN, LOOK AT HOW MUCH YOU IMPROVED BY THE END OF THE GAME.
ALSO, IT'S HARD TO KICK A MOVING BALL AS A BEGINNER.
DIDN'T YOU FIND LEARNING A NEW SKILL FUN?
...!
SO WHAT IF I IM-PROVED?

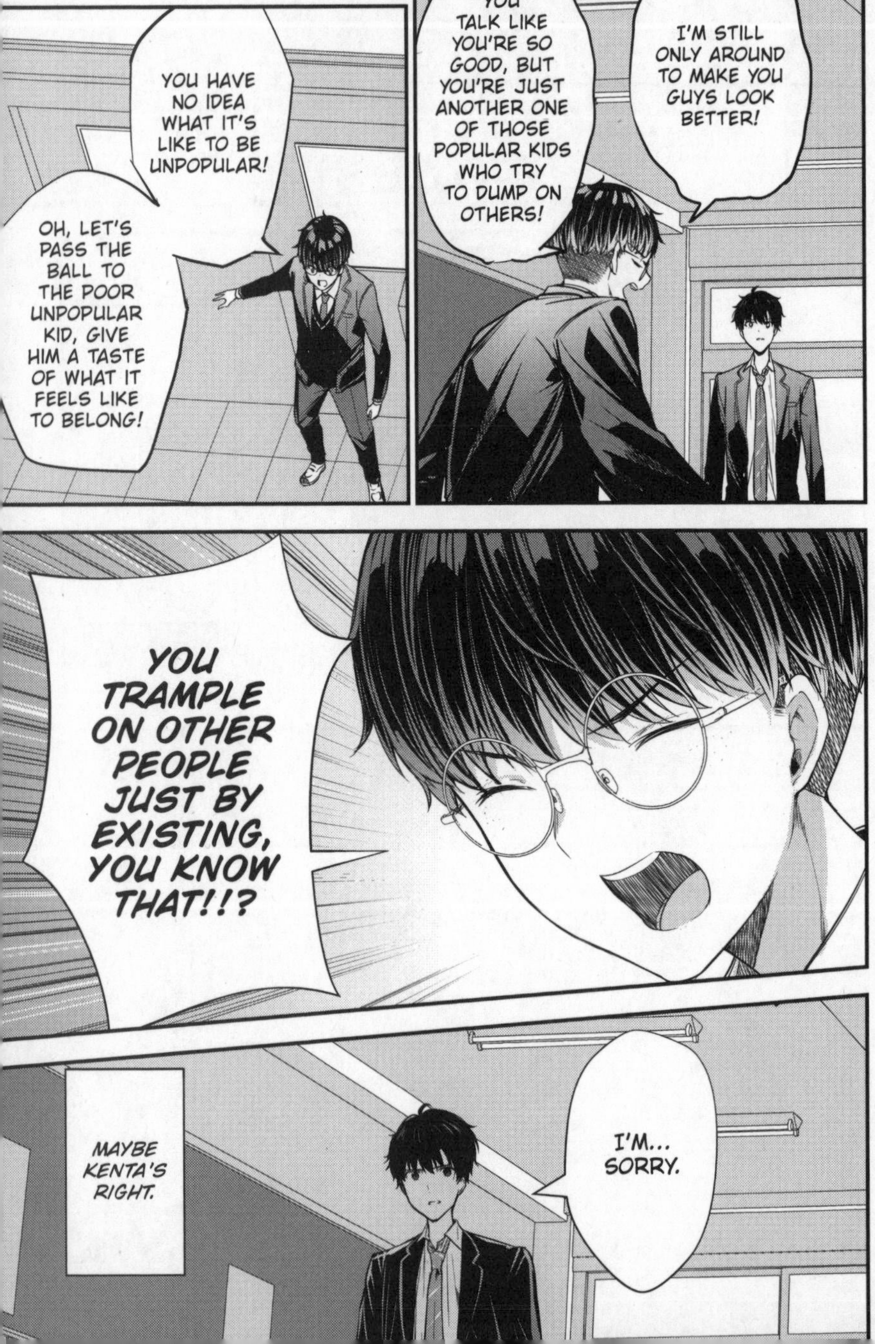
I'M STILL ONLY AROUND TO MAKE YOU GUYS LOOK BETTER!
YOU TALK LIKE YOU'RE SO GOOD, BUT YOU'RE JUST ANOTHER ONE OF THOSE POPULAR KIDS WHO TRY TO DUMP ON OTHERS!
YOU HAVE NO IDEA WHAT IT'S LIKE TO BE UNPOPULAR!
OH, LET'S PASS THE BALL TO THE POOR UNPOPULAR KID, GIVE HIM A TASTE OF WHAT IT FEELS LIKE TO BELONG!
YOU TRAMPLE ON OTHER PEOPLE JUST BY EXISTING, YOU KNOW THAT!!?
I'M... SORRY.
MAYBE KENTA'S RIGHT.

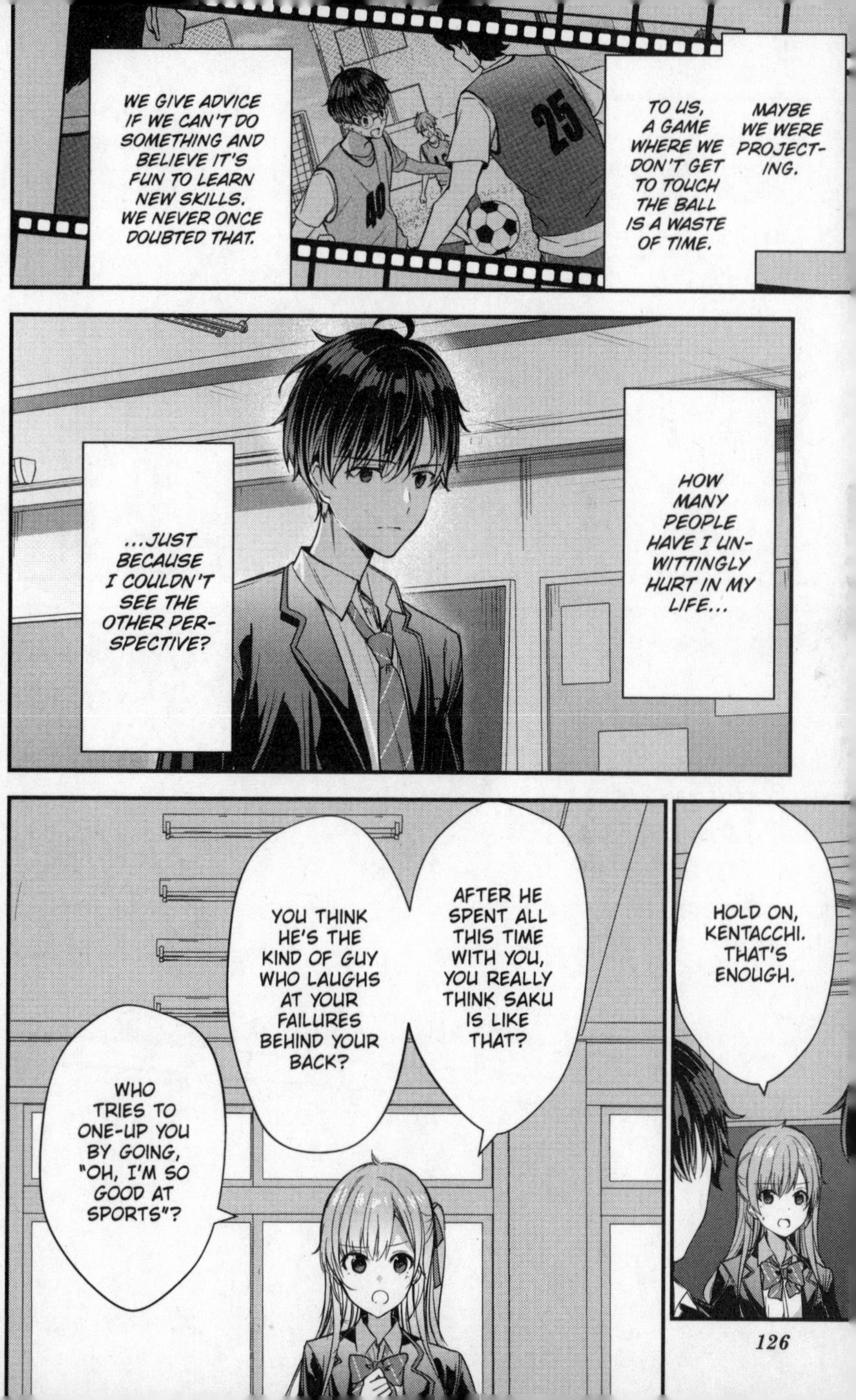
MAYBE WE WERE PROJECT-ING.
TO US, A GAME WHERE WE DON'T GET TO TOUCH THE BALL IS A WASTE OF TIME.
WE GIVE ADVICE IF WE CAN'T DO SOMETHING AND BELIEVE IT'S FUN TO LEARN NEW SKILLS. WE NEVER ONCE DOUBTED THAT.
HOW MANY PEOPLE HAVE I UN-WITTINGLY HURT IN MY LIFE...
...JUST BECAUSE I COULDN'T SEE THE OTHER PER-SPECTIVE?
HOLD ON, KENTACCHI. THAT'S ENOUGH.
AFTER HE SPENT ALL THIS TIME WITH YOU, YOU REALLY THINK SAKU IS LIKE THAT?
YOU THINK HE'S THE KIND OF GUY WHO LAUGHS AT YOUR FAILURES BEHIND YOUR BACK?
WHO TRIES TO ONE-UP YOU BY GOING, "OH, I'M SO GOOD AT SPORTS"?

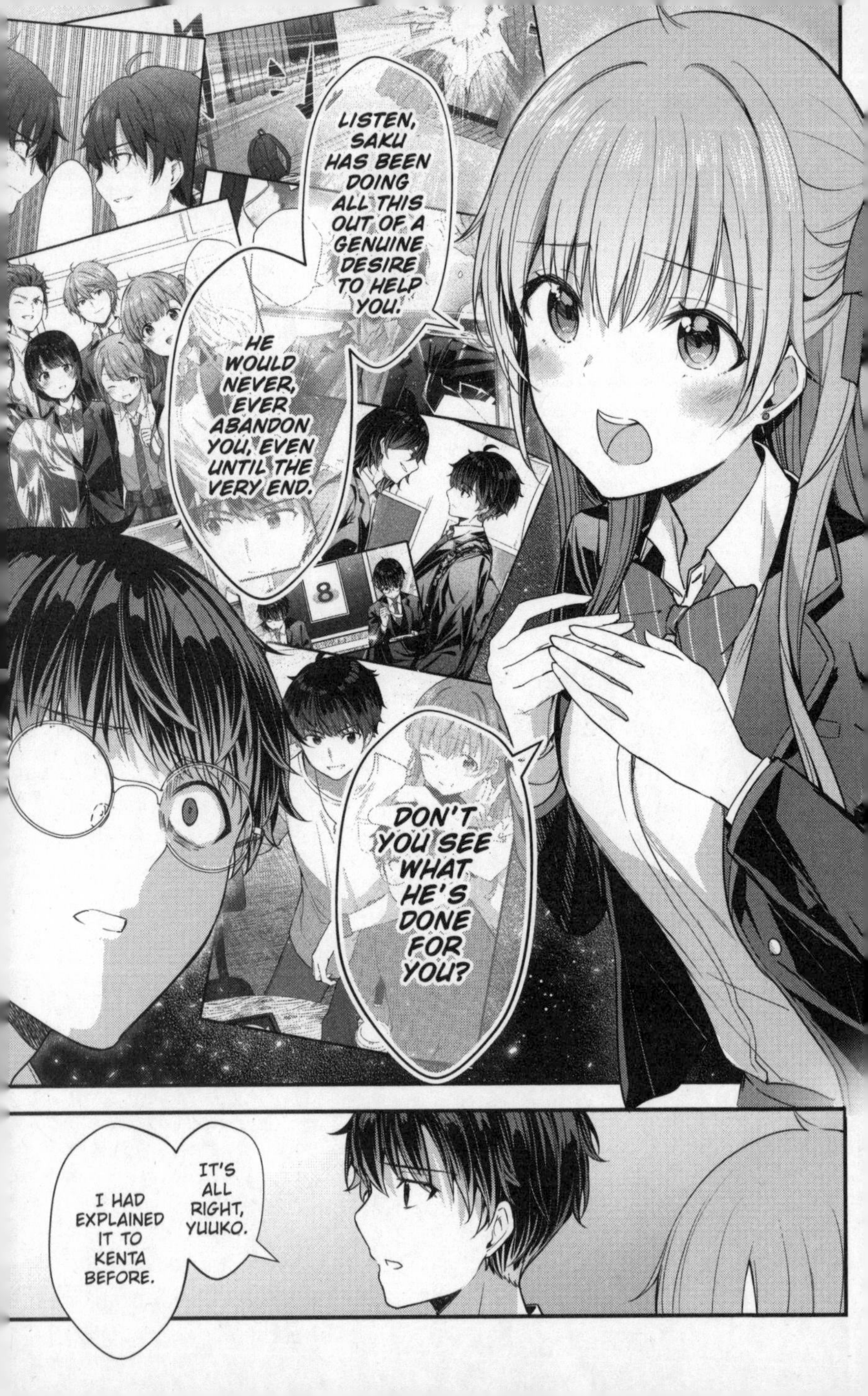
LISTEN, SAKU HAS BEEN DOING ALL THIS OUT OF A GENUINE DESIRE TO HELP YOU.
HE WOULD NEVER, EVER ABANDON YOU, EVEN UNTIL THE VERY END.
DON'T YOU SEE WHAT HE'S DONE FOR YOU?
IT'S ALL RIGHT, YUUKO.
I HAD EXPLAINED IT TO KENTA BEFORE.

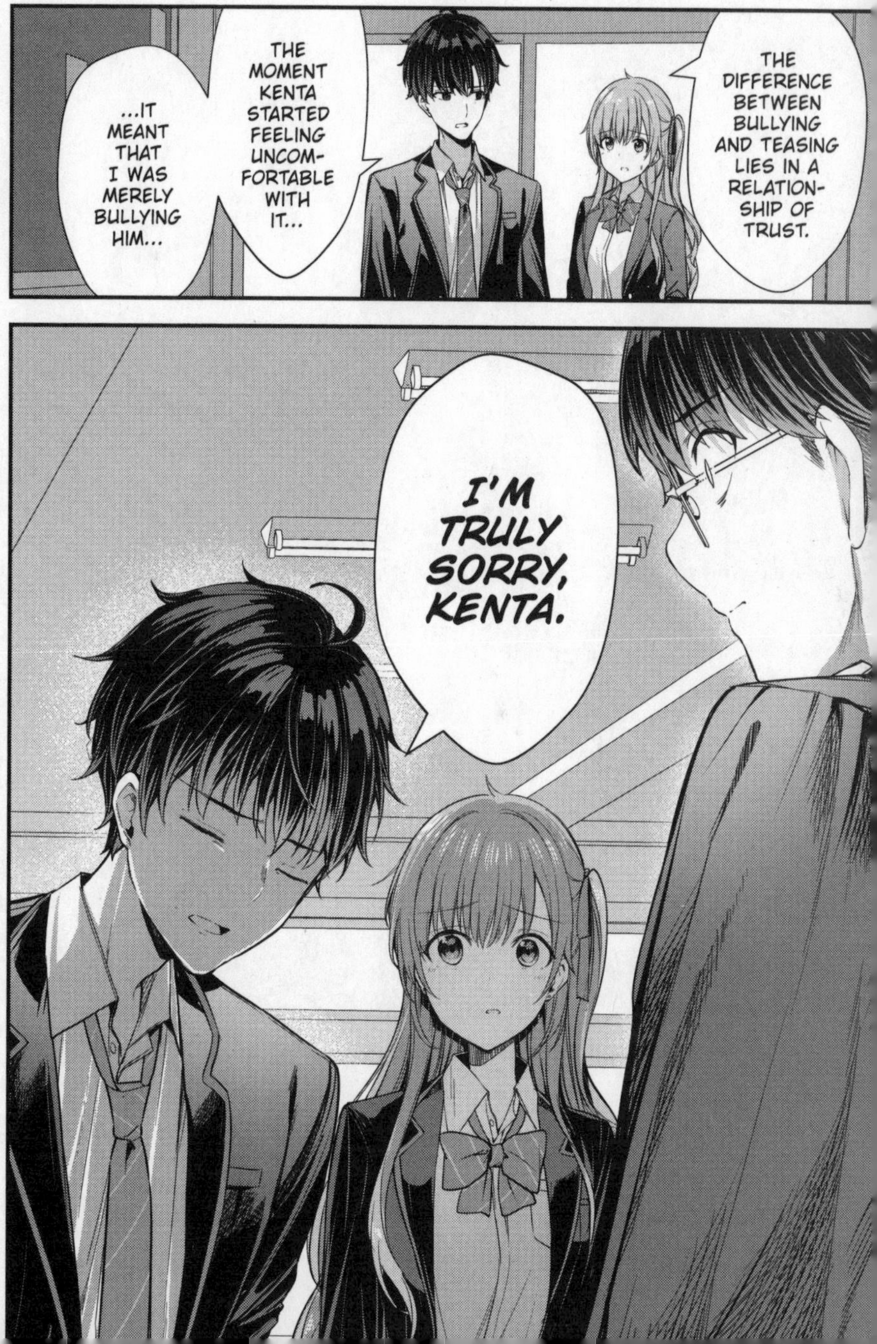
THE DIFFERENCE BETWEEN BULLYING AND TEASING LIES IN A RELATION-SHIP OF TRUST.
THE MOMENT KENTA STARTED FEELING UNCOM-FORTABLE WITH IT...
...IT MEANT THAT I WAS MERELY BULLYING HIM...
I'M TRULY SORRY, KENTA.

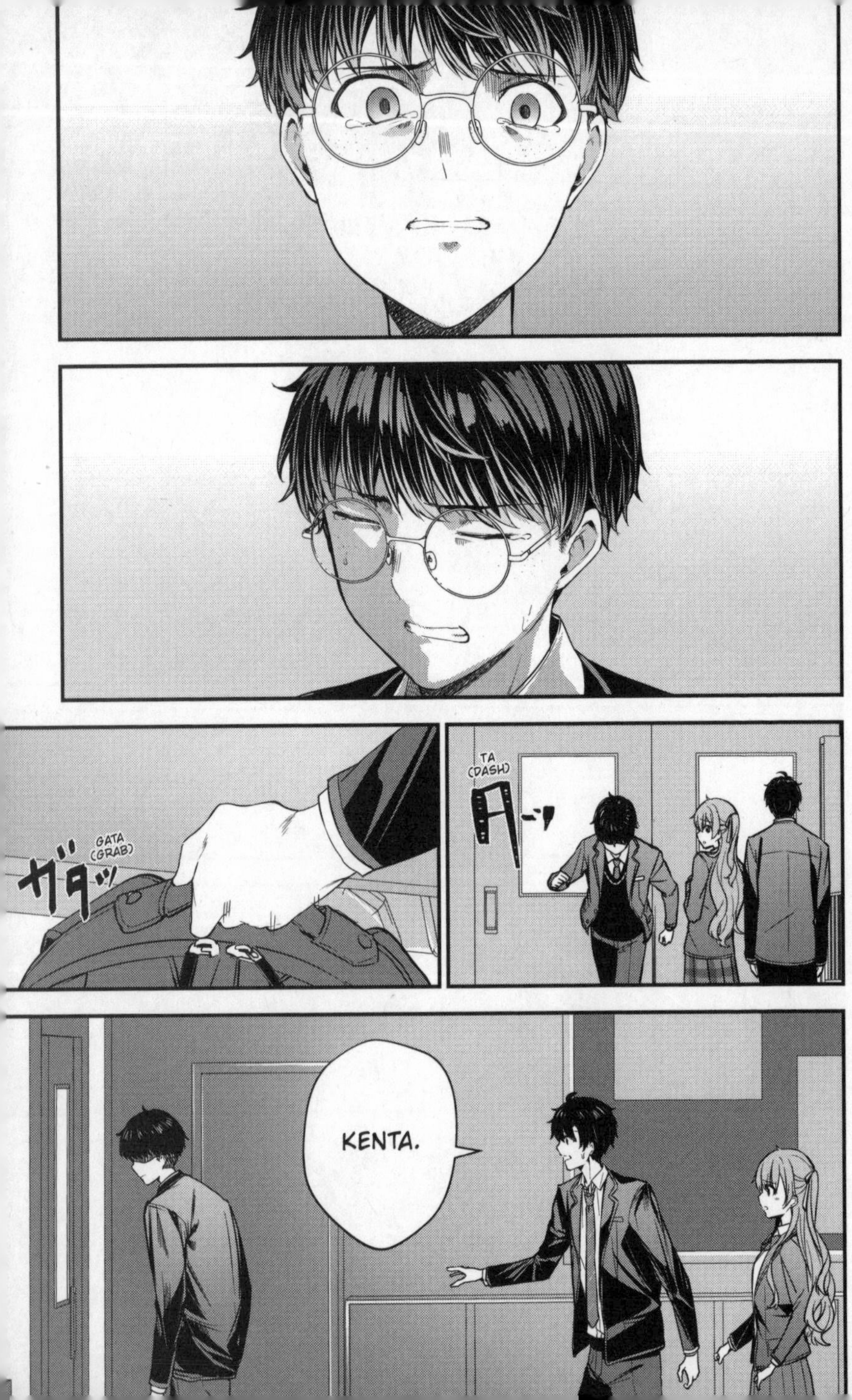
TA (DASH)
GATA (GRAB)
KENTA.

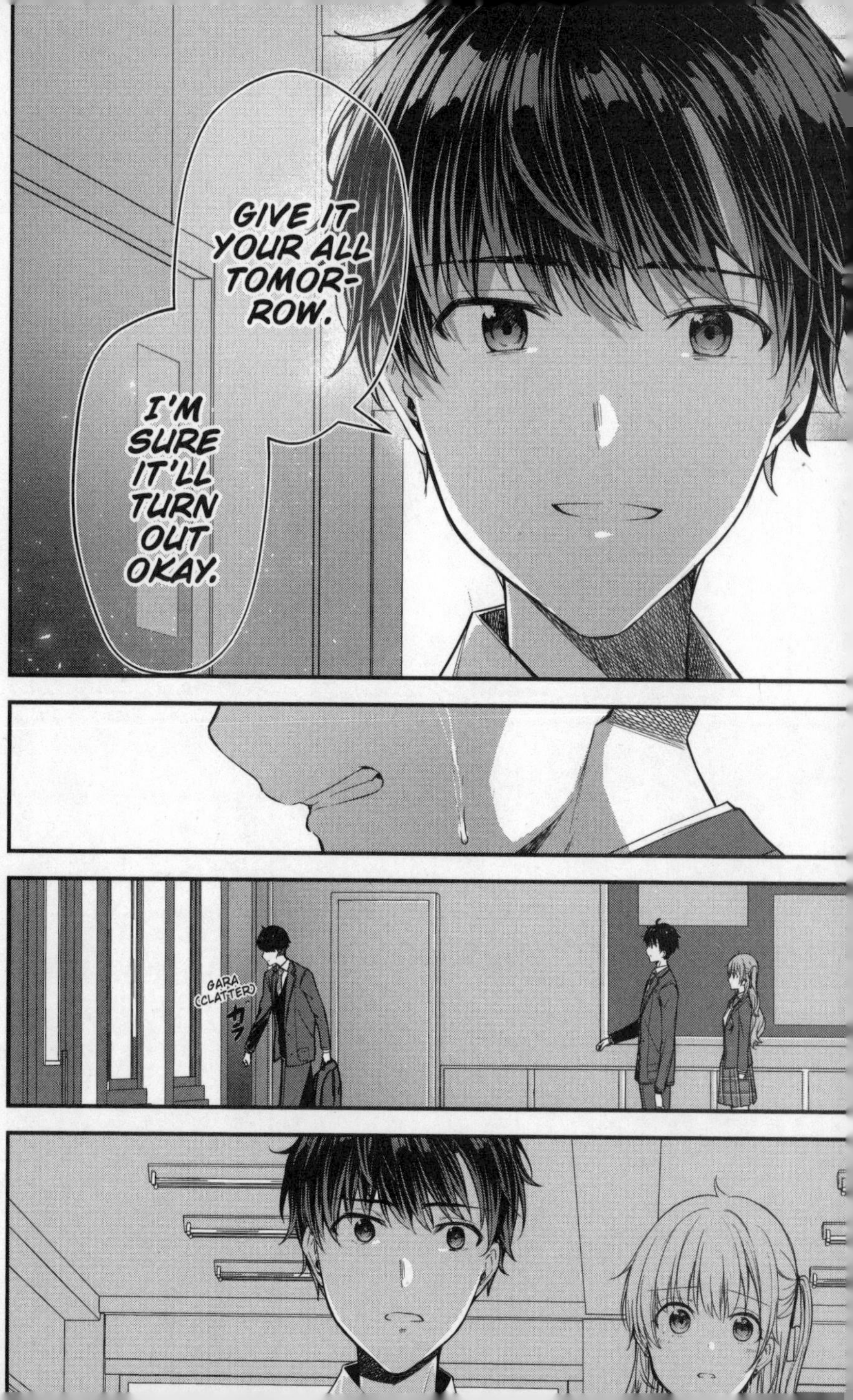
GIVE IT YOUR ALL TOMOR-ROW.
I'M SURE IT'LL TURN OUT OKAY.
GARA (CLATTER)
ガラ

Chitose Is in the Ramune Bottle

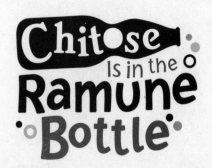

CHARACTER PROFILE

Kuranosuke Iwanami

Age: 38 years old

Height: 5’9” (177 cm)

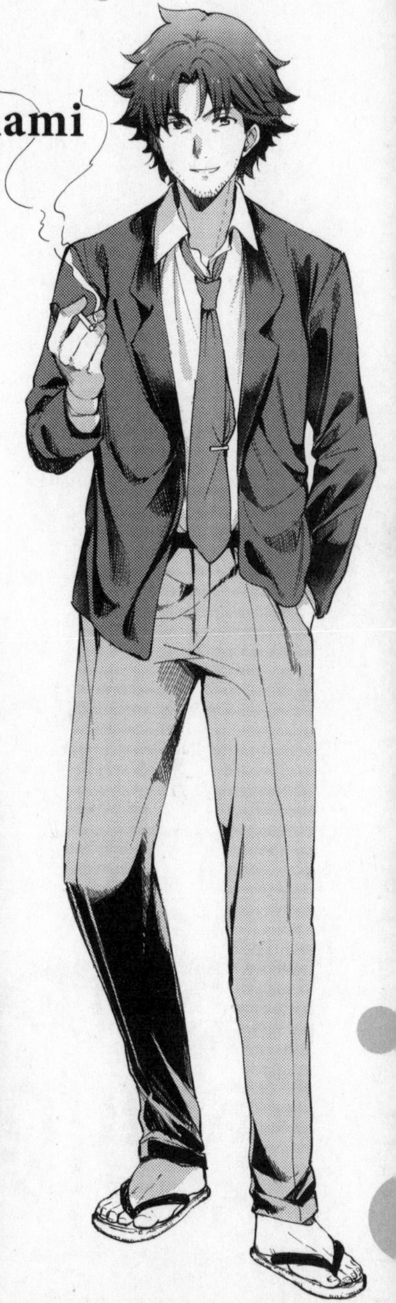

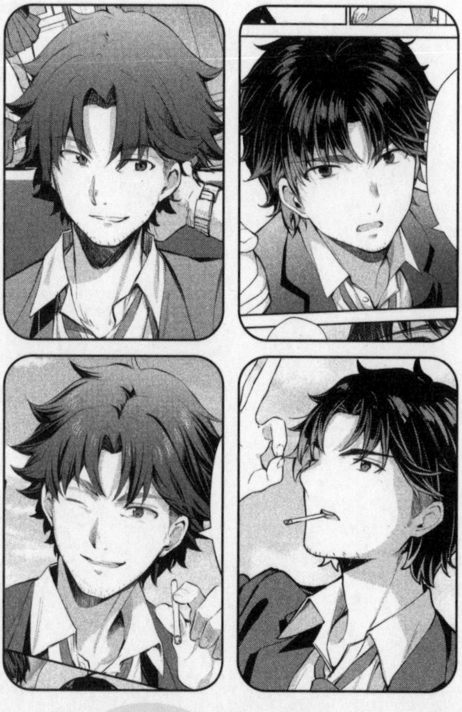

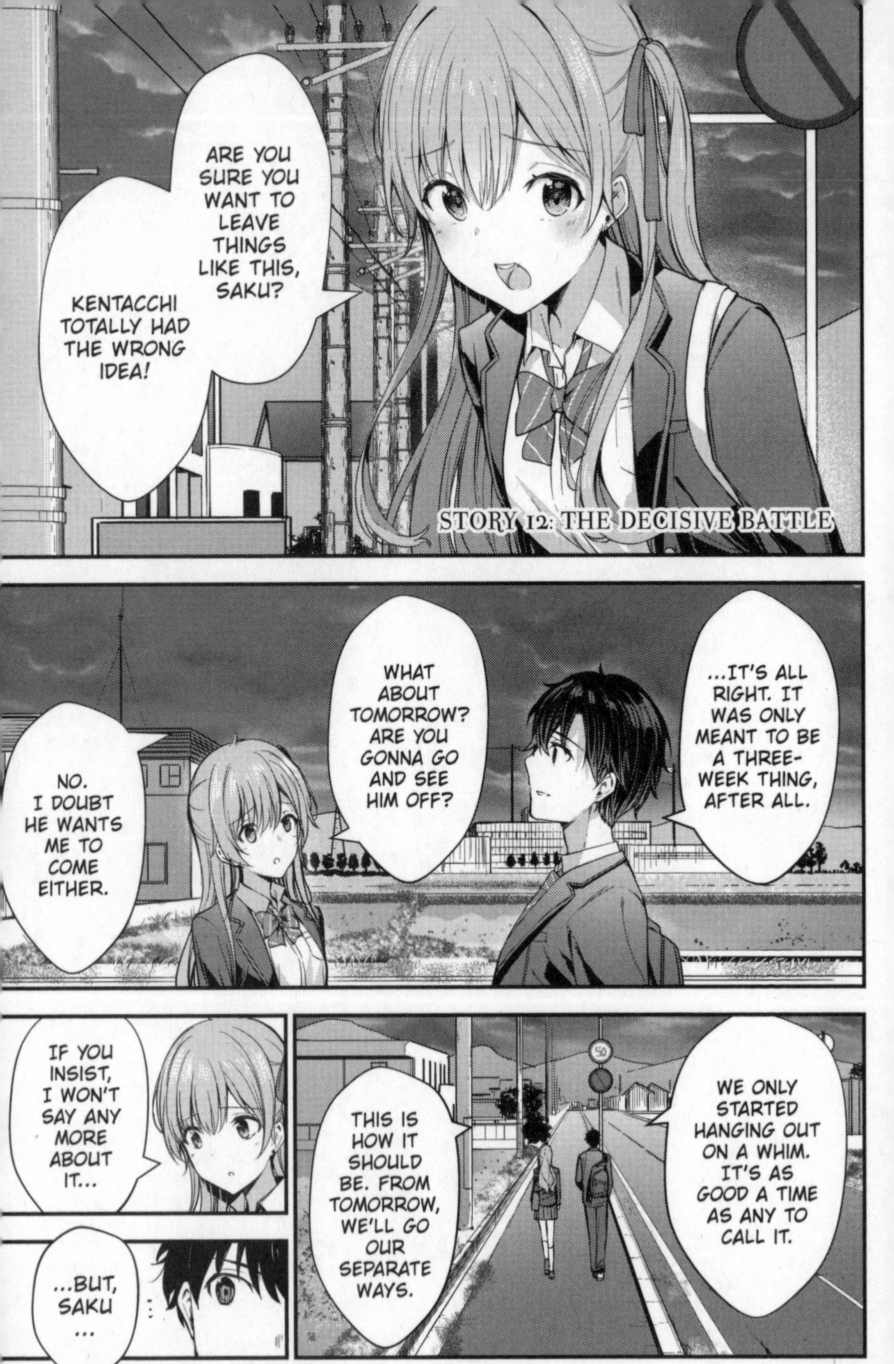
ARE YOU SURE YOU WANT TO LEAVE THINGS LIKE THIS, SAKU?
KENTACCHI TOTALLY HAD THE WRONG IDEA!
STORY 12: THE DECISIVE BATTLE
...IT'S ALL RIGHT. IT WAS ONLY MEANT TO BE A THREE-WEEK THING, AFTER ALL.
WHAT ABOUT TOMORROW? ARE YOU GONNA GO AND SEE HIM OFF?
NO. I DOUBT HE WANTS ME TO COME EITHER.
WE ONLY STARTED HANGING OUT ON A WHIM. IT'S AS GOOD A TIME AS ANY TO CALL IT.
THIS IS HOW IT SHOULD BE. FROM TOMORROW, WE'LL GO OUR SEPARATE WAYS.
IF YOU INSIST, I WON'T SAY ANY MORE ABOUT IT...
...BUT, SAKU ...
...

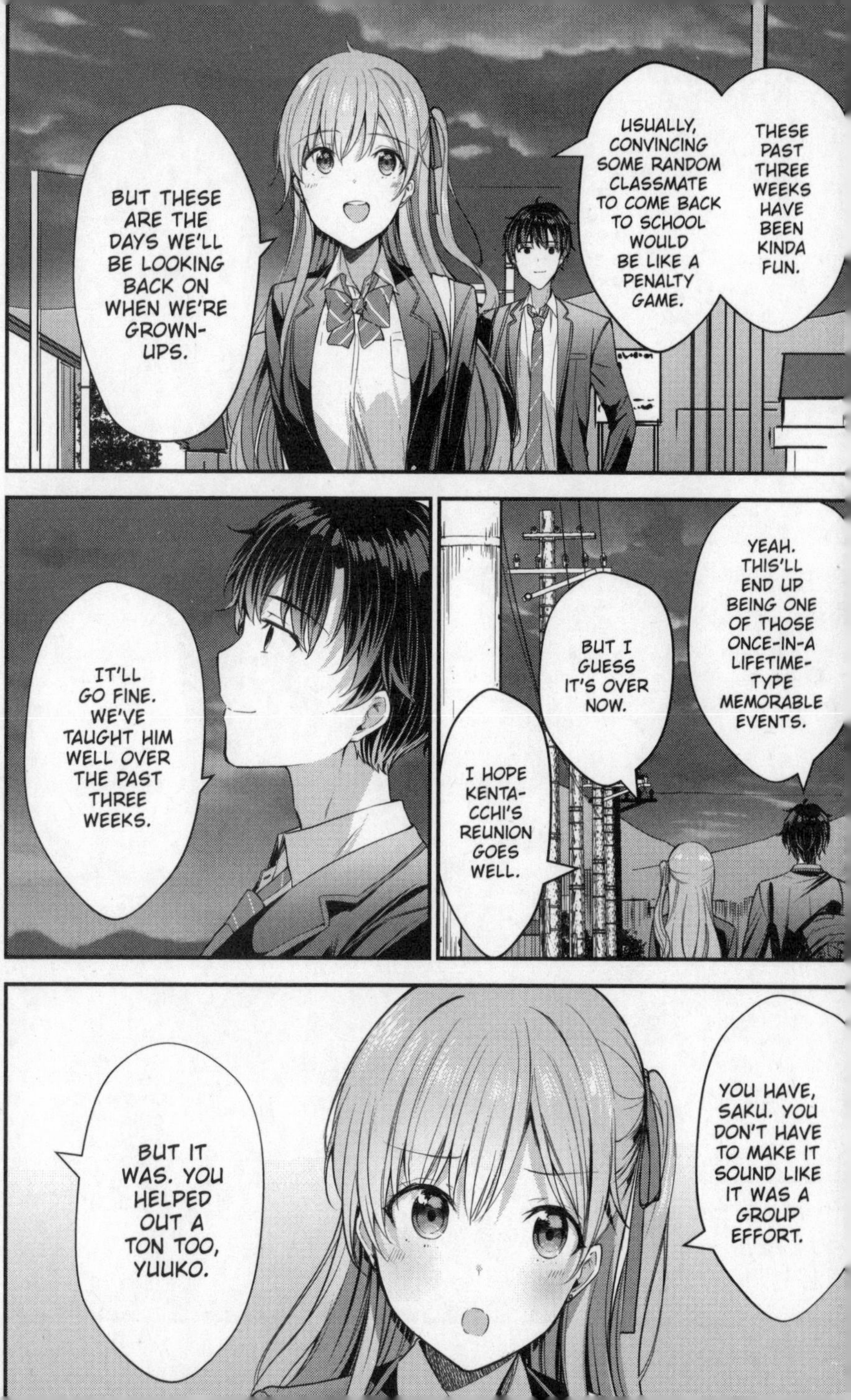
THESE PAST THREE WEEKS HAVE BEEN KINDA FUN.
USUALLY, CONVINCING SOME RANDOM CLASSMATE TO COME BACK TO SCHOOL WOULD BE LIKE A PENALTY GAME.
BUT THESE ARE THE DAYS WE'LL BE LOOKING BACK ON WHEN WE'RE GROWN-UPS.
YEAH. THIS'LL END UP BEING ONE OF THOSE ONCE-IN-A LIFETIME-TYPE MEMORABLE EVENTS.
BUT I GUESS IT'S OVER NOW.
I HOPE KENTA-CCHI'S REUNION GOES WELL.
IT'LL GO FINE. WE'VE TAUGHT HIM WELL OVER THE PAST THREE WEEKS.
YOU HAVE, SAKU. YOU DON'T HAVE TO MAKE IT SOUND LIKE IT WAS A GROUP EFFORT.
BUT IT WAS. YOU HELPED OUT A TON TOO, YUUKO.

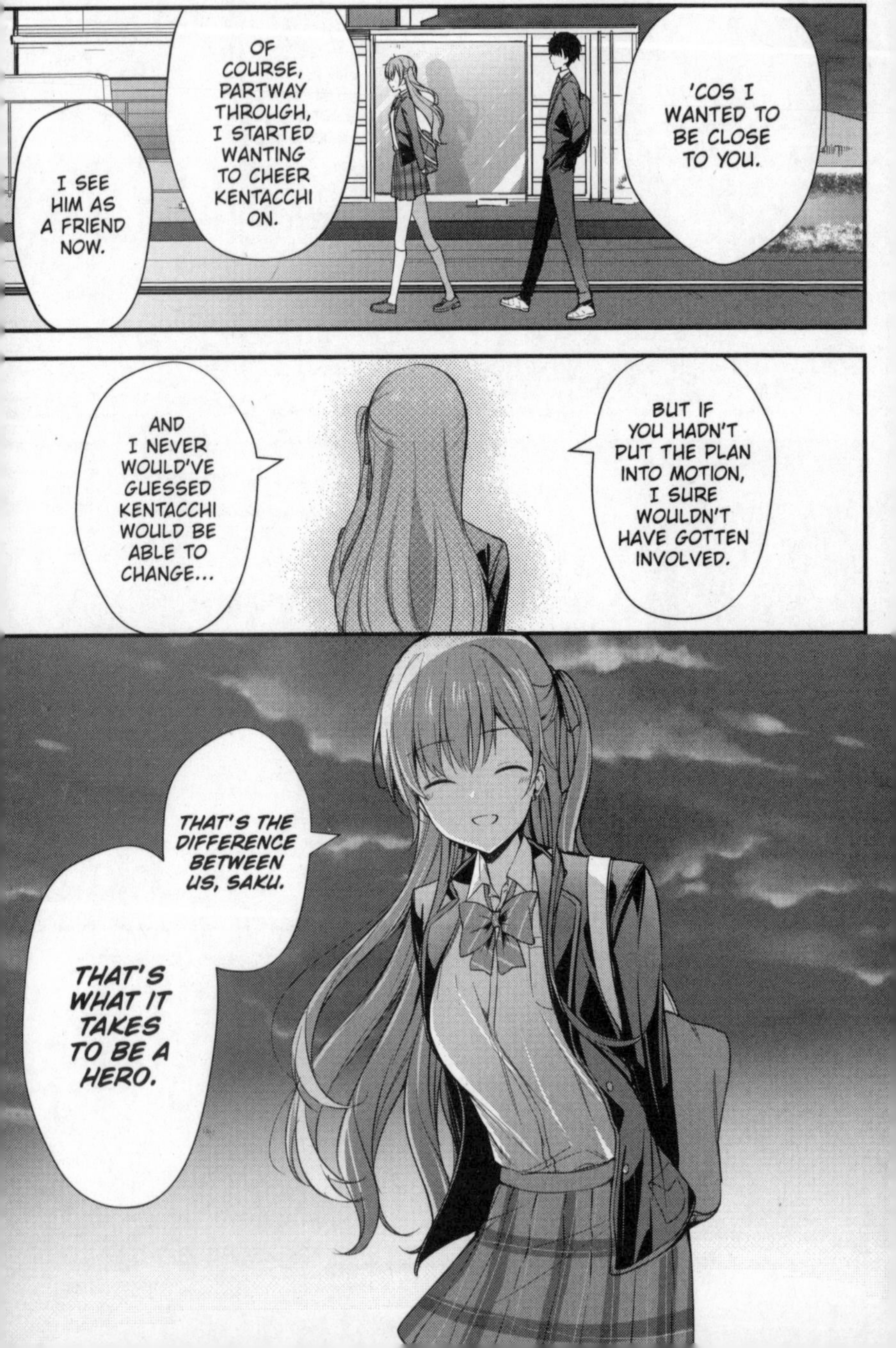
'COS I WANTED TO BE CLOSE TO YOU.
OF COURSE, PARTWAY THROUGH, I STARTED WANTING TO CHEER KENTACCHI ON.
I SEE HIM AS A FRIEND NOW.
BUT IF YOU HADN'T PUT THE PLAN INTO MOTION, I SURE WOULDN'T HAVE GOTTEN INVOLVED.
AND I NEVER WOULD'VE GUESSED KENTACCHI WOULD BE ABLE TO CHANGE...
THAT'S THE DIFFERENCE BETWEEN US, SAKU.
THAT'S WHAT IT TAKES TO BE A HERO.

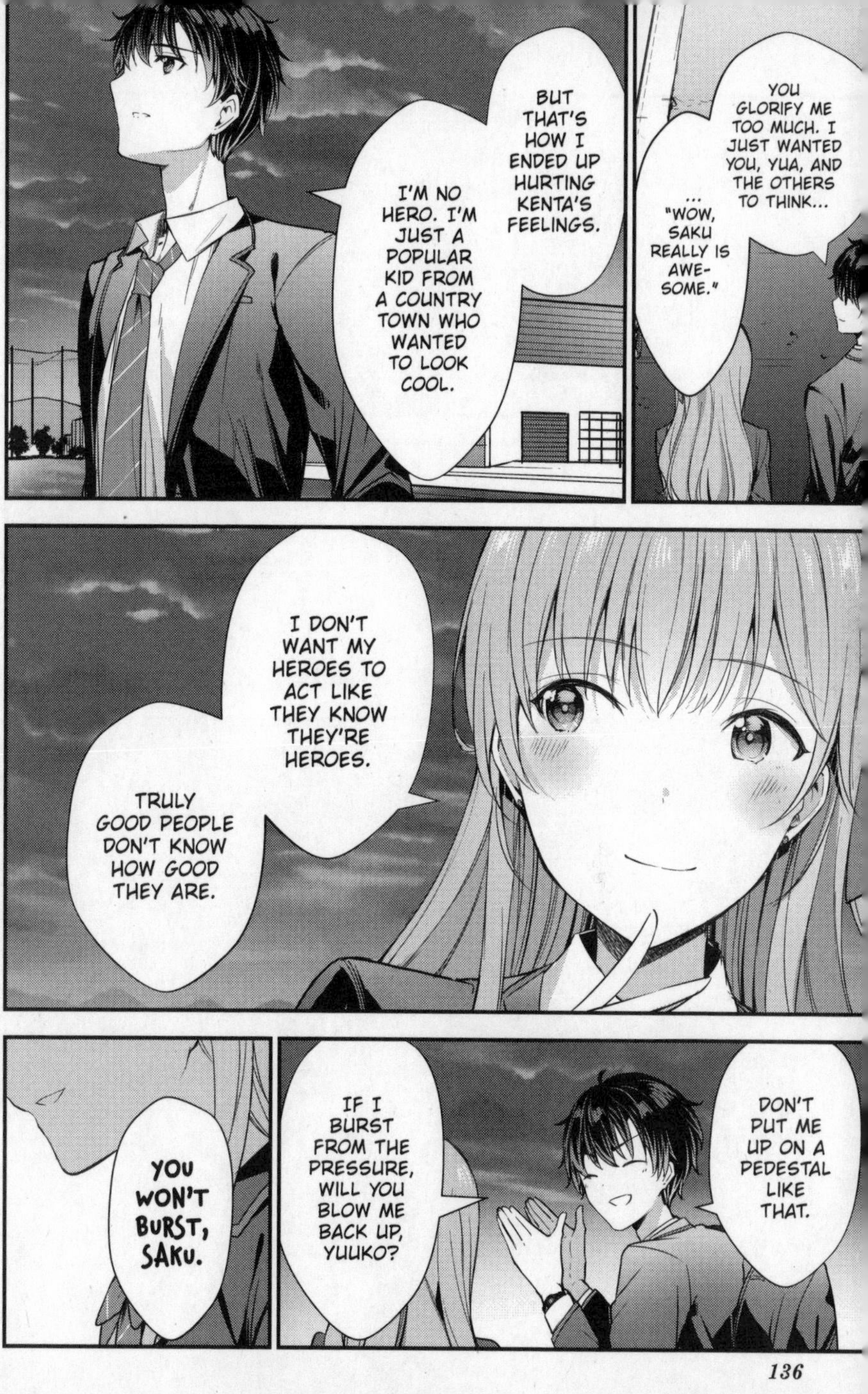
YOU GLORIFY ME TOO MUCH. I JUST WANTED YOU, YUA, AND THE OTHERS TO THINK...
... "WOW, SAKU REALLY IS AWE-SOME."
BUT THAT'S HOW I ENDED UP HURTING KENTA'S FEELINGS.
I'M NO HERO. I'M JUST A POPULAR KID FROM A COUNTRY TOWN WHO WANTED TO LOOK COOL.
I DON'T WANT MY HEROES TO ACT LIKE THEY KNOW THEY'RE HEROES.
TRULY GOOD PEOPLE DON'T KNOW HOW GOOD THEY ARE.
DON'T PUT ME UP ON A PEDESTAL LIKE THAT.
IF I BURST FROM THE PRESSURE, WILL YOU BLOW ME BACK UP, YUUKO?
YOU WON'T BURST, SAKU.

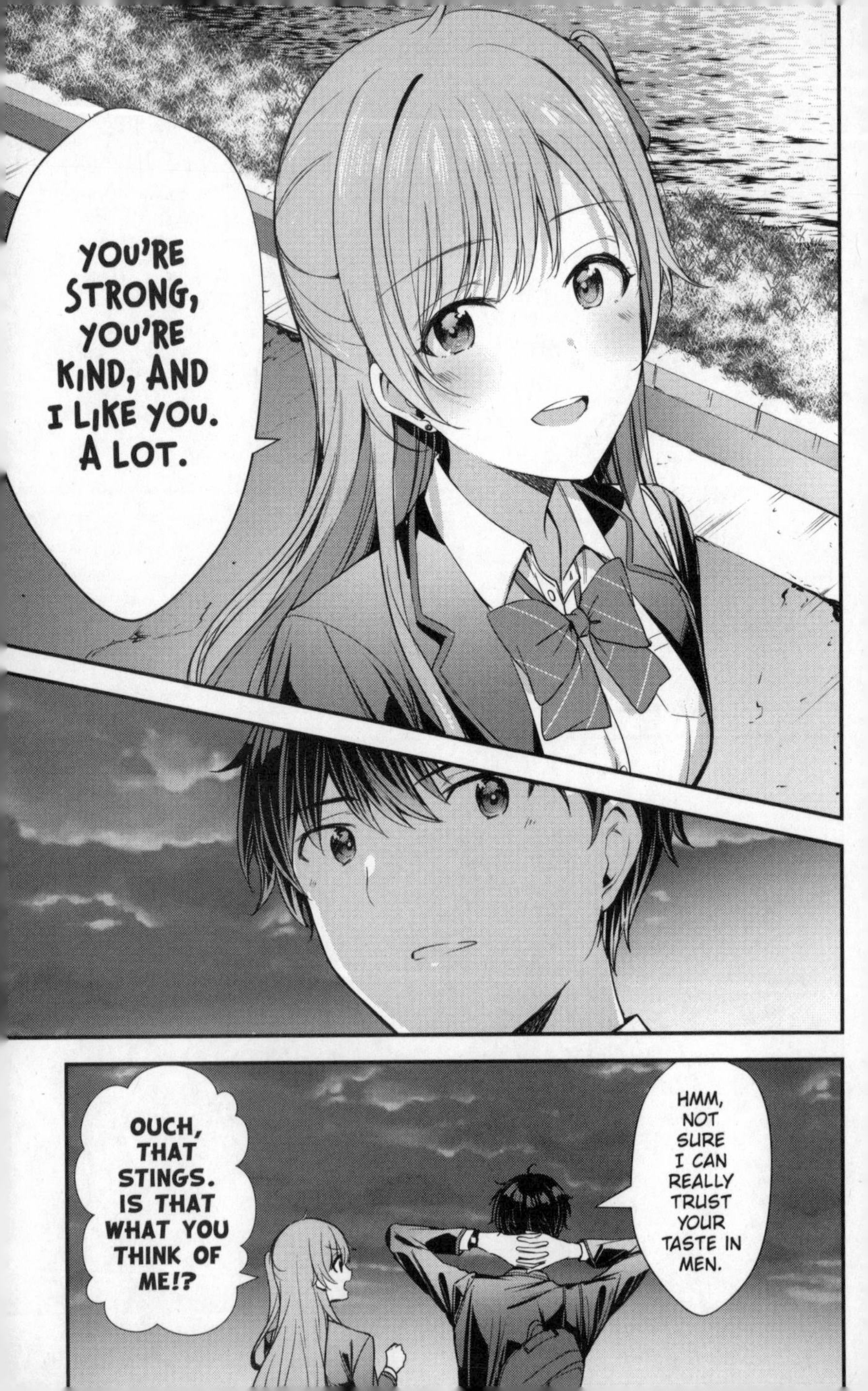
YOU'RE STRONG, YOU'RE KIND, AND I LIKE YOU. A LOT.
HMM, NOT SURE I CAN REALLY TRUST YOUR TASTE IN MEN.
OUCH, THAT STINGS. IS THAT WHAT YOU THINK OF ME!?

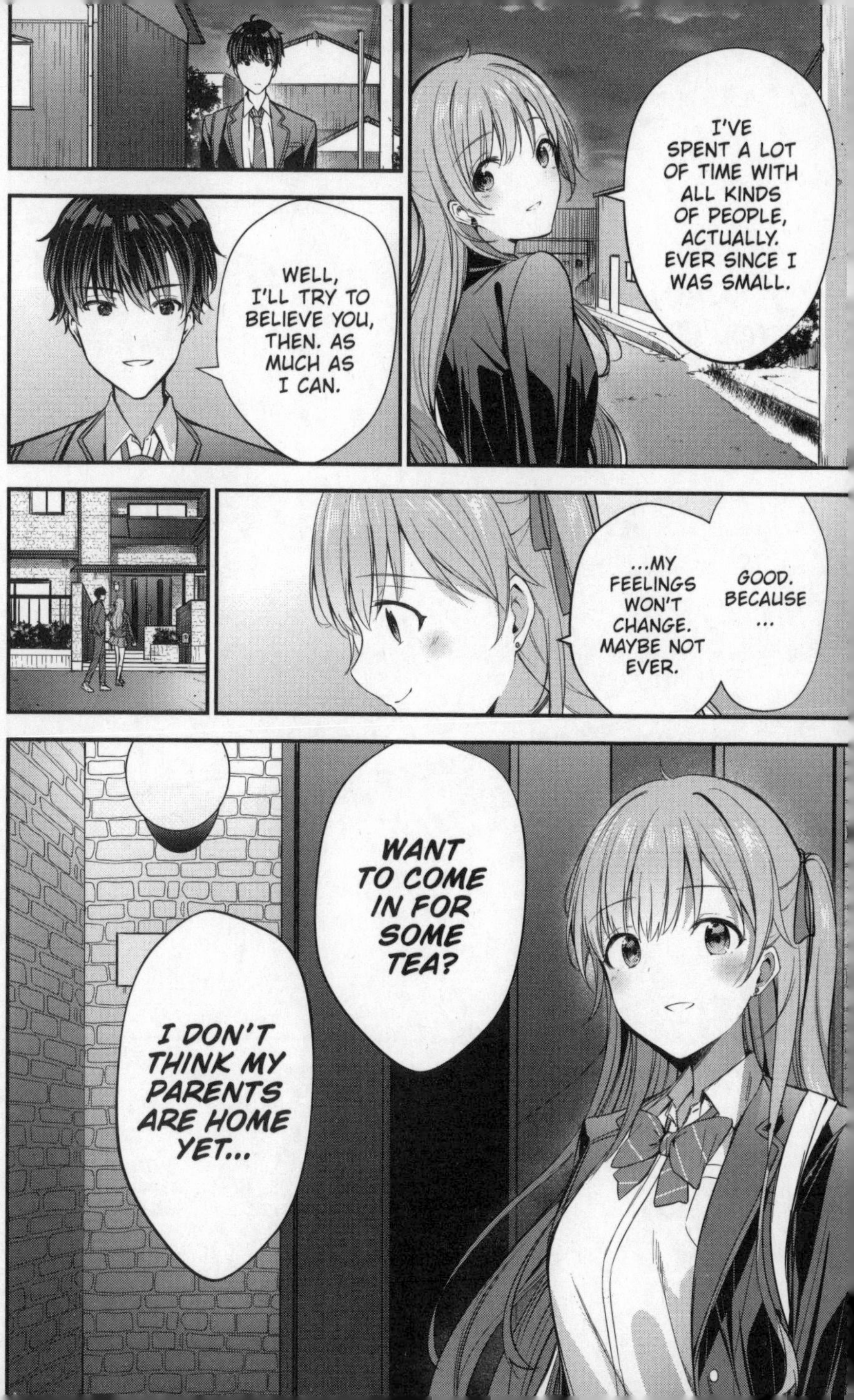
I'VE SPENT A LOT OF TIME WITH ALL KINDS OF PEOPLE, ACTUALLY. EVER SINCE I WAS SMALL.
WELL, I'LL TRY TO BELIEVE YOU, THEN. AS MUCH AS I CAN.
GOOD. BECAUSE ...
...MY FEELINGS WON'T CHANGE. MAYBE NOT EVER.
WANT TO COME IN FOR SOME TEA?
I DON'T THINK MY PARENTS ARE HOME YET...

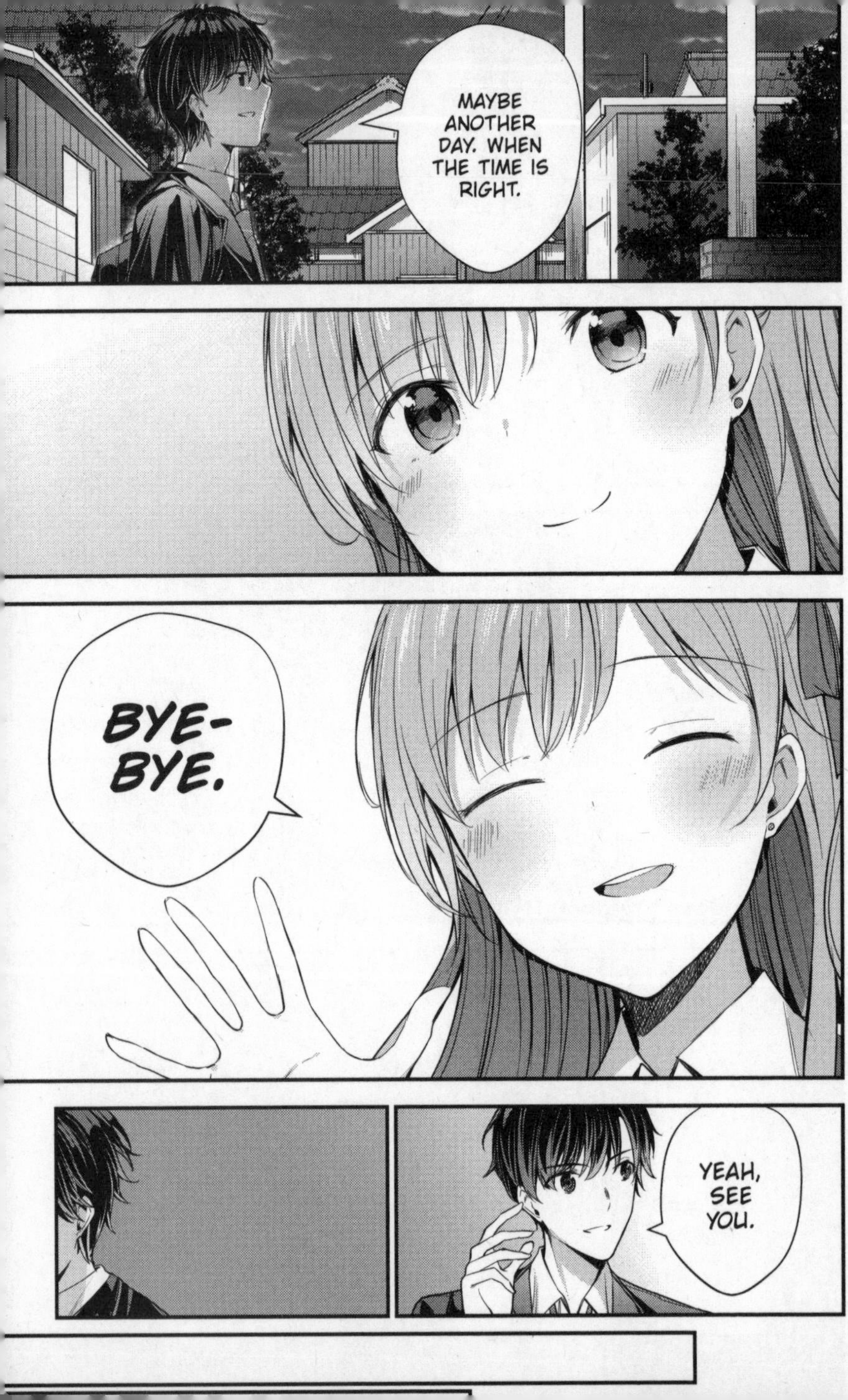
MAYBE ANOTHER DAY. WHEN THE TIME IS RIGHT.
BYE-BYE.
YEAH, SEE YOU.

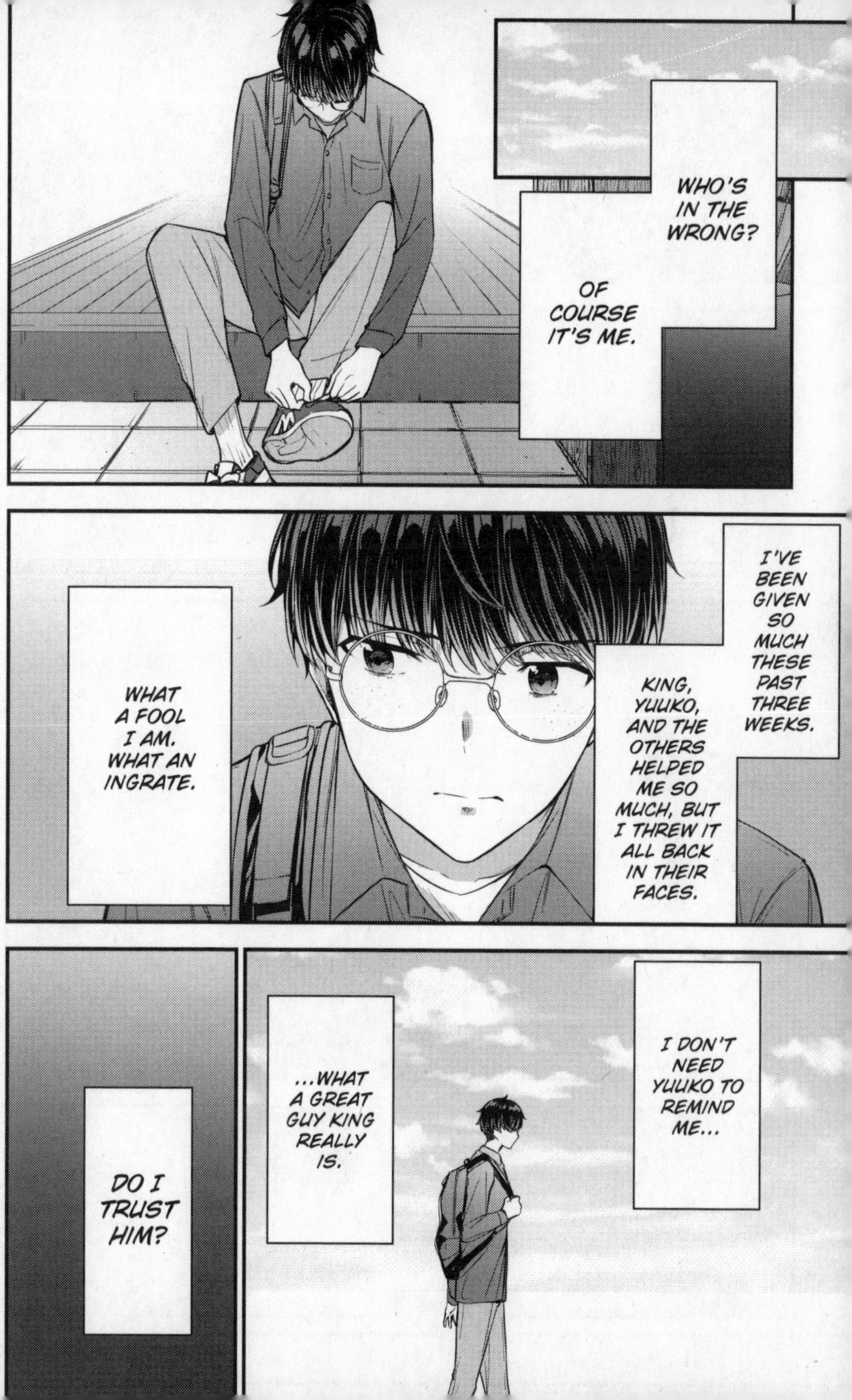
WHO'S IN THE WRONG?
OF COURSE IT'S ME.
I'VE BEEN GIVEN SO MUCH THESE PAST THREE WEEKS.
KING, YUUKO, AND THE OTHERS HELPED ME SO MUCH, BUT I THREW IT ALL BACK IN THEIR FACES.
WHAT A FOOL I AM. WHAT AN INGRATE.
I DON'T NEED YUUKO TO REMIND ME...
...WHAT A GREAT GUY KING REALLY IS.
DO I TRUST HIM?

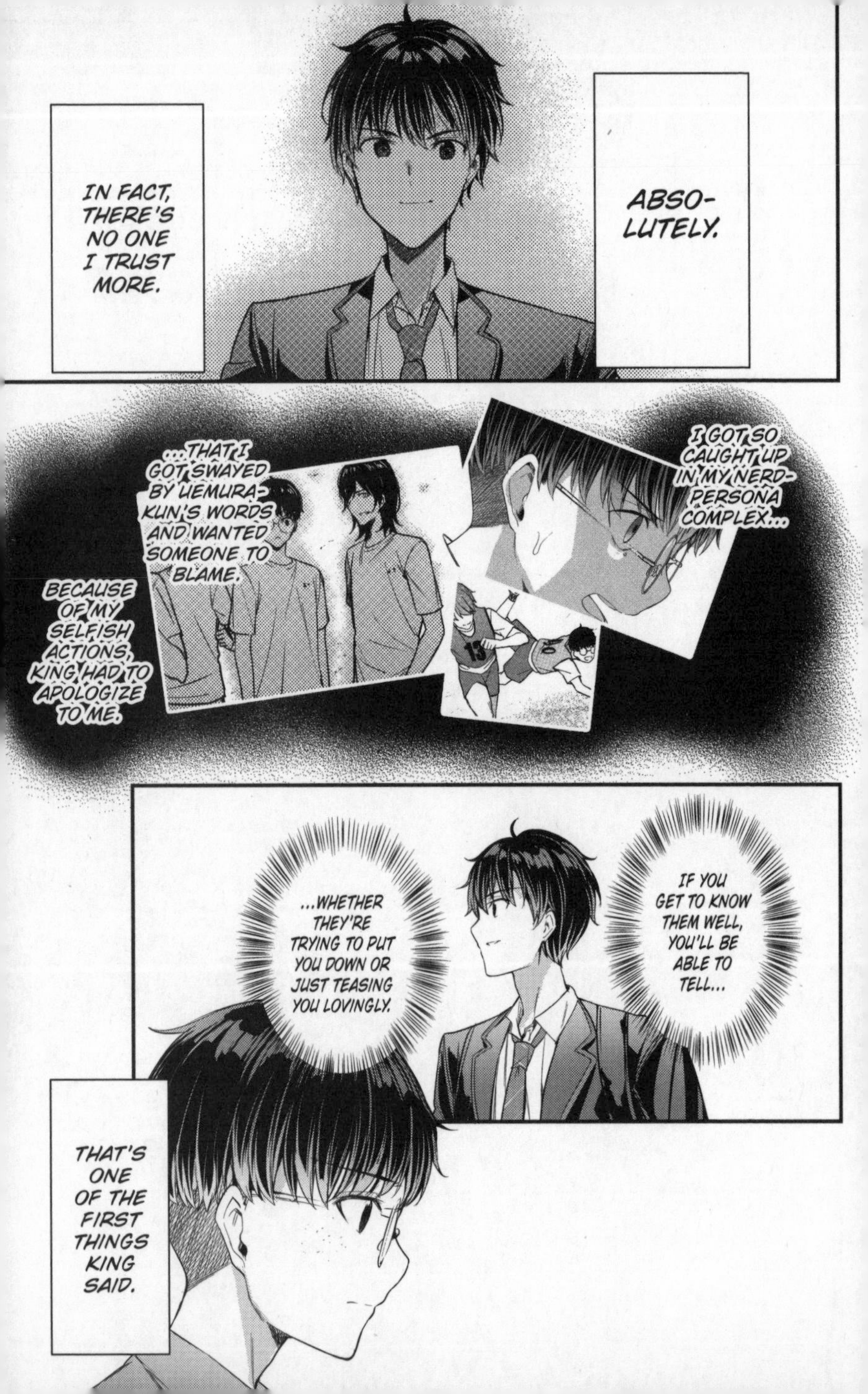
ABSO-LUTELY.
IN FACT, THERE'S NO ONE I TRUST MORE.
I GOT SO CAUGHT UP IN MY NERD-PERSONA COMPLEX...
...THAT I GOT SWAYED BY UEMURA-KUN'S WORDS AND WANTED SOMEONE TO BLAME.
BECAUSE OF MY SELFISH ACTIONS, KING HAD TO APOLOGIZE TO ME.
IF YOU GET TO KNOW THEM WELL, YOU'LL BE ABLE TO TELL...
...WHETHER THEY'RE TRYING TO PUT YOU DOWN OR JUST TEASING YOU LOVINGLY.
THAT'S ONE OF THE FIRST THINGS KING SAID.

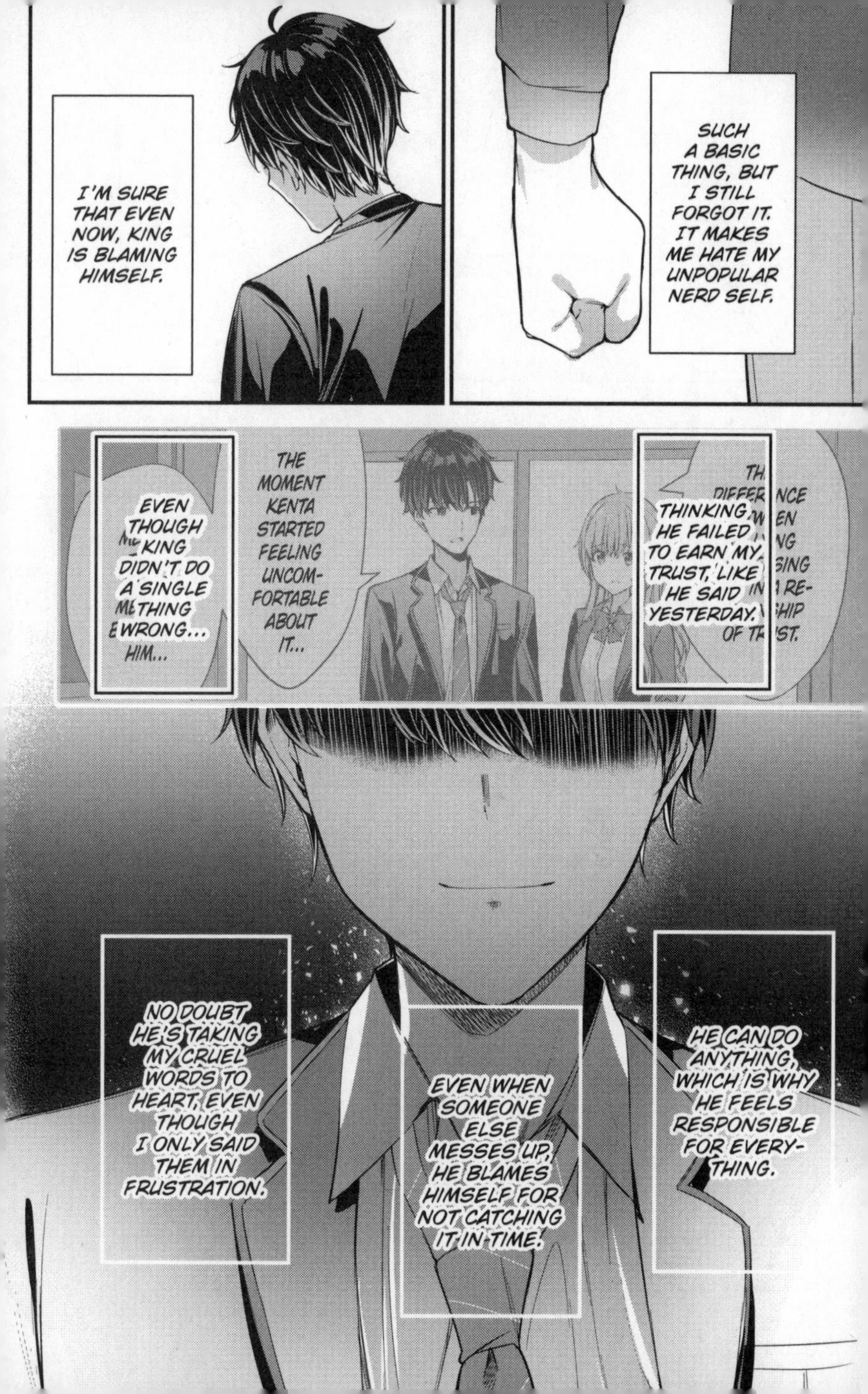
SUCH A BASIC THING, BUT I STILL FORGOT IT. IT MAKES ME HATE MY UNPOPULAR NERD SELF.
I'M SURE THAT EVEN NOW, KING IS BLAMING HIMSELF.
THINKING HE FAILED TO EARN MY TRUST, LIKE HE SAID YESTERDAY.
THE MOMENT KENTA STARTED FEELING UNCOM-FORTABLE ABOUT IT...
EVEN THOUGH KING DIDN'T DO A SINGLE THING WRONG...
HE CAN DO ANYTHING, WHICH IS WHY HE FEELS RESPONSIBLE FOR EVERY-THING.
EVEN WHEN SOMEONE ELSE MESSES UP, HE BLAMES HIMSELF FOR NOT CATCHING IT IN TIME.
NO DOUBT HE'S TAKING MY CRUEL WORDS TO HEART, EVEN THOUGH I ONLY SAID THEM IN FRUSTRATION.

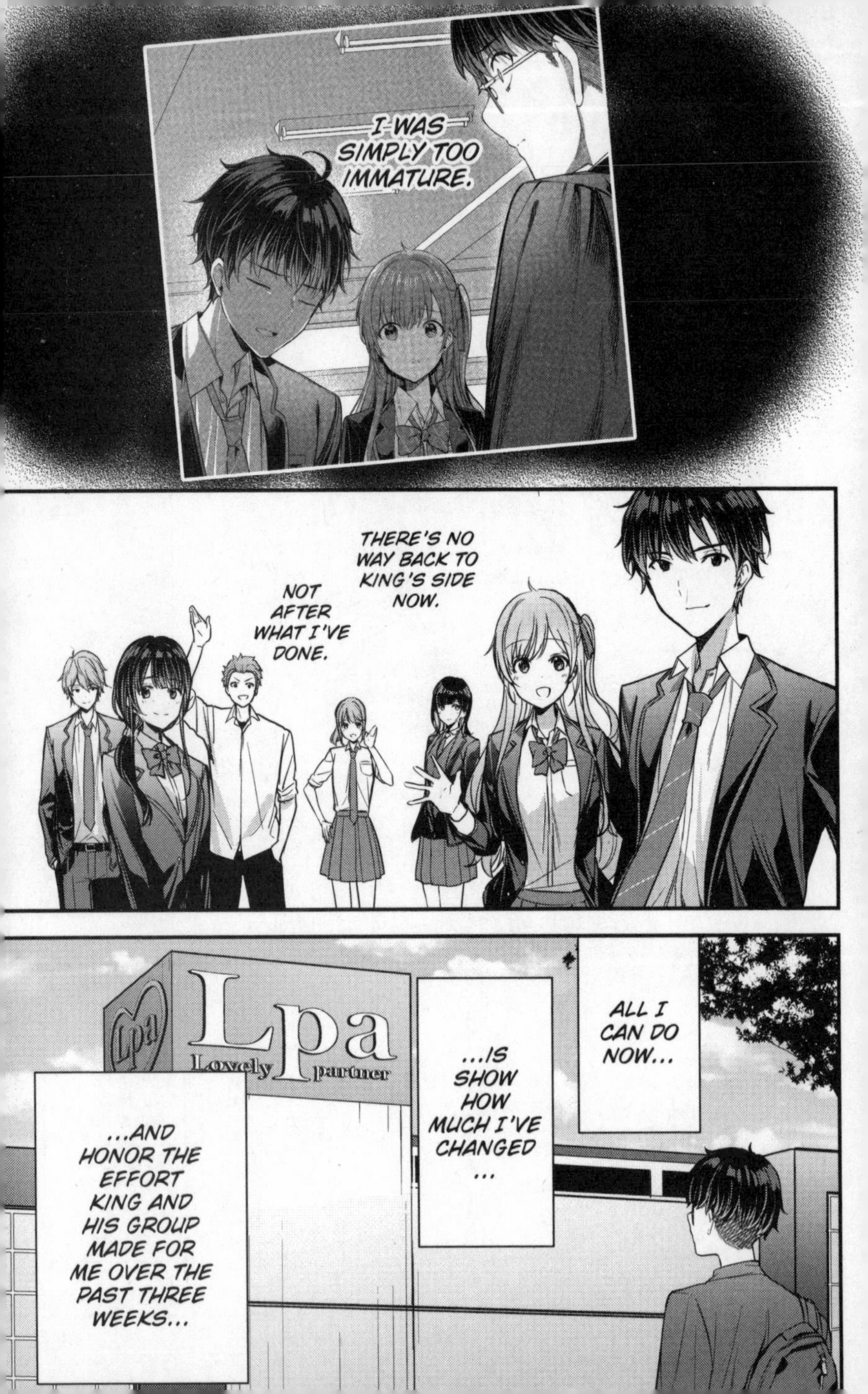
I WAS SIMPLY TOO IMMATURE.
THERE'S NO WAY BACK TO KING'S SIDE NOW.
NOT AFTER WHAT I'VE DONE.
ALL I CAN DO NOW...
...IS SHOW HOW MUCH I'VE CHANGED ...
Lpa
Lovely partner
...AND HONOR THE EFFORT KING AND HIS GROUP MADE FOR ME OVER THE PAST THREE WEEKS...

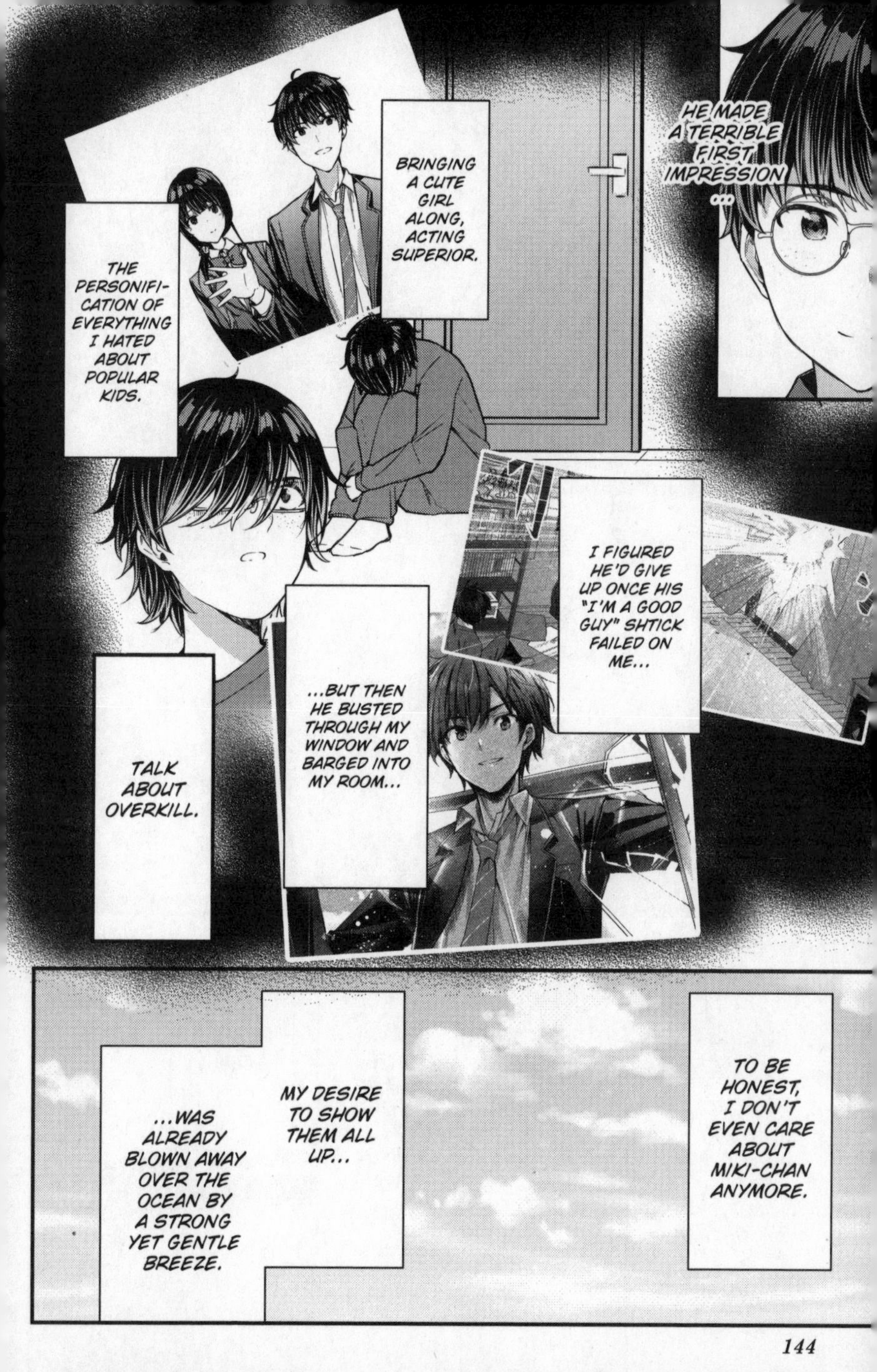
HE MADE A TERRIBLE FIRST IMPRESSION...
BRINGING A CUTE GIRL ALONG, ACTING SUPERIOR.
THE PERSONIFICATION OF EVERYTHING I HATED ABOUT POPULAR KIDS.
I FIGURED HE'D GIVE UP ONCE HIS "I'M A GOOD GUY" SHTICK FAILED ON ME...
...BUT THEN HE BUSTED THROUGH MY WINDOW AND BARGED INTO MY ROOM...
TALK ABOUT OVERKILL.
TO BE HONEST, I DON'T EVEN CARE ABOUT MIKI-CHAN ANYMORE.
MY DESIRE TO SHOW THEM ALL UP...
...WAS ALREADY BLOWN AWAY OVER THE OCEAN BY A STRONG YET GENTLE BREEZE.

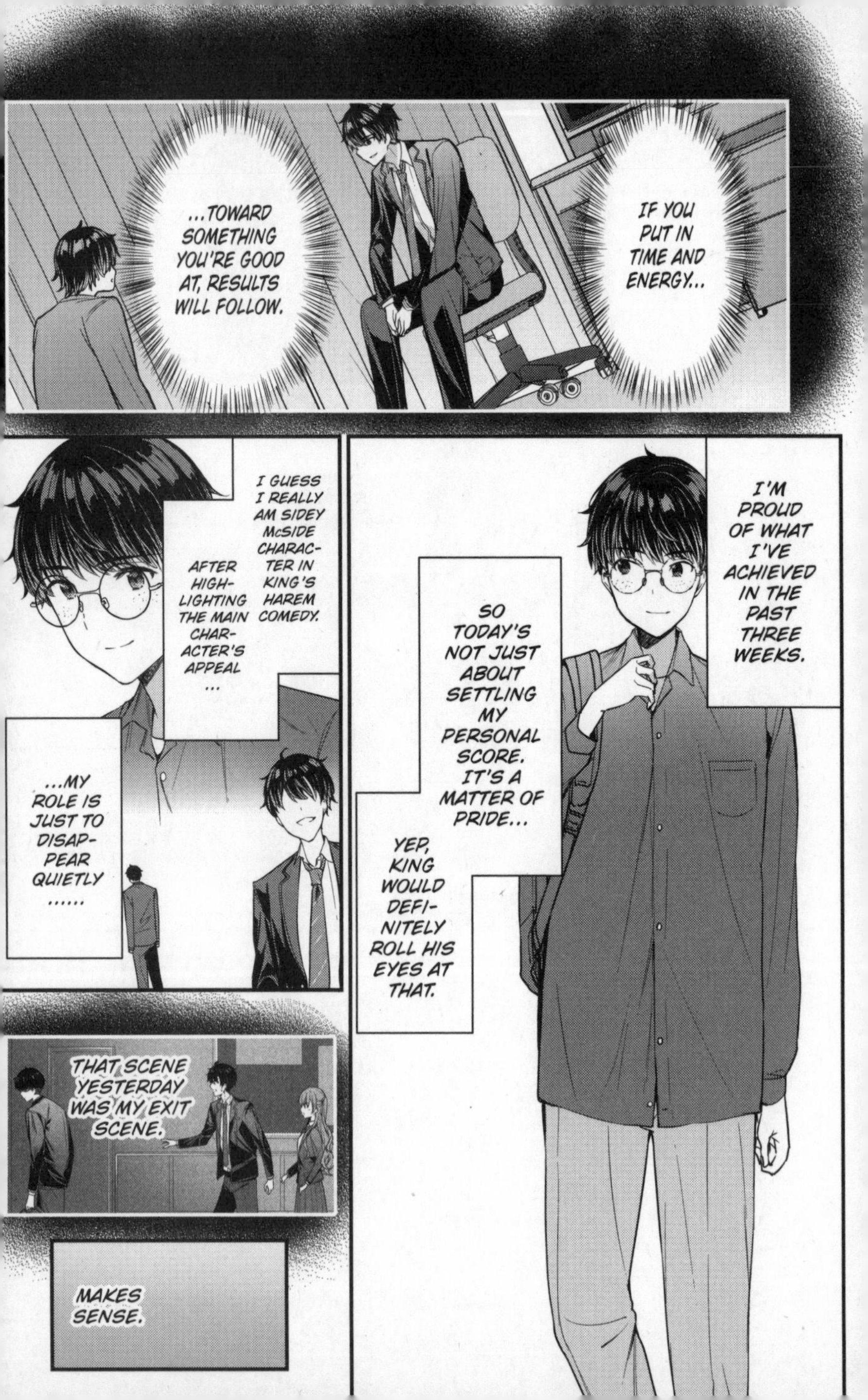
IF YOU PUT IN TIME AND ENERGY...
...TOWARD SOMETHING YOU'RE GOOD AT, RESULTS WILL FOLLOW.
I'M PROUD OF WHAT I'VE ACHIEVED IN THE PAST THREE WEEKS.
SO TODAY'S NOT JUST ABOUT SETTLING MY PERSONAL SCORE. IT'S A MATTER OF PRIDE...
YEP, KING WOULD DEFINITELY ROLL HIS EYES AT THAT.
I GUESS I REALLY AM SIDEY McSIDE CHARACTER IN KING'S HAREM COMEDY.
AFTER HIGHLIGHTING THE MAIN CHARACTER'S APPEAL...
...MY ROLE IS JUST TO DISAPPEAR QUIETLY......
THAT SCENE YESTERDAY WAS MY EXIT SCENE.
MAKES SENSE.

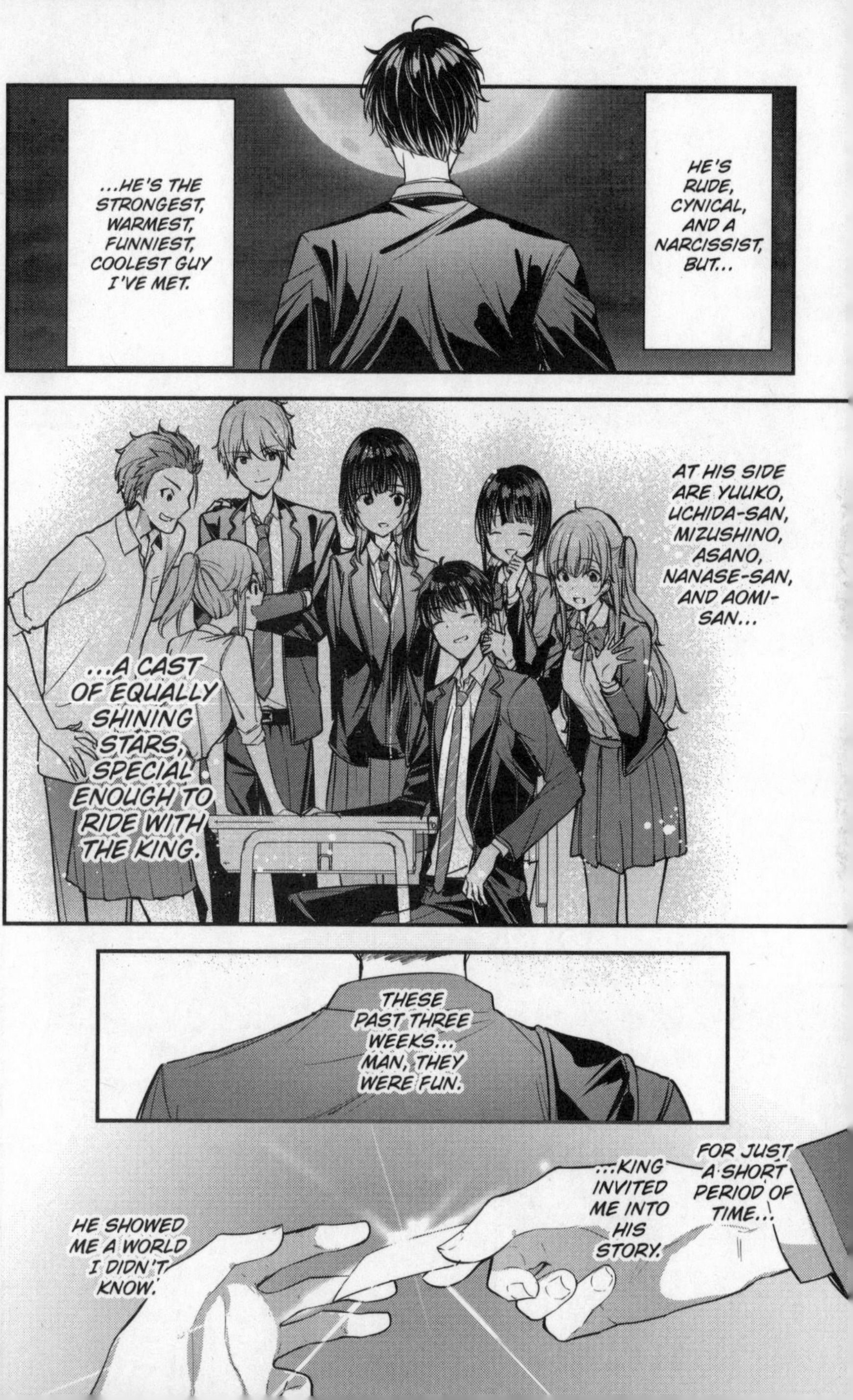
HE'S RUDE, CYNICAL, AND A NARCISSIST, BUT...
...HE'S THE STRONGEST, WARMEST, FUNNIEST, COOLEST GUY I'VE MET.
AT HIS SIDE ARE YUUKO, UCHIDA-SAN, MIZUSHINO, ASANO, NANASE-SAN, AND AOMI-SAN...
...A CAST OF EQUALLY SHINING STARS, SPECIAL ENOUGH TO RIDE WITH THE KING.
THESE PAST THREE WEEKS... MAN, THEY WERE FUN.
FOR JUST A SHORT PERIOD OF TIME...
...KING INVITED ME INTO HIS STORY.
HE SHOWED ME A WORLD I DIDN'T KNOW.

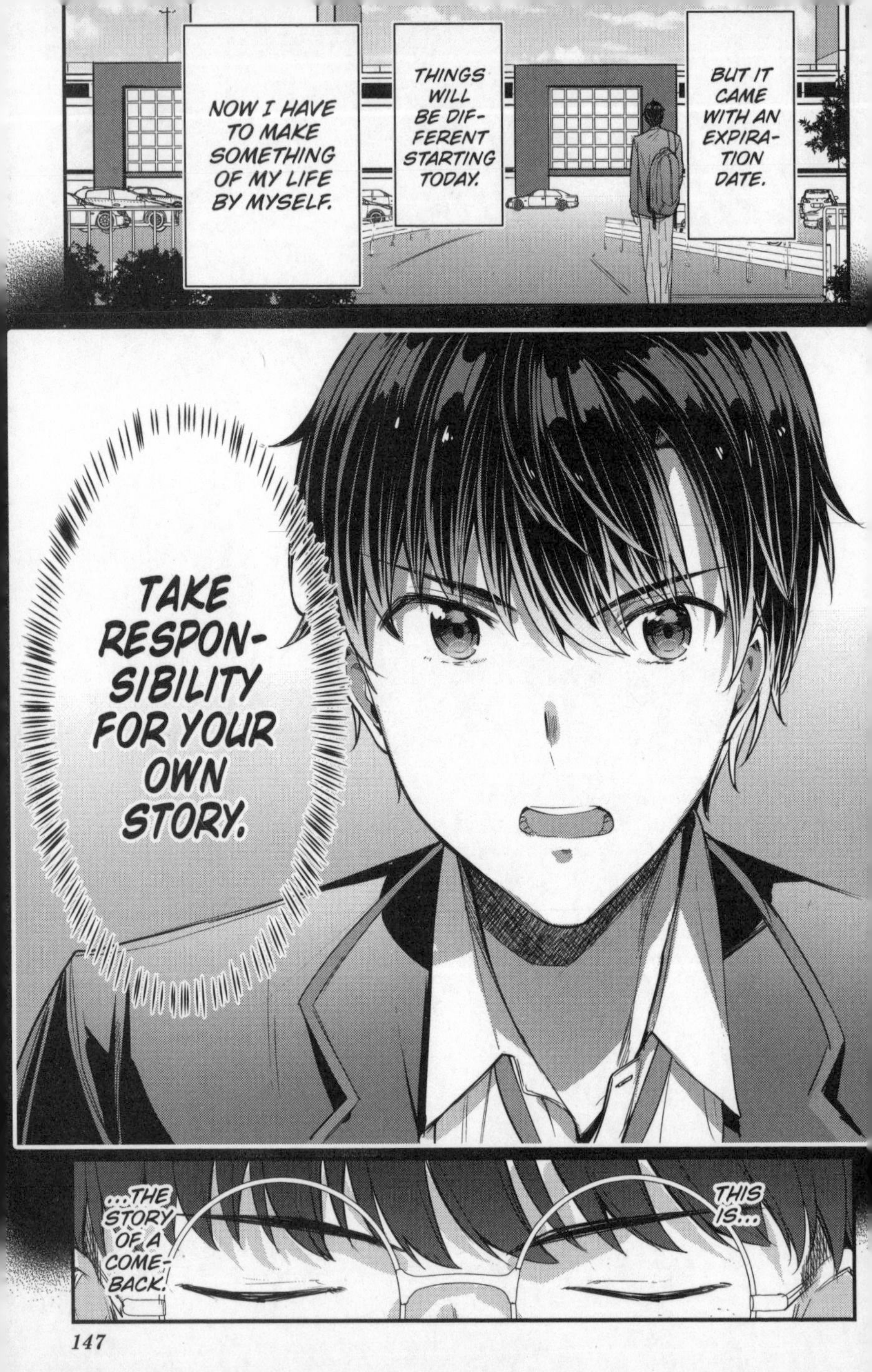
BUT IT CAME WITH AN EXPIRATION DATE.
THINGS WILL BE DIFFERENT STARTING TODAY.
NOW I HAVE TO MAKE SOMETHING OF MY LIFE BY MYSELF.
TAKE RESPONSIBILITY FOR YOUR OWN STORY.
THIS IS...
...THE STORY OF A COMEBACK.

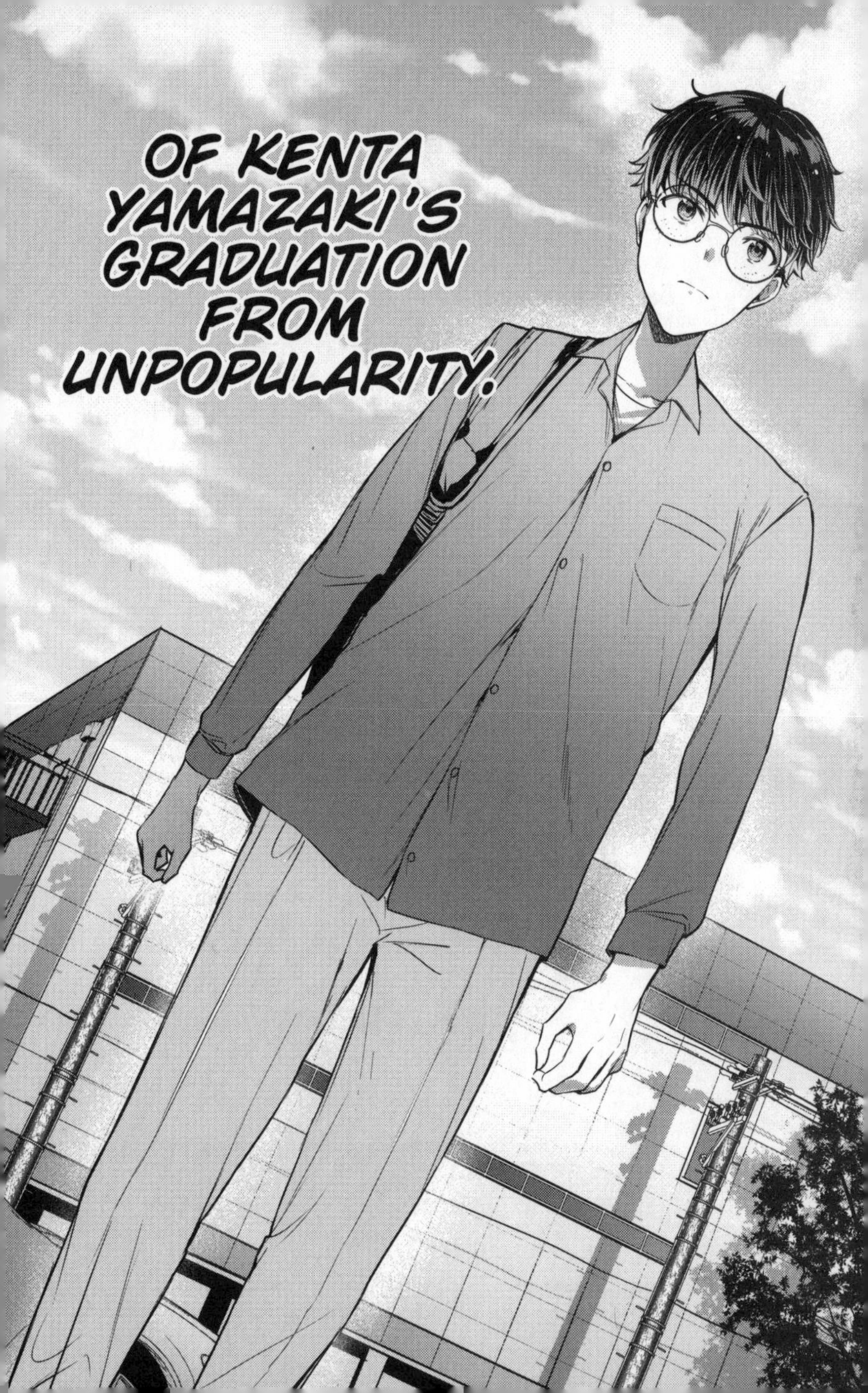
OF KENTA YAMAZAKI'S GRADUATION FROM UNPOPULARITY.

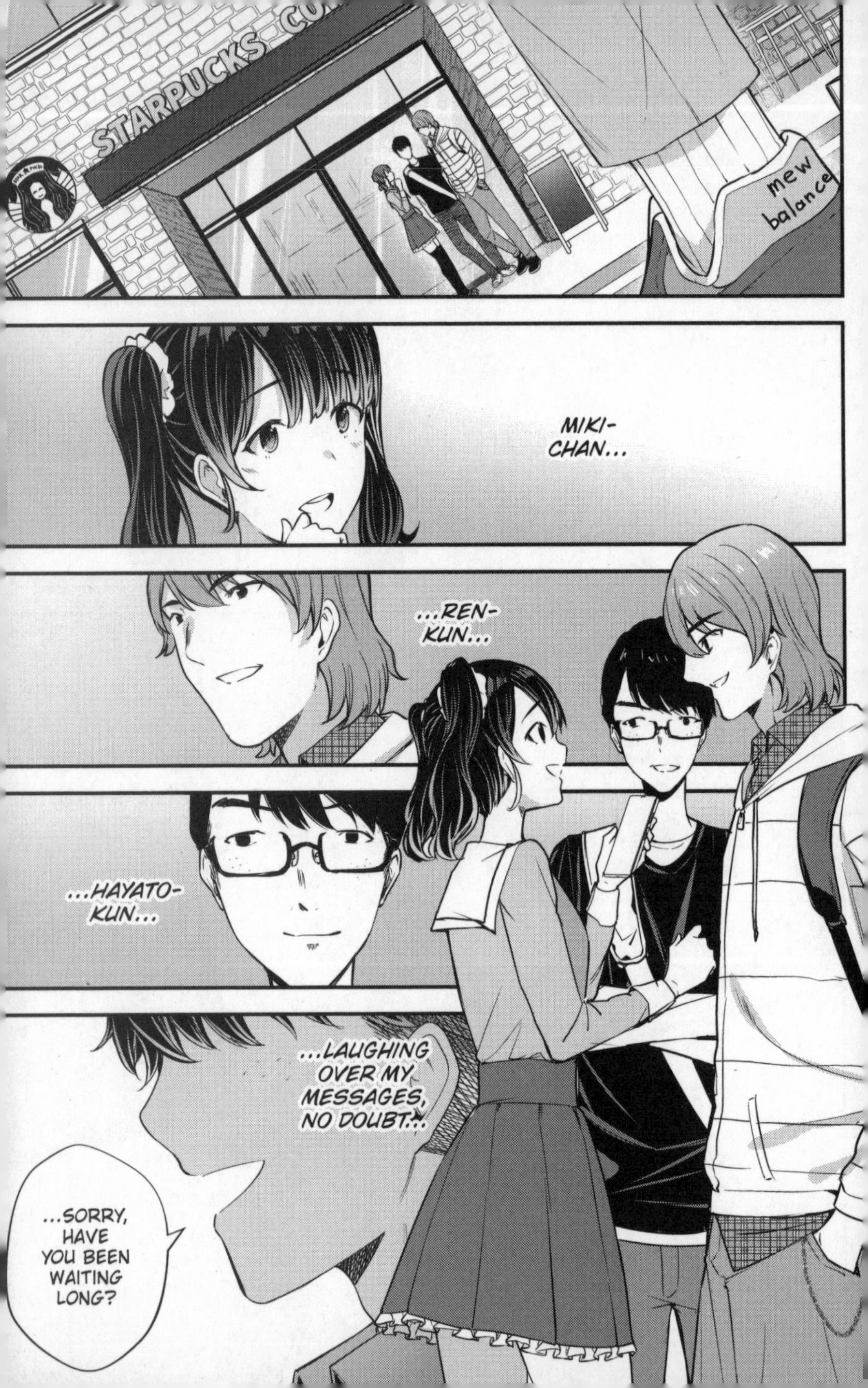
STARPUCKS CO
mew balance
MIKI-CHAN...
...REN-KUN...
...HAYATO-KUN...
...LAUGHING OVER MY MESSAGES, NO DOUBT...
...SORRY, HAVE YOU BEEN WAITING LONG?

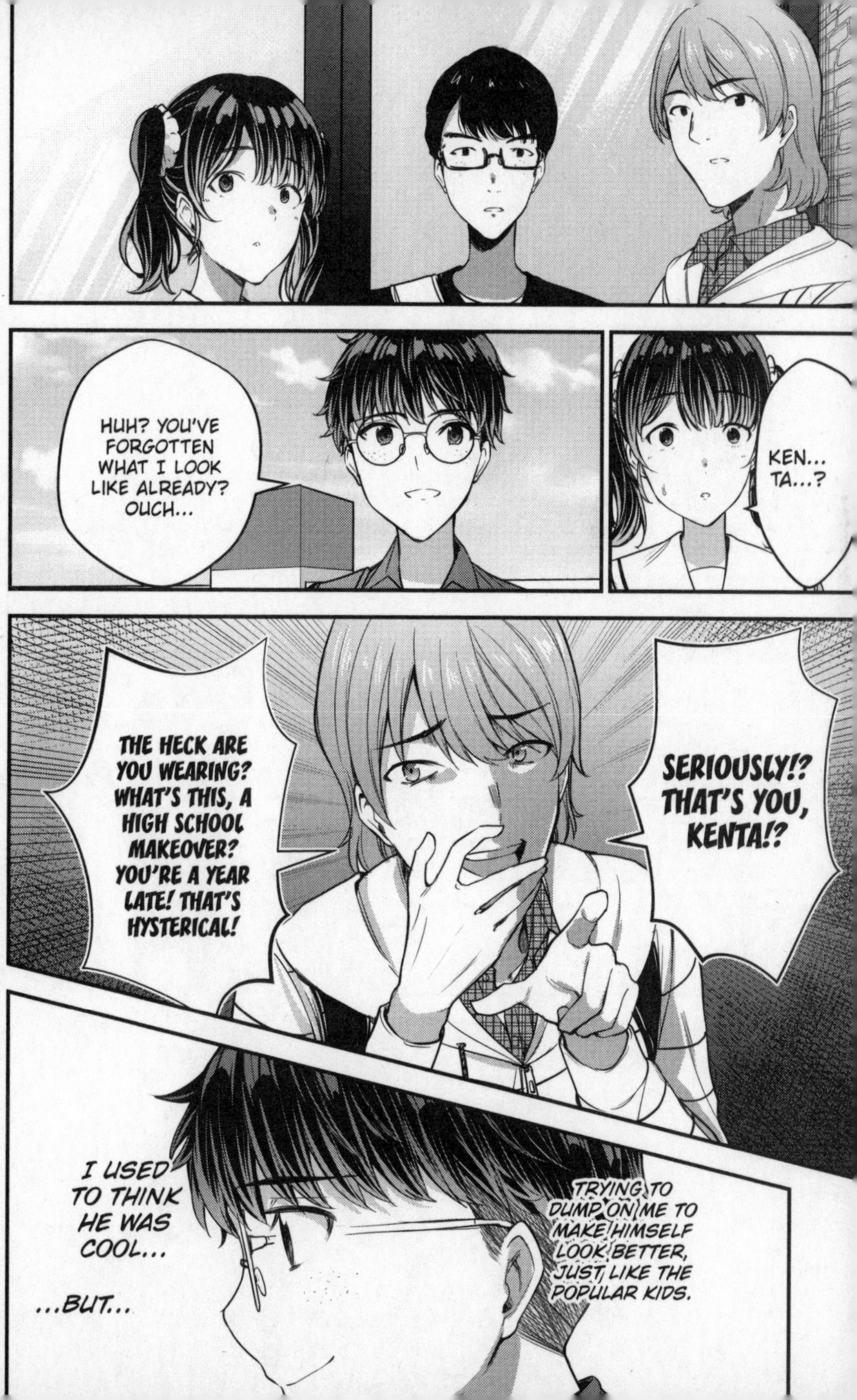
KEN... TA...?
HUH? YOU'VE FORGOTTEN WHAT I LOOK LIKE ALREADY? OUCH...
SERIOUSLY!? THAT'S YOU, KENTA!?
THE HECK ARE YOU WEARING? WHAT'S THIS, A HIGH SCHOOL MAKEOVER? YOU'RE A YEAR LATE! THAT'S HYSTERICAL!
TRYING TO DUMP ON ME TO MAKE HIMSELF LOOK BETTER, JUST LIKE THE POPULAR KIDS.
I USED TO THINK HE WAS COOL...
...BUT...

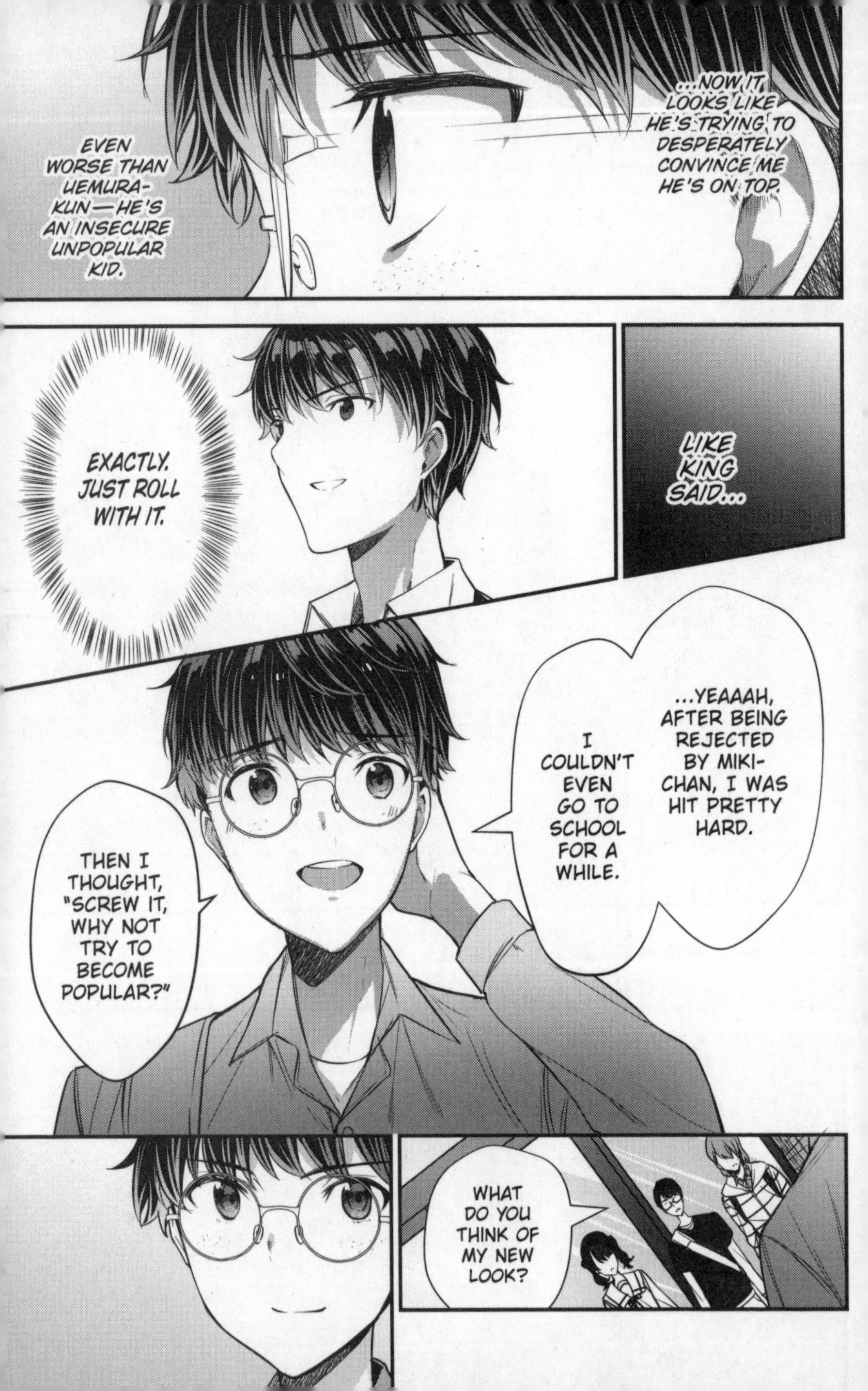
...NOW IT LOOKS LIKE HE'S TRYING TO DESPERATELY CONVINCE ME HE'S ON TOP.
EVEN WORSE THAN UEMURA-KUN—HE'S AN INSECURE UNPOPULAR KID.
LIKE KING SAID...
EXACTLY. JUST ROLL WITH IT.
...YEAAAH, AFTER BEING REJECTED BY MIKI-CHAN, I WAS HIT PRETTY HARD.
I COULDN'T EVEN GO TO SCHOOL FOR A WHILE.
THEN I THOUGHT, "SCREW IT, WHY NOT TRY TO BECOME POPULAR?"
WHAT DO YOU THINK OF MY NEW LOOK?

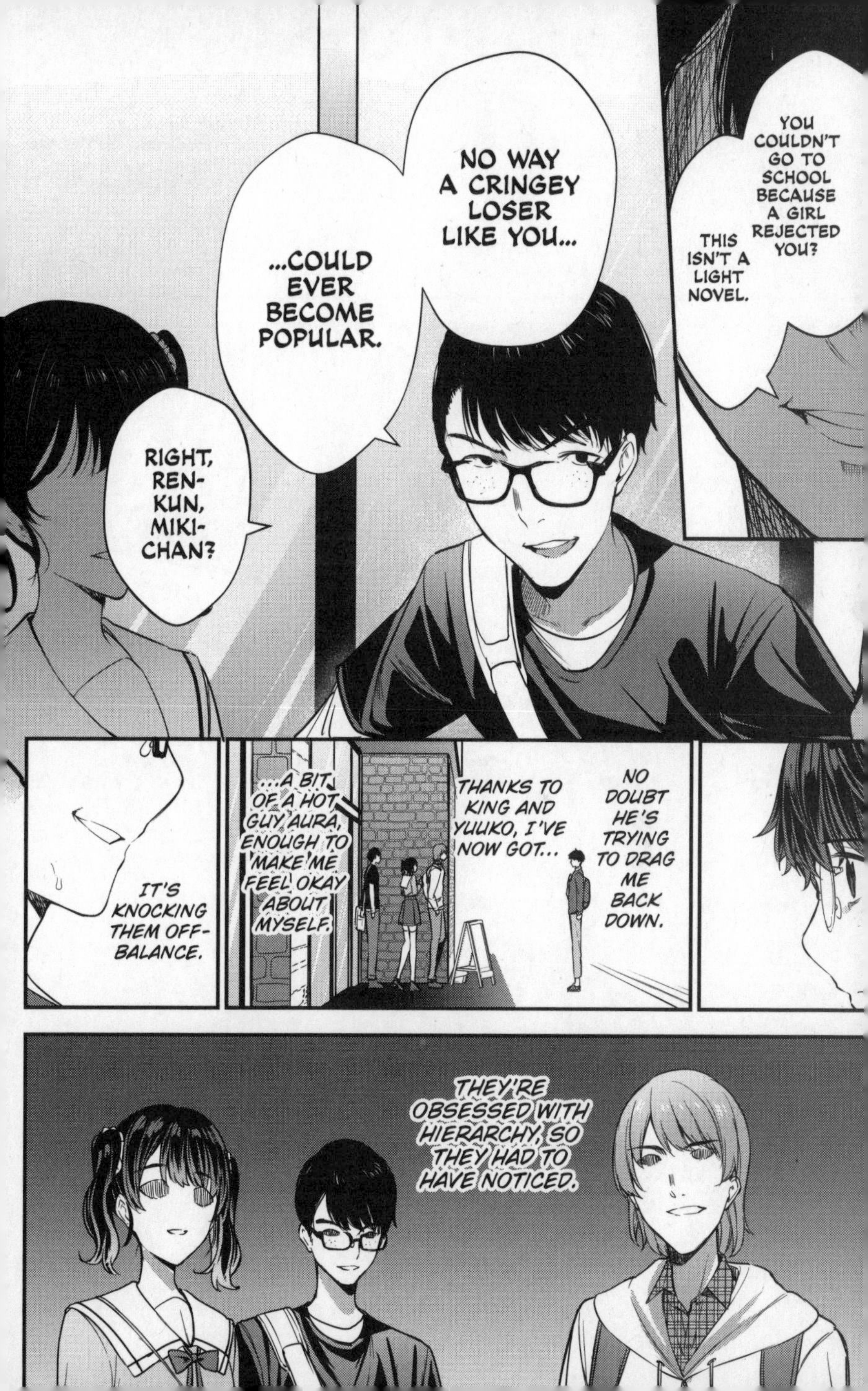
YOU COULDN'T GO TO SCHOOL BECAUSE A GIRL REJECTED YOU?
THIS ISN'T A LIGHT NOVEL.
NO WAY A CRINGEY LOSER LIKE YOU...
...COULD EVER BECOME POPULAR.
RIGHT, REN-KUN, MIKI-CHAN?
NO DOUBT HE'S TRYING TO DRAG ME BACK DOWN.
THANKS TO KING AND YUUKO, I'VE NOW GOT...
...A BIT OF A HOT GUY AURA, ENOUGH TO MAKE ME FEEL OKAY ABOUT MYSELF.
IT'S KNOCKING THEM OFF-BALANCE.
THEY'RE OBSESSED WITH HIERARCHY, SO THEY HAD TO HAVE NOTICED.

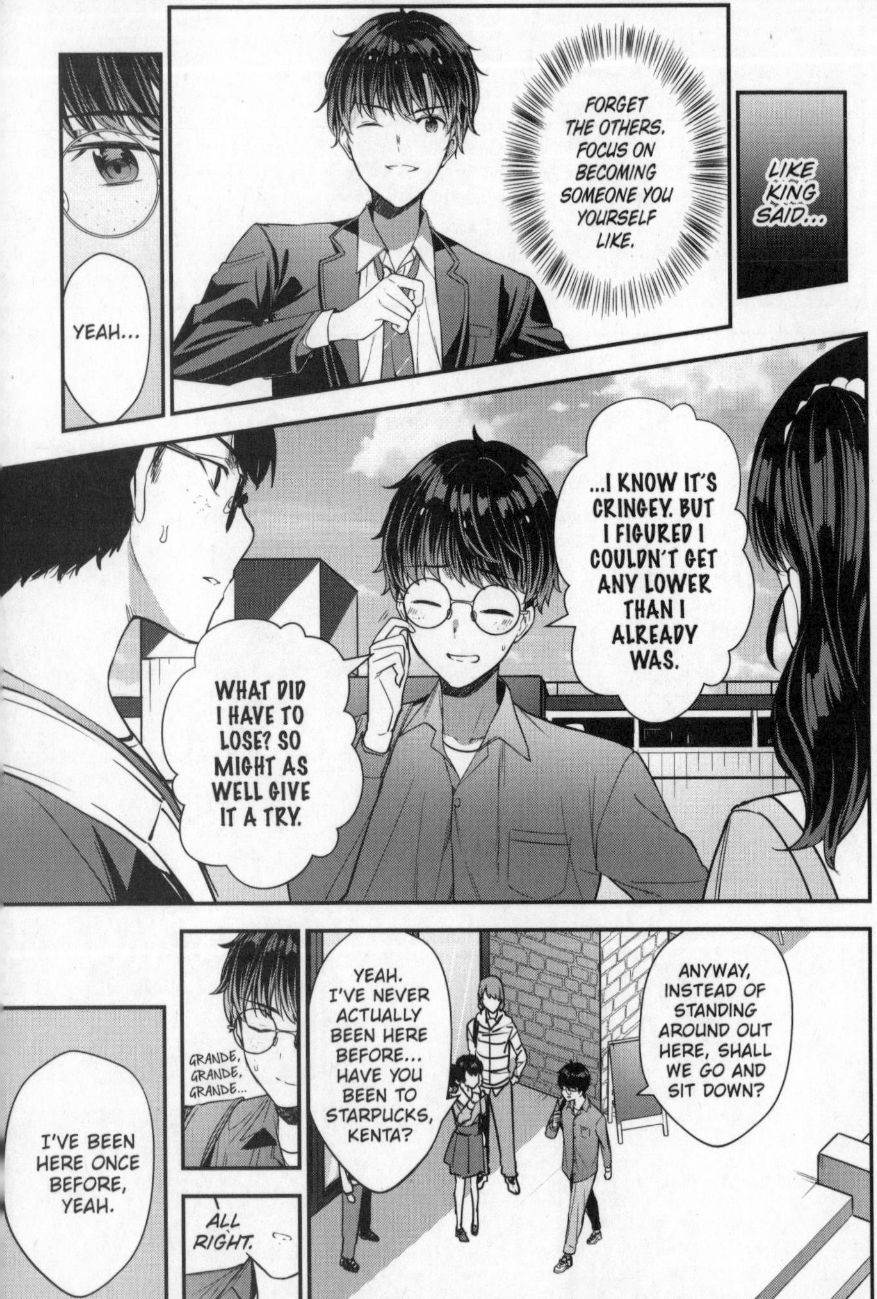
LIKE KING SAID...
FORGET THE OTHERS. FOCUS ON BECOMING SOMEONE YOU YOURSELF LIKE.
YEAH...
...I KNOW IT'S CRINGEY. BUT I FIGURED I COULDN'T GET ANY LOWER THAN I ALREADY WAS.
WHAT DID I HAVE TO LOSE? SO MIGHT AS WELL GIVE IT A TRY.
ANYWAY, INSTEAD OF STANDING AROUND OUT HERE, SHALL WE GO AND SIT DOWN?
YEAH. I'VE NEVER ACTUALLY BEEN HERE BEFORE... HAVE YOU BEEN TO STARPUCKS, KENTA?
GRANDE, GRANDE, GRANDE...
ALL RIGHT.
I'VE BEEN HERE ONCE BEFORE, YEAH.

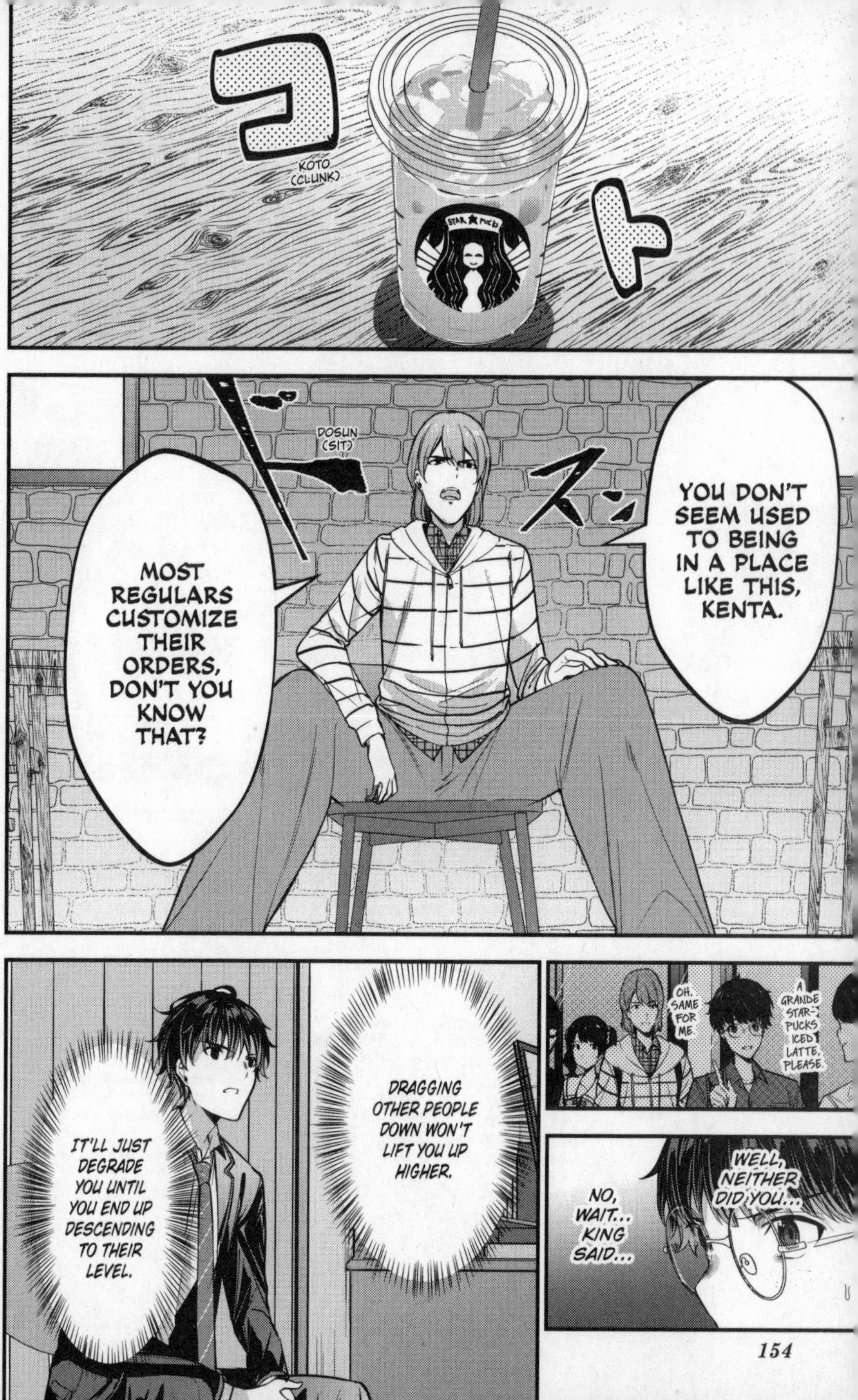
KOTO (CLUNK)
STAR PUCKS
YOU DON'T SEEM USED TO BEING IN A PLACE LIKE THIS, KENTA.
DOSUN (SIT)
MOST REGULARS CUSTOMIZE THEIR ORDERS, DON'T YOU KNOW THAT?
A GRANDE STAR-PUCKS ICED LATTE, PLEASE.
OH. SAME FOR ME.
WELL, NEITHER DID YOU...
NO, WAIT... KING SAID...
DRAGGING OTHER PEOPLE DOWN WON'T LIFT YOU UP HIGHER.
IT'LL JUST DEGRADE YOU UNTIL YOU END UP DESCENDING TO THEIR LEVEL.

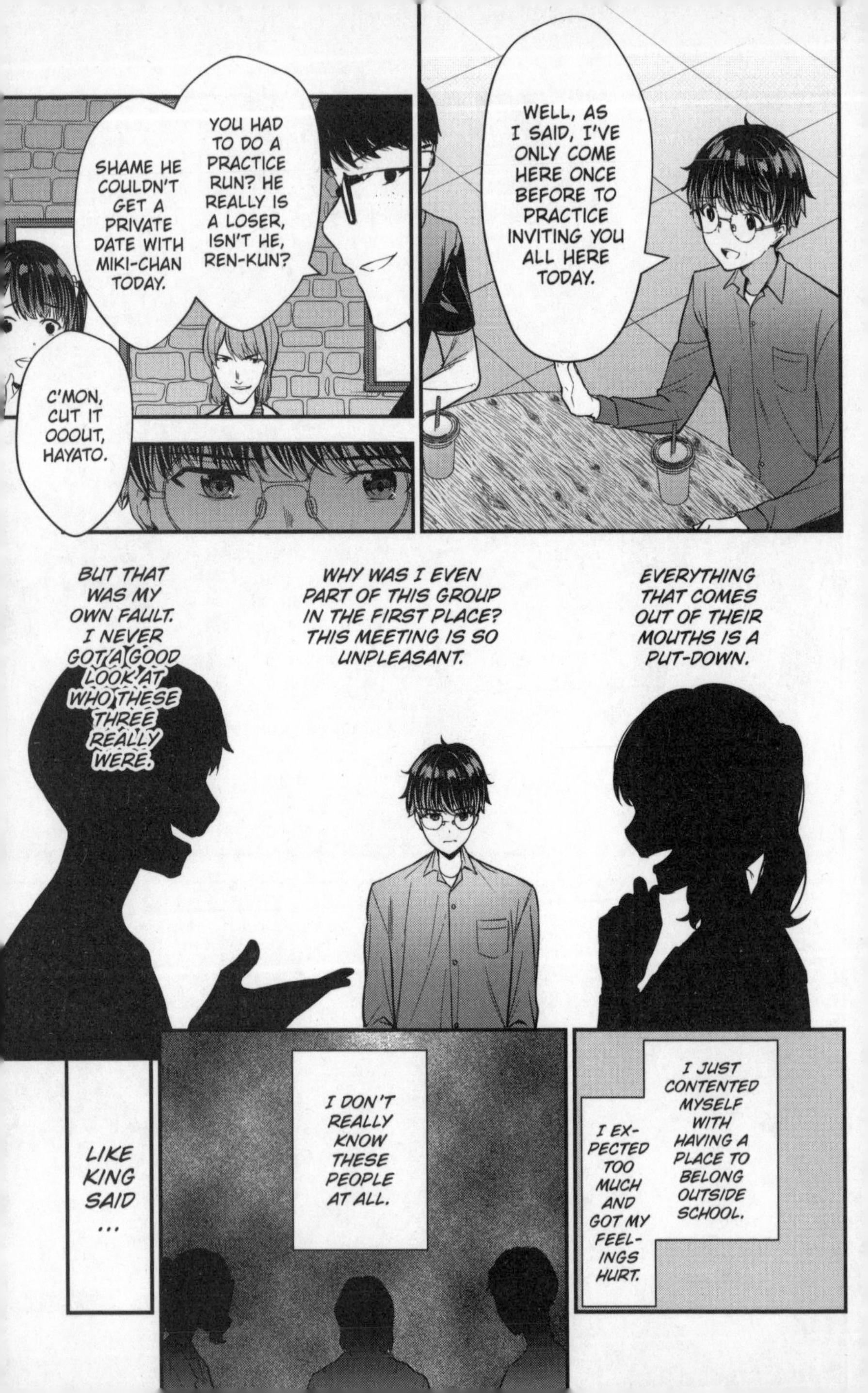
WELL, AS I SAID, I'VE ONLY COME HERE ONCE BEFORE TO PRACTICE INVITING YOU ALL HERE TODAY.
YOU HAD TO DO A PRACTICE RUN? HE REALLY IS A LOSER, ISN'T HE, REN-KUN?
SHAME HE COULDN'T GET A PRIVATE DATE WITH MIKI-CHAN TODAY.
C'MON, CUT IT OOOUT, HAYATO.
EVERYTHING THAT COMES OUT OF THEIR MOUTHS IS A PUT-DOWN.
WHY WAS I EVEN PART OF THIS GROUP IN THE FIRST PLACE? THIS MEETING IS SO UNPLEASANT.
BUT THAT WAS MY OWN FAULT. I NEVER GOT A GOOD LOOK AT WHO THESE THREE REALLY WERE.
I JUST CONTENTED MYSELF WITH HAVING A PLACE TO BELONG OUTSIDE SCHOOL.
I EXPECTED TOO MUCH AND GOT MY FEELINGS HURT.
I DON'T REALLY KNOW THESE PEOPLE AT ALL.
LIKE KING SAID...

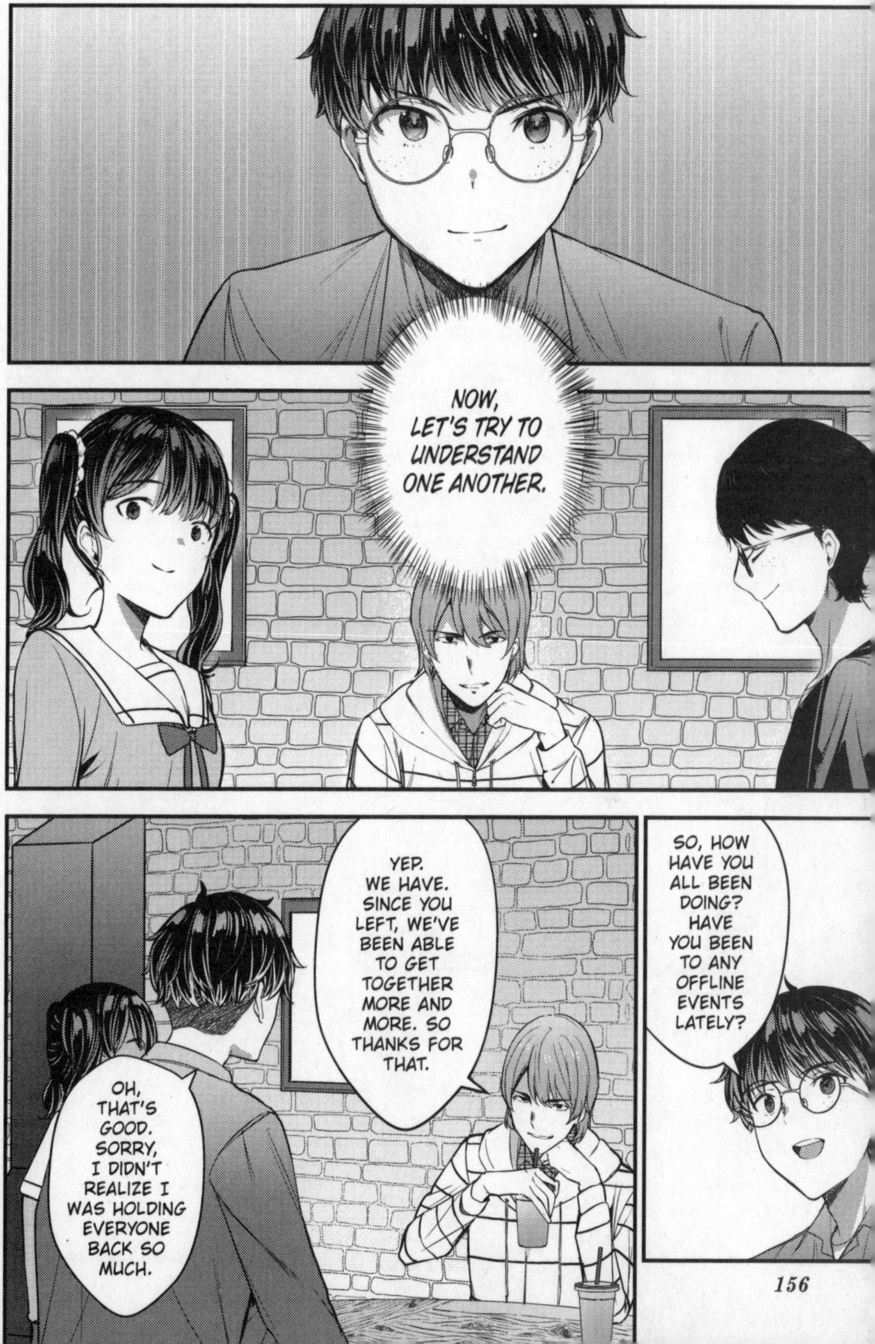
NOW, LET'S TRY TO UNDERSTAND ONE ANOTHER.
SO, HOW HAVE YOU ALL BEEN DOING? HAVE YOU BEEN TO ANY OFFLINE EVENTS LATELY?
YEP. WE HAVE. SINCE YOU LEFT, WE'VE BEEN ABLE TO GET TOGETHER MORE AND MORE. SO THANKS FOR THAT.
OH, THAT'S GOOD. SORRY, I DIDN'T REALIZE I WAS HOLDING EVERYONE BACK SO MUCH.

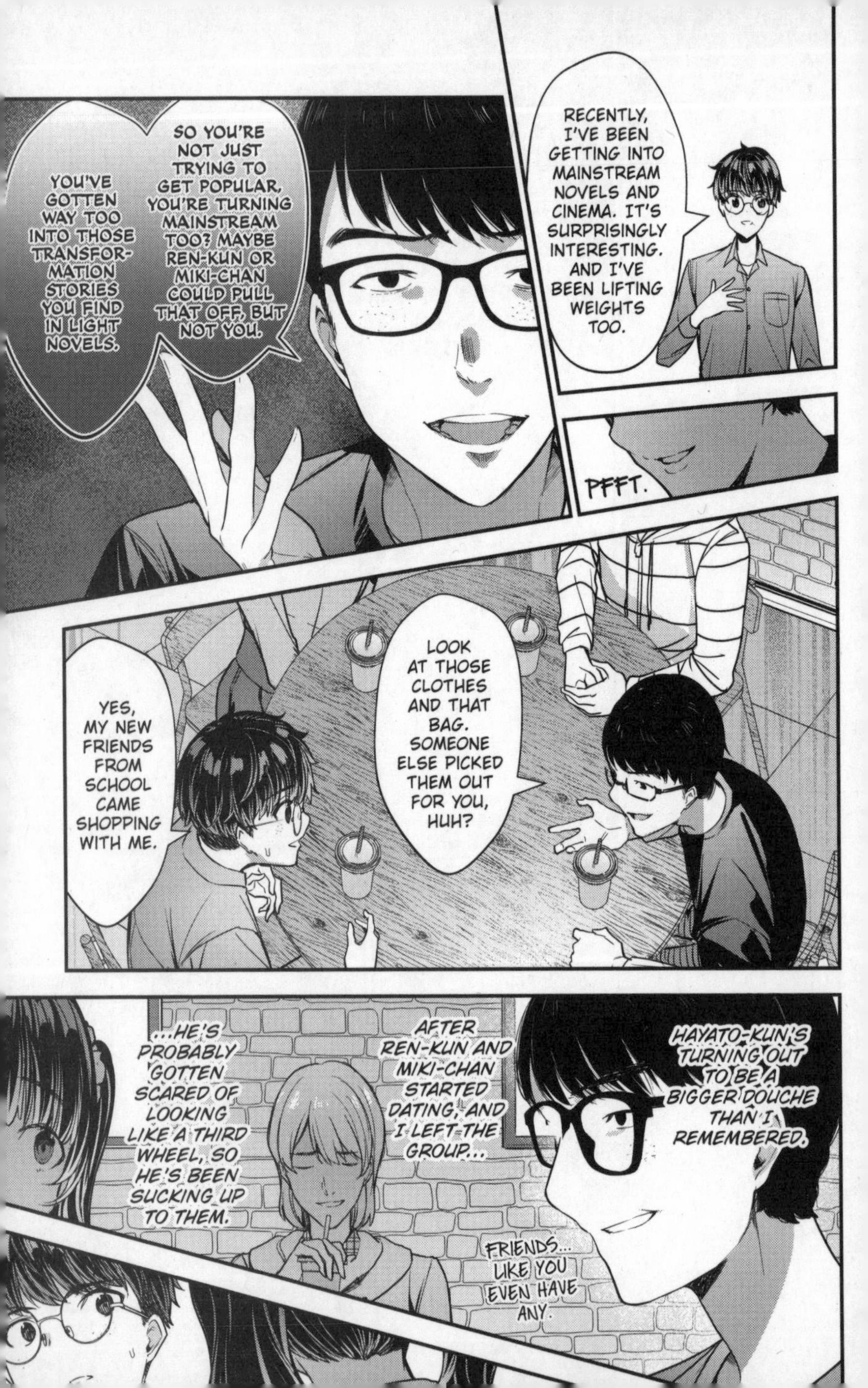
RECENTLY, I'VE BEEN GETTING INTO MAINSTREAM NOVELS AND CINEMA. IT'S SURPRISINGLY INTERESTING. AND I'VE BEEN LIFTING WEIGHTS TOO.
PFFT.
SO YOU'RE NOT JUST TRYING TO GET POPULAR, YOU'RE TURNING MAINSTREAM TOO? MAYBE REN-KUN OR MIKI-CHAN COULD PULL THAT OFF, BUT NOT YOU.
YOU'VE GOTTEN WAY TOO INTO THOSE TRANSFOR-MATION STORIES YOU FIND IN LIGHT NOVELS.
LOOK AT THOSE CLOTHES AND THAT BAG. SOMEONE ELSE PICKED THEM OUT FOR YOU, HUH?
YES, MY NEW FRIENDS FROM SCHOOL CAME SHOPPING WITH ME.
HAYATO-KUN'S TURNING OUT TO BE A BIGGER DOUCHE THAN I REMEMBERED.
AFTER REN-KUN AND MIKI-CHAN STARTED DATING, AND I LEFT THE GROUP...
...HE'S PROBABLY GOTTEN SCARED OF LOOKING LIKE A THIRD WHEEL, SO HE'S BEEN SUCKING UP TO THEM.
FRIENDS... LIKE YOU EVEN HAVE ANY.

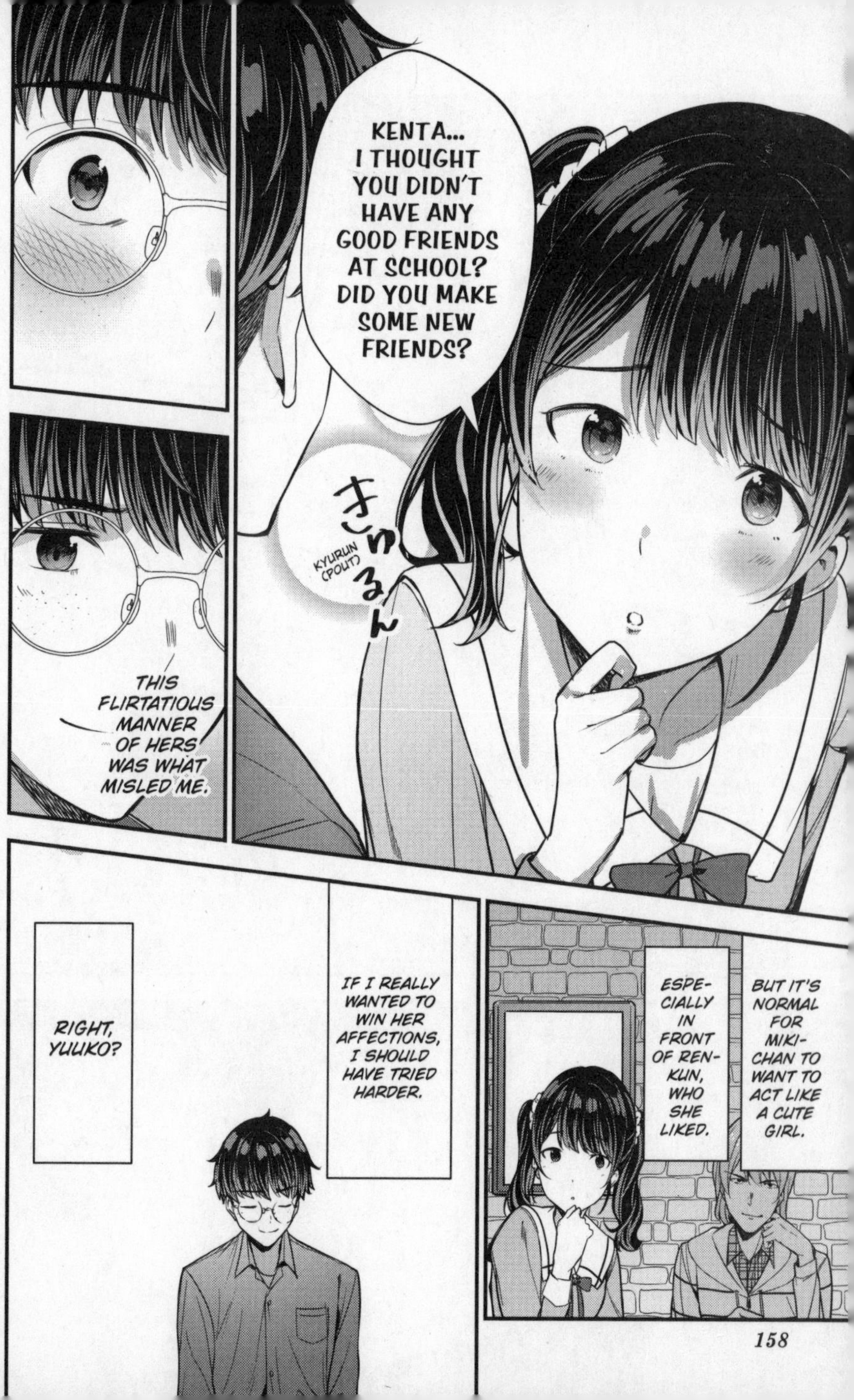
KENTA... I THOUGHT YOU DIDN'T HAVE ANY GOOD FRIENDS AT SCHOOL? DID YOU MAKE SOME NEW FRIENDS?
きゅるん
KYURUN (POUT)
THIS FLIRTATIOUS MANNER OF HERS WAS WHAT MISLED ME.
BUT IT'S NORMAL FOR MIKI-CHAN TO WANT TO ACT LIKE A CUTE GIRL.
ESPE-CIALLY IN FRONT OF REN-KUN, WHO SHE LIKED.
IF I REALLY WANTED TO WIN HER AFFECTIONS, I SHOULD HAVE TRIED HARDER.
RIGHT, YUUKO?

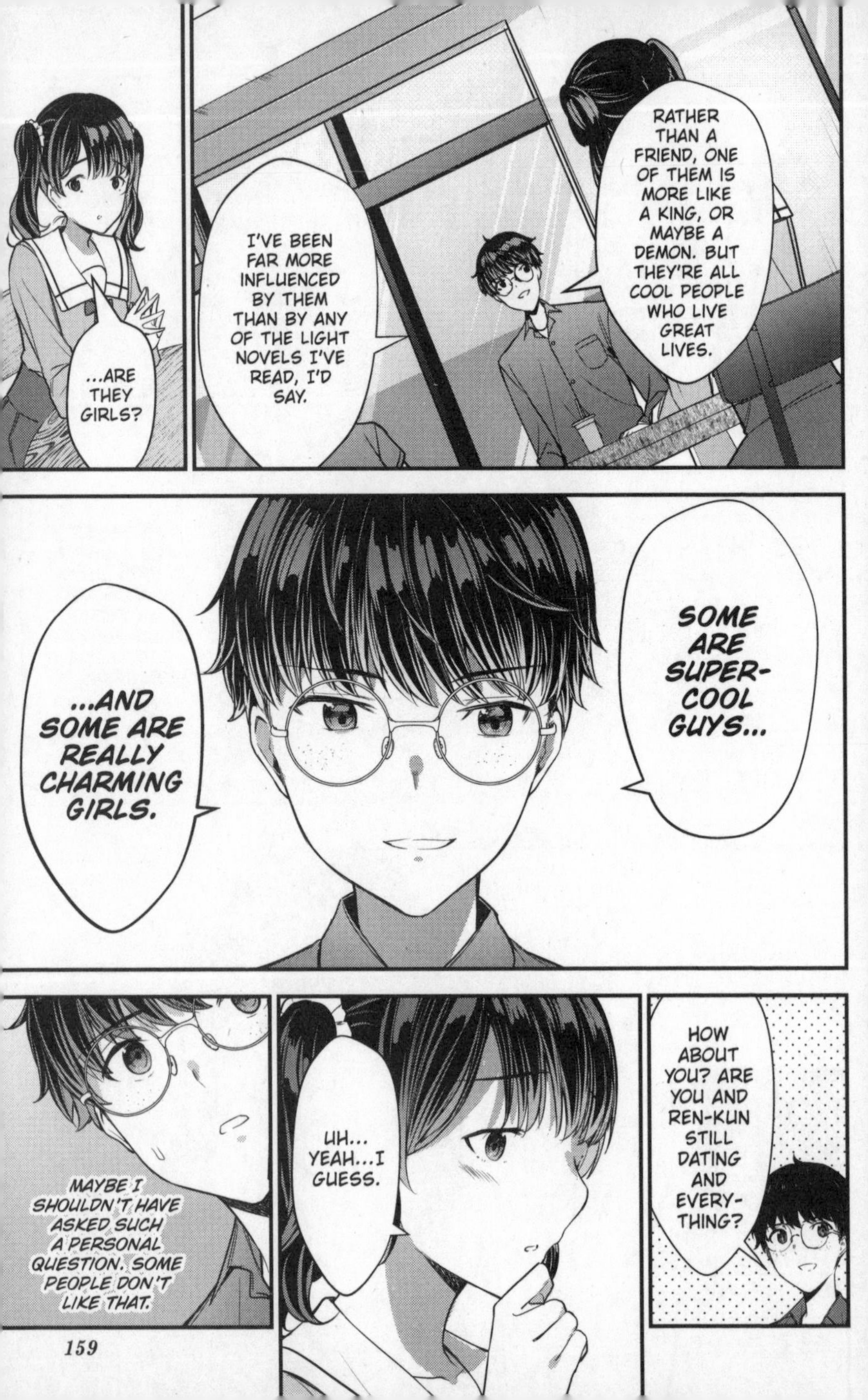
RATHER THAN A FRIEND, ONE OF THEM IS MORE LIKE A KING, OR MAYBE A DEMON. BUT THEY'RE ALL COOL PEOPLE WHO LIVE GREAT LIVES.
I'VE BEEN FAR MORE INFLUENCED BY THEM THAN BY ANY OF THE LIGHT NOVELS I'VE READ, I'D SAY.
...ARE THEY GIRLS?
SOME ARE SUPER-COOL GUYS...
...AND SOME ARE REALLY CHARMING GIRLS.
HOW ABOUT YOU? ARE YOU AND REN-KUN STILL DATING AND EVERYTHING?
UH... YEAH...I GUESS.
MAYBE I SHOULDN'T HAVE ASKED SUCH A PERSONAL QUESTION. SOME PEOPLE DON'T LIKE THAT.

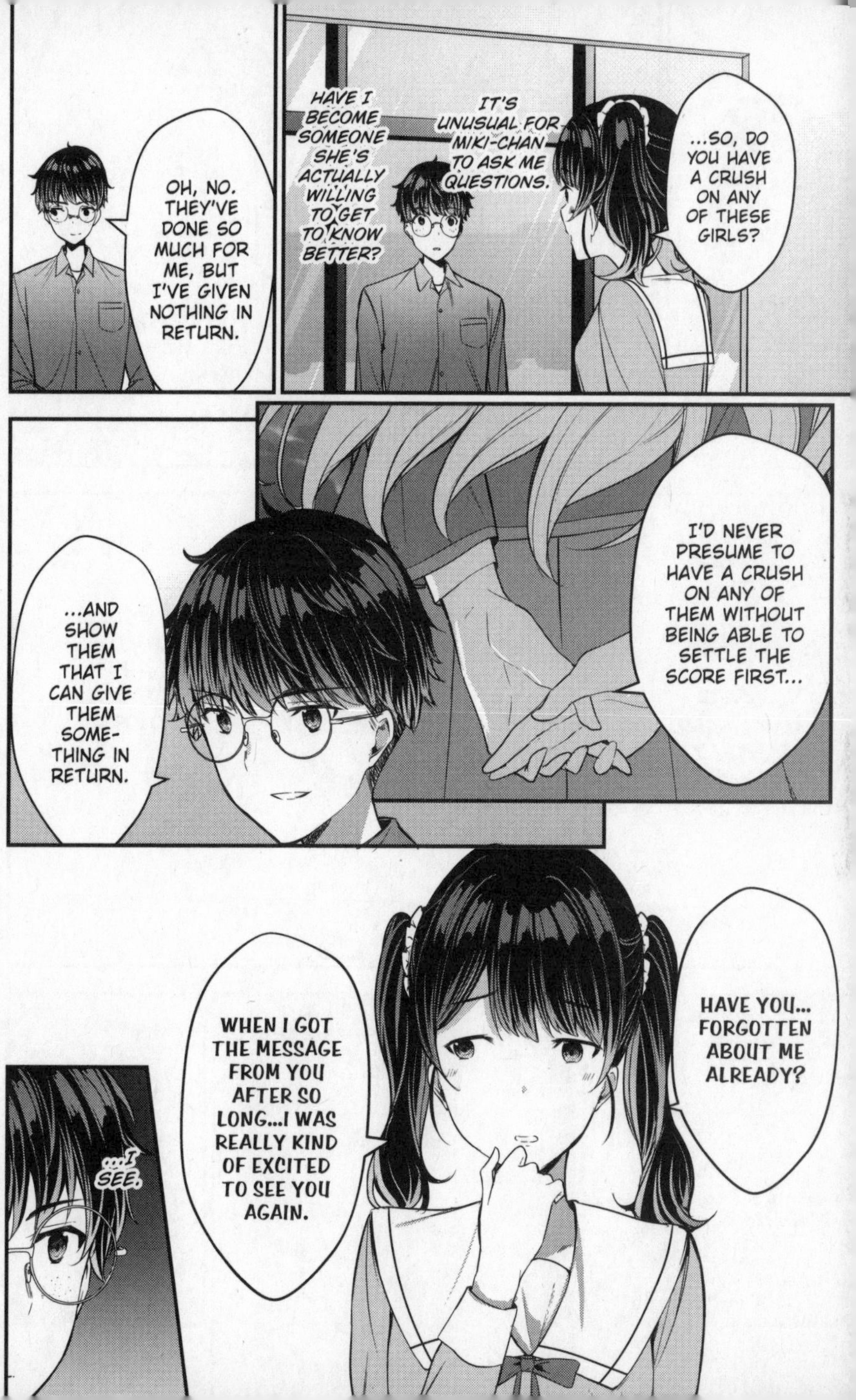
...SO, DO YOU HAVE A CRUSH ON ANY OF THESE GIRLS?
IT'S UNUSUAL FOR MIKI-CHAN TO ASK ME QUESTIONS.
HAVE I BECOME SOMEONE SHE'S ACTUALLY WILLING TO GET TO KNOW BETTER?
OH, NO. THEY'VE DONE SO MUCH FOR ME, BUT I'VE GIVEN NOTHING IN RETURN.
I'D NEVER PRESUME TO HAVE A CRUSH ON ANY OF THEM WITHOUT BEING ABLE TO SETTLE THE SCORE FIRST...
...AND SHOW THEM THAT I CAN GIVE THEM SOME-THING IN RETURN.
HAVE YOU... FORGOTTEN ABOUT ME ALREADY?
WHEN I GOT THE MESSAGE FROM YOU AFTER SO LONG...I WAS REALLY KIND OF EXCITED TO SEE YOU AGAIN.
...I SEE.

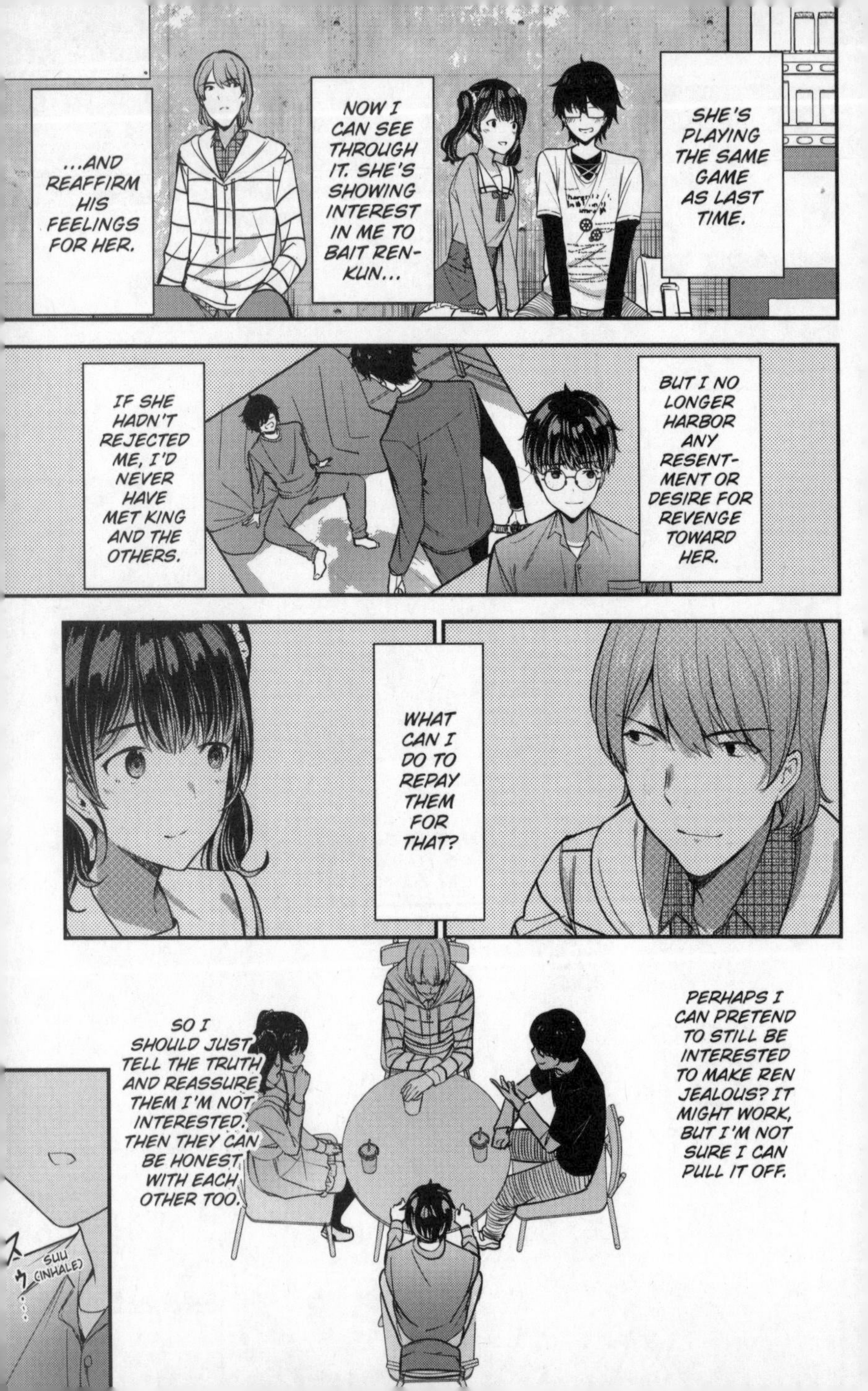
SHE'S PLAYING THE SAME GAME AS LAST TIME.
NOW I CAN SEE THROUGH IT. SHE'S SHOWING INTEREST IN ME TO BAIT REN-KUN...
...AND REAFFIRM HIS FEELINGS FOR HER.
BUT I NO LONGER HARBOR ANY RESENT-MENT OR DESIRE FOR REVENGE TOWARD HER.
IF SHE HADN'T REJECTED ME, I'D NEVER HAVE MET KING AND THE OTHERS.
WHAT CAN I DO TO REPAY THEM FOR THAT?
PERHAPS I CAN PRETEND TO STILL BE INTERESTED TO MAKE REN JEALOUS? IT MIGHT WORK, BUT I'M NOT SURE I CAN PULL IT OFF.
SO I SHOULD JUST TELL THE TRUTH AND REASSURE THEM I'M NOT INTERESTED. THEN THEY CAN BE HONEST WITH EACH OTHER TOO.
スウ…
SUU (INHALE)

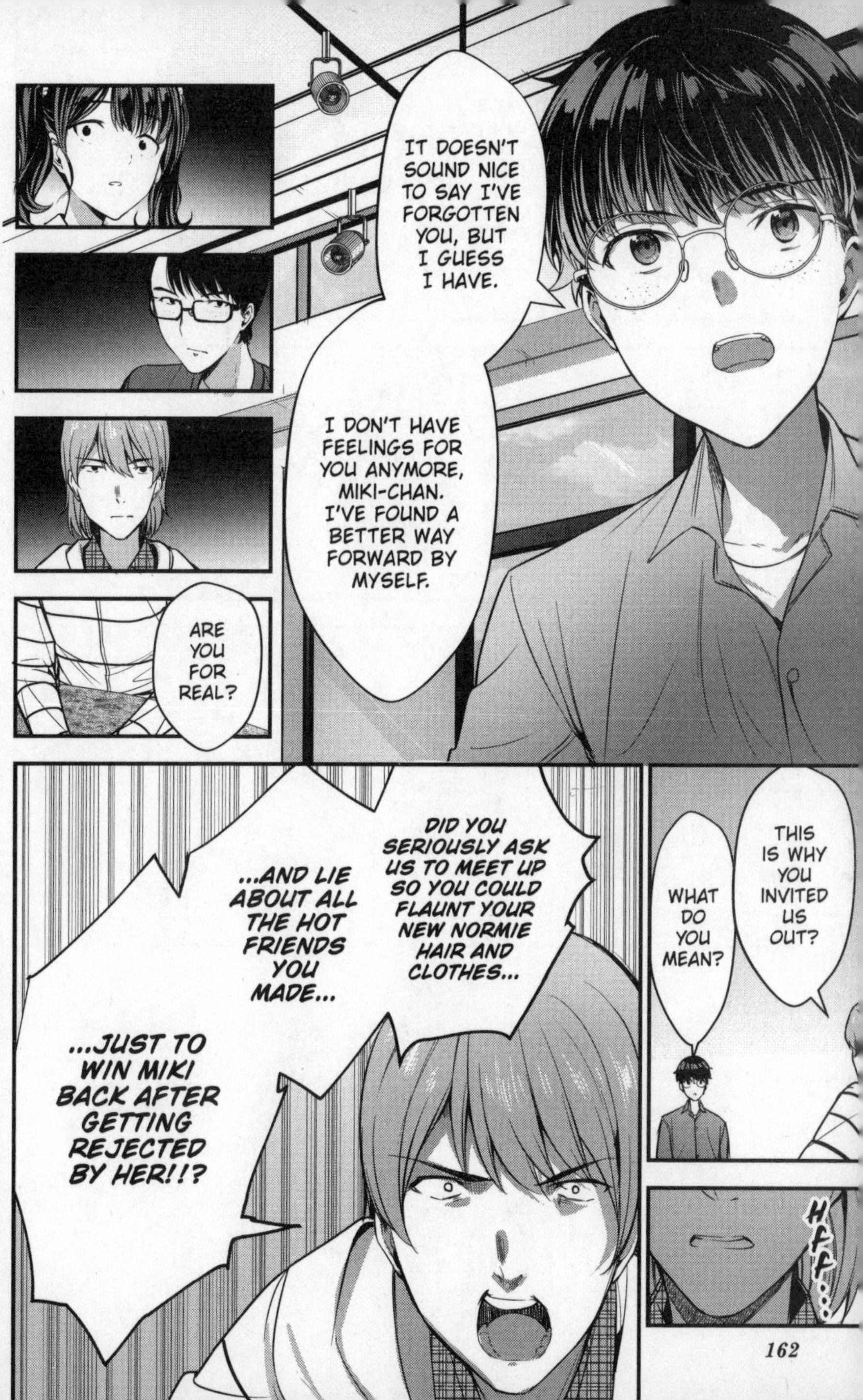
IT DOESN'T SOUND NICE TO SAY I'VE FORGOTTEN YOU, BUT I GUESS I HAVE.
I DON'T HAVE FEELINGS FOR YOU ANYMORE, MIKI-CHAN. I'VE FOUND A BETTER WAY FORWARD BY MYSELF.
ARE YOU FOR REAL?
THIS IS WHY YOU INVITED US OUT?
WHAT DO YOU MEAN?
HFF...
DID YOU SERIOUSLY ASK US TO MEET UP SO YOU COULD FLAUNT YOUR NEW NORMIE HAIR AND CLOTHES...
...AND LIE ABOUT ALL THE HOT FRIENDS YOU MADE...
...JUST TO WIN MIKI BACK AFTER GETTING REJECTED BY HER!!?

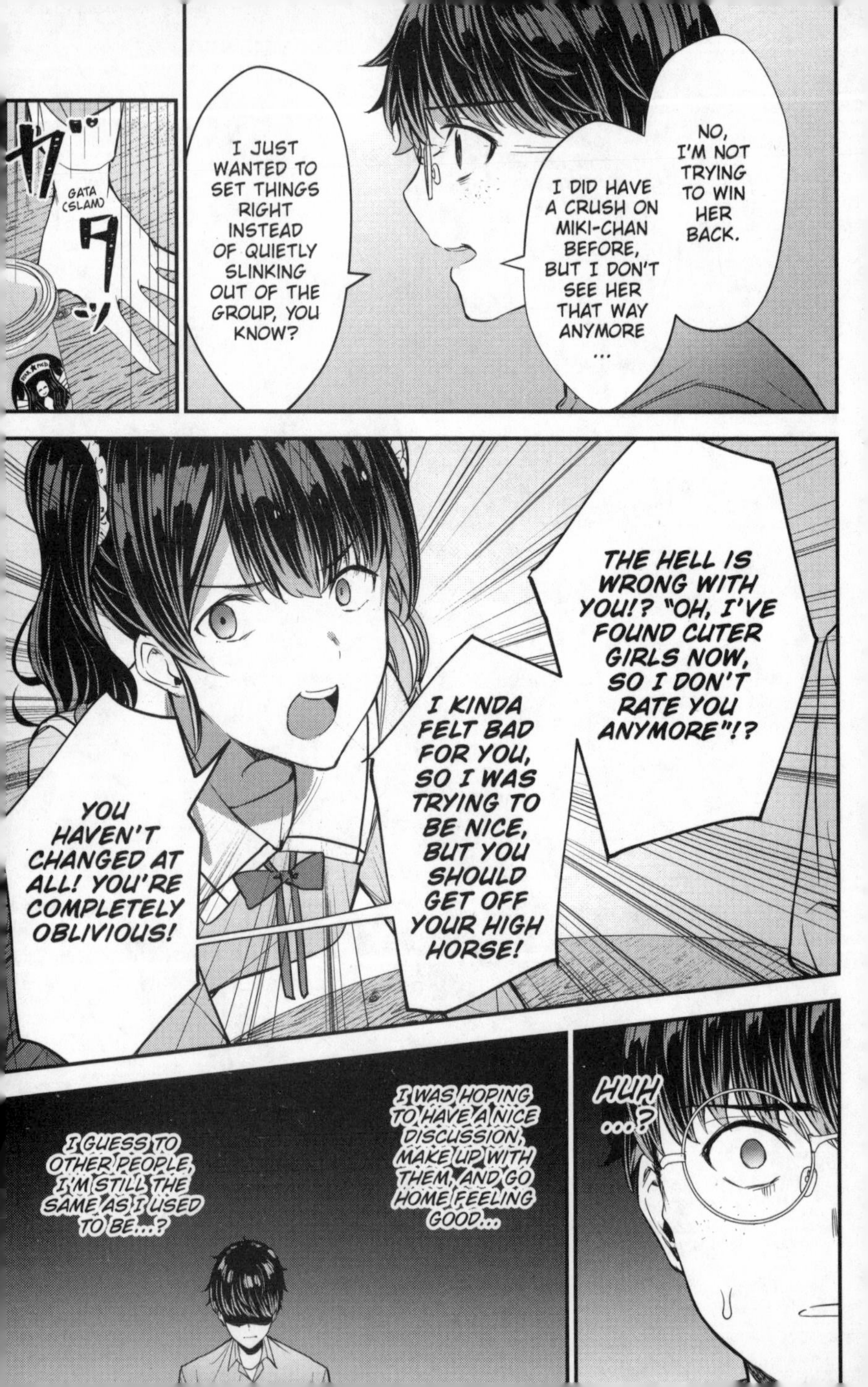
NO, I'M NOT TRYING TO WIN HER BACK.
I DID HAVE A CRUSH ON MIKI-CHAN BEFORE, BUT I DON'T SEE HER THAT WAY ANYMORE ...
I JUST WANTED TO SET THINGS RIGHT INSTEAD OF QUIETLY SLINKING OUT OF THE GROUP, YOU KNOW?
GATA (SLAM)
THE HELL IS WRONG WITH YOU!? "OH, I'VE FOUND CUTER GIRLS NOW, SO I DON'T RATE YOU ANYMORE"!?
I KINDA FELT BAD FOR YOU, SO I WAS TRYING TO BE NICE, BUT YOU SHOULD GET OFF YOUR HIGH HORSE!
YOU HAVEN'T CHANGED AT ALL! YOU'RE COMPLETELY OBLIVIOUS!
HUH ...?
I WAS HOPING TO HAVE A NICE DISCUSSION, MAKE UP WITH THEM, AND GO HOME FEELING GOOD...
I GUESS TO OTHER PEOPLE, I'M STILL THE SAME AS I USED TO BE...?

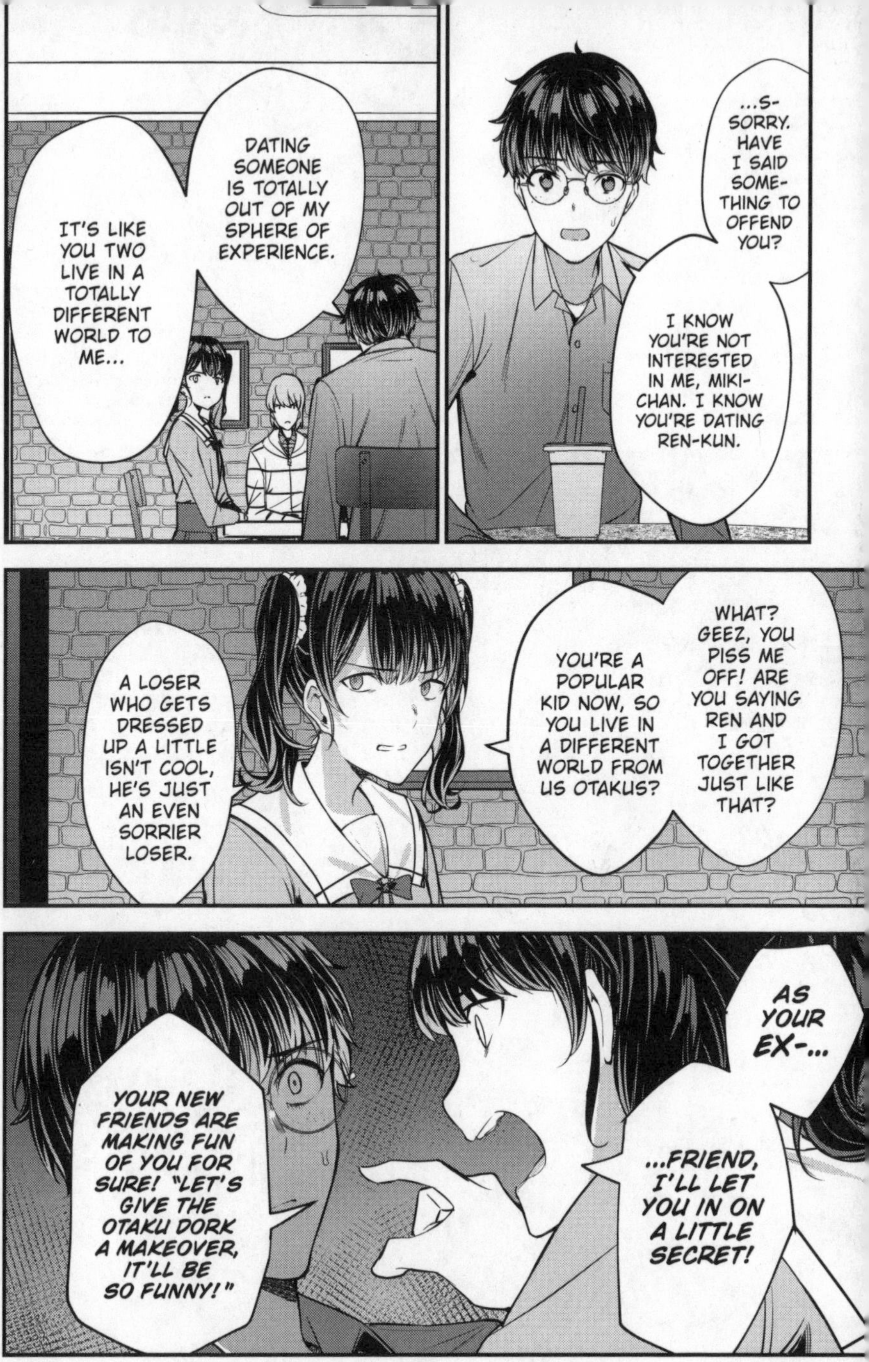
...S-SORRY. HAVE I SAID SOME-THING TO OFFEND YOU?
I KNOW YOU'RE NOT INTERESTED IN ME, MIKI-CHAN. I KNOW YOU'RE DATING REN-KUN.
DATING SOMEONE IS TOTALLY OUT OF MY SPHERE OF EXPERIENCE.
IT'S LIKE YOU TWO LIVE IN A TOTALLY DIFFERENT WORLD TO ME...
WHAT? GEEZ, YOU PISS ME OFF! ARE YOU SAYING REN AND I GOT TOGETHER JUST LIKE THAT?
YOU'RE A POPULAR KID NOW, SO YOU LIVE IN A DIFFERENT WORLD FROM US OTAKUS?
A LOSER WHO GETS DRESSED UP A LITTLE ISN'T COOL, HE'S JUST AN EVEN SORRIER LOSER.
AS YOUR EX-...
...FRIEND, I'LL LET YOU IN ON A LITTLE SECRET!
YOUR NEW FRIENDS ARE MAKING FUN OF YOU FOR SURE! "LET'S GIVE THE OTAKU DORK A MAKEOVER, IT'LL BE SO FUNNY!"

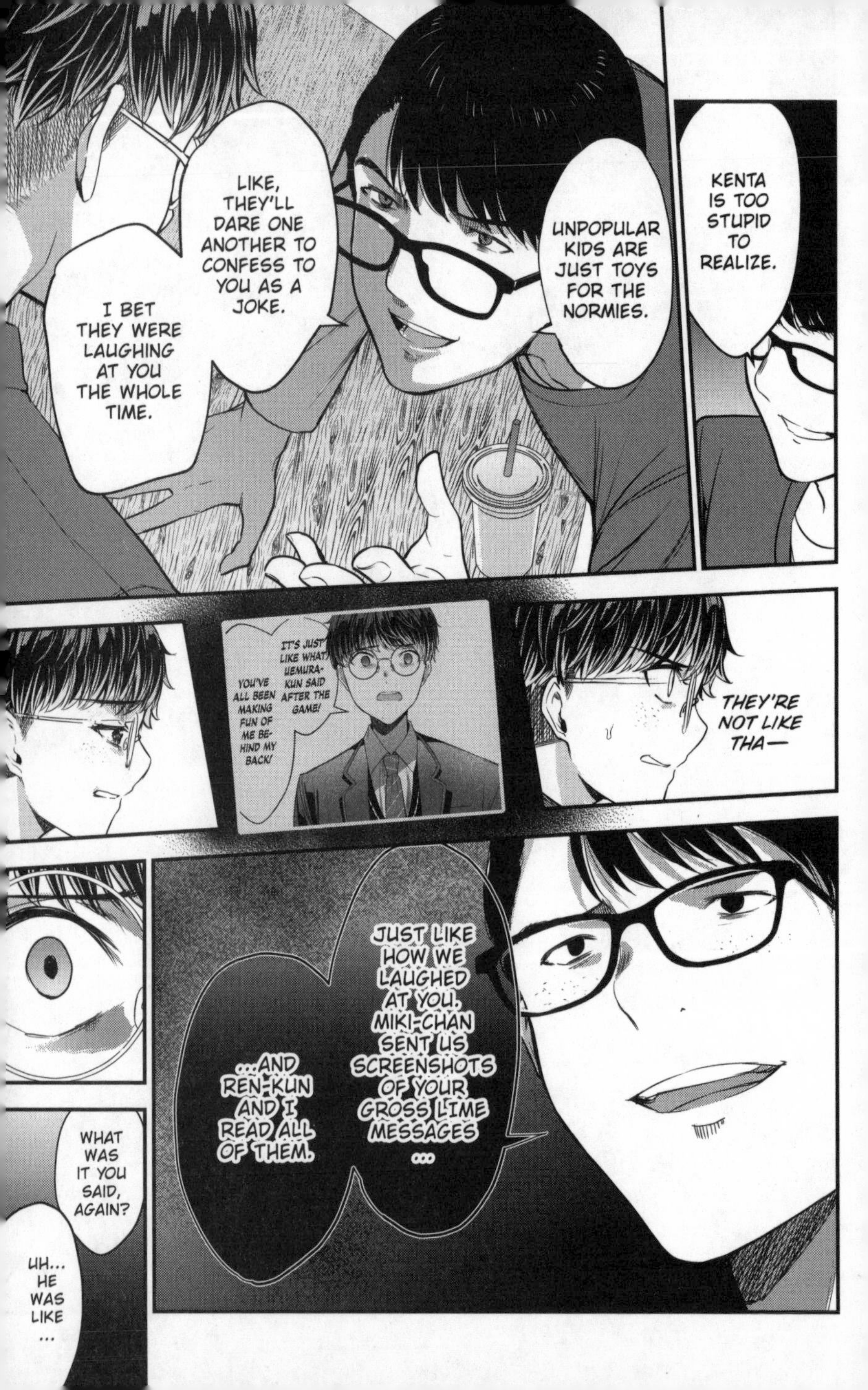
KENTA IS TOO STUPID TO REALIZE.
UNPOPULAR KIDS ARE JUST TOYS FOR THE NORMIES.
LIKE, THEY'LL DARE ONE ANOTHER TO CONFESS TO YOU AS A JOKE.
I BET THEY WERE LAUGHING AT YOU THE WHOLE TIME.
THEY'RE NOT LIKE THA—
IT'S JUST LIKE WHAT UEMURA-KUN SAID AFTER THE GAME!
YOU'VE ALL BEEN MAKING FUN OF ME BEHIND MY BACK!
JUST LIKE HOW WE LAUGHED AT YOU, MIKI-CHAN SENT US SCREENSHOTS OF YOUR GROSS LIME MESSAGES...
...AND REN-KUN AND I READ ALL OF THEM.
WHAT WAS IT YOU SAID, AGAIN?
UH... HE WAS LIKE...

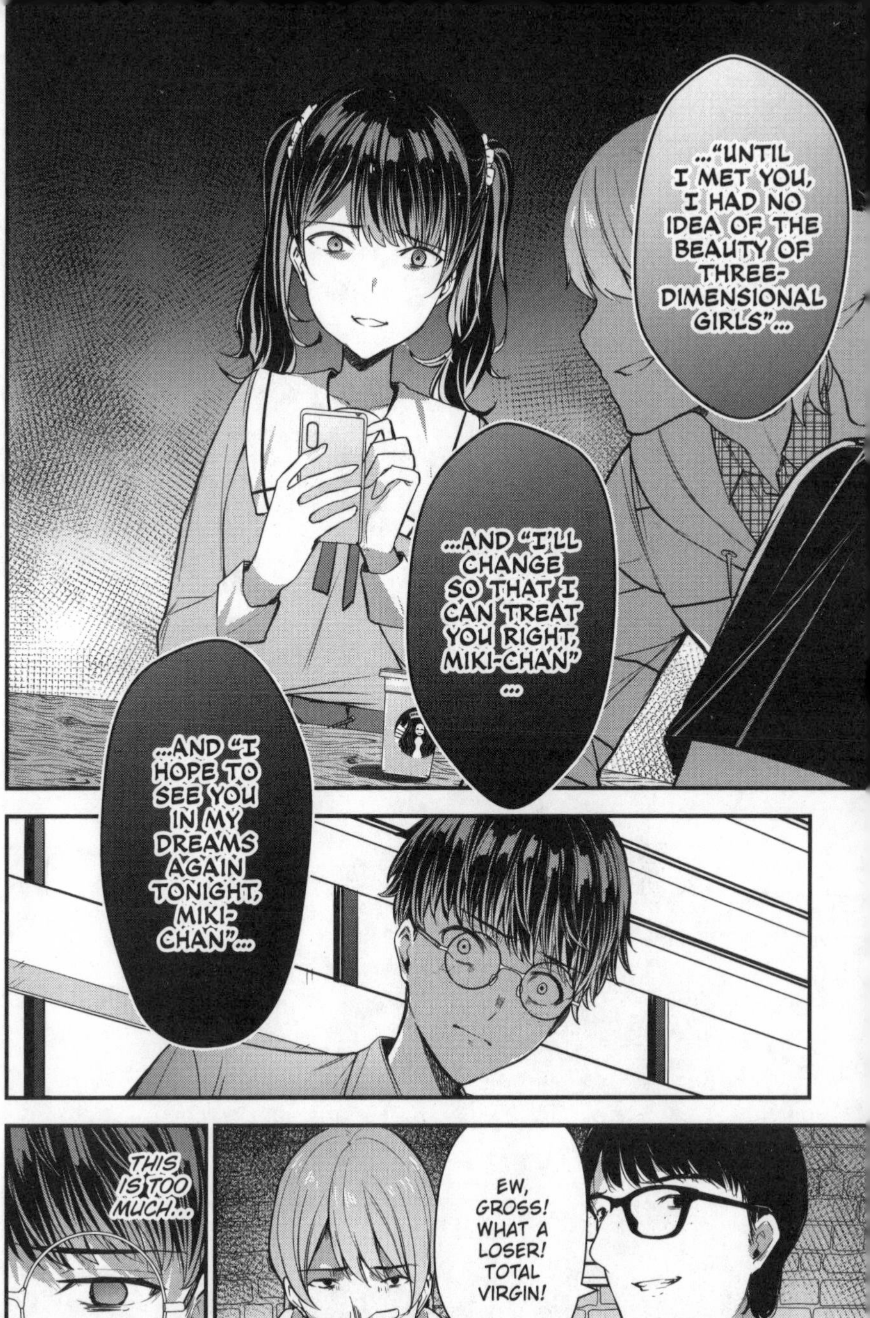
..."UNTIL I MET YOU, I HAD NO IDEA OF THE BEAUTY OF THREE-DIMENSIONAL GIRLS"...
...AND "I'LL CHANGE SO THAT I CAN TREAT YOU RIGHT, MIKI-CHAN"...
...AND "I HOPE TO SEE YOU IN MY DREAMS AGAIN TONIGHT, MIKI-CHAN"...
EW, GROSS! WHAT A LOSER! TOTAL VIRGIN!
THIS IS TOO MUCH...

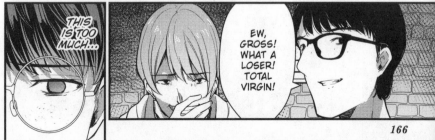

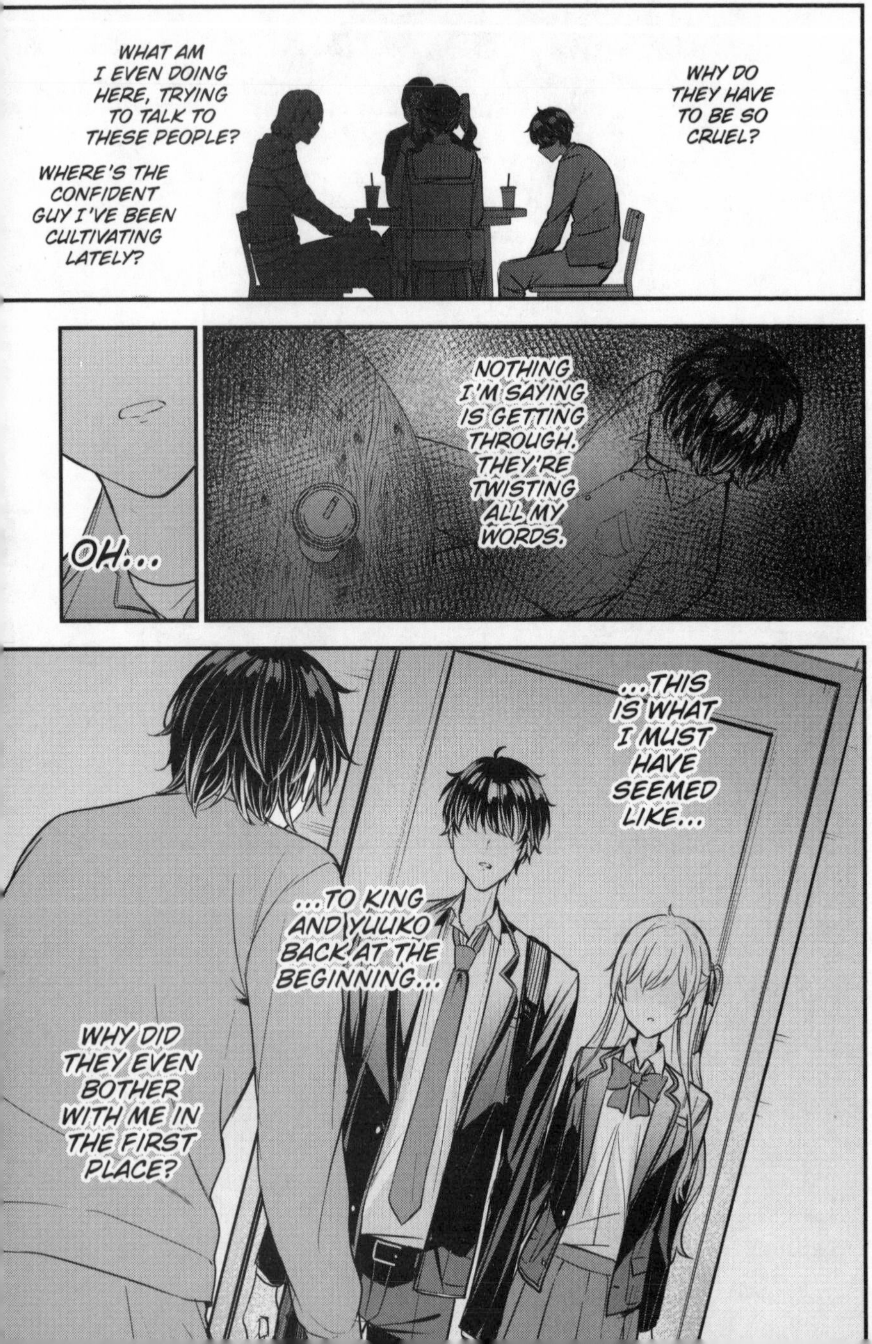
WHY DO THEY HAVE TO BE SO CRUEL?
WHAT AM I EVEN DOING HERE, TRYING TO TALK TO THESE PEOPLE?
WHERE'S THE CONFIDENT GUY I'VE BEEN CULTIVATING LATELY?
NOTHING I'M SAYING IS GETTING THROUGH. THEY'RE TWISTING ALL MY WORDS.
OH...
...THIS IS WHAT I MUST HAVE SEEMED LIKE...
...TO KING AND YUUKO BACK AT THE BEGINNING...
WHY DID THEY EVEN BOTHER WITH ME IN THE FIRST PLACE?

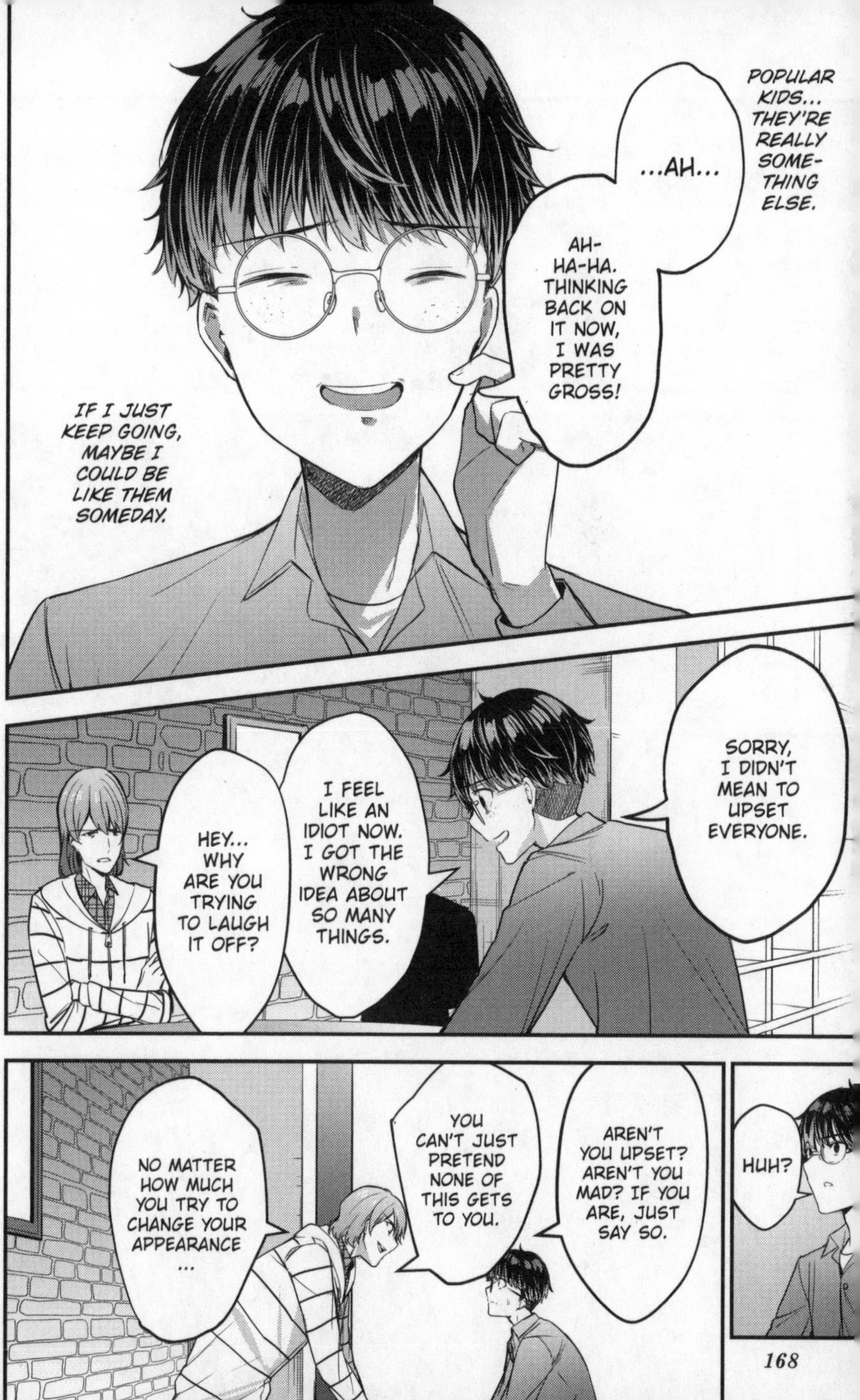
POPULAR KIDS... THEY'RE REALLY SOME-THING ELSE.
...AH...
AH-HA-HA. THINKING BACK ON IT NOW, I WAS PRETTY GROSS!
IF I JUST KEEP GOING, MAYBE I COULD BE LIKE THEM SOMEDAY.
SORRY, I DIDN'T MEAN TO UPSET EVERYONE.
I FEEL LIKE AN IDIOT NOW. I GOT THE WRONG IDEA ABOUT SO MANY THINGS.
HEY... WHY ARE YOU TRYING TO LAUGH IT OFF?
HUH?
AREN'T YOU UPSET? AREN'T YOU MAD? IF YOU ARE, JUST SAY SO.
YOU CAN'T JUST PRETEND NONE OF THIS GETS TO YOU.
NO MATTER HOW MUCH YOU TRY TO CHANGE YOUR APPEARANCE ...

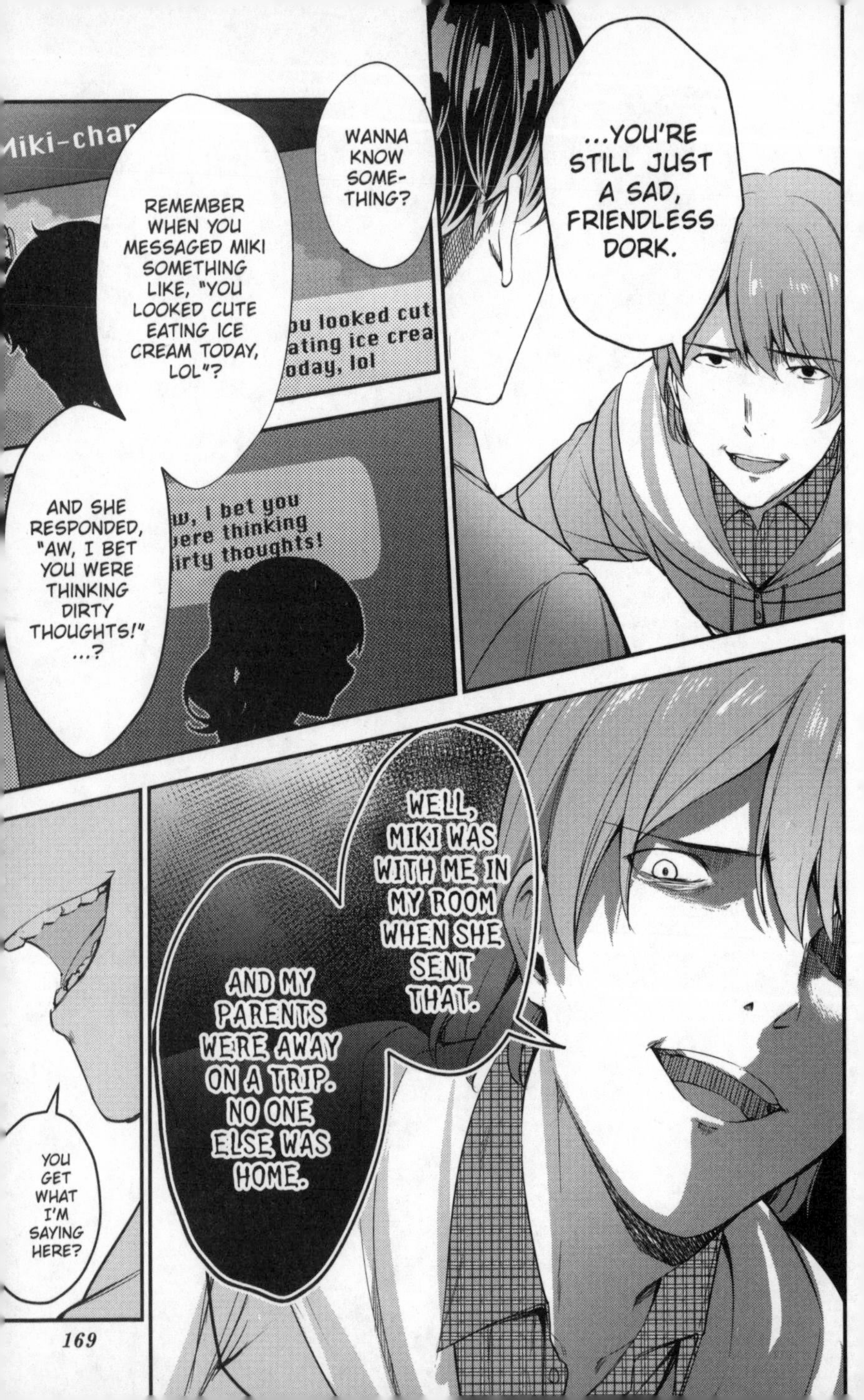
...YOU'RE STILL JUST A SAD, FRIENDLESS DORK.
WANNA KNOW SOMETHING?
Miki-chan
REMEMBER WHEN YOU MESSAGED MIKI SOMETHING LIKE, "YOU LOOKED CUTE EATING ICE CREAM TODAY, LOL"?
ou looked cut
ating ice crea
oday, lol
AND SHE RESPONDED, "AW, I BET YOU WERE THINKING DIRTY THOUGHTS!" ...?
w, I bet you
ere thinking
irty thoughts!
WELL, MIKI WAS WITH ME IN MY ROOM WHEN SHE SENT THAT.
AND MY PARENTS WERE AWAY ON A TRIP. NO ONE ELSE WAS HOME.
YOU GET WHAT I'M SAYING HERE?

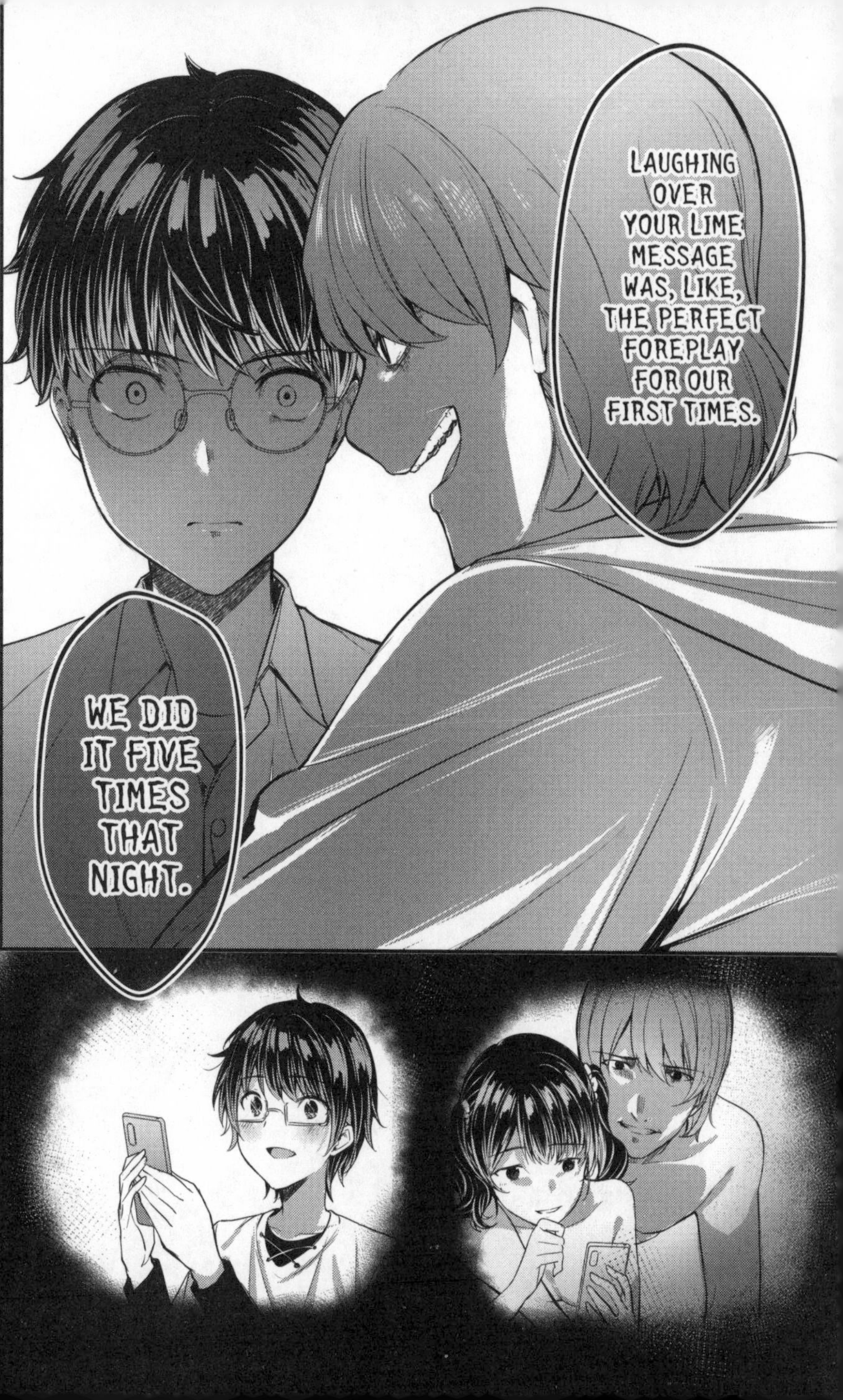
LAUGHING OVER YOUR LIME MESSAGE WAS, LIKE, THE PERFECT FOREPLAY FOR OUR FIRST TIMES.
WE DID IT FIVE TIMES THAT NIGHT.

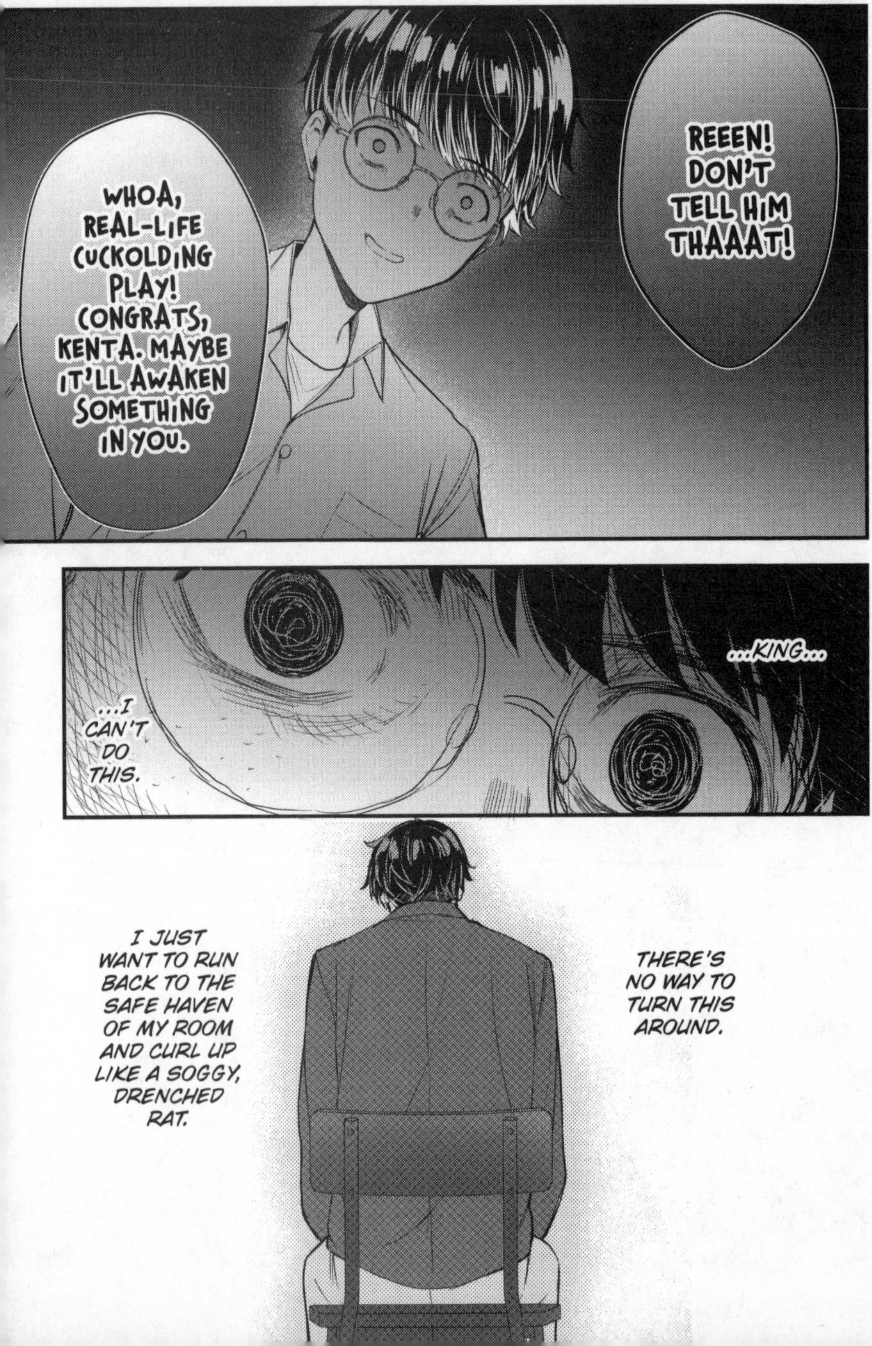
REEEN! DON'T TELL HIM THAAAT!
WHOA, REAL-LIFE CUCKOLDING PLAY! CONGRATS, KENTA. MAYBE IT'LL AWAKEN SOMETHING IN YOU.
...KING...
...I CAN'T DO THIS.
THERE'S NO WAY TO TURN THIS AROUND.
I JUST WANT TO RUN BACK TO THE SAFE HAVEN OF MY ROOM AND CURL UP LIKE A SOGGY, DRENCHED RAT.

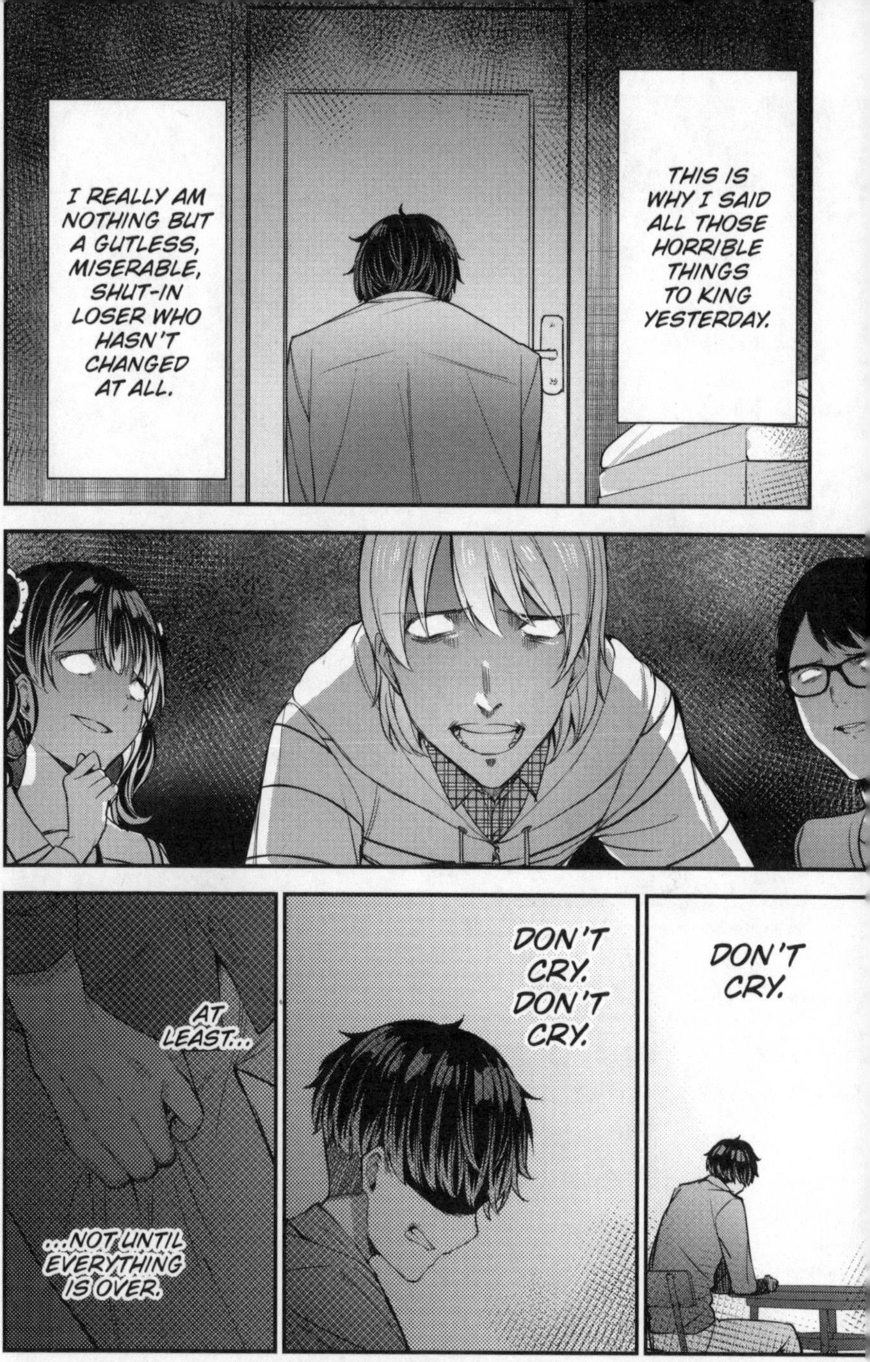
THIS IS WHY I SAID ALL THOSE HORRIBLE THINGS TO KING YESTERDAY.
I REALLY AM NOTHING BUT A GUTLESS, MISERABLE, SHUT-IN LOSER WHO HASN'T CHANGED AT ALL.
DON'T CRY.
DON'T CRY. DON'T CRY.
AT LEAST...
...NOT UNTIL EVERYTHING IS OVER.

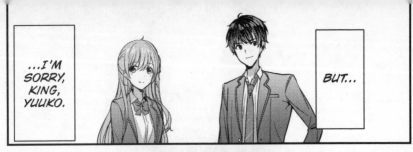

...I'M SORRY, KING, YUUKO.

BUT...

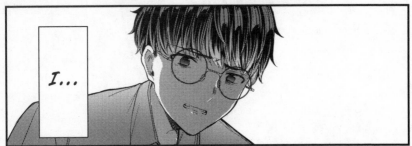

I...

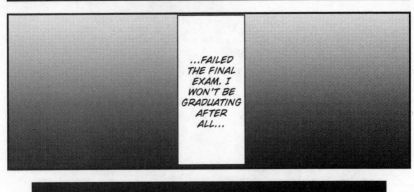

...FAILED THE FINAL EXAM. I WON'T BE GRADUATING AFTER ALL...

LIKE KING SAID...

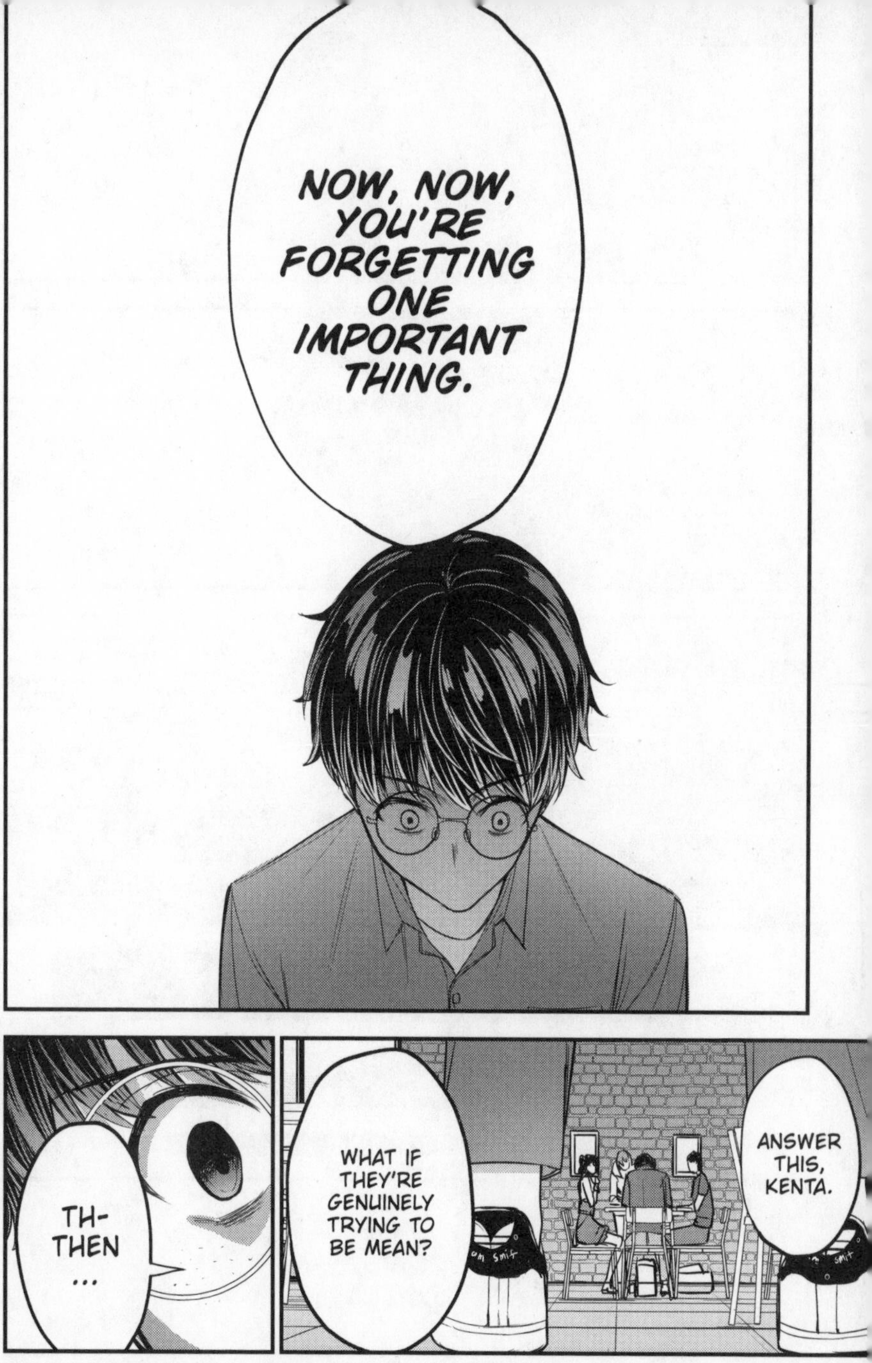
NOW, NOW, YOU'RE FORGETTING ONE IMPORTANT THING.
ANSWER THIS, KENTA.
WHAT IF THEY'RE GENUINELY TRYING TO BE MEAN?
TH-THEN ...

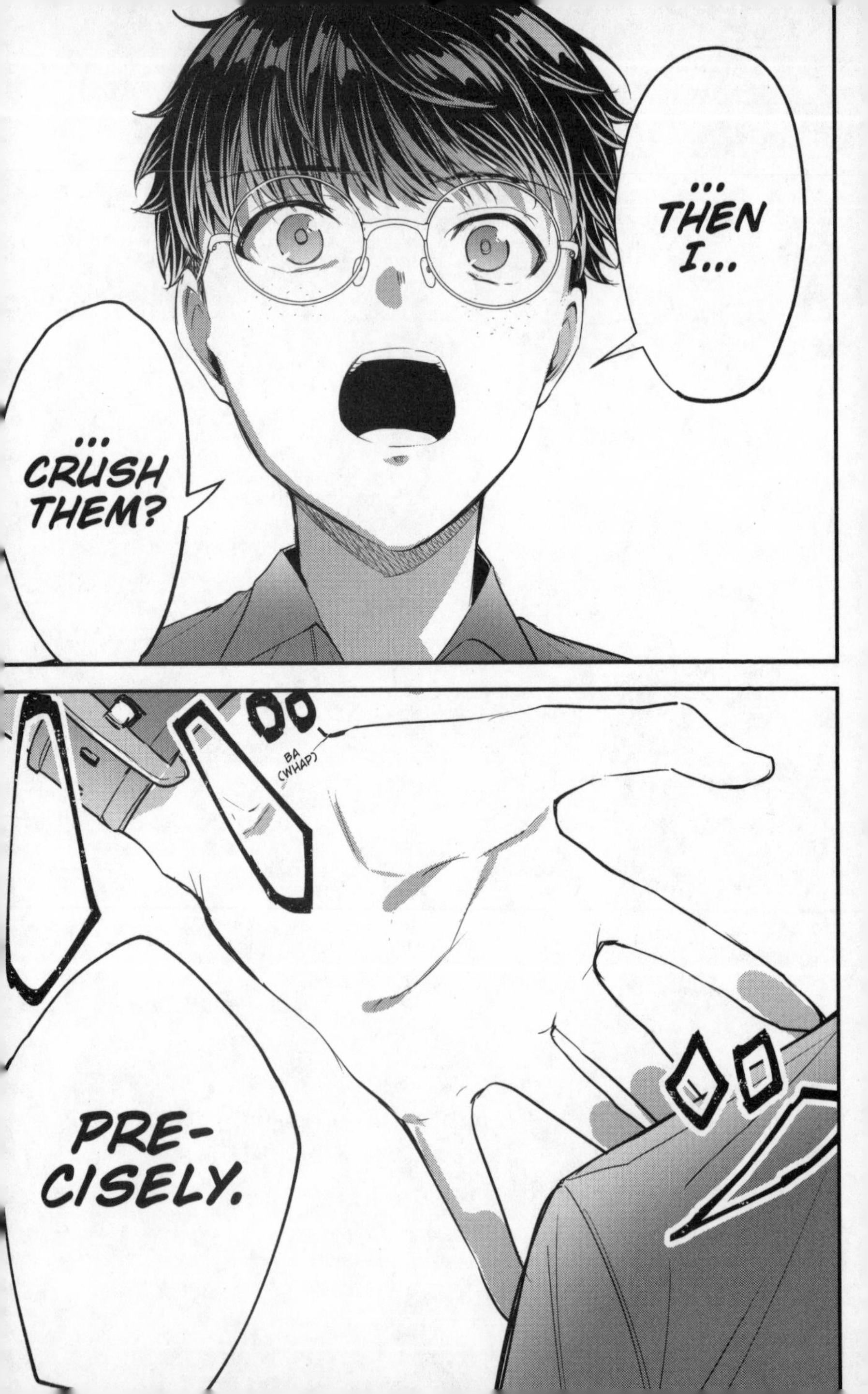
... THEN I...
... CRUSH THEM?
BA (WHAP)
PRE-CISELY.

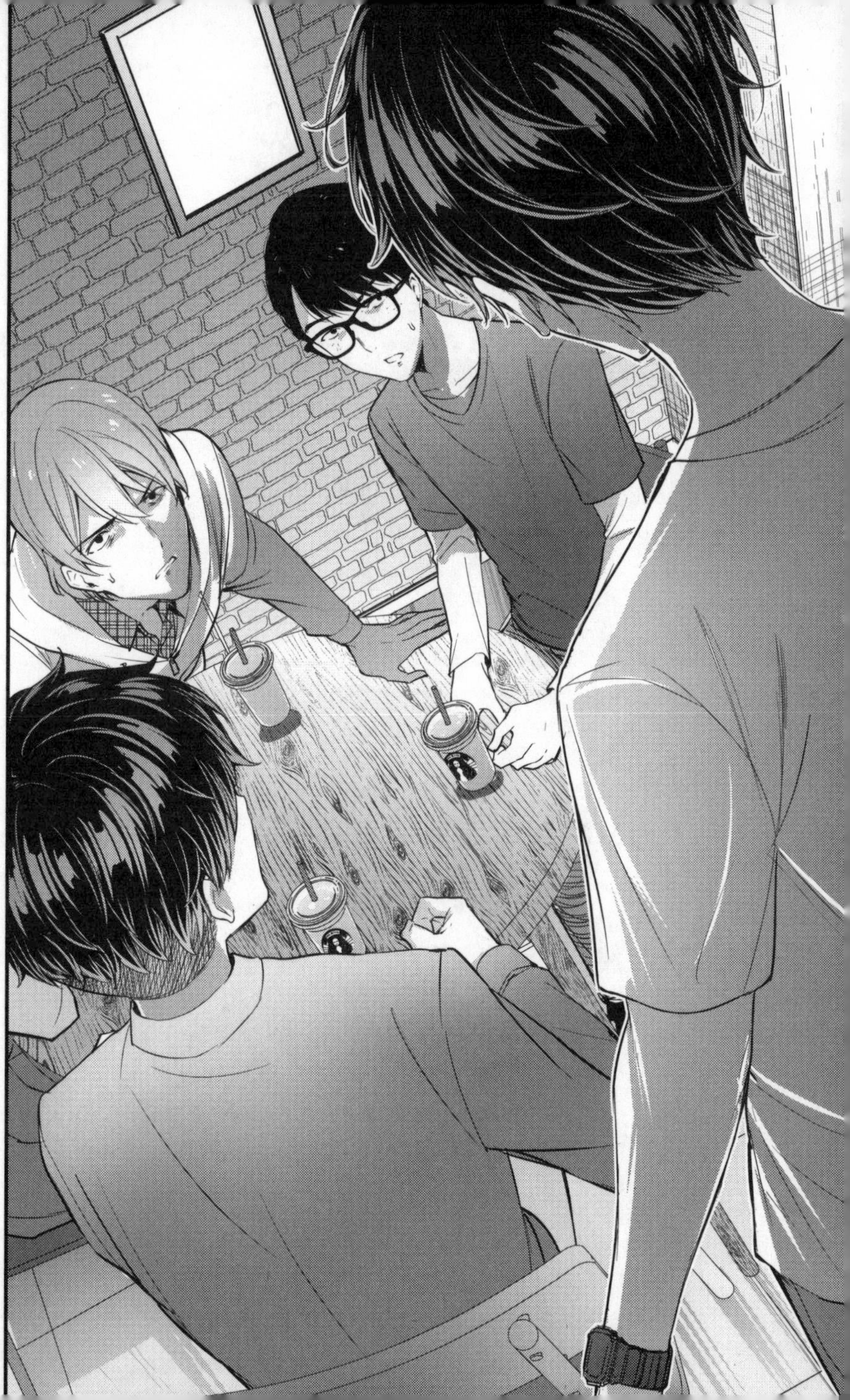

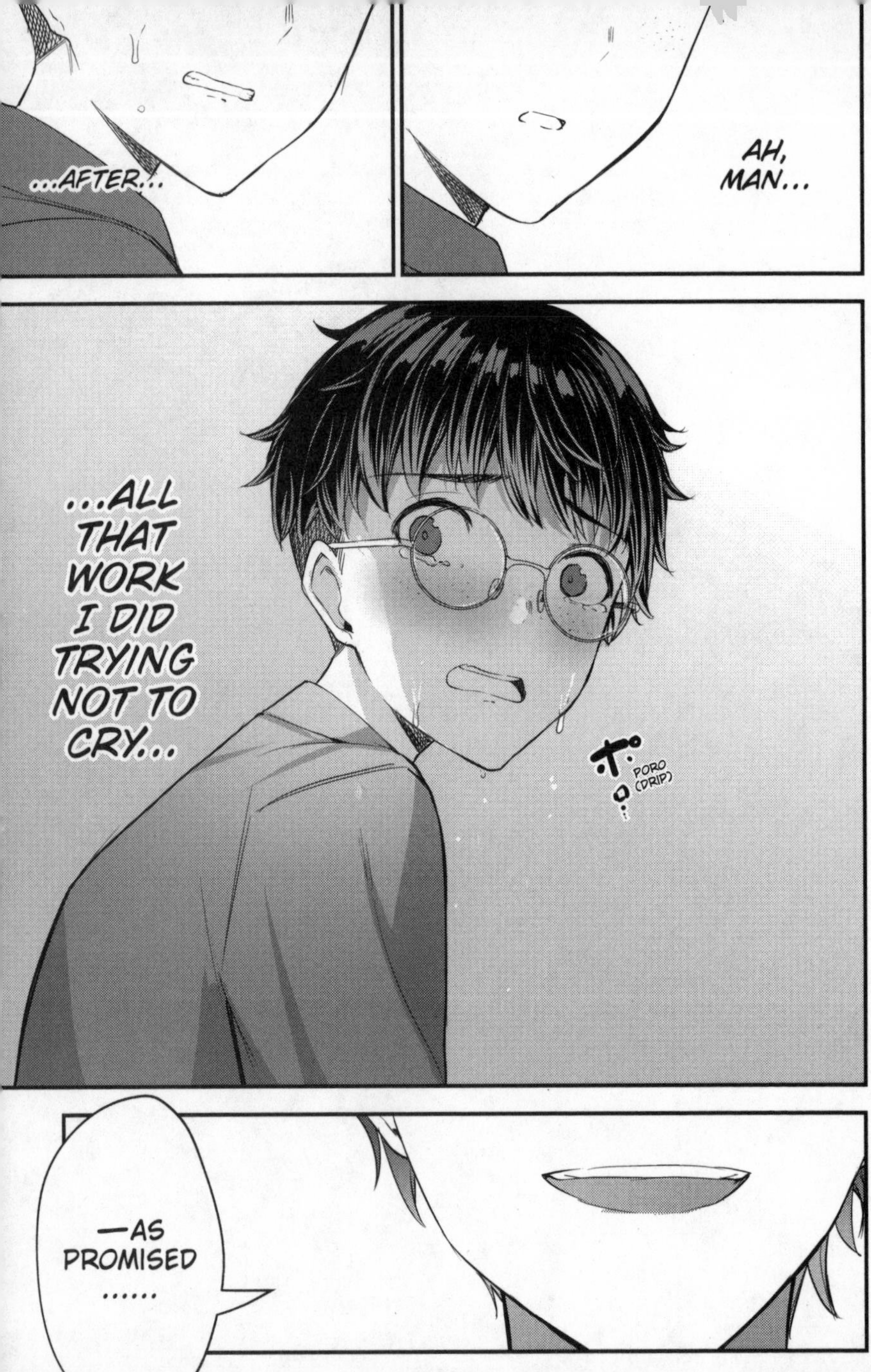
AH, MAN...
...AFTER...
...ALL THAT WORK I DID TRYING NOT TO CRY...
PORO (DRIP)
—AS PROMISED ......

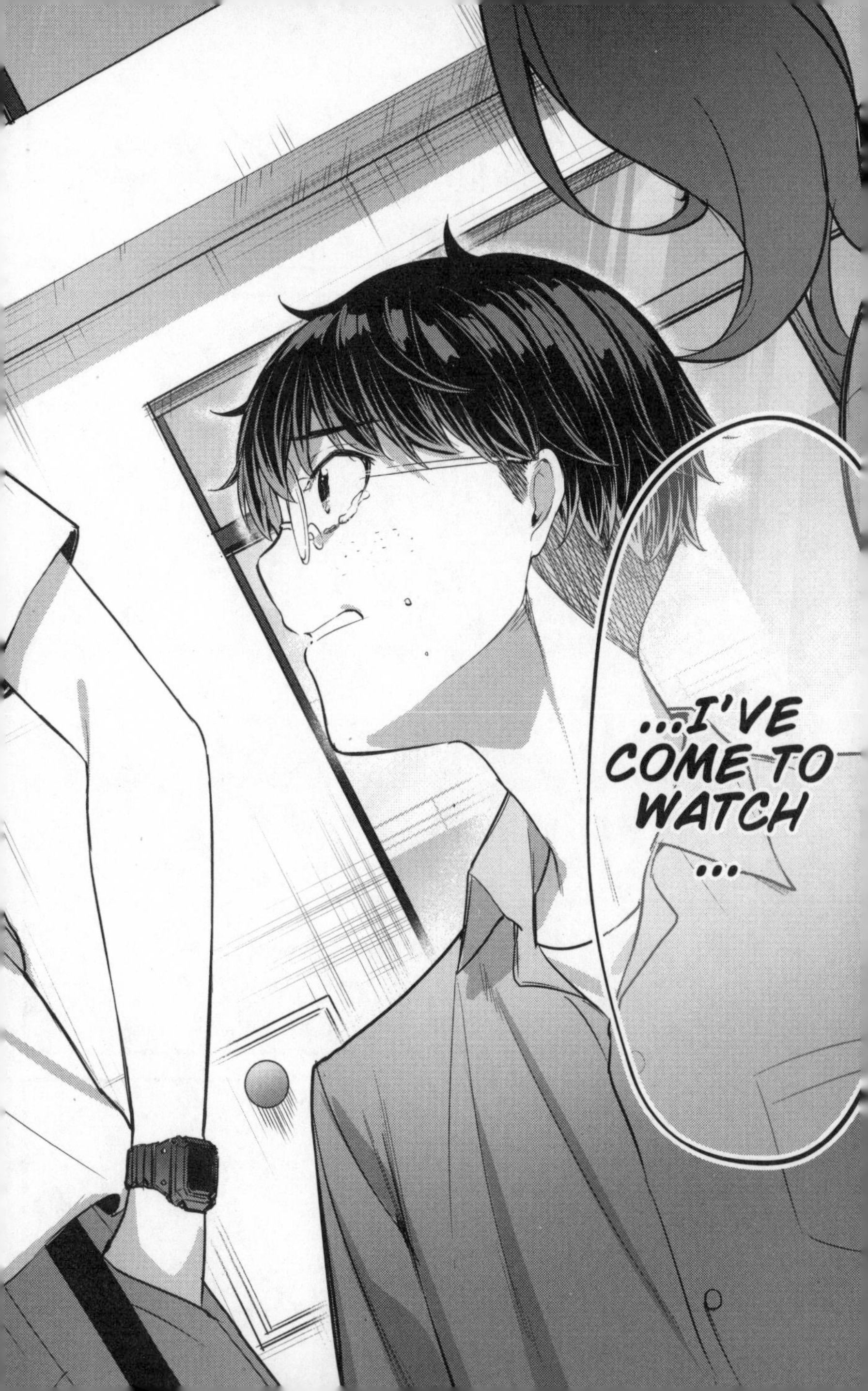
...I'VE COME TO WATCH ...

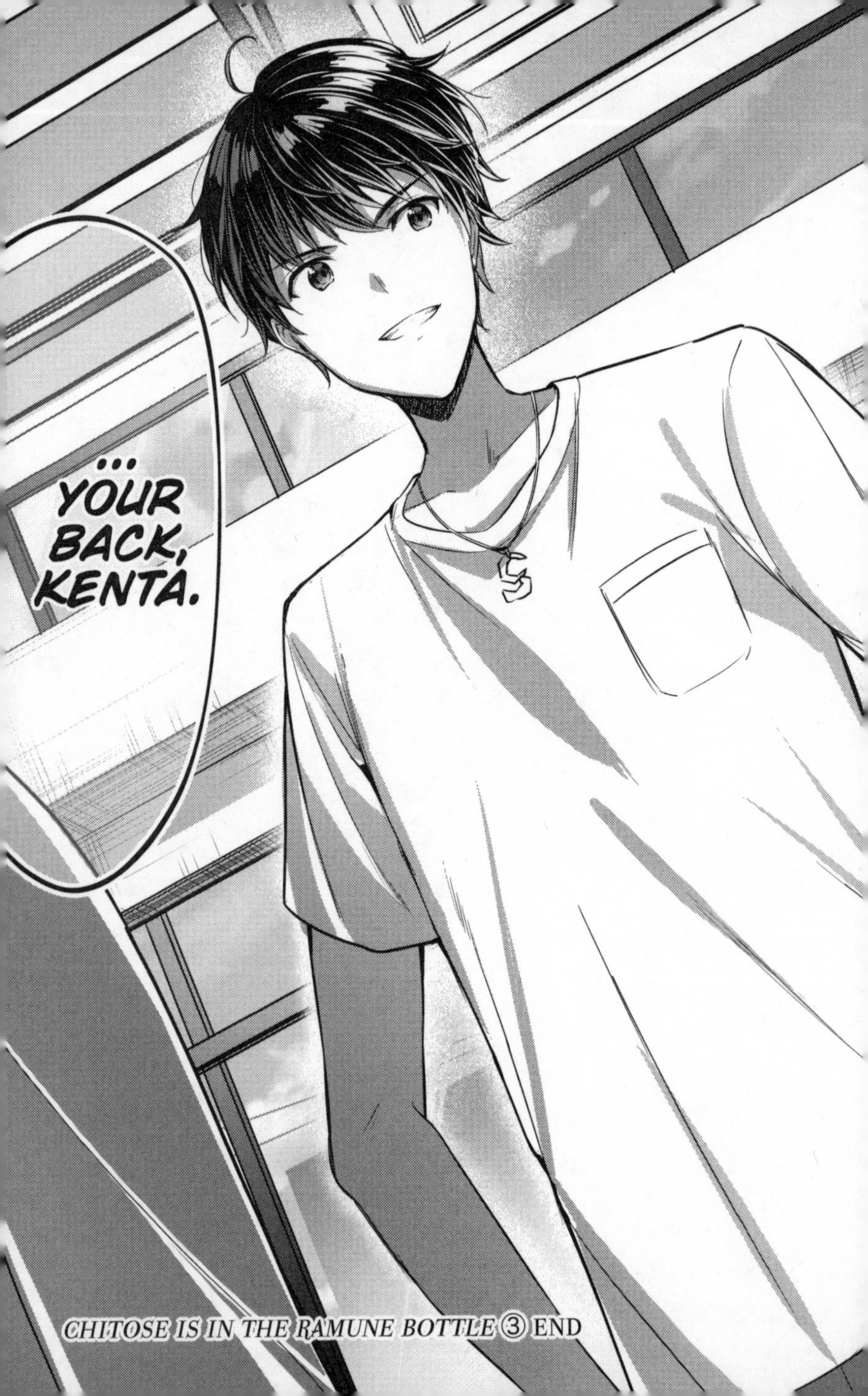
...YOUR BACK, KENTA.

CHITOSE IS IN THE RAMUNE BOTTLE ③ END

Chitose Is in the Ramune Bottle

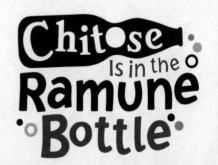

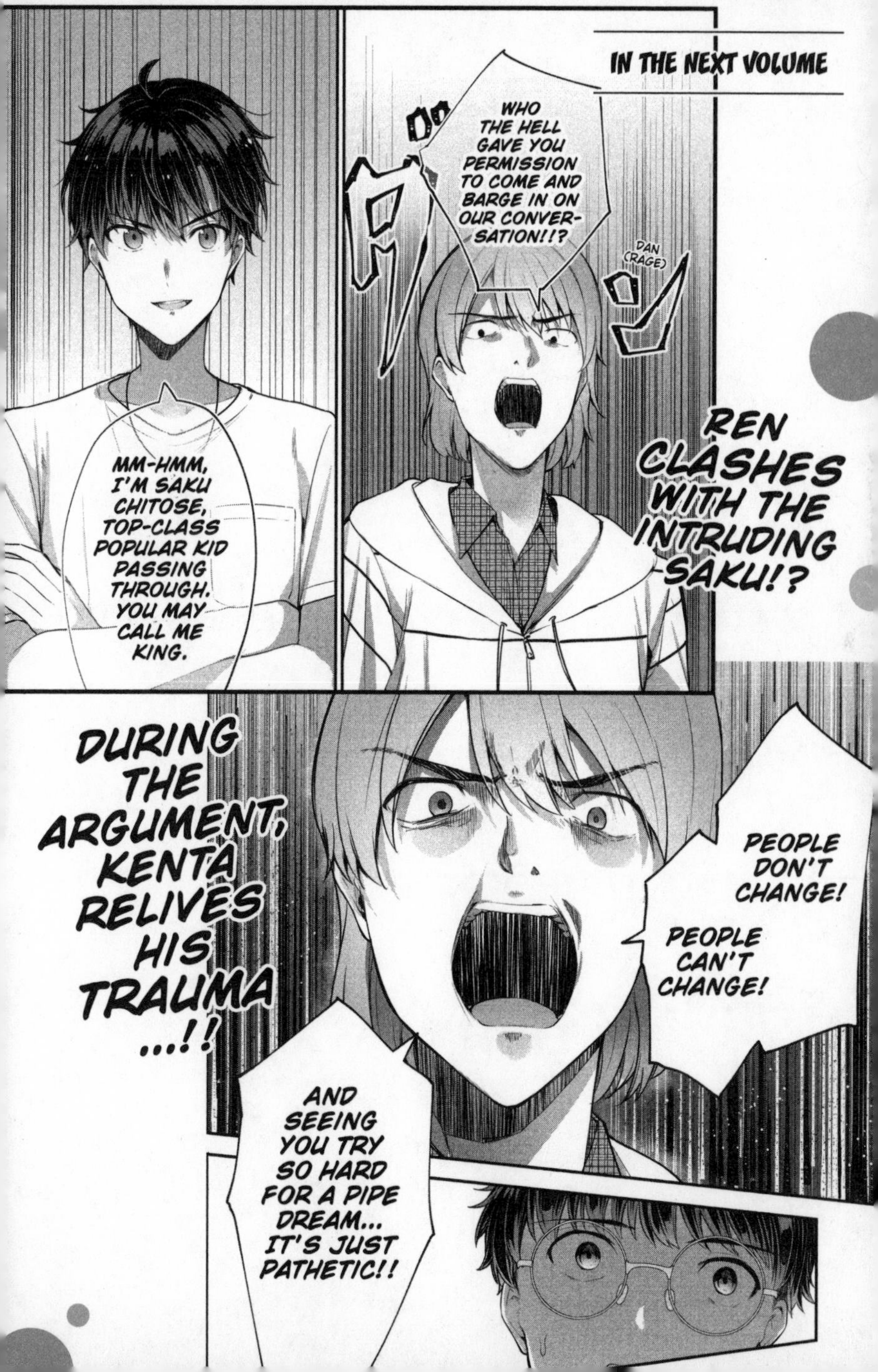
IN THE NEXT VOLUME
WHO THE HELL GAVE YOU PERMISSION TO COME AND BARGE IN ON OUR CONVER-SATION!!?
DAN (RAGE)
REN CLASHES WITH THE INTRUDING SAKU!?
MM-HMM, I'M SAKU CHITOSE, TOP-CLASS POPULAR KID PASSING THROUGH. YOU MAY CALL ME KING.
PEOPLE DON'T CHANGE!
PEOPLE CAN'T CHANGE!
DURING THE ARGUMENT, KENTA RELIVES HIS TRAUMA ...!!
AND SEEING YOU TRY SO HARD FOR A PIPE DREAM... IT'S JUST PATHETIC!!

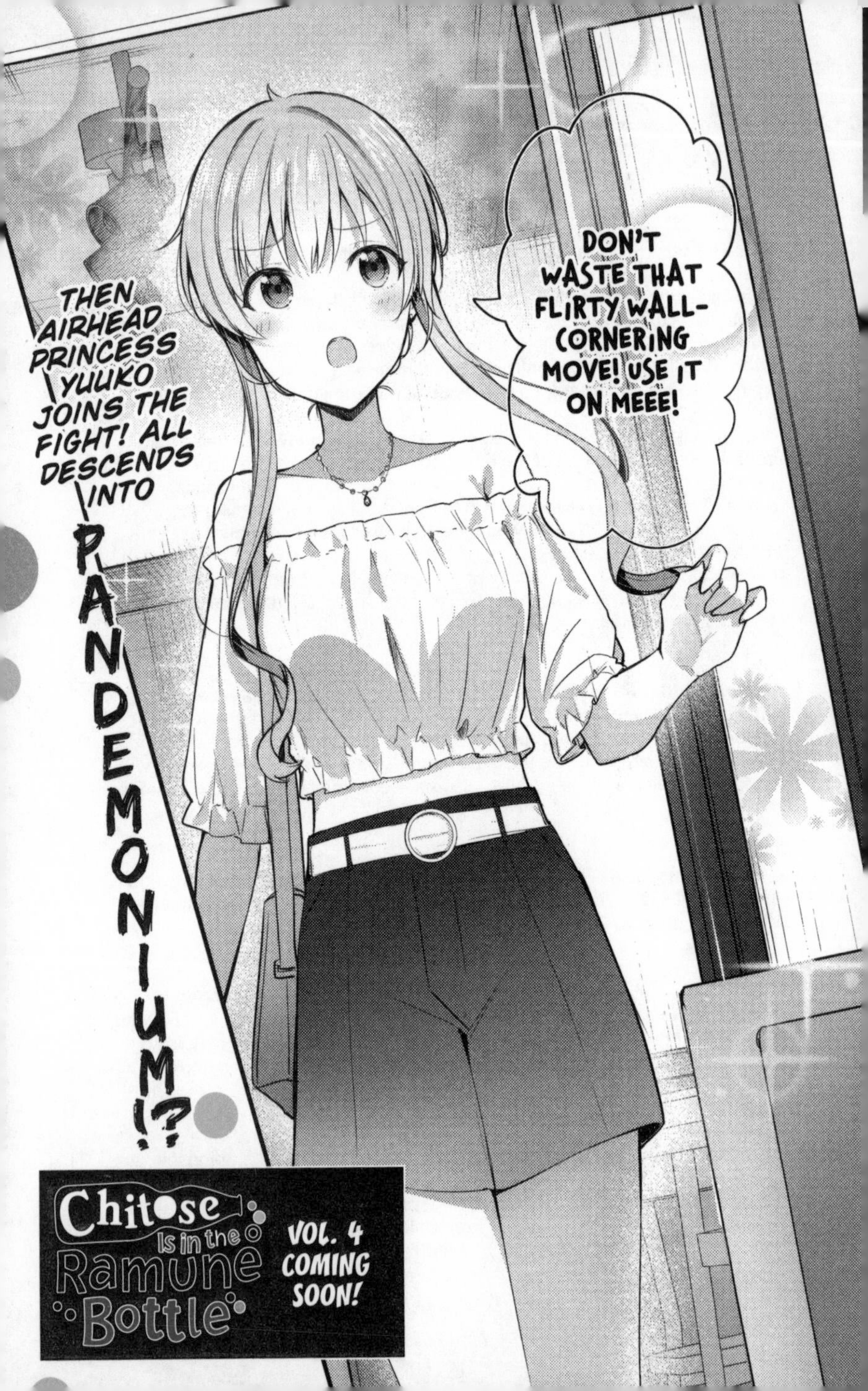
DON'T WASTE THAT FLIRTY WALL-CORNERING MOVE! USE IT ON MEEE!
THEN AIRHEAD PRINCESS YUUKO JOINS THE FIGHT! ALL DESCENDS INTO
PANDEMONIUM!?
Chitose Is in the Ramune Bottle
VOL. 4 COMING SOON!

Translation Notes

Common Honorifics

-san: The Japanese equivalent of Mr./Mrs./Miss. If a situation calls for politeness, this is the fail-safe honorific.

-kun: Used most often when referring to boys, this indicates affection or familiarity. Occasionally used by older men among their peers, but it may also be used by anyone referring to a person of lower standing.

-chan: An affectionate honorific indicating familiarity used mostly in reference to girls; also used in reference to cute persons or animals regardless of gender.

-sensei: A respectful term for teachers, artists, or high-level professionals.

-sen: A shortened version of the honorific '-sensei'. This suggests that students have a very casual and friendly relationship with their teacher.

-nii-san/aniki and **nee-san/aneki**: A term of endearment meaning "big brother" or "big sister" that may be used to address anyone regardless of whether they are related or not.

No honorific: Indicates familiarity or closeness; if used without permission or reason, addressing someone in this manner would be interpreted as an insult or disrespectful.

Title

Ramune bottle: *Ramune* is a carbonated soft drink from Japan that comes in a variety of flavors. The glass bottles use a glass marble in the opening instead of a cap to trap the pressurized contents. A plastic device comes with the bottle, and it can be used to push the glass marble free and allow consumers to enjoy the beverage. It is impossible to open the bottle in order to remove the marble.

Page 5

Straight man: Called *tsukkomi* in Japanese, one member of a comedy duo (the other being the "funny man" or *boke*) whose role is to misinterpret jokes or act more serious.

Page 6

Shut-in: Also called *hikikomori*, these are people who have separated themselves from society by closing themselves off in their rooms and refusing to leave the house to attend work or school. This situation is an increasing problem in Japan, and many believe it to be a result of bullying or social anxiety.

Page 13

Koushien refers to Japan's National High School Baseball Championship, an annual event held in the Hanshin Koushien Stadium. The Inter-High refers to Japan's Inter-High School Championships, an annual competition covering a variety of sports events. The U-17 refers to the FIFA U-17 World Cup, the world championship of soccer players under the age of seventeen.

Page 16
Lpa: Also known as "Lovely Partner." It is a large shopping mall located in Fukui, Japan, with various clothing stores, restaurants, and entertainment options.

Otaku: *Otaku* is a slang term for people who are generally known as avid fans of something, such as computer *otaku* or camera *otaku*. *Otaku* by itself is typically used to refer to fans of manga and anime.

Page 17
Light novels: Also called *ranobe*, novels that are often adapted into manga or anime series in Japan. They have rapidly increased in popularity over the past few years.

Page 24
Normie: A slang term used by people of certain subcultures (like *otaku*) to describe people who are part of mainstream culture and generally follow more "acceptable" cultural norms.

Page 28
First year: The Japanese school system is organized in such a way that high school and middle school each comprise three years.

Page 44
Go-home club: In Japan, students who do not participate in any club activities after school and return home immediately are colloquially known as belonging to the "go-home club."

Page 54
Castle fish ornaments: Saku is referring to the *shachihoko*, a sea monster in Japanese folklore that is often used as an ornament on rooftops. It is typically depicted with its head down and tail curled high in the air.

Page 76
LIME: A reference to LINE, an instant messaging app on which users can text, share images or videos, and make phone calls. It is the most popular social media app in Japan.

Page 98
"Monkey, gorilla, chimpanzee" song: An alternate version of a classic march known as the Colonel Bogey March with the nonsense lyrics "Monkey, gorilla, chimpanzee" inserted into the melody. It is widely known in Japan.

Back cover
Gyaru: A transliteration of the English "gal," referring to a fashion subculture for young women in Japan who rebel against traditional beauty standards.

Chitose Is in the Ramune Bottle

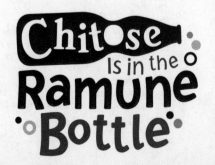

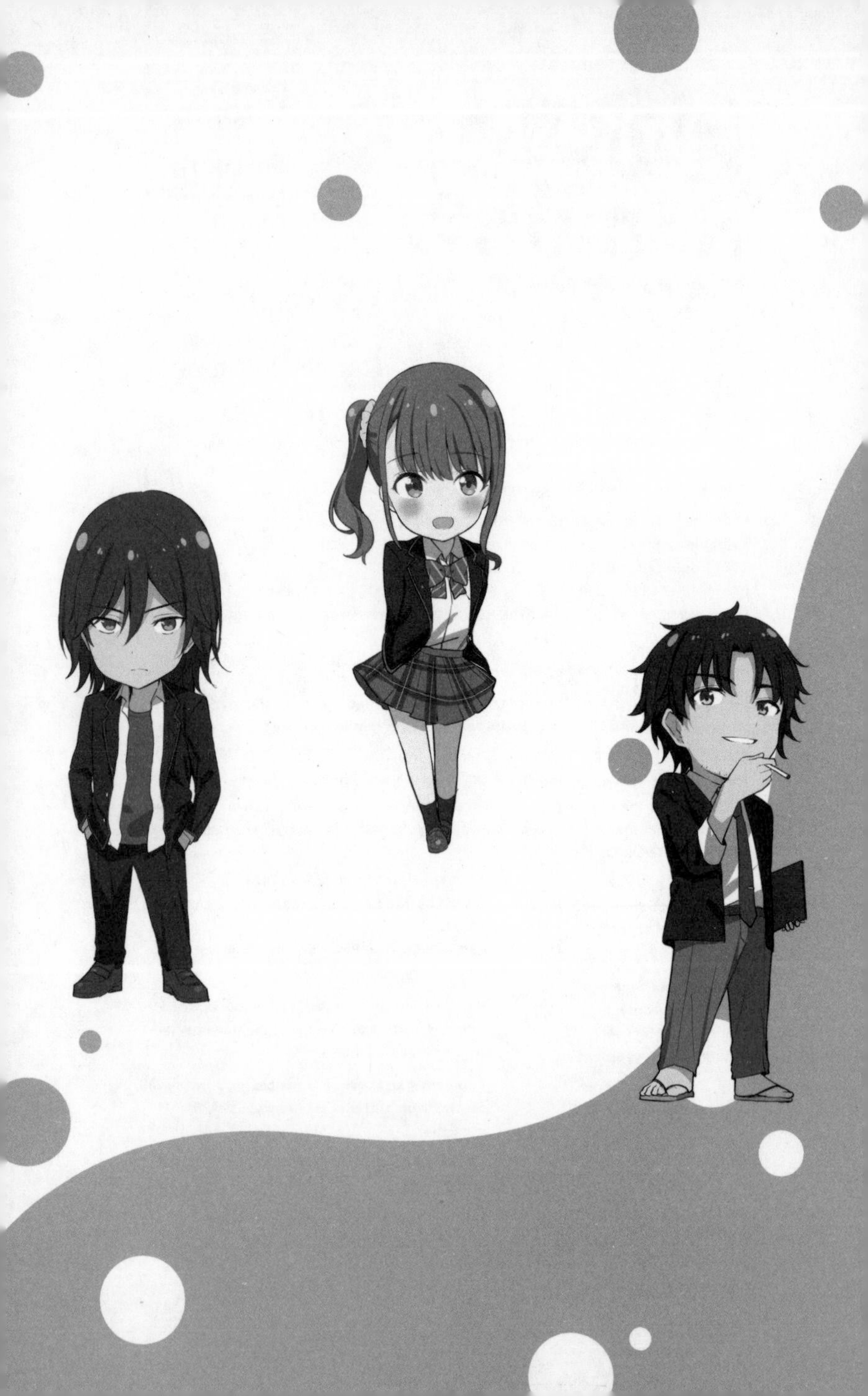

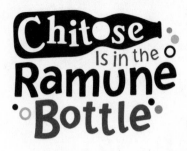

Chitose Is in the Ramune Bottle

3

Original Story
Hiromu

Art
Bobkya

Character Design
raemz

Translation
Evie Lund

Lettering
Rachel J. Pierce

CHITOSE-KUN WA RAMUNE-BIN NO NAKA vol. 3
©Hiromu, raemz/Shogakukan Inc.(Gagaga Bunko)
©2021 Bobkya/SQUARE ENIX CO., LTD.
First published in Japan in 2021 by SQUARE ENIX CO., LTD. English translation rights arranged with SQUARE ENIX CO., LTD. and Yen Press, LLC through Tuttle-Mori Agency, Inc.

English translation ©2023 by SQUARE ENIX CO., LTD.

Yen Press
150 West 30th Street, 19th Floor
New York, NY 10001

Visit us at yenpress.com
facebook.com/yenpress
twitter.com/yenpress
yenpress.tumblr.com
instagram.com/yenpress

First Yen Press Edition: May 2023
Edited by Yen Press Editorial: Jacquelyn Li, Carl Li
Designed by Yen Press Design: Jane Sohn, Andy Swist

Yen Press is an imprint of Yen Press, LLC.
The Yen Press name and logo are trademarks of Yen Press, LLC.

The publisher is not responsible for websites (or their content) that are not owned by the publisher.

Library of Congress Control Number: 2022934292

ISBNs: 978-1-9753-6137-2 (paperback)
        978-1-9753-6138-9 (ebook)

10 9 8 7 6 5 4 3 2 1

WOR

Printed in the United States of America

Please flip to the back to read an exclusive, new short story.